Meditation Sickness

Meditation Sickness

A Sourcebook on the Dangers of Buddhist Practice

Edited by C. Pierce Salguero

University of Hawaiʻi Press
Honolulu

Printed in the United States of America

First printed, 2026

Library of Congress Cataloging-in-Publication Data

Names: Salguero, C. Pierce editor
Title: Meditation sickness : a sourcebook on the dangers of Buddhist practice / edited by C. Pierce Salguero.
Other titles: Sourcebook on the dangers of Buddhist practice
Description: Honolulu : University of Hawaiʻi Press, [2026] | Includes bibliographical references and index.
Identifiers: LCCN 2025042389 | ISBN 9798880702633 hardback
Subjects: LCSH: Meditation—Buddhism—Health aspects—History—Sources | Meditation—Buddhism—Psychological aspects—History—Sources | Mental illness—Religious aspects—Buddhism—History—Sources | Buddhist literature—Translations into English
Classification: LCC BQ9289 .M366 2026
LC record available at https://lccn.loc.gov/2025042389

The manufacturer's authorized representative in the EU for product safety is Mare Nostrum Group B.V., Doelen 72, 4831 GR Breda, The Netherlands. Email: gpsr@mare-nostrum.co.uk

Profuse thanks to Raymond Chang and the Institute of East-West Medicine for generously funding the publication of this project.

Cover art: Broken Buddha (Borobudur, Indonesia). Photograph by C. Pierce Salguero ©2025.

University of Hawaiʻi Press books are printed on acid-free paper and meet the guidelines for permanence and durability of the Council on Library Resources.

Contents

Introduction

C. PIERCE SALGUERO

In the summer of 2021, a user submitted a post to the Dharma Overground website (www.dharmaoverground.org) asking for help and advice.[1] Founded by Daniel M. Ingram, the author of a popular Buddhist meditation guidebook, this online discussion board's home page describes itself as a forum and support group for "pragmatic" and "diligent" meditators. The user wrote seeking help with recent difficulties that had arisen in their "heart chakra" after participating in a twelve-day solo meditation retreat. They described what was occurring:

> I have this anxious ball of energy on my spine leveled around the nipples. Maybe size of a fist, localized, always there. If I focus on it, it intensifies, one time even got a round burning feeling on the spine. Usually radiating this anxious energy to my chest, giving the general feeling of anxiousness.[2]

This user was not alone. Reports of "energetic symptoms," "anxiety," "depression," "psychosis," "hallucinations," and other adverse effects from practicing intensive meditation have been seen frequently on the forum since its founding in 2008. Just a few months later, another member reported that she was experiencing kundalini as a result of "pretty intensively" practicing meditation and qigong. It was bad enough that witnesses had called paramedics for her on at least one occasion:

> I started having what I can only describe as seizures. . . . The energy starts pumping through my heart and forcefully through my navel area and this sets off all kinds of spontaneous movement, a lot of uncontrollable shaking, eyes roll in the back of my head, big intakes of breath, big vibrations up my central channel. Inside I feel quite ecstatic and also vulnerable as people around me often are a little freaked out.[3]

While some reports of meditation side effects have come from meditators practicing on their own without supervision from qualified teachers, such effects have also been noted within the context of formal retreats. For example, another long-term meditator on the forum reported that he had been hospitalized due to symptoms that began during a ten-day *vipassanā* meditation course. The insomnia and energy flows intensified when he returned home, ultimately leading to pronounced "sexual weirdness" and bizarre behavioral symptoms:

> Suddenly my body starts rolling around on the bed all on its own. . . . Pretty soon I'm up off the bed and dancing. Then I'm spinning my arms all around. . . . Then I felt strong hands push me onto the bed and begin to ravish me sexually. . . . I could feel my gender changing from male to female and back again. . . . All night long I had these bizarre sexual experiences with my ghost lover even though I was exhausted. . . . What the hell was going on? . . . Was I possessed by a fucking spirit? . . . [Sleep was] impossible, and on the third day I had my friends take me to the hospital. . . . A week later I was discharged with a prescription for a powerful antipsychotic in hand. After a month or so I could sleep without the drugs but I became severely depressed. It's only in the last few weeks I've felt like I've come out of the depression and started meditating again.[4]

It is not only on Dharma Overground that one finds firsthand reports from meditators in crisis. The website of Cheetah House (www.cheetahhouse.org), an organization that describes itself as offering "resources and support for those with adverse meditation experiences," features a number of self-reports as well. One of the anonymous accounts on that site tells of terrifying symptoms during a sixty-day retreat in Myanmar:

> Within the first few days my body began an intense physical purge, I experienced deep states of concentration, began hallucinating and experiencing visions of what I can only describe as past traumas resurfacing. I experienced myself transforming into a bird and an extremely dark disturbing figure, I felt sensations in my brain that almost felt like it was being reprogrammed. . . . The sensations would become so intense it was almost as if something was trying to make its way out of me as it thrashed my body in all different directions. . . . Visions, voices, paranoia, I began having trouble walking and holding my limbs in place. All of my senses were incredibly heightened. . . . Something felt terribly wrong. . . . I began to fear for my life. The mental health states I began to experience were terrifying. I cried a lot. Everything became dark and depressing.[5]

Similar reports can be found on numerous other websites, forums, subReddits, and social media groups where meditators gather and discuss their experiences. Perhaps the most well-known account of meditation gone wrong, which has been repeated and referenced in the media many times, is the story of Megan Vogt, a young woman who committed suicide after undergoing a mental breakdown during a meditation retreat.[6] The specter of Vogt's experience seems to be raised most frequently as an example of the worst-case scenario: the potentially deadly combination of irresponsible teachers, negligent retreat centers, and vulnerable practitioners.

What is going on here? Isn't meditation supposed to be good for the mind, body, and spirit, as we constantly have been hearing in the popular media? Isn't it "beneficial in the beginning; beneficial in the middle; beneficial in the end," as the Buddhist sutras put it? How can people be having such distressing experiences? How can meditation possibly go this wrong?

Contemporary Western Perspectives on the Potential Dangers of Meditation

The positive effects of mindfulness and other Buddhist meditation practices have been enthusiastically studied by many types of researchers for several decades now. On the plus side, this has resulted in enormous benefits for those seeking stress-reduction techniques. On the downside, something of a popular media juggernaut has occurred in which mindfulness is too often characterized as a panacea.[7] While the benefits have gotten all the press, the potential for adverse side effects has received far less attention.[8] Nevertheless, the potential troubles arising from intensive meditation have been acknowledged in Buddhist literature written in English for many decades, including in guidebooks by some of the most popular meditation teachers.[9]

Recently, those "meditation-related challenges" or "practice-related challenges" have become more prominent in the popular consciousness. A big part of the reason for this is a recent uptick in scientific attention to this phenomenon. The center of gravity for that new research agenda has undoubtedly been the Varieties of Contemplative Experience study led by Willoughby Britton and Jared Lindahl (see chapter 21). Britton, Lindahl, and colleagues have now published a series of qualitative and clinical studies identifying a spectrum of potential negative side effects from meditation, ranging from gastrointestinal disorders to anxiety, depression, psychosis, delusions, terror, dissociation, depersonalization, and suicidality.[10]

As other researchers have joined in the examination of these effects over the past few years, the types of phenomena being studied and the methods being used to measure them have varied, leading to differences in their findings. For example, one study by Britton et al. (2021) found that adverse effects "with durations of 1 day to 1 week were reported by 11 (14.1%) participants, with durations of 1 week to 1 month by seven (9.0%) participants, and with durations of 1 to 5 months or ongoing by five (6.4%) participants." Meanwhile, Baer et al. (2020) found that 73 percent of participants in their study reported "having unpleasant experiences associated with mindfulness practice at least 'occasionally' during the 6-week follow-up period." Goldberg et al. (2021) found that 32.3 percent of the meditators in their study experienced "meditation-related adverse effects," with 10 percent ongoing for a month or longer. Other major survey-based studies include Cebolla et al. (2017) and Schlosser et al. (2019), but each of these uses divergent terminology and criteria for inclusion. To date there is still no agreed-upon definition of what constitutes negative outcomes and no universally consistent statistics on their prevalence.

An additional complication is that many of these scientific studies have presented meditation experiences through biomedical frameworks and terminology, which can often clash with Buddhist meditation theory. For example, Farias et al. (2020) included among their list of adverse events auditory and visual hallucinations, perceptual hypersensitivity, an "altered sense of self and world," and out-of-body experiences—all of which many groups of practitioners could actually count as desirable, or at least unsurprising, signs of meditation attainments.[11] Uniquely, Britton and Lindahl's project has undertaken extensive ethnographic interviews with Buddhist meditation teachers and practitioners, enabling less biomedically focused approaches and more "person-centered" perspectives in their analyses.[12] Their studies are therefore more sensitive to whether certain phenomena are desirable or detrimental, based on the practitioners' own understandings and expectations.

All this research is still in a nascent phase. However, it seems safe to say that despite some variance, a consensus is emerging that intensive meditation practice may not be a good fit for everyone. Rather than a universal panacea or a completely safe spiritual practice, it seems clear that some people are in danger of experiencing unwanted mental, physical, and behavioral side effects from meditation—beyond the normal and expected challenges of the practice—and that sometimes these symptoms can be terrifying, debilitating, and even life-threatening.

In tandem with the emerging academic research, public awareness of the potential dangers of meditation has also recently risen. High-profile media outlets as varied as *Harper's*, *Esquire*, *Daily Mail*, *Vice*, *The Atlantic*, and *The Guardian* began featuring meditation-gone-wrong stories as far back as the mid-2000s, and the frequency of such reports seems to have increased over time.[13] Public awareness has been fueled in part by Britton and Lindahl themselves, who have distributed press releases about their research and appeared on podcasts, social media, and in other popular media venues. Britton herself founded the aforementioned Cheetah House to help meditators in crisis connect with resources, video consultations, and personalized guidance for dealing with their symptoms. This organization is also involved in raising public awareness of the potential problems connected with meditation practice through social media campaigns and other methods of outreach. While still a relatively new organization, its website was on average receiving 73,000 visits from 56,000 unique visitors annually, and its consultants were seeing about 150 cases per month in 2024.[14]

Meanwhile, additional public attention has been drawn to these issues through the efforts of Ingram. The founder of the previously mentioned Dharma Overground forum (which at the beginning of 2024 had over 178,000 posts by nearly 3,900 users) and a regular guest on podcasts devoted to Buddhism and spirituality, Ingram's widely read meditation guide strongly warns readers about the "difficult" experiences they can encounter as a result of "hardcore" practice.[15] Ingram, a retired emergency physician, founded a research consortium in 2020 and a charitable organization in 2021 dedicated to promoting and financially supporting scientific and academic research focused on "emergent phenomena."[16] Echoing the notion of "spiritual emergence" pioneered by Christina and Stanislav Grof, Ingram's term explicitly encompasses energetic symptoms, kundalini, visions, spirit possession, and other "highs, lows, and weirds" that may arise as a result of spiritual practice—whether interpreted positively or negatively by practitioners.[17]

In numerous public interviews, Ingram has stated that one of his chief goals is to ensure that people become aware of the possibilities of emergent phenomena, including potentially adverse effects, before they start meditating. He expresses the wish that would-be practitioners were allowed to give "informed consent" concerning the risks, benefits, and alternatives to meditation based on outcomes data, just as they would when undertaking any other therapeutic activity or medical intervention.[18] The Cheetah House website vision statement similarly reads, "We envision an environment where communities and professionals are equipped with the knowledge and skills to prevent and mitigate adverse meditation experiences" and highlights the need for informed consent in the meditation industry.[19]

Whereas the potential dangers of meditation are coming under increasing scrutiny in research labs and growing more widely known by the public, a number of high-profile Western Buddhist teachers and leaders have weighed in with contrary viewpoints.[20] In general, these defenders of meditation have acknowledged that practitioners occasionally face challenges but have emphasized the following counterarguments:

1. Adverse effects do not happen when one is properly instructed in the practice of meditation by a legitimate teacher with genuine insight.
2. They primarily affect Western meditators who are too culturally unprepared and doctrinally uninformed to successfully participate in meditation retreats.
3. They are the result of latent psychological issues that may emerge during meditation but are not necessarily caused by it.

The overall message of these doctrinally centered responses is that well-prepared and well-trained practitioners can safely engage in properly structured and well-led meditation retreats without concern for adverse effects. They often also argue that meditation centers already put adequate measures in place to screen out practitioners who may potentially be harmed, such that no further safeguards are necessary.

The Origins and Purposes of This Volume

As neither a clinician, a Buddhist, nor a participant in long-term intensive meditation retreats, I have no strong personal stake in the outcome of the debates over the dangers of Buddhist meditation outlined above. However, as a scholar of Buddhism and medicine in Asia, the more I have read the more I have felt that both researchers of adverse effects and defenders of meditation would benefit from opening up to non-Western voices and perspectives. Commentators have periodically cited famous Asian meditation teachers as authorities (e.g., S. N. Goenka, Mahāsī Sayādaw, and others) or introduced passages from ancient Buddhist scripture or commentaries to bolster their arguments (such as the *Visuddhimagga,* an oft-cited fifth-century Pāli text). Many of the Western meditators interviewed in studies by Lindahl and others use Asian vocabularies and doctrines (qi, winds, chakras, energies, kundalini, etc.) to frame their experiences, and researchers have also used these words.[21] Notwithstanding, the vast majority of the research subjects participating in these studies have been of European descent, and neither side in the debate has engaged deeply with non-Western, non–English-speaking voices on the question of the potential dangers of meditation. Given that the vast majority of adept Buddhist meditators are now and have always been Asian, it seems to me that this blind spot is a major hindrance to understanding emergent phenomena.

In contrast, as a scholar of Chinese religion I first encountered the notion that undesirable mental or physical symptoms could arise from the practice of meditation long before this research and media attention began. Back in 2010 I had already written briefly about this in my analysis of a fifth-century sutra dedicated to this topic.[22] Shortly after that, in 2012, I translated a brief chapter of a meditation manual by the famous monk Zhiyi (538–597) that discusses these dangers in detail.[23] Then, in 2017, I published an edited volume including Eric Greene's translation of an excerpt from that fifth-century sutra, Juhn Ahn's translation of Hakuin Ekaku's (1686–1769) description of his bout with "meditation sickness," and a republication of my translation of Zhiyi.[24]

In addition to knowing about historical texts such as these, I was also aware that the dangers of spiritual practice are discussed freely by contemporary

Buddhists in the Chinese cultural context. In the Chinese language, one term for the negative side effects of spiritual or energetic practices (*zouhuorumo*) has even entered the everyday lexicon as an idiom meaning "madness" or "obsession." The notion that intensive spiritual practice is risky has a broad cultural acceptance in martial arts films and other areas of Chinese popular culture (see the discussion in chapter 17). Anecdotally, whenever I have raised the topic of the potential dangers of meditation with Chinese-speaking monks and nuns, I have invariably been told that this is a well-known phenomenon discussed openly within monastic institutions in Asia.

Thus, when I initially encountered first-person accounts of contemporary Western meditators in distress, such as those with which this book opens, it was not so much their novelty that struck me as their similarity to the descriptions I already knew from the Chinese contexts. These similarities prompted me to wonder what, if anything, translating historical Chinese perspectives into English might be able to contribute to our contemporary Western understandings of the potential dangers of meditation. In 2023 I published an article that began to map out some of those connections more explicitly.[25] As I argued in that piece, translations of what Asian meditation teachers and historical Buddhist writings have had to say about the prevention and treatment of meditation-related adverse effects would likely be of immense value to English-language readers. That idea formed the origin of this book.

Even before the publication of the present volume, some of these missing Asian voices were already sporadically available through the works of individual academic historians and ethnographers. While not a comprehensive list, extant scholarship touching on the adverse effects of spiritual practice has included studies of premodern Buddhist writings on meditation sickness from China and Japan,[26] descriptions of "wind disorders" in premodern meditation manuals from Southeast Asia,[27] and ethnographic studies conducted among Tibetan Buddhists.[28] (Casting the net more widely, comparative material has been published on the side effects that reportedly can result from Daoist "inner alchemy,"[29] qigong,[30] Christian prayer,[31] and other forms of intensive spiritual practices around the globe.) Because these preexisting studies do not seem to be influencing the current debates over meditation sickness in any appreciable way, I felt that it would be valuable to bring together in one place a selection of voices from across the Buddhist world on this topic.

With this material already available from humanistic scholars, one might ask why contemporary Western Buddhist institutions, teachers, and practitioners are not more familiar with Asian perspectives on the topic of the potential dangers of meditation. Are they protecting themselves by eliding these viewpoints, or are they simply unaware? Do they have an ethical obligation to be better informed and to be more forthcoming with the public about the dangers? On the latter question, I would like to argue yes. However, I recognize that significant barriers presently stand in the way of these materials being widely accessible and their knowledge being widely applied in the West. Some of the main barriers, in my view, are the disciplinary norms that deter scholars from engaging with contemporary issues, and I have discussed this problem in more detail in my previous publication on this topic.[32] My hope is that this book can begin to overcome some of this compartmentalization by making reliable scholarly translations widely available in an accessible and affordable format. No easy answers lie within these pages, but my sincere hope is that this collection may serve to stimulate conversation and to enrich our Western understanding of the nuances and complexities of meditation.

Overview of Contents

This book is divided into three principal sections, the first containing translations of scriptures, the second historical texts, and the third contemporary ethnographic materials.

Part I includes a cluster of translations from the Buddhist scriptural canons. In chapter 1, Bryan De Notariis translates from the Pāli the Buddha's account of the physical and mental challenges he himself faced when he engaged in excessively austere spiritual practice prior to his enlightenment. Here, the Buddha describes the sound of winds in his ears, headaches, heat, and sweating, but he also makes a point of mentioning that they were temporary afflictions.

In chapter 2, Bhikkhu Anālayo translates one of the most famous accounts of meditation gone wrong from the earliest layer of historical Buddhist writings. This narrative, which appears in a sutra with both Pāli and Chinese versions, tells of the time the community of monks followed the Buddha's meditation instructions and became so distressed that they committed suicide en masse.

A translation from a Sanskrit Perfection of Insight text, which warns of Māra demons attacking meditators who lack resolve, faith, or a proper understanding of doctrine, is the subject of chapter 3. In this context, Charles DiSimone tells us, these demons are to be understood as both external entities and as personifications of one's own unawakened delusions of grandeur, which can lead to becoming an unethical, narcissistic teacher.

Chapter 4 includes Eric M. Greene's translation of a text called *Secret Essential Methods for Curing Meditation Sickness.* This sutra presents a panoply of severe mental and physical ailments that can befall meditators and prescribes complex visualizations to either counteract or soothe the symptoms.

The last chapter in the group, chapter 5, contains James A. Benn's translation of an excerpt from the *Śūraṃgama Sūtra,* an important meditation text in East Asian Buddhism. The passages included here introduce a series of phenomena that can occur during meditation whose misinterpretation can lead one into a "demonic state," which frequently involves mental imbalances.

Part II includes translations of historical commentaries and reflections on the dangers of meditation. This portion of the book begins with two meditation manuals composed by the aforementioned sixth-century master Zhiyi, who founded the Tiantai (Jp. Tendai) school and became highly revered in Chan (Jp. Zen). Zhiyi's *Longer Treatise on Śamatha and Vipaśyanā* is translated in chapter 6 by Paul Swanson. Here the reader is treated to a detailed account of Zhiyi's system, including how to distinguish between ailments caused by medical conditions versus those caused by meditation, the signs and symptoms of the latter, and a range of techniques to treat problems once they arise.

In chapter 7, David Carpenter translates passages from Zhiyi's *Sequential Gate of Meditation* that distinguish between the signs of proper meditative absorption (Skt. *dhyāna;* Pāli *jhāna*) and the signs of "deviant practice." Taken together, these two chapters paint the fullest picture we have of a premodern author's understanding of how to recognize, treat, and prevent the dangers of meditation.

After these chapters focusing on Zhiyi are four texts written in the second millennium of the Common Era. In chapter 8, Michael R. Sheehy presents translations from Tibetan obstacle-elimination (*geksel*) texts dating from the twelfth to the fifteenth century. These brief instructions for advanced meditators provide pithy advice for dealing with all kinds of troubles one may encounter in the course of spiritual practice, including various ailments.

Next, in chapter 9, Juhn Ahn provides a translation of the abovementioned text by Hakuin, a famous passage in which he describes both his symptoms of meditation sickness as well as the "butter meditation" he learned in order to cure it. In a portion of the text not translated here, Hakuin traces the lineage of this practice back to Zhiyi, and beyond, to the sutra translated in chapter 4.

Coauthors Leslie E. de Vries and Leo W. Lok move us forward to the seventeenth to nineteenth century in chapter 10. Here, we are introduced to two texts from the classical Chinese medical tradition that clearly indicate that meditation-induced ailments were known to and treated by formally trained Chinese physicians in the premodern period.

In chapter 11, Swe Swe Mon and Daniel M. Stuart translate some of the teachings of one of the most significant forefathers of modern Western Buddhism, the *vipassanā* teacher Sayagyi U Ba Khin (1899–1971). The stories U Ba Khin tells in these passages reveal his understanding of *vipassanā* as a purificatory practice and indicate some of the highly uncomfortable experiences beginning meditators might have in releasing their impurities during his trainings.

In chapter 12, Melissa Anne-Marie Curley translates a chilling memoir written by the Japanese author Kurata Hyakuzō (1891–1943). Kurata describes how meditation-induced obsessive thinking drove him to the brink of madness, as well as his personal quest to overcome this condition.

Finally, chapter 13 presents three short translations of monastic experts' teachings about the dangers of meditation by Francisco Figueroa Medina, Dixuan Chen, and Trang T. D. Nguyen. The first of these is an excerpt of a book by the Rinzai Zen master Yamada Mumon (1900–1988), the second a chapter from a book by the revered Taiwanese meditation master Sheng Yen (1931–2009), and the third a transcript of a YouTube video by the venerable Thích Nhật Từ (1969–), a monastic reformer in Vietnam.

Part III of this book contains ethnographic materials, interviews, and other contemporary accounts. In this section, instead of being presented chronologically, the chapters are clustered by cultural zones. In chapter 14, Céline Coderey starts off the first batch of chapters pertaining to Southeast Asia with some field notes about an episode of meditation-induced madness—or was it an attack by evil spirits?—that she witnessed during her time in Myanmar. This chapter portrays a community's struggles to deal with and to make sense of extreme spiritual experiences in terms of traditional religious and medical ideas.

In chapter 15, Daphne Weber takes us to Thailand, where a female monastic meditation teacher shares her insights into the visual phenomena that can arise during practice (Pāli: *nimitta*). By skillfully navigating these experiences—and, importantly, by not taking them literally—Luang Pi teaches meditators how to avoid problematic occurrences.

Chapter 16 then takes us to Japan, where Nathan Jishin Michon interviews Asahi Seichō, a Shingon priest and abbot of a temple in Hiroshima. This chapter presents a glimpse into esoteric Japanese Buddhism's repertoire of deities, rituals, and other practices to prevent and manage problems caused by meditation.

In chapter 17, Kin Cheung introduces the perspective of a Cantonese-speaking community ritualist and healer who lives in the New York City area. The conversation centers on the abovementioned Chinese notion of *zouhuo-rumo,* which literally translates to "losing control of the fire and entering a demonic state" but commonly refers to cases of madness caused by meditation, qigong, martial arts, and other spiritual practices.

Chapter 18 then takes us to the Tibetan cultural area of Amdo, where Susannah Deane presents excerpts from six interviews she conducted with Buddhist and medical specialists in the region. Here we learn about the physical and mental health dangers of tantric practices as well as the Tibetan theoretical models used to explain and manage such phenomena.

Tibetan cultural understandings continue as the focus in chapter 19, a contribution by Ben P. Joffe. This time the translation is of an extended interview with the well-known Buddhist teacher and traditional medical doctor Nida Chenagtsang, who shares his perspective on how best to mitigate harm to participants in intensive meditation.

In the penultimate chapter 20, Ira Helderman interviews a biomedical doctor and researcher, Pawan Sharma, who shares stories about his encounters with the adverse effects of meditation in India and Nepal. Sharma's reflections point to important cultural differences in how meditation is understood even within the biomedical establishment and how such understandings can influence medical research and the treatment of patients.

Last but by no means least, chapter 21 provides the reader with a glimpse into the data collected by the aforementioned Varieties of Contemplative Experience Study at Brown University, the preeminent Western study of meditation-related challenges. Jared R. Lindahl, Nathan E. Fisher, David J. Cooper, and Willoughby B. Britton provide transcripts of three interviews from their dataset, introducing us to three Western meditators who detail their harrowing experiences.

These contents, while expansive, are unavoidably limited to the scope and expertise of the contributors who agreed to participate in the current project. We are under no illusions that we have managed to represent all Buddhist perspectives on the dangers of meditation. Conspicuously missing are materials from Korea, Mongolia, Bhutan, Cambodia, Laos, and Singapore, as well as from Asian diasporic communities in most parts of the world. Of course, there are millions of practitioners of Buddhism of all races and cultural backgrounds around the globe whose ideas about this topic would be valuable to include alongside the translations offered here. It is hoped that the present volume inspires scholars to conduct future research and produce translations that will continue to add more voices to the conversation.

Macro-Level Observations

Having briefly surveyed the contents of this volume, permit me to conclude this introduction with a general consideration of how these materials might, in the aggregate, contribute to the contemporary Western conversation about the potential dangers of meditation. Let me begin by noting that as a scholar of Buddhism and not a devotee, I treat all Buddhist texts, regardless of their origins, not as unassailable spiritual truths but rather as documents produced by particular authors and communities in certain times and places in order to pursue specific rhetorical purposes. Seen through that lens—and despite whatever other messages they were intended to convey—the materials translated in this book are unambiguously communicating the fact that an overwhelming number of Buddhists across space and time have considered spiritual practice to be a potential cause of behavioral anomalies, mental illness, and physical disease. Adverse experiences that cross the line from expected challenges to acute problems appear in scriptures and early commentaries written in Pāli, Sanskrit, Chinese, and Tibetan and in interviews with contemporary Burmese, Chinese, Japanese, Nepali, Thai, Tibetan, Vietnamese, and American practitioners. They appear in practice manuals, case studies, oral teachings, autobiographies, YouTube videos, and everyday conversations among neighbors.

In almost all the historical and contemporary discourses recorded here, the potential adverse effects of meditation are explained according to elemental, demonic, karmic, and traditional medical models that differ markedly from scientific biomedicine and modern Western psychology. Occasionally, the definition of meditation-induced sickness expressed in these sources includes heterodox beliefs, behaviors, or proclivities that in the modern Western context would not be recognized as conditions necessitating treatment. However, most of these sources provide descriptions of symptoms that seem to jibe with modern Western descriptions of obsessive-compulsive disorder, anxiety, psychosis, and other mental and physical conditions. This cross-cultural similarity raises many complex theoretical and practical questions about the translation of disease categories that remain beyond the scope of the current volume. Sorting through these issues in a rigorous way would necessitate detailed study by a transdisciplinary collaboration of historians, ethnographers, clinical researchers, medical professionals, Dharma teachers, longtime meditators, and other interested parties.

Even while this kind of research team is still a desideratum, we can nonetheless identify similarities in the phenomenology of the symptoms being experienced by meditators in distress across time, space, and cultural divides. We can plainly see that adverse experiences such as strange sensations, unexplained pains, psychological instability, undesired hallucinations, sexual anomalies, uncontrollable behaviors, demonic possession, suicidality, and so forth have been well-known and well-documented across the Buddhist world.

What are the implications of this information? In my view, at the very least, we need to lay to rest once and for all the notion that adverse side effects are a problem that affects only "culturally unprepared" Western practitioners who naively jump into serious meditation. Far from being a modern Western problem, it is not at all a stretch to say that the physical, mental, and emotional dangers of meditation are well-known among communities of Buddhists everywhere—and always have been. In addition, we can clearly see that while many Asian Buddhists stress the importance of having good teachers, the possibility of experiencing adverse effects from meditation is not entirely mitigated by the teacher's legitimacy, authenticity, or level of enlightenment. If teachings coming from the Buddha himself can cause suicidality (see chapter 2), then no teacher is above the possibility. Nor do these sources suggest that it comes down to the question of students being doctrinally, culturally, or psychologically unprepared. While meditation can trigger preexisting psychological problems, the majority of the sources introduced here suggest that unwanted side effects can happen to anyone. If they can occur to Siddhartha Gautama himself on his way to becoming the Buddha (see chapter 1) and to other masterful meditators who were his direct disciples (see chapter 4), then surely the practitioner is not to blame. I think any reasonable reader will agree that these sources clearly refute the main arguments of contemporary Western commentators who are dismissive of the dangers of meditation.

In terms of the specific causes of meditation ailments, there is no consensus between all of the perspectives presented in these chapters. One of the causes most commonly mentioned in these pages is overly strenuous practice that exceeds one's natural capacities, especially when a single technique is practiced to an extreme level. Other common causes include giving undue importance to passing phenomena that arise during the course of practice, mismanaging bodily energies, experiencing the effects of unfortunate karma, and being assailed by spirits.

It is crucial to underscore that nearly all forms of Buddhism acknowledge difficulties or challenges will arise along the path to enlightenment. There is an expectation that meditation will bring up latent traumas, difficult memories, strong emotions, and other "mental imprints" (Skt. *saṃskāra*) or "defilements" (Skt. *kleśa*)—indeed, the release or purification of such materials is often considered to be the very point of meditation. But there is also recognition across Buddhist cultures that sometimes a line can be crossed. Sometimes, people experience radically destabilizing results that can be classified as illnesses needing treatment. The texts translated here remind us that it is important to discriminate between expected difficulties or challenges versus true health crises. The fact that different authors draw that line in different places due to varying cultural, doctrinal, and other sensibilities suggests that there are no universal answers to such questions.

Whatever factors they identify as the causes of medical crises and however they distinguish these from ordinary meditation challenges, many of the texts in this volume also provide a panoply of potentially valuable advice on prevention and treatment. Some texts prescribe specific meditation techniques or visualizations as antidotes to certain types of ailments. Understanding the potential signs of danger enables the practitioner to switch up their practice as soon as symptoms arise, thereby nipping in the bud more serious disorders. These texts also advise rituals, meritorious actions, shifts in perspective, conventional medical treatments, and other interventions. Many underscore the preservation of a stable foundation of morality (*śila*) as the essential prerequisite for any contemplative practice. Despite this range of possibilities, alas, these pages offer no easy answers or infallible formulas for success. The purpose of this volume is not to narrow the field of solutions down to a "silver bullet" that will be universally applicable. Rather, the goal is to present a wealth of different opinions and approaches to meditation-induced illness, to explore the resources and repertoires other cultures have to offer for understanding and coping with these conditions.

The details of cross-cultural translation are complex, the barriers to understanding are formidable, and the Buddhist world is not univocal in its understanding of meditation ailments. Nonetheless, while giving all those caveats, I personally feel that some of the knowledge contained in the translations in this book may be able to be adapted for use in the contemporary West. For those who prefer to work within Buddhist frameworks, I believe that some of these texts might provide meditation teachers with practical and actionable techniques that could be taught to students in retreat settings to help prevent or ameliorate the kinds of disastrous side effects discussed in the opening of this chapter. I believe it may also be possible for meditators to self-administer these or similar techniques at the first sign of symptoms, before they are overcome by anxiety, depression, psychosis, and other severe psychological and physical ailments. Likewise, I believe that those working outside Buddhist frameworks—whether medical doctors, psychiatric professionals, or practitioners of contemporary Asian medical systems such as acupuncture or yoga therapy—might also be able to adapt some of these methods to enhance their current repertoires of interventions. I believe that these texts could also contribute to the development of diagnostic models that help modern clinicians and researchers discriminate between normal signs of meditation progress, adverse effects that can be managed by making changes to the meditation regimen, and genuine psychiatric crises.

I am obviously not suggesting that all those benefits can be straightforwardly gained merely by reading the pages of this book. Much cross-cultural and transdisciplinary interpretive work remains to be done. Nor should we assume that Buddhism necessarily has all the answers. The tradition is not univocal, and texts often contradict one another. Moreover, it is a distinct possibility that following advice from Asian Buddhists could be counterproductive for contemporary Western meditators—either because these remedies are simply impossible to fit within mainstream Western worldviews or for any number of other reasons. How helpful the approaches presented in these texts will be in practice remains to be determined. The principal point I wish to make here is simply that these historical and contemporary perspectives from across the Buddhist world can and should play an important role in any conversation about the potential dangers of meditation taking place in the West.

To read the firsthand reports quoted at the beginning of this chapter and elsewhere in this volume (see, particularly, chapters 12, 14, and 21) is to be moved by the palpable anguish and long-term harm that such experiences can cause. As meditation becomes ever more popular in the West, it is being learned primarily via apps, websites, workplace workshops, self-retreats, AI guidance, and countless other ways outside traditional Buddhist institutional structures. That means that a growing number of practitioners will not only inevitably experience mental and physical symptoms caused or exacerbated by practices they were led to believe could only be beneficial, but also that they will not necessarily turn to Buddhist teachers or communities for support or remedies to their ailments.

I am in no way arguing that people should stop meditating. The physical and mental health benefits of Buddhist and Buddhist-derived meditation practices such as mindfulness have been exceedingly well-documented for decades now. The spiritual benefit of these practices goes without saying. Let us not hold to the black-and-white position that either meditation is an unassailable good or it should be thrown out entirely just because there may be some undesirable side effects. That being said, given the materials presented in this volume, I do believe it is an ethical imperative that researchers, teachers, and practitioners educate themselves about the dangers and reflect on how Asian perspectives might inform contemporary Western approaches to meditation. I also believe that discovering within these pages new frameworks that make sense of anomalous meditation experiences may benefit sufferers. Just knowing that meditators from Buddhist traditions all over the world have, through no fault of their own, encountered challenging experiences and found solutions may, in itself, be therapeutic. In these many ways, I hope that this book can serve as a catalyst for a wider discussion to take place and thus contribute to the alleviation of suffering.

Notes

1. This chapter is based on Salguero (2023).
2. Dharma Overground, accessed January 28, 2024, https://www.dharmaoverground.org/discussion/-/message_boards/message/22886952.

3. Dharma Overground, accessed January 28, 2024, https://www.dharmaoverground.org/discussion/-/message_boards/message/23092082.
4. Dharma Overground, accessed January 28, 2024, https://www.dharmaoverground.org/discussion/-/message_boards/message/21772129.
5. Cheetah House, accessed January 28, 2024, https://www.cheetahhouse.org/rising-falling.
6. See, e.g., Kortava (2021).
7. Wilson (2014).
8. Lutkajtis (2020).
9. Kornfield (1993, 119–156).
10. See Lindahl et al. (2017) and other publications from the Brown University lab listed here: https://www.cheetahhouse.org/vce, last accessed January 28, 2024.
11. For example, Ingram's meditation manual interprets such events as signs the meditator has attained a stage called the second *vipassanā jhāna*. See Ingram (2018, pt. 4, sect. 30.4), available in an open-access updated version, accessed January 28, 2024, at MCTB.org, https://www.mctb.org/mctb2/table-of-contents/part-iv-insight/30-the-progress-of-insight/4-the-arising-and-passing-away/.
12. See, most notably, Lindahl et al. (2017, 2020, 2021).
13. See a listing of articles at Cheetah House, accessed January 28, 2024, https://www.cheetahhouse.org/media. See the discussion and analysis in Helderman (2024).
14. Lindahl, personal communication with author, January 11, 2025.
15. Ingram (2018). See, particularly, pt. 4, sect. 30.5–10, accessed January 28, 2024, beginning at https://www.mctb.org/mctb2/table-of-contents/part-iv-insight/30-the-progress-of-insight/5-dissolution-entrance-to-the-dark-night.
16. See Emergence Benefactors, https://www.emergencebenefactors.com, and Emergent Phenomenology Research Consortion, https://theeprc.org, respectively. See a detailed introduction to the goals of these organizations in the YouTube video, https://www.youtube.com/watch?v=Q1F2eTYVvr0&t=3840s, accessed January 28, 2024. In the interest of full disclosure, I should note that I joined the research consortium in 2021.
17. See a discussion of the affordances provided by this term in Sandilands and Ingram (2024).
18. See e.g., EPRC White Paper, "Ethics and Informed Consent," accessed January 28, 2024, https://hypernotes.zenkit.com/i/UFIY1UO1cp/WUSs7pr1o/ethics-and-informed-consent.
19. Cheetah House, accessed January 28, 2024, https://www.cheetahhouse.org/about-us.
20. A range of opinions are summarized in Love (2018); Agsar (2021); Anālayo (2021b); Rosenthal (2021).
21. See, for example, Lindahl (2017); Cooper et al. (2021); Lindahl et al. (2021).

22. The discussion of the *Secret Essentials for Curing Meditation Sickness* appeared in Salguero (2014, 85–86).
23. Salguero (2012), edited and republished in Salguero (2017).
24. Salguero (2017).
25. Some of that publication is repeated here in this introduction but not the portion of the paper that analyzes four medieval Chinese sources on meditation sickness and its remedies (Salguero 2023). All four of the texts discussed in the earlier version of the essay are translated in this book. However, some valuable points were made in my discussion in the previous publication that are not repeated here, and thus I encourage the reader to access the original.
26. In addition to the works cited in note 22–24, see also Ahn (2007, 2021); Curley (2024).
27. Mettanando (1999).
28. Deane (2018, 2025); Samuel (2019).
29. Eskildsen (2008).
30. N. Chen (2003).
31. Luhrmann and Morgain (2012); Fisher (2021).
32. Again, see Salguero (2023), particularly pp. 200–201.

Part I

Scriptures

Chapter 1

Discomforts Caused by Meditation in the Buddha's Own Life

An Excerpt from the Pāli Canon

BRYAN DE NOTARIIS

It is apparent that relaxation was not the primary aim for people involved in meditation practices in ancient India. While they had a soteriological goal, it seems that some types of meditators were comparable to modern practitioners of extreme sports, dedicating themselves to a potentially dangerous and deadly activity as they tried to escape from the infinite cycle of birth, death, and rebirth known as saṃsāra.

Such people were referenced in Pāli with the term *samaṇa* (Skt. *śramaṇa*), a word connected with the act of straining or exerting oneself. We can say that they were "ascetics," as this word's Greek etymology shares the same meaning. The Buddha, at the beginning of his career as a meditator, joined the ascetic community active in that historical period in India, adopting its customs and practices. However, given the extremely mortifying nature of the ascetic and meditative exercises he undertook, he eventually abandoned this to find his own way.

The risks of these kinds of asceticism reach us through the testimony of the Pāli literature, which openly address potential problems with these practices, including their symptoms, treatments, and prevention strategies. The Pāli canon is widely recognized as the only canon composed in an Indian language that came down to us in its entirety.[1] This canonical literature is stratified and usually quite difficult to date with certainty. The first century BC is considered the period in which the texts were written down in Sri Lanka, an event concomitant with a certain closure in doctrinal terms.[2] The Theravāda tradition preserved canonical texts along with a huge body of exegetical literature initiated by Buddhaghosa in the fifth century AD and continued in the following centuries by other commentators.

The text translated here is the *Great Discourse to Saccaka* (*Mahāsaccaka Sutta*), in which the Buddha details his experience with strenuous ascetic practices (*dukkara-kārikā*).[3] Among these, we find mention of "breathless meditations" (*appānakaṃ jhānaṃ*), which are comparatively close to what in other Indian contexts it is called *prāṇāyāma*. These ascetic exercises are said to promote the arising of energy (*viriya*) and the establishment of mindfulness (*sati*), which are among the factors that contribute to awakening.[4] Nonetheless, they provoked some unpleasant side effects to the Buddha-to-be, namely sweating, the sound of winds in the ears, head pains, and the arising of a body's temperature in, perhaps, a feverish-like manner. These strong, and of course undesirable, effects are in sharp contrast with the general sense of ease which seems to emerge from the accounts of the Buddhist meditative absorptions (*jhāna*) and were a part of the pre-Buddhist ascetic background from which the Buddha distanced himself. The moral of the story is that austerities lead to painful feelings without being conducive to awakening, whereas the form of meditation experienced by the Buddha in his childhood is not only pleasant but also leads to awakening.

Further Reading

Anālayo, Bhikkhu. 2017. *A Meditator's Life of the Buddha, Based on the Early Discourses.* Windhorse.

Anālayo, Bhikkhu. 2021. "The Buddha's Pre-Awakening Practices and Their Mindful Transformation." *Mindfulness* 12:1892–1898.

Anālayo, Bhikkhu. 2022. "Asceticism in Early Buddhist Thought." In *Encyclopedia of Mindfulness, Buddhism, and Other Contemplative Practices,* edited by Nirbhay N. Singh. Springer. https://doi.org/10.1007/978-3-030-90465-4_2-1.

Bronkhorst, Johannes. 1993. *The Two Traditions of Meditation in Ancient India.* Motilal Banarsidass.

Excerpts from the *Great Discourse to Saccaka*[5]

O Aggivessana,[6] I thought: "What if I, after having clenched the teeth and placed the tongue on the palate, clashed, confronted, collided the mind with the mind?" Then, after having clenched the teeth and placed the tongue on the palate, I clashed, confronted, collided the mind with the mind. In the process, sweat was released from my armpits.

As if there were, Aggivessana, a strong man who grappled a weaker man by the head or by the shoulders and clashed, confronted, collided with him. In the same way, after having clenched the teeth and placed the tongue on the palate, I clashed, confronted, collided the mind with the mind, and sweat was released from my armpits. I had an increasing energy that did not decrease, an established mindfulness that was relentless, but nonetheless I had an agitated body that was unquiet, while I was harassed by exertion, by painful exertion. A painful feeling like that arose, but it did not seize my mind and endure.

O Aggivessana, I thought: "What if I would enter an absorption meditation which is breathless?" Thus, Aggivessana, I suppressed airflow from both the mouth and nose. Then, Aggivessana, once I suppressed airflow from both the mouth and nose, there was a boisterous sound of winds coming out from my ear canal.[7] As if there were, Aggivessana, a boisterous sound when smith's bellows are blown. . . .

O Aggivessana, I thought: "What if I entered an absorption meditation that is truly breathless?" Thus, Aggivessana, I suppressed airflow from mouth, nose, and ears.[8] Then, Aggivessana, once I suppressed airflow from mouth, nose, and ears there were boisterous winds afflicting my head.[9] As if there were, Aggivessana, a strong man who pressed my head with a sword point. . . .[10]

O Aggivessana, I thought: "What if I entered an absorption meditation that is truly breathless?" Thus, Aggivessana, I suppressed airflow from mouth, nose, and ears. Then, Aggivessana, once I suppressed airflow from mouth, nose, and ears there were head pains in my head. As if there were, Aggivessana, a strong man who wrapped my head with a firm strip of leather. . . .

O Aggivessana, I thought: "What if I entered an absorption meditation that is truly breathless?" Thus, Aggivessana, I suppressed airflow from mouth, nose, and ears. Then, Aggivessana, once I suppressed airflow from mouth, nose, and ears, boisterous winds ran through the abdomen. As if there were, Aggivessana, a dexterous butcher or a butcher's apprentice who would run through the abdomen with a sharp meat cleaver. . . .

O Aggivessana, I thought: "What if I entered an absorption meditation that is truly breathless?" Thus, Aggivessana, I suppressed airflow from mouth, nose, and ears. Then, Aggivessana, once I suppressed airflow from mouth, nose, and ears there was an extreme heat in my body.[11] As if there were, Aggivessana, two strong men who seized a weaker man by each arm and burned and torched him in a charcoal pit.

O Aggivessana, even the gods, after having seen me, said: "The ascetic Gotama passed away!" Some gods said: "The ascetic Gotama has not passed away, but he is passing away!" Some other gods said: "The ascetic Gotama has not passed away nor is he passing away; the ascetic Gotama is an arahant, and an arahant indeed has a way of persisting like this!" . . .

Whatever ascetics or brahmanas now experience sharp, stinging, painful feelings caused by self-mortification, this is the maximum degree, there is no higher than this. But, by these sharp strenuous ascetic practices, I have not definitely attained qualities which are beyond [the average reach of] human beings or an excellence in knowledge and vision worthy enough. Could there be another path that leads to enlightenment?

O Aggivessana, I thought: "I remember that when my father Sakka was carrying out his duties, I sat in the refreshing shadow of a *jambu* tree, and, detached from sensual pleasures and from unwholesome states, reached and dwelled in the first meditative absorption, with applied and sustained thought, with joy and happiness born of seclusion. Could this be the path to enlightenment?"

O Aggivessana, I had an awareness prompted by memory: "This is, indeed, the path to enlightenment!"

Notes

1. Norman's (1984/1992, 39–40) observations, which suggest caution in the attribution of adjectives such as "intact" and "complete" to the Pāli canon, should not deter us from considering its value as an organic collection.
2. Anālayo (2012).
3. Dutoit (1905).
4. Gethin (2001).
5. *Majjhima-nikāya* I 242–246; also translated in Ñāṇamoli and Bodhi (1995/2009, 337–340). The passage occurs in an abbreviated form at *Majjhima-nikāya* II 93 and *Majjhima-nikāya* II 212. For a comparison with other versions of this account preserved by other Buddhist traditions, see Anālayo (2011, 232–246).
6. Aggivessana (also known as Saccaka) was the son of two Jains. In our text he asks the Buddha if any pleasant or painful feeling had ever arisen in him that "seized his mind and endured." The Buddha then presents his experience with strenuous ascetic practices as an example of painful feelings.
7. We might wonder whether this was a case of tinnitus.
8. A few lines above, we read that when the Buddha suppressed airflow from his mouth and nose, he heard the sound of wind, as if the air were venting from his ears. Therefore, the rationale for this next step was to close off the ears as well. In so doing, as we will read soon, the boisterous winds remained in the head, without finding a way out.
9. It is worth noting that the verb *ūhanati* can also have meanings related to "to rise" or "lift up," so we might wonder whether this indicates that some winds that were supposed to stay in the lower part of the body rose up to the head.
10. This simile occurs in other contexts, and these are, notably, connected with sick people (e.g., *Saṃyutta-nikāya* IV 56; *Aṅguttara-nikāya* III 380).
11. The Pāli word *ḍāha* translates as "heat" and can among various meanings indicate fever.

Chapter 2

Meditation Leading to Suicide

A Discourse from the Saṃyukta-Āgama

BHIKKHU ANĀLAYO

What is about the worst thing that could happen to a meditation teacher? When considering different possibilities, the most unfortunate scenario may be recommending a particular meditation practice to someone and then finding out that the practitioner who followed this recommendation became so unbalanced as to commit suicide.

Early and later Buddhist texts agree that the Buddha was an exceptionally gifted teacher. The standard form of recollecting the Buddha by way of his qualities mentions his unsurpassable skill in guiding others in his role as a teacher of celestials and humans.[1] Yet a specimen found among the earliest strata of Buddhist texts, a discourse in the Pāli *Nikāyas* with a counterpart in the Chinese *Āgamas*, reports a mass suicide of monastics after having received the Buddha's recommendation on the meditative cultivation of the lack of attractiveness of the human body (*asubha*). The translation below takes up a version of this episode found in a topically organized collection of discourses extant in Chinese translation, the *Saṃyukta-āgama,* which has a parallel in a similar discourse collection extant in Pāli, the *Saṃyutta-nikāya.*

In addition to these two discourse versions, the same episode is also found in a range of texts on monastic discipline, the *Vinaya.* These show various stages of exaggeration and dramatization, evidently reflecting the needs of the ancient reciters to engage their audiences. Nevertheless, even with the more dramatic elements set aside, the basic storyline remains the same. The Buddha recommends the meditation practice of seeing the body as bereft of beauty to newly ordained monastics, presumably to help them maintain their celibacy. Ostensibly due to not having received more detailed instructions on the matter, the monastics engage in the practice in an unbalanced manner, in line with the fairly prevalent negative attitude toward the body in ancient Indian ascetic circles. As a result of their unbalanced practice, they develop such a degree of aversion toward their own bodies that a substantial number commit suicide. When informed of what has happened, the Buddha is on record for giving detailed instructions on another form of meditation—namely, the mindfulness of breathing.[2] In particular, the scheme of sixteen steps described in the early discourses involves experiences of joy, happiness, and gladness, counterbalancing any negativity toward the body.

The episode reflects the potential problem of general recommendations that are not followed by detailed instructions or supervision of novice meditators. This makes this tale remarkably relevant to contemporary times, where especially in the Western setting those who are fairly new to meditation and have little knowledge of Buddhism can occasionally experience destabilizing consequences when undertaking intensive and prolonged silent meditation retreats.[3]

Further Reading

Anālayo, Bhikkhu. 2014a. "The Mass Suicide of Monks in Discourse and Vinaya Literature." *Journal of the Oxford Centre for Buddhist Studies* 7:11–55.

Anālayo, Bhikkhu. 2014b. "Perspectives on the Body in Early Buddhist Meditation." In *Buddhist Meditative Traditions: Their Origin and Development,* edited by Chuang Kuo-pin. Shin Wen Feng Print.

Mills, Laurence C. R. 1992. "The Case of the Murdered Monks." *Journal of the Pali Text Society* 16:71–75.

Wiltshire, Martin G. 1983: "The 'Suicide' Problem in the Pāli Canon." *Journal of the International Association of Buddhist Studies* 6 (2): 124–140.

The Mass Suicide of Monks[4]

Thus have I heard. At one time the Buddha was staying in a Sāla tree grove alongside the river Vaggumudā, by a village of the Vajjīs.[5] At that time the Blessed One spoke to the monastics on contemplating the absence of beauty; he praised contemplating the absence of beauty, saying: "Monastics, one who cultivates contemplating the absence of beauty, cultivates it much, attains great fruit and great benefit."[6]

Then, having cultivated contemplating the absence of beauty, the monastics exceedingly loathed their bodies. Some killed themselves with a knife, some took poison, some hanged themselves with a rope or committed suicide by throwing themselves down from a crag, some got another monastic to kill them.[7]

A certain monastic, who had given rise to excessive loathing and aversion on being exposed to the absence of beauty, approached Deer Park, the son of a brahmin. He said to Deer Park, the son of a brahmin: "Venerable, if you can kill me, my robes and bowl will belong to you."[8]

Then Deer Park, the son of a brahmin, killed that monastic. Carrying the knife, he went to the bank of the river Vaggumudā. When he was washing the knife, a Māra deity, who stood in midair, praised Deer Park, the son of a brahmin:

"It is well, it is well, venerable one. You are attaining innumerable merits by being able to cause recluses, sons of the Sakyan, upholders of morality and endowed with virtue, who have not yet crossed over to cross over, who have not yet been liberated to be liberated, causing those who have not yet been stilled to attain stillness, causing those who have not yet [attained] nirvana to attain nirvana; and all their monastic possessions, robes, bowls, and various things, they all belong to you."

Then, having heard this praise, Deer Park, the son of a brahmin, further increased his evil and wrong view, having this thought: "I am truly creating great merit now by causing recluses, sons of the Sakyan, upholders of morality and [endowed] with virtue, who have not yet crossed over to cross over, who have not yet been liberated to be liberated, causing those who have not yet been stilled to attain stillness, causing those who have not yet [attained] nirvana to attain nirvana; and their robes, bowls, and various things all belong to me."

Thereupon he went around the living quarters, the areas for walking meditation, the individual huts, and the meditation huts, holding in his hand a sharp knife. On seeing monastics, he spoke in this way: "Which recluses, upholders of morality and endowed with virtue, who have not yet crossed over can I cause to cross over, who have not yet been liberated can I cause to be liberated, who have not yet been stilled can I cause to attain stillness, who have not yet [attained] nirvana can I cause to attain nirvana?"

Then all the monastics who loathed their bodies came out of their monastic living quarters and said to Deer Park, the son of a brahmin: "I have not yet attained the crossing over, you should [cause] me to cross over, I have not yet attained liberation, you should liberate me, I have not yet attained stillness, you should cause me to attain stillness, I have not yet attained nirvana, you should cause me to attain nirvana." Then Deer Park, the son of a brahmin, killed the monastics one after another with his sharp knife, until he had killed sixty persons.

At that time, on the fifteenth day, at the time for reciting the rules, the Blessed One sat in front of the community and said to the venerable Ānanda: "What is the reason, what is the cause that the monastics have come to be few, have come to decrease, have come to disappear?"

Ānanda said to the Buddha: "The Blessed One spoke to the monastics on cultivating contemplation of the absence of beauty, he praised contemplating the absence of beauty. Having cultivated contemplation of the absence of beauty, the monastics exceedingly loathed their bodies . . . *to be spoken in full up to* . . . he killed sixty monastics.[9] Blessed One, this is the reason and the cause why the monastics have come to be few, have come to decrease, have come to disappear. May the Blessed One give them another teaching causing the monastics, on having heard it, to cultivate wisdom diligently and delight in receiving the true Dharma, delight in abiding in the true Dharma."

The Buddha said to Ānanda:[10] "Therefore, I will now teach you step by step [how] to abide in a subtle abiding that inclines to awakening and that quickly causes the stilling of already arisen and not yet arisen evil and unwholesome states. It is just as a heavy rain from the sky can cause the stilling of arisen and not yet arisen dust. In the same way, monastics, cultivating this subtle abiding can cause the stilling of all [already] arisen and not yet arisen evil and unwholesome states. Ānanda, what is the subtle abiding which, being much cultivated, inclines to awakening, and which can cause the stilling of already arisen and not yet arisen evil and unwholesome states? It is abiding in mindfulness of breathing."

Ānanda said to the Buddha: "How does cultivating an abiding in mindfulness of breathing incline one to awakening and [how] can it cause the stilling of already arisen and not yet arisen evil and unwholesome states?"[11]

The Buddha said to Ānanda: "Suppose a monastic dwells in dependence on a village . . . *to be spoken in full as above up to* . . . he trains to be mindful of breathing out [contemplating] cessation."[12] When the Buddha had spoken this discourse, hearing what the Buddha had said the venerable Ānanda was delighted and received it respectfully.

Notes

1. An example is *Aṅguttara-nikāya* 6.10 at *Aṅguttara-nikāya* III 285,5, with parallels in *Saṃyukta-āgama* 931 at *Taishō Tripiṭaka* no. 99, 2: 237c23 (hereafter, *T*) and the other *Saṃyukta-āgama* 156 at *T* no. 100, 2: 432c11; on the apparent error underlying the

Chinese rendering, see Nattier (2003, 227) and on recollection of the Buddha in later texts, Harrison (1978).

2. In questioning the historical reliability of this episode, Dhammajoti (2021, 5) takes it to convey that mindfulness of breathing had not been taught at all before, which he correctly shows would not square well with other passages related to this practice. Yet the relevant passage only conveys that the practice was newly introduced to those present on this particular occasion, rather than being the first-ever instance of such instructions. Other arguments raised by Dhammajoti (2021, 4–5) include the following: the discourse versions are derivatives of the *Vinaya* accounts, which are known for a tendency to not be "wholly factual" and to be "partly fabricated," as well as the conflict between the narrative and the idea that the Buddha was a supreme teacher. Even though the extant *Vinaya* versions of this episode do indeed at times reflect a tendency to exaggeration, the fact remains that all extant versions, found among the *Vinaya*s and the discourses, agree on the basic storyline, which clearly was passed on in spite of the problems it creates with idealized depictions of the Buddha. This is as far as we can go with the material at hand, and the question of historical authenticity is to some extent beside the point, as this cannot be definitively established based on texts resulting from centuries of oral transmission; see Anālayo (2022) for more detail. In other words, it is no longer possible to ascertain what may or may not have happened on the ground in ancient India twenty-five hundred years ago, and this holds for the present case just as much as for episodes showcasing the Buddha's superb teaching skills. What can be ascertained is the narrative nucleus shared by the different extant versions of the present tale in order to try to determine its main message. Dhammajoti (2021, 5) notes that the contemplation of the lack of attractiveness of the human body is often praised elsewhere in early textual sources and only combined with a word of warning in a few later texts. This would be in line with the impression that in the context of *Vinaya* and discourse material, the present story fulfills precisely the function of sounding a warning of the possible pitfalls of this type of practice.
3. On the social dimensions of silent retreat participation that can be challenging, see Pagis (2014) and on a case of destabilization resulting in suicide, Rosenthal (2021).
4. Translation of *Saṃyukta-āgama* 809 at *T* no. 99, 2: 207b21–208a8; the title given above is not found in the original. This translation previously appeared in Anālayo (2014) and is reproduced here with permission from the publisher.
5. For reconstructing the name of the river given in *Saṃyukta-āgama* 809 at *T* no. 99, 2: 207b21, I follow Akanuma (1930/1994, 725). The location in *Saṃyutta-nikāya* 54.9 at *Saṃyutta-nikāya* V 320,7 is the Hall with the Peaked Roof in the Great Wood.
6. *Saṃyutta-nikāya* 54.9 does not report any direct speech and thus only has a counterpart to the preceding sentence, according to which the Buddha spoke in praise of cultivating *asubha*.
7. *Saṃyutta-nikāya* 54.9 at *Saṃyutta-nikāya* V 320,23, reports that on a single day ten, twenty, or thirty monks committed suicide.

8. Such a tale is not found in *Saṃyutta-nikāya* 54.9, although it does occur in the Theravāda *Vinaya* III 68,21.
9. The reference "to be spoken in full up to" is an instruction to the reciters of the discourse to supplement the full text given earlier. This type of abbreviation is frequently found in *Āgama* literature; for more detail, see Anālayo (2020).
10. In *Saṃyutta-nikāya* 54.9 at *Saṃyutta-nikāya* V 321,10, the Buddha has Ānanda first convene all the monks who live in the area.
11. In *Saṃyutta-nikāya* 54.9 at *Saṃyutta-nikāya* V 322,3, this question is part of the Buddha's own speech, instead of being posed by Ānanda.
12. The reference is to a preceding discourse in the *Saṃyukta-āgama* collection, which gives the sixteen-step scheme for mindfulness of breathing in full; for a translation and comparative study, see Anālayo (2019a).

Chapter 3

The Danger of Pride

The Twenty-Fourth Chapter of The Perfection of Insight in 8,000 Lines

CHARLES DISIMONE

The following pages consist of a translation of a chapter from *The Perfection of Insight in 8,000 Lines* (*Aṣṭasāhasrikāprajñāpāramitā*). The Perfection of Insight (Prajñāpāramitā) literature is a foundational genre of Mahāyāna sutras consisting of a voluminous assortment of works, ranging from very short to incredibly long, on the practices required of a bodhisattva mahāsattva, a person who has taken up the resolution to become a buddha, on their long path to perfect awakening (*saṃbodhi*) spanning the course of many lives over countless eons. *The Perfection of Insight in 8,000 Lines* is one of the earliest examples of Perfection of Insight literature and indeed is among the earliest known works to be definitively considered a Mahāyāna discourse. It is one of the earliest Mahāyāna works translated into Chinese.[1] It is also one of the relatively few Mahāyāna works to have very early witnesses still extant, with fragments of an early version of the work in the Gāndhārī language dating from the first through second centuries of the Common Era as well as witnesses surviving from the first millennium CE in Sanskrit.[2] It has continued to be a highly influential work to this day throughout Asia and eventually across the globe. Nonetheless, it has only been translated from the Sanskrit into European languages twice, with an English translation by Edward Conze (1958) and a French translation by Eugène Burnouf (2022).[3] For the translation here, I have relied upon the editions of the Sanskrit created by previous scholars and have consulted these against the Tibetan from the Dergé Kangyur (Sde dge bka' 'gyur).[4]

Below we find a complete translation of the twenty-fourth chapter, the "Chapter on Pride" (Abhimānaparivarta). This chapter takes the form of a discourse between the Buddha Gautama and one of his foremost disciples,

Ānanda. This discussion deals with the dangers of pride that can afflict a bodhisattva after they have made progress in their spiritual, meditative pursuits but are still far from the goal. *The Perfection of Insight in 8,000 Lines,* concerned with the practice of successfully navigating the path to buddhahood, acts as a sort of manual instructing bodhisattvas how to act and progress in this pursuit. Throughout this text and the Perfection of Insight literature as a whole, the act of hearing, memorizing, reciting, and writing the Perfection of Insight is taught as an imperative spiritual practice. It can be seen as a fundamental type of meditative practice itself. We see this clearly in the translation below, where hearing or teaching the Perfection of Insight is discussed only in terms used to describe Buddhist meditation practices.[5]

In this chapter we see bodhisattvas who have been training deeply in the Perfection of Insight, whose success in this activity begins to attract the attention of Māra, the god of temptation and illusion, drawing his ire. Māra preys on the bodhisattva's weaknesses by gaining influence over them and directing them toward vain pridefulness, viewing themselves as better than other Buddhists. This includes not only those who follow the Mainstream Buddhist vehicles, the Vehicle of the Hearers (Śrāvakayāna), which leads to becoming an arhat, and the Vehicle of the Solitary Buddhas (Pratyekayāna), which leads to becoming a *pratyekabuddha*—but also other followers of the Vehicle of the Bodhisattvas (Bodhisattvayāna),[6] their own colleagues on the long and extremely difficult road to awakening. Surprisingly, while Māra is evidently unable to influence bodhisattvas who have become irreversible (*avinivartanīya;* i.e., no longer liable to sliding into births worse than the one before and assured to complete the Bodhisattvayāna as opposed to settling for the the Śrāvakayāna or Pratyekayāna), he is able to sway those who have had their own future buddhahood predicted by a buddha during a previous life in the distant past. Even, or perhaps especially, those who know they will eventually succeed in perfect awakening are susceptible to falling victim to their own opinion of themselves as they progress toward their goal, thus moving that goal ever further away.

Within the cosmological understanding laid out in Buddhist traditions, a world system, or universe (*lokadhātu*), is made up of three realms of existence, the desire realm (*kāmadhātu*), the form realm (*rūpadhātu*), and the formless realm (*arūpadhātu*). Within these three a number of realms exist concurrently, ranging from hells to ghostly spheres of existence, the animal world, and the human world, up to various heavenly realms. Multiple world systems exist simultaneously and independent from one another, each with buddhas, deities, and living beings residing in the various realms.[7] Many deities and divine figures feature heavily within the Buddhist traditions and travel between these realms. Among them, Māra is portrayed as an antagonistic figure toward the Buddha and his Dharma. It was Māra who is famously portrayed as the one who attempted to stop the ascetic Siddhārtha Gautama as he sat under the bodhi tree from realizing perfect awakening to finally become the Buddha.

Māra is a somewhat ambiguous character within the Buddhist cosmology. While he is definitely portrayed as an existing, divine being who attempts to thwart the Buddha and those who follow his teachings, he may simultaneously be seen as what has been called a "personification of subjective mental conditions."[8] It is perhaps best to view the figure of Māra in both of these lights: an antagonist toward the Buddha and the Dharma who is the cause and yet also the embodiment of negative mental states and hallucinations, or what may be thought of today as psychological afflictions. In this particular instance, Māra specifically embodies destructive narcissistic tendencies. We see this tension in Māra's role both as an agent and a result of illusion within the translation below. Māra is dismayed to see bodhisattvas progressing in their practice of the Perfection of Insight and gains influence over them, allowing negative mental states to appear that thwart both their own goals and even the spiritual progress of those who may be charmed by their words and become their students. The only way to free oneself from this, the Buddha explains to Ānanda, is to confess these negative mental states to the monastic community, to remorsefully reprimand oneself for these past actions, and to refocus oneself on the goal of omniscience, or buddhahood, by striving to view others as if they were no other than the Teacher, the Buddha, himself.

The Perfection of Insight literature was produced by and for bodhisattvas at a time when this term referred to a community of Buddhist cultivators who viewed their goal and purpose as the highest among human endeavors. This endeavor is long and arduous, spanning an incalculable amount of time and, as such, progress is considered difficult. A real fear throughout the literature is that any hard-won progress can be subverted to regress, and this is what we see here, where fear and pride indicate a mental imbalance that can hinder not only the bodhisattva but also those around them. In the beginning of the chapter, we find various Māras of many world systems focus their attention upon a bodhisattva who is making progress in meditative cultivation toward complete awakening through following the Perfection of Insight, a state free from negative mental afflictions and thus one loathed by all Māras in any world system. They first seek to thwart this by causing the meditating bodhisattva to become fearful, to the point of breaking their psyche by creating an apocalyptic scene in the form of meteors in the sky. This may be viewed as a distressing hallucination that can arise in meditation and potentially cause severe mental harm to the person who perceives them. It is important to note that negative mental states do not arise in everyone but rather fall upon those whom Māra sees as vulnerable to his influence, those who are unnerved by uncertainty and engaged in unhealthy relationships. A similar profile applies to many who may suffer from poor mental health today.

In the end, those afflicted by narcissistic traits prove the most susceptible to the mental imbalance personified by Māra. While the Perfection of Insight literature served as a guidebook for those who chose to be bodhisattvas, the mental dangers of pride are just as real for any meditator. Even though a meditator may have gained significant experience and discipline in their mental cultivation, based upon their personality and previous experiences they are potentially liable to succumb to the alluringly pleasant feeling of superiority over others. This way of being prizes the individual's self and personality to the point of allowing them to view others with contempt, making it dangerously easy to commit abuse and violence toward them, whether it is spiritual, psychological, or physical. As is noted in the chapter, this can be especially dangerous for those who begin to fill the role of a teacher with responsibility over others. In recent years many disturbing revelations have come to light about spiritual teachers in Mahāyāna communities who are continuing the very bodhisattva traditions fundamental to the Perfection of Insight. While appearing to hold great spiritual authority and power over their community, they have been outed as narcissistic manipulators who abused the very people they were charged with guiding toward awakening. As we can see from this chapter from *The Perfection of Insight in 8,000 Lines,* this danger of cultivation has been known all too well within the Buddhist community for millennia and is becoming more widely known among those engaging in meditative practices today.

Further Reading

Anālayo. 2019. "Brahmā, Śakra, and Māra." In *Brill's Encyclopedia of Buddhism.* Vol. 2, *Lives,* edited by Jonathan A. Silk, Richard Bowring, Vincent Eltschinger, and Michael Radich. Brill.

Burnouf, Eugène. 2022. *Aṣṭasāhasrikā Prajñāpāramitā: La perfection de sagesse en huit mille stances.* Edited by Guillaume Ducoeur. Université de Strasbourg.

Conze, Edward. 1958. *Aṣṭasāhasrikā Prajñāpāramitā: The Perfection of Wisdom in Eight Thousand Slokas.* Asiatic Society.

Zacchetti, Stefano. 2015. "Prajñāpāramitā Sūtras." In *Brill's Encyclopedia of Buddhism.* Vol. 1, *Literature and Languages,* edited by Jonathan A. Silk, Oskar von Hinüber, and Vincent Eltschinger. Brill.

Pride, the Twenty-Fourth Chapter in the Noble *Perfection of Insight in 8,000 Lines*

Then the Blessed One again addressed the Venerable Ānanda: At a time, Ānanda, when a bodhisattva mahāsattva trains in the Perfection of Insight, engages in the yoga of the Perfection of Insight, cultivates the Perfection of Insight, at this time, Ānanda, those evil Māras in the triple thousand great thousand world system, are hesitant. "Will this bodhisattva mahāsattva directly realize the final goal while in the midst of the *śrāvaka* stage or *pratyeka* stage? Or will he even thoroughly realize unsurpassed, complete and perfect awakening!?"

Moreover, at a time when a bodhisattva mahāsattva dwells in the refuge of the Perfection of Insight, at this time those evil Māras are pierced by arrows of affliction.

Moreover, Ānanda, at a time when a bodhisattva mahāsattva practices the Perfection of Insight, engages in the yoga of the Perfection of Insight, cultivates the Perfection of Insight, at this time those evil Māras cause him harm, they produce fear in him, they let fly a shower of meteors in all directions causing him to perceive an unnaturally red glow upon the horizon. Saying: "Perhaps this bodhisattva mahāsattva might cower down or his hair may stand on end, and with this his production of a single-minded fixation upon unsurpassed, complete and perfect awakening might be diminished." In that case, Ānanda, Māra, that evil one, does not attack with the intention to harm every bodhisattva mahāsattva, rather some he attacks and others he does not.

Ānanda said: Blessed One, which type of bodhisattva mahāsattva does Māra, that evil one, attack intending to harm?

The Blessed One said: Ānanda, a bodhisattva mahāsattva who has not already in the past aroused a resolve [toward awakening] when speaking the Perfection of Insight. This, Ānanda, is the bodhisattva mahāsattva who Māra, that evil one, attacks intending to harm, and he finds the opportunity to influence him.

Moreover, Ānanda, a bodhisattva mahāsattva who is filled with hesitation when speaking of the Perfection of Insight, who produces uncertainty, saying: "Perhaps this is the Perfection of Insight. Perhaps it is this way, perhaps it is not." This also, Ānanda, is the bodhisattva mahāsattva who Māra, that evil one, attacks intending to harm, and he finds the opportunity to influence him.

Moreover, Ānanda, a bodhisattva mahāsattva who is without a good friend, who is held back by evil friends, who does not listen to its deeply profound subjects when speaking the Perfection of Insight. He did not listen and so does not know. He did not know and so does not ask: "How is the Perfection of Insight to be cultivated?" This also, Ānanda, is the bodhisattva mahāsattva who

Māra, that evil one, attacks intending to harm, and he finds the opportunity to influence him.

Moreover, Ānanda, a bodhisattva mahāsattva who hangs on to one who adheres to false Dharma, saying: "He is my companion, and in all matters, he does not forsake me. There are many other bodhisattva mahāsattvas whom I might accompany. However, they do not fulfill my purpose, so I have kept him as a suitable companion. He will fulfill my purpose." This also, Ānanda, is the bodhisattva mahāsattva who Māra, that evil one, attacks intending to harm, and he finds the opportunity to influence him.

Moreover, Ānanda, a bodhisattva who, when this profound Perfection of Insight is being spoken, might say this to another bodhisattva: "Profound indeed is this Perfection of Insight. Why do you bother with listening to it? When, although I apply myself to other discourses as they were spoken by the Tathāgata, I cannot attain even a taste of its depth! Why do you bother with listening to it or with writing it?" In this way he dissuades other bodhisattva mahāsattvas. This also, Ānanda, is the bodhisattva mahāsattva who Māra, that evil one, attacks intending to harm, and he finds the opportunity to influence him.

Moreover, Ānanda, at a time when a bodhisattva mahāsattva holds other bodhisattvas in contempt, thinking: "I dwell in a state of detachment. The others do not dwell in a state of detachment. For the others, states of detachment do not exist." At this time, Ānanda, Māra, that evil one, is pleased, satisfied, glad, delighted, elated, excited, titillated, and enraptured. Why is this? Because this bodhisattva is now far from unsurpassed, complete and perfect awakening.

Moreover, Ānanda, at a time when a bodhisattva mahāsattva mentions his name, mentions his lineage, or proclaims ascetic qualities for himself, he may regard that as sufficient reason to hold in contempt other bodhisattva mahāsattvas who are clever and virtuous in character. The qualities of irreversible bodhisattva mahāsattvas who practice the Perfection of Insight do not exist for him, nor do their traits, signs, or marks exist for him.

When these qualities of irreversibility do not exist, he produces defilements. That is to say, he esteems himself and disparages others, thinking: "Certainly, they do not appear to be my equal regarding these Dharmas." In that case those evil Māras conclude: "The realms of Māra will not be empty, they will swell. The great hot hells, the animal world, the sphere of hungry ghosts, and the host of *āsuras* will become swollen."

As Māra, that evil one, becomes more empowered, so those bodhisattva mahāsattvas likewise will be trampled over by honor and gain. They will become crafters of pleasant speech. They will captivate many people with this pleasant speech. The public will regard them as being worth listening to and worth believing. They will fall into the misfortune of imitating them in what they have seen and heard. Falling into this misfortune of imitating what they have seen and heard, they will not train for suchness. They will not practice for suchness. They will fall into the misfortune of not engaging in yoga for suchness. In this way, not training in suchness, not practicing in suchness, and falling into the misfortune of not engaging in yoga in suchness, their defilements will increase. In this way, whatever actions they even whisper toward with their inverted mentality—whether by body, speech, or mind—will turn out unpleasant, disagreeable, disgusting, and repulsive. In this way the great hot hells will become swollen, the animal world, the sphere of hungry ghosts, and the host of *āsuras*—the realms of Māra—will become swollen. Ānanda, recognizing this state of affairs, Māra, that evil one, is pleased, satisfied, glad, delighted, and elated.

Moreover, Ānanda, at a time when a bodhisattva mahāsattva fights with a person following the Vehicle of the Hearers, rebukes or alienates him, may despise, may revile, may be malicious, or produces hatred toward him, at this time Māra, that evil one, concludes: "Far indeed will this son of a good family remain from omniscience. He will remain further still from omniscience if a person following the Vehicle of the Bodhisattvas fights with another person following the Vehicle of the Bodhisattvas, rebukes or alienates him, may despise, may revile, may be malicious, or produces hatred toward him." In that case, Māra, that evil one, is especially pleased, is especially satisfied, glad, delighted, and elated. He thinks in this way: "Both of these bodhisattvas will remain far from omniscience."

Moreover, Ānanda, if a bodhisattva mahāsattva who has had a prediction [of his own future awakening] were to fight with a bodhisattva mahāsattva who has not had a prediction, rebuke or alienate him, despise, revile, show malice, produce hatred toward him, or harbor ill-will toward him, this bodhisattva mahāsattva is to arm himself with arousing the resolve [toward awakening] for as many eons it takes if omniscience is not to be abandoned.

Thus addressed, the Venerable Ānanda spoke to the Blessed One: Blessed One, is there some escape for those who arouse resolve? Or must this bodhisattva mahāsattva inevitably arm himself so for as many eons as it takes?

The Blessed One said: Ānanda, I have taught Dharma allowing for such escape for people who are followers of the Vehicle of the Hearers, the Vehicle of the Solitary Buddhas, and the Vehicle of the Bodhisattvas. In that case, Ānanda, a person who is a follower of the Vehicle of the Bodhisattvas who, having fought with a person who is a follower of the Vehicle of the Bodhisattvas, having rebuked or alienated him, despised, reviled, shown malice, or produced hatred toward him, who does not confess [his transgressions], who does not practice restraint in the future, who bears this latent proclivity, who dwells bound to this proclivity, to this person, Ānanda, I do not say there is an escape. Rather, this person must inevitably arm himself so for as many eons as it takes.

However, Ānanda, a person who is a follower of the Vehicle of the Bodhisattvas who, having fought with a person who is a follower of the Vehicle of the Bodhisattvas, having rebuked or alienated him, despised, reviled, shown malice, or produced hatred toward him, who does confess, and having confessed who does practice restraint in the future, he arouses the following resolve: "I am supposed to eliminate, eradicate, and pacify alienation, rebuke, and conflict from all beings, and yet I myself rebuke [others]. I find loss and not gain when I am one who responds in the way I am spoken to. I am supposed to cultivate remaining within the sea of transmigration for all beings, and yet I say to others 'you!,' giving a sharp or harsh reply. I am not supposed to speak to others like this. In the face of fighting, alienation, and rebuke I am supposed to seem apathetic, as silent as a sheep. Hearing someone saying offensive, abusive, or insulting words I am not supposed to harbor ill-will. I am one who recognizes the faults within another, and it is not proper or agreeable for me to do so in the presence of others. Nor is it agreeable that I think that the faults of others are worth hearing about.

"Why is this? As one with the highest intentions, I am not the one to disturb others. I, the one who is supposed to gladden all beings by providing the basis of all happiness. Who, having thoroughly realized unsurpassed, complete and perfect awakening, is supposed to lead them to *parinirvāṇa*. Nevertheless, I show malice. I am not supposed to show malice toward others even when they wrong me. Nevertheless, I become perturbed. I am not supposed to do that. I am supposed to be firmly and resolutely disciplined. I am not to become perturbed even if my life is in danger and without a frown upon my face."

To this bodhisattva mahāsattva, Ānanda, I say there is an escape. In this way, Ānanda, a bodhisattva mahāsattva is to stand in the presence of people who follow the Vehicle of the Hearers. That is to say, he should not become perturbed in the presence of any beings whatsoever. In this very way, he is to stand in the presence of all beings. How, Ānanda, is a bodhisattva mahāsattva to stand in the presence of people following the Vehicle of the Bodhisattvas? Just as if, Ānanda, he was in the presence of the Teacher [the Buddha]. He is to stand thinking in this way: "These bodhisattva mahāsattvas are my teachers. Certainly, these bodhisattva mahāsattvas enter the one and the same vehicle as mine. Certainly, these bodhisattva mahāsattvas enter the one and the same path as mine. Certainly, these bodhisattva mahāsattvas have intentions concordant with mine. Certainly, these bodhisattva mahāsattvas have set out on a vehicle concordant with mine. In whatever way they are to train is how I am to train. As they train so I shall train. If, however, one of them will dwell in confusion, I am not to dwell in confusion. If, however, they will dwell unconfused, concentrating upon concern with omniscience, then I am to train in that way." Training in omniscience in this way, Ānanda, there is no hindrance to unsurpassed, complete and perfect awakening for a bodhisattva mahāsattva. He swiftly thoroughly realizes unsurpassed, complete and perfect awakening.

Notes

1. *Taishō Tripiṭaka* no. 224, translated by Lokakṣema in 179 CE, the first of many translations into Chinese, Tibetan, and many other languages.
2. See Falk and Karashima (2012, 2013) on the Gāndhārī fragments, Sander (2000, 2002) on an early Kuṣāṇa-period Sanskrit witness likely found around Bāmiyān in Afghanistan, DiSimone (2023) on a fifth- or sixth-century Sanskrit witness recently excavated from the ancient city of Mes Aynak in Afghanistan, and Ye (2013) for a fragment from the eighth or ninth centuries found in Xinjiang. These all predate the earliest witnesses of this work extant via Nepal by centuries.
3. Unfortunately, both of these translations are not without their problems. Conze's, despite his occasionally great eloquence and deep knowledge of the *Prajñāpāramitā* corpus, is not always a literal translation and not without inaccuracies. Burnouf's, while finally published in 2022, was produced in the 1840s and suffers from being created during a period when the academic study of Buddhism was in its infancy. Nevertheless, Burnouf's efforts are highly impressive. Both Conze's and Burnouf's translations are from the Sanskrit. No complete translation exists from the Chinese, but an English translation by Matthew Orsborn and Lewis Lancaster of Kumārajīva's translation (*Taishō Tripiṭaka* no. 227) is near completion and will be published in the BDK English Tripiṭaka Project. A French translation has been made from the Tibetan (Driessens 2007), although its quality is not known to me, and an English translation is currently in progress by Greg Seton for the 84000 project to translate the words of the Buddha.
4. Mitra (1888); Wogihara (1932–1935); and Vaidya (1960). I have primarily favored Wogihara's edition, which faithfully responds to Mitra's. Vaidya's edition is more a reediting of Mitra than a new edition based off of manuscripts and should not be relied upon by itself. For the Tibetan, I utilized the scans from the Dergé Kangyur (Dergé ka 226a5–229b4) of the *'phags pa shes rab kyi pha rol tu phyin pa brgyad stong pa* available from the Buddhist Digital Resource Center.
5. Variously, engaging in the yoga of the Perfection of Insight (*prajñāpāramitāyāṃ yogam apadyate*), cultivating the Perfection of Insight (*prajñāpāramitāṃ bhāvayati*), practicing it (*carati*), dwelling in a state of detachment (*vivekavihāreṇa viharanti*), and proclaiming ascetic qualities (*dhutaguṇaparikīrtanam*). For the bodhisattva, maintaining

attention toward the Perfection of Insight is often described as the recommended best form of meditation to which they should dedicate themselves.

6. An earlier term for the Mahāyāna.
7. As we see in the beginning of the translation, all the Māras of many world systems are dismayed when bodhisattvas engage in the practice of the Perfection of Insight.
8. Anālayo (2019b), 88. Although it should be noted that Anālayo himself favors the interpretation of Māra as a physical entity directly responsible for his actions.

Chapter 4

Therapies for Contemplation Gone Wrong

Secret Essential Methods for Curing Meditation Sickness

ERIC M. GREENE

Secret Essential Methods for Curing Meditation Sickness (hereafter, *Methods for Curing*), translated below, is a Chinese Buddhist text, in the form of a sutra, preserved in the East Asian Buddhist canon. It is one of the oldest and most comprehensive premodern Buddhist texts to take up the topic of meditation sickness (*chanbing*). Taken as a whole, *Methods for Curing* suggests that while meditation can lead to serious problems that can damage both the body and the mind, with the proper methods these problems can be overcome.

Bibliographic sources state that *Methods for Curing* was translated into Chinese in the year 455 CE, at a nunnery near the southern Chinese capital of Jiankang (modern Nanjing), by a layman named Juqu Jingsheng who obtained the original text from an Indian meditation teacher in the Central Asian city of Khotan along the Silk Road. This Juqu Jingsheng was, supposedly, a refugee member of the royal family of the Northern Liang kingdom (based in present-day Gansu Province) that in the year 439 had been conquered by the rival Northern Wei. Although this story probably tells us the rough date at which it entered wider circulation, a careful analysis of the content of *Methods for Curing* suggests that it was, in fact, not the direct translation of a single original text written in an Indian language. Like a number of other new meditation texts that appeared in China in the 400s, *Methods for Curing* seems rather to have been the product of a murky process in which the legacies of various Indian and Central Asian teachers of Buddhist meditation who were then living in China—a time when the practice of Buddhist meditation was rapidly increasing in prominence among Chinese Buddhists and there appeared many new meditation texts—were recorded, compiled, edited, and perhaps expanded. To this extent, *Methods for Curing* is a document that emerged at the intersection of the Indian (or at least, non-Chinese) and Chinese Buddhist worlds. Although it is thus an example of what is traditionally called an *apocryphal* Chinese Buddhist text, it does not reflect the thinking of Chinese Buddhists alone but rather reveals aspects of a wider, cosmopolitan, and transnational culture of Buddhist meditation that during this time existed, in various forms, across India, central Asia, and China.

Methods for Curing takes the form of two short, nominally independent sutras written in a style resembling the sutras of the Indian Buddhist Āgama/Nikāya collections. Notable is the presence, within the framing narratives, of protagonists such as the prince Virūḍhaka and the monk Lekuñcika, who are known personages from Indian Buddhist lore but appear here in unusual contexts different from the traditional stories concerning them. The Chinese compilers of *Methods for Curing* evidently took the trouble to populate their new sutra with minor yet authentically Indian Buddhist characters whose presence would lend authenticity to the text. And, indeed, the status of *Methods for Curing* as an Indian sutra was never questioned in later Chinese Buddhism.

Originally, it seems that *Methods for Curing* was connected to a larger set of meditation texts that provided a path to awakening based on a variety of meditation techniques in a distinctly "visionary" vein (that is, techniques that both make use of imagery-rich imagination and are said to produce visions as a result).[1] *Methods for Curing* was perhaps originally a kind of appendix to that larger treatise, spelling out problems that could arise for those following this path. These problems are divided between techniques for curing meditation-induced "sicknesses" (*bing*), in the first sutra, and methods, in the second sutra, for countering the attacks of certain "demons" (*mo*), to which meditators are, apparently, particularly susceptible.

The first sutra begins with the story of a group of meditators who are driven to madness when a loud noise disturbs them as they engage in the "contemplation of the wind element," which is implied here to be an advanced meditation practice. The Buddha then supplies a method for "curing" this situation by imagining a soundproof dome (§ 2). Later passages repeat this pattern of first explaining a scenario in which a meditator succumbs to either madness or a bodily illness, followed by a technique for resolving the issue. Sometimes, it is relatively clear that the "sickness" in question is what we would call psychological in character, such as the case of a meditator who has horrific hallucinations (§ 14). In other cases, they are decidedly physical. When one undertakes meditation on the fire element, for example, one can inadvertently overheat the body's "fire channels" (*huomai*), resulting in difficulty hearing or headaches (§ 13). Entering the "*samādhi* of the water element," on the other hand, can lead to a "continual diarrhea" (§ 12). Here it seems that meditation practices whose object is the material element of one's own body (a common object of meditative contemplation) can accidently provoke sickness. The details of *why* this is so are not specified, but the underlying theory must be a version of the standard Buddhist idea that bodily illness results from imbalance within the four material elements of the body (earth, water, wind, and fire).[2]

Portions of the text not included here (§ 7–11) but translated elsewhere warn that moral failings or lapses in discipline may derail the meditator, including lust, greed, violating the precepts, relishing pleasing sounds, and being enamored with melodic chanting and religious poetry. That moral failings such as these will impede meditation is a standard idea within Buddhist thought. The present text, however, emphasizes the way these failings produce illness-like symptoms in meditators that must be "cured" as part of one's forward progress along the path. Also not included here is the second and much shorter sutra of *Methods for Curing*. This text provides only two methods: one for banishing a demon who causes nocturnal emissions and a second for countering demons who harass meditators by causing "aching joints, itchy palms, pain on the soles of the feet," and other similar discomforts such as numbness in the legs.

In its presentation of meditation sickness, *Methods for Curing* provides an early example of an eventually common idea in Chinese religious culture—that the methods of mental and bodily cultivation that lead to awakening or transcendence can also, if wrongly performed, provoke illness, madness, or even death. As a primarily practical guide to curing such problems, *Methods for Curing* does not explain why its methods work. But we can discern a few patterns. Frequently, sickness that is generated by a given meditation practice is treated by developing or visualizing an opposing quality or state, thereby, it seems, restoring balance. Thus, for example, meditators who are dangerously disturbed by noise should visualize ghee coating their eardrums (§ 2); madness caused by a disturbance of the heart channels is cured when the meditator imagines those channels being irrigated with divine milk (§ 3); and excessive heat in the body is cured when one imagines being bathed a cooling light (§ 4). Some methods also involve the imaginative performance of real medical procedures such as trepanation and acupuncture (§ 5), suggesting that the authors here wanted to connect their methods to "medicine" in its strict sense. Similarly, in some cases *Methods for Curing* also recommends what it calls "worldly medicines" (§ 6; § 12) such as milk, honey, and the *harītakī* (myrobalan plum) fruit (§ 2).

Although *Methods for Curing* introduces most of its methods as ways of countering problems or obstacles generated by meditation, many if not most sections end up implying that these methods will also lead the adept forward on the path to awakening. The link that is in this way established between healing the body and progress toward liberation reflects what we might call a somatic soteriology, eventually a frequent theme within the literature of Indian Tantra, Buddhist and otherwise. *Methods for Curing* is notable for containing some of the earliest known Buddhist claims to this effect.

These ideas inform many parts of *Methods for Curing,* including the frame story of the first sutra in which the method for "softening and curing the internal wind element" first heals monks of their immediate ailment but then leads them to arhatship (§ 3). Section 4 presents a four-part sequence initially introduced as a means of curing imbalances in the four elements provoked by meditation, which then leads to progressively more advanced soteriological attainments, culminating in an encounter with the seven buddhas of the past. Similarly, the "enveloping butter contemplation" of section 5 is initially prescribed for meditators beset by the seemingly physical malady of excessive gas (caused, again, by an imbalance in the four elements) but concludes with a visionary consecration by the god Brahmā that "tames the ninety-eight defilements." A meditator assailed by cold winds that lead to "blockage"—a term of art described in a highly medicalized idiom—is treated by a long sequence of techniques by which he eventually becomes either an arhat or firmly established on the bodhisattva path (§ 6). The method prescribed for curing diarrhea ultimately "eliminates the ocean of karmic obstructions," thereby placing the meditator near to awakening (§ 12).

All these passages seem to imply that there is a distinctly somatic element to the meditative path to liberation, an idea rarely mentioned in classic Indian Buddhist meditation manuals. *Methods for Curing,* to this extent, foreshadows the development of such ideas within Tantra, such as the various "subtle body" processes well-known from those traditions.[3] Though it remains difficult to locate any specific prehistories of those later traditions, a few tantalizing passages are worthy of further investigation, such as section 7 (not included in the excerpts here), which sketches out some kind of connection, through the bodily channels, between the (male) sexual organs and the crown of the head, a circuit that is the subject of much discussion in both Daoist and Tantric methods of physiological cultivation. *Methods for Curing,* as a text composed or compiled in China, reflects conditions in India only imperfectly. Still, the presence of these ideas suggests that by as early as the turn of the fifth century at least some Indian Buddhist traditions had come to conceive of the path from ordinary being to liberated saint, as developed through meditation, as something involving all aspects of one's person. Those who undertake the path of meditation must thus be prepared to face, and then overcome, the kinds of sicknesses that *Methods for Curing* describes.

Further Reading

Greene, Eric M. 2016. "Visions and Visualizations: In Fifth-Century Chinese Buddhism and 19th-Century Experimental Psychology." *History of Religions* 55 (3): 289–328.

Greene, Eric M. 2021a. *Chan Before Chan: Meditation, Repentance, and Visionary Experience in Chinese Buddhism*. University of Hawai'i Press.

Greene, Eric M. 2021b. *The Secrets of Buddhist Meditation: Visionary Meditation Texts from Early Medieval China*. University of Hawai'i Press.

O'Brien-Kop, Karen. 2022. "Meditation, Idealism and Materiality: Vivid Visualization in the Buddhist 'Qizil Yoga Manual' and the Context of Caves." *Journal of Indian Philosophy* 50:223–244.

Yamabe, Nobuyoshi. 2005. "Visionary Repentance and Visionary Ordination in the Brahma Net Sutra." In *Going Forth: Visions of Buddhist Vinaya*, edited by William M. Bodiford. University of Hawai'i Press.

Excerpts from *Secret Essential Methods for Curing Meditation Sickness:*[4]

Methods for Curing the Seventy-Two Sicknesses That Disturb the Minds of Forest-Dwelling Meditators:[5] Questions of the Venerable Śāriputra from the Forest-Dwelling Section of the *Connected Discourses*[6]

[1. Introduction]

Thus have I heard. Once, the Buddha was dwelling in Śrāvasti, in Sudatta's park in the grove of Prince Jeta, together with one thousand two hundred fifty monks. It was summer, the fifteenth day of the fifth month. Five hundred monks of the Śākya clan were dwelling in the bamboo grove cultivating the forest dwellers' practice. Cultivating their minds through meditation on the twelve links of dependent origination while performing breath meditation, they entered the beryl *samādhi*.

Just then Virūḍhaka, son of King Prasenajit,[7] was riding on a great fragrant elephant accompanied by five hundred other sons of prominent men. Near the edge of Jeta's grove, they put on a performance by getting their elephants drunk and staging an elephant fight in which a troupe of black-lotus elephants made horrid roars, like thunderclaps interspersed with the faint screeching of a cat.

The Śākya monks, including Nandi the Meditator and Upanandi, were startled, their hair standing on end, and being immersed in the contemplation of the wind element, were driven mad. Emerging from trance, they were unrestrained like drunken elephants.

The venerable Ānanda ordered the other monks: "Lock the doors! These Śākyas have gone mad and might cause harm."

The other monks went to Śāriputra and said: "O Venerable One, your wisdom is unobstructed, and fear vanishes in your wake as from the victory banner of lord Indra. Please have compassion and rescue these Śākyas from the suffering of their madness!"

At that, Śāriputra got up from his seat and led Ānanda by the hand to the Buddha. He circled the Buddha three times, and after making prostrations, knelt down before the Buddha with joined palms and addressed him: "O World-honored One, may you, honored by the gods, bestow your compassion on all. In forest-dwelling monks of the future, madness may arise in five different ways: one, because of loud sounds; two, because of bad reputation;[8] three, because of desire for personal gain; four, because of external winds; five, because of internal winds. May you, honored by the gods, please explain to me, for the sake of people such as this, how these five illnesses may be cured!

The World-honored One smiled and a five-colored light emerged from his mouth, circled him seven times, and reentered his body through the crown of the head. Then he said to Śāriputra: "Listen carefully, listen carefully, and reflect on it well. I will now explain this to you."

[2. The Method for Curing a Perturbed Mind]

When a practitioner is practicing the forest dwellers' way and cultivating his mind by the contemplation of the twelve links, if his mind organ is touched within by an unpleasant external noise, the four hundred and four channels will at once become agitated owing to excess tension in his heart. Because wind is the strongest [of the four elements], it is the first to produce madness, shaking the heart channels and causing the five kinds of wind to enter the throat, where they initially produce evil speech.

In this case the practitioner must be instructed to consume milk, honey, and myrobolan plum and to fix his mind on a single thing. He must first imagine a crystal mirror and contemplate himself within the mirror performing various deeds of madness, that is to say, transgressions. When he sees this, he should be further instructed with the following words: "You now see yourself within the clear mirror performing deeds of madness and delusion. Your parents and kinsmen also see you doing these wicked things. I will now teach you how to separate yourself from madness and delusion. You must remember this."

The practitioner must first be taught to remove the sound.[9] The method for removing the sound is as follows. He must press his tongue upward against his palate. Then he should imagine a *maṇi* pearl within each of his ears. From the tips of these wish-fulfilling pearls, which are like droplets of milk, ghee flows out and coats the eardrums so that they no longer register sound. Even if there is a loud noise, they will remain unmoving, as if coated in thick oil.

When this meditation is complete, the practitioner should next imagine a nine-layered adamantine canopy emerging from the royal wish-fulfilling pearls and covering his body. An adamantine flower appears below, upon which he sits. Adamantine mountains with no gap between them surround him on all four sides, so that external sounds are completely blocked. Within each of the mountains are seven seated buddhas, who instruct him in the four bases of mindfulness. There is now total silence. He hears no external sounds. He follows only the teachings of these buddhas.

This is called the method for removing disturbance, the meditation that removes evil sounds. The Buddha said to Śāriputra: You practitioners must cultivate this and not forget it. This is called the method for curing a perturbed mind.

[3. The Method for Softening and Curing the Internal Wind Element]

Next, Śāriputra, having removed external sounds, one must remove internal sounds. Internal sounds occur when the six sensory organs, having been shaken by external sounds, perturb the heart channel and cause five kinds of evil wind to enter and stir the heart, causing singing, dancing, and all sorts of strange behavior.

You must teach this person the heart-cleansing contemplation. For the heart-cleansing contemplation, the practitioner first contemplates his heart, making it gradually brighter until it is a fire jewel, its four hundred and four channels, like the leaves of the trunk of a beryl-gold plantain tree, reaching to the tip. The fire jewel heart emits a vapor (qi), neither cold nor hot, neither thick nor thin, that wafts into the channels. The practitioner now imagines Lord Brahmā holding a wish-fulfilling jewel mirror,[10] reflecting the practitioner's chest. He sees his own chest as a royal wish-fulfilling jewel, beautiful and pure, with a fire jewel as the heart.

Lord Brahmā holds an imperial seal, within which is a white lotus flower. Atop the white lotus flower is a divine boy. Holding up fresh milk in his hands, he emerges from the royal wish-fulfilling jewel and pours the milk into the channels of the practitioner's heart. The milk drips downward to the tip of the heart. The divine boy then holds two needles, one golden and one blue. He places two gold flowers against the sides of the heart and runs the needles through them seven times.[11] When he has finished, the heart returns to its former state of relaxation. He further rinses the heart with the milk. The milk drips into the large intestine, and when the large intestine is full it flows into the small intestine.[12] When the small intestine is full, the milk drips from it, drop by drop, into the mouths of the eighty families of worms.[13] When the worms are full, the milk circulates throughout the body, irrigating the three hundred thirty-six bones.

Next, the practitioner must imagine a pond of milk with a white lotus flower growing in it, upon which he sits, bathing himself with milk. He imagines a cotton cloth, white like a lotus flower, wrapping around his body seven times. Lord Brahmā takes milk from his own body and rinses out the practitioner's mouth. Having done this, Lord Brahmā takes a parasol and holds it above the practitioner's head. Seeing many amazing confirmatory visions in Lord Brahmā's parasol, the practitioner regains his sanity and is no longer disturbed.[14]

When the Buddha had spoken these words, the five hundred Śākya monks followed the Buddha's instructions exactly. Their minds became clear, and they contemplated the five aggregates of matter, sensations, perceptions, volitional formations, and consciousness as impermanent, suffering, empty, and non-self. No longer clinging to the world, they understood the truth of emptiness and regained their sanity in a flash, smashing the raging defilements of eighty million and becoming stream-enterers, certain to continue their cultivation and become arhats endowed with the three wisdoms, six powers, and eight deliverances.

At that time the monks, hearing what the Buddha had said, joyfully undertook to carry it out. This is called the method for softening and curing the internal wind element.

[4. Curing Imbalances in the Four Elements]

Further, Śāriputra, one who wishes to practice meditation should skillfully contemplate the four great elements and adjust according to the season.

In spring he should enter the fire *samādhi,* thereby warming his body. If the fire becomes too strong, his body will overheat, and he must correct this by imagining the flames of the fire as wish-fulfilling jewels. They emerge from his pores, and in the midst of the flames he imagines golden lotus flowers, upon which sit transformation buddhas who preach the curing of illness with three different jewels: a "moon essence" wish-fulfilling jewel, a "starlight" wish-fulfilling jewel that is blue in color with a white glow, like a star, and a crystal wish-fulfilling jewel. He imagines the three jewels, one shining on top of his head, one shining on his left shoulder, and one shining on his right shoulder. When he has seen the three jewels, he then imagines the light of the jewels emerging from the pores of his body, extremely cool and refreshing. With his body and mind relaxed, he can enter the fire *samādhi* without incurring harm.

This is called the method for curing [imbalances resulting from] the *samādhi* of the fire element.

Further, Śāriputra, in autumn one should enter the earth *samādhi*. Immersed in the earth *samādhi*, the practitioner will see the many forms of earth: a hundred thousand stone mountains, iron mountains, encircling iron mountains, and adamantine mountains. Each of the three hundred thirty-six bones of his body becomes hundreds of thousands of mountains, steep and jagged in appearance.

To cure this, he must imagine and carefully contemplate these mountains as being as insubstantial as the trunk of a plantain tree. He must contemplate them one by one in this manner, using the ten similes for emptiness from the sutras. He then sees the great earth, in all directions, becoming white beryl and white jewel flowers. He sees Śāriputra, Maudgalyāyana, Kāśyapa, and Kātyāyana sitting within caves of white adamant, sunk within the earth as if it were water.[15] They preach for the practitioner the "separation and coming together of the five" and the impermanence of the earth element.[16] When the practitioner sees these things, his body and mind become relaxed and he regains his sanity.

This is called the method for curing [imbalance of] the earth element.

Further, Śāriputra, if the practitioner enters the water *samādhi* and sees his body as a giant surging fountain of water, his three hundred thirty-six bones all washed away, and if he sees the world in all directions filled with blue, white, or red water, then he must quickly be cured.

The method for curing [this imbalance in the] water element is as follows. First, he must contemplate his body and make it an auspicious wish-fulfilling jewel vase, with golden flowers covering the top. He must then make the waters of the ten directions flow into the vase. Seven flowers emerge from the auspicious vase, their seven stalks each clearly apparent. Within each stalk are seven jets of water. Within each jet of water are seven golden flowers, and upon each flower sits a buddha preaching the seven limbs of awakening.

This is called the method for curing [imbalance in the] water element.

Further, Śāriputra, if a practitioner who enters the wind *samādhi* sees his body as a nine-headed snake, each head with nine hundred ears and innumerable mouths, its pores, ears, and mouths like deep gorges emitting violent winds, then he must quickly be cured.

The method for curing is as follows. The practitioner must be taught to contemplate his body, making for it an adamantine seat.[17] On each side he imagines an adamantine wheel to block the wind. Seven adamantine flowers emerge from the adamantine wheels,[18] upon which are transformation buddhas holding pitchers of water. Within each pitcher is a six-headed dragon that moves about inhaling the winds of the ten directions and making them still. The practitioner then sees the seven buddhas and the four great voice-hearers,[19] who again explain for him the seven limbs of awakening and then gradually reveal the eightfold holy path.

This is called the method for curing [imbalance in] the internal wind element.

[5. The Enveloping Butter Contemplation to Soften the Four Elements and Allow the Gradual Attainment of the Confirmatory Visions of Sanctity]

Further, Śāriputra, if the four elements of the practitioner's body become imbalanced, he may become alternately angry and happy, or sad and joyful. Or he may begin to crawl about on his stomach, or else may pass gas. He must be taught to immediately cure such sicknesses.

The method for curing this is as follows. First, he must, beginning from the tip of his toe, contemplate the outer layer of his skin. He sees this outer layer of skin, itself ninety-nine layers thick, swelling up as if filled with air. Next he must contemplate the inner layer of skin, also ninety-nine layers thick, like the [layered leaves of the trunk of] a plantain tree. Next he must contemplate the thin membrane [between the inner and outer layers of skin]. As thin as a cataract on the eye, composed of ninety-nine layers, it bulges outward to the verge of tearing.

Next he must contemplate his muscles, which also have ninety-nine layers, like the leaves of the trunk of a plantain tree. Within the muscles are worms, as tiny as autumn goose down. Each worm has four heads, four mouths, and ninety-nine tails. Next he must contemplate his bones, shining white like white beryl, ninety-eight layers thick, like the leaves of the trunk of a plantain tree. The four hundred four channels reach into the bones transmitting fluids up and down. Next he must contemplate the bone marrow, ninety-eight layers thick and like a cobweb in appearance.

When he has contemplated all of his bones, he must next contemplate his skull. Beneath each strand of hair there are four hundred four channels that go straight into the brain. Everything else—such as the outer layer of skin, the inner layer of skin, the bones—is here just as it is elsewhere in the body. The only difference is that the brain membrane has only fourteen layers. The brain itself has four sections, ninety-eight layers, and four hundred four channels that flow directly into the heart.

The meditator must carefully contemplate his stomach, intestines, spleen, kidneys, liver, lungs, heart, gallbladder, throat, lung-point,[20] the receptacles of undigested and digested food and the eighty families of worms, causing everything to become transparent, glimmering white, and pure, bright and pure like white beryl encased within layers of the skin.

In this manner he must contemplate each bone of his body, making all three hundred thirty-six bones clear and apparent and concentrating his mind upon them. He should repeat this one thousand nine hundred ninety-nine times. Then he should gather his breath and smoothly count his inhalations and exhalations. He should then imagine Lord Brahmā holding a divine water pitcher. Together with a host of brahma gods, Lord Brahmā approaches and gives the practitioner an adamantine sword. Taking the sword, he should slice a piece off the top of his own skull the size of a piece of agate and then place it on his left knee.[21]

Within the water pitcher grow nine white lotus flowers. A boy emerges from the first flower and falls in line behind Lord Brahmā. This boy is white in color, like a white-jade man. He holds a white pitcher full of ghee. The magic jewel in Lord Brahmā's topknot then exudes medicinal herbs that mix into the ghee, and the boy pours the ghee into the practitioner's skull. It enters the channels within the brain and flows downward, reaching all the way to the tip of his left big toe. His body becomes entirely filled, saturated out to the outer layer of skin. Bit by bit, half his body is filled. When half has been filled, it continues until his entire body is filled. When his entire body is filled, the medicines flow through the four hundred four channels, irrigating and filling his three hundred thirty-six bones.

He should then pick up the piece of his skull and put it back on his head. The boy then takes a blue medicine and spreads it on the practitioner's head. The medicine seeps into his pores. Fearing that external winds might enter the practitioner, Lord Brahmā then prepares some Himalayan butter, fresh and pure, dripping with ghee. Like a barrier of crystal, the butter envelops the practitioner's body forty-nine times. It then grows larger, becoming a lake of pure ghee. The practitioner sits on a lotus flower made of white butter under a canopy of butter within a cave of butter. Lord Brahmā's medicine of compassion is mixed throughout the butter.

He must carefully contemplate this nine hundred ninety-nine times.

He must next imagine that within the second lotus flower there is a red boy. This boy spreads a red medicine through the practitioner's hair and all over the pores of his body. The red medicine is absorbed through the outer layer of his skin, eventually reaching the marrow of his bones. His belly becomes bright, and his entire body gradually becomes soft and supple.

From the third lotus flower a golden boy emerges, who spreads a yellow medicine through the practitioner's hair and over all the pores of his body. The yellow medicine is absorbed through his outer skin, eventually reaching the marrow of his bones. His belly becomes blue, and his entire body gradually becomes more and more supple.

In the fourth lotus flower, there is a beryl-colored boy who spreads blue medicine with his right hand through the practitioner's hair and over all the pores of his body. The blue medicine is absorbed through his outer skin, eventually reaching the marrow of his bones. His belly becomes red.

Into each of his pores the boy inserts a needle pointing downward, and through the soles of his feet he inserts two needles pointing upward.[22] Three lotus flowers, containing three fire jewels radiating red light, appear above the practitioner's heart. The light shines upon his heart, gently warming the belly area beneath it.

The boy then inserts three needles into each of the joints of the practitioner's two palms, upward or downward depending on the channel in question.[23] This balances the various qi, makes the four hundred four channels free of turmoil, and strengthens the large intestine and kidney channels. Taking five needles, the boy then stimulates the left intestine channel, manipulating the needles with inconceivable skill and refinement. Then he removes them and hides them beneath his fingernails. With his hands he massages the practitioner's body all over.

In the fifth lotus flower, there is a green boy who pours a jade pitcher of green medicine into the practitioner's anus. It fills his large and small intestines, his five viscera, and all the channels of his body. Then it flows back out through his anus, carrying with it various worms and impurities while not diminishing the previously applied ghee. When the worms are entirely removed, the liquid stops flowing. The boy then spreads a dry green medicine through the practitioner's hair and over all the pores of his body. The dry green medicine is absorbed through the outer skin, eventually reaching the marrow of his bones. His belly becomes white, and his entire body gradually becomes even more soft and supple.

In the sixth lotus flower, there is a purple boy who cleans the channels with rosewater from a rose-jewel pitcher. Then the rose-colored water is made to exit the practitioner's body through the pores, carrying with it all the worms living beneath his body hair. The boy spreads a dry rose-colored medicine through his hair and over all the pores of his body. The dry rose-colored medicine is absorbed through his outer skin, eventually reaching the marrow of his bones. His belly becomes even brighter, like gleaming white snow, and his entire body gradually becomes even more soft and supple.

In the seventh flower, there is a yellow boy who pierces the practitioner's hands, feet, and the two sides of his heart with adamantine nails. Then he rubs the practitioner's six organs with a royal wish-fulfilling jewel, making the organs experience the bliss of the highest level of trance.[24] [The practitioner's body] becomes thoroughly soft and supple, as if all his wrinkles were smeared with pure fat.

In the eighth flower, there is an adamant-colored boy who pours adamant-colored medicine from two pitchers into the practitioner's ears and pores. Just as when being massaged each of the body's joints are adjusted in turn, so too does this medicine travel through each joint of his chain-like body.

In the ninth flower, there is a boy the color of a wish-fulfilling jewel. He emerges from the mouth of Lord Brahmā's pitcher and comes before the practitioner. He places the five fingers of his right hand inside the practitioner's mouth, and a five-colored medicine flows from the tips of his five fingers. When the practitioner contemplates his body after consuming this medicine, his heart and its channels are as pure as a clear mirror, surpassing even crystal or wish-fulfilling jewels. Then the boy feeds the practitioner the flower stalks. They are crunchy like lotus root, and their juices are ambrosia.

When he has eaten the stalks, only the nine flowers remain. Within each flower there is a Lord Brahmā. They give the practitioner a Brahmā throne to sit upon. When he sits on it, a great canopy made of the seven precious substances extends above him, and the Lords Brahmā each instruct the practitioner in the method for cultivating love. By the power of these lords, the buddhas of the ten directions arrive before the practitioner and preach for him [the method for cultivating] love, pity, mutual joy, and equanimity.[25] In accordance with his capacity they give him medicine that makes the four elements of his body soft and supple.

The Buddha said to Śāriputra: "You must preserve and preach for the four groups of Buddhists this method for contemplating Lord Brahmā's consecration of the crown of the head with enveloping butter, which makes the four elements of the body soft and supple and tames the ninety-eight defilements and all illness, both internal and external."

When Śāriputra and the venerable Ānanda heard what the Buddha had said, they joyfully undertook to carry it out.

[6] The Method for Curing Blockage[26]

Further, Śāriputra, if a forest-dwelling monk employs his mind with too much tension, is too rough with his breathing, or sleeps in too spartan conditions, he will, owing to external winds, become afflicted by cold. As a result, his stomach tube and spleen and kidney channels will become agitated, and wind will stir within his tendons. A reverse qi will stagnate in his chest. All his joints will leak water, which will accumulate in his chest. His blood will roil, his qi will erupt, his head will ache, his back will swell, and all his tendons will seize up. This must be treated quickly.

The method for curing it is as follows. First, the practitioner must take excellent, nourishing worldly medicine. He should then lie down on his back, count his breaths, and settle himself.

He should then imagine Lake Anavatapta,[27] its waters reaching a mile in breath. The bottom of the lake is golden sand, and there is a golden wheel as big as a chariot's made of four precious substances. From it grows a golden flower, within which are four jeweled animal heads: an elephant's, whose trunk spouts water, as well as those of a lion, a horse, and a bull, all of whose mouths spout water. These waters circle the lake seven times. In the middle of the four animal heads is the dragon king of Lake Anavatapta in a palace made of the seven precious substances.

By his power, fifteen hundred lotus flowers of various colors grow from the wish-fulfilling jewel on the crown of the dragon king's head. Five hundred are blue lotus flowers, upon which are seated Piṇḍola and the remainder of the five hundred arhats. The flowers close at sunset and open again at dawn. The canopies above the monks' heads are made of the seven precious substances, as are their seats on the lotus flowers below.

Upon five hundred golden lotus flowers sit Cundrava and the remainder of the five hundred novices. The flowers close at sunset and open again at dawn. The canopies above the novices' heads are made of the seven precious substances, as are their seats on the lotus flowers below.

Upon five hundred red lotus flowers sit Upananda, Vasumitra, and the other great arhats. Some say this is the five-hundred-person retinue of the great bodhisattva, [the dragon king]. The flowers close at sunset and open again at dawn. The canopies above the monks' heads are made of the seven precious substances, as are their seats on the lotus flowers below.

There is further a tall dais made of the seven precious substances, eight thousand feet wide, extending upward directly in front of the palace of the dragon king of Anavatapta. Upon this dais are five hundred boys, their bodies the color of pure gold. The first is named Jīvaka,[28] the second is named Good Fortune, and the last is named Empowered by Consecration.

One who wishes to cure the illness of blockage should first bring to mind the venerable Piṇḍola and the fifteen hundred people mentioned previously. When he sees them all clearly, the venerable Piṇḍola will bring forward the boy Jīvaka, who holds out the white medicinal herb named *abaddha* used by the dragon king of Anavatapta.[29] The *abaddha* herb tastes like sugarcane and is shaped like a lotus root. Its flavor is also like rock sugar. When the practitioner has consumed this medicine, his blockage will be cured, his four bodily elements will be balanced, and his vision will become clear.

For one who aspires to the Great Vehicle, Jīvaka, Good Fortune, and the remainder of the five hundred boys will preach the teachings of the Great Vehicle. As a result, the practitioner will be able to see the sixteen noble ones led by Bhadrapāla, as well as Maitreya and the remainder of the one thousand bodhisattvas of this auspicious eon. By means of this, the practitioner will produce the aspiration for the complete, perfect awakening of a buddha, and he will become fully endowed with the six *pāramitās*.

For one who aspires to become a voice-hearer, the venerable Piṇḍola will preach the four bases of mindfulness and the other factors of awakening up to the eightfold holy path.[30] After ninety days, the practitioner will become an arhat.

The Buddha said to Śāriputra: "You must preserve this method for curing blockage. Do not forget it." When Śāriputra and Ānanda heard what the Buddha said, they joyfully undertook to carry it out.

[12] Curing Diarrhea Resulting from Excess of the Water Element[31]

Further, Śāriputra, there may be a Buddhist practitioner who enters the *samādhi* of the water element such that water emerges from all over his body and he can no longer see his body or mind, which become like giant oceans. Emerging from trance, he feels no desire to eat or drink and suffers from a burning sensation in the stomach region. His water channels become increasingly agitated, and he suffers from continual diarrhea. This must quickly be cured.

The method for curing this is as follows. The practitioner must imagine a golden-winged bird upon which rides a monk.[32] They fly at ease over the great ocean, the various dragons and *rākṣasa*-demons fleeing in terror. The bird catches a dragon, and the frightened dragon, about to be eaten, drinks up all the water [of the ocean] and turns into four snakes. This royal golden-winged bird grasps the four snakes in his beak. The monk sits on it, unable to find any water. The royal golden-winged bird shoots fire from his eyes to burn the snakes. The snakes are afraid, and like the magical creations of a conjurer they suddenly disappear and enter the monk's body.

The practitioner should then emerge from trance and consume worldly medicines for curing diarrhea. He should imagine two fire jewels, like hot rocks, one in his stomach tube, where it warms the channels, and one at the anus. He should imagine the god of the Himalayas, Uttaraga,[33] who is six feet tall and as white as shell or snow. He bestows upon the practitioner a fragrant medicine named Sahanaka.[34]

Before taking this medicine the practitioner must first produce the aspiration for unsurpassed awakening. After taking it, he will be free not only from diarrhea, but from all four hundred four illnesses for the rest of his life.

One who wishes to make this god come with all due haste must first purify himself through bathing and refrain from eating the five pungent foods, drinking alcohol, or consuming meat. Dwelling in a quiet place, he should concentrate his mind by counting his breaths, and for seven days he should chant this god's name and bring to mind his image.

This great god of the Himalayas, [Uttaraga], will then come before the practitioner together with the remainder of the twelve radiant gods. These gods first preach the Dharma, after which they will bestow medicine and also teach the twelve gates of trance.[35]

These gods are all great fifth-stage bodhisattvas. One who is sick should first bring to mind the god Uttaraga, and next bring to mind the remainder of the twelve radiant gods: Vigor, Strength, Might, Wisdom, Power, Strong-arms, Kumāra, Unconquerable, Radiance, Radiance King, and Medicine King.

When [the practitioner] sees these gods, he inquires about a different teaching with each of them. They first cause the practitioner to see the bodhisattva Maitreya, and in Maitreya's abode he sees Mañjuśrī and all the other bodhisattvas, as well as the buddhas of the ten directions.

If the practitioner has not violated the four grave prohibitions, either in this life or past lives, then when he sees these gods, he will immediately realize the path.

If, however, he has violated the precepts, then after the gods have instructed him, he must perform repentance rituals for one thousand days. Only after this will he be able to see Maitreya bodhisattva, Mañjuśrī, and the other great saints, and then finally attain the path.

The Buddha said to Śāriputra: "As a result of water, diarrhea may arise for a practitioner and the four hundred four illnesses may then stir. If he wishes to cure this, he must promptly take this medicine of Sahanaka and do the other things. When his sickness is completely removed and he has eliminated the ocean of karmic obstructions, he will quickly realize the path. Therefore, you all must diligently remember this method. Do not forget it."

When Śāriputra and Ānanda heard what the Buddha said, they joyfully undertook to carry it out.

[13] The Method for Curing Pain in the Head and Eyes and Deafness in the Ears Resulting from the Fire Element

Further, Śāriputra, if flames emerge from a practitioner's joints when he enters the fire *samādhi,* and fire arises simultaneously in his large and small intestines, thereby heating and stimulating his fire channels, when he emerges from trance his head will ache slightly, all his channels will tense and contract, his eyes will become red, and he will have difficulty hearing. One who becomes sick in this manner must quickly be cured.

The method for curing this is as follows. He should first imagine a beryl vase filled with multicolored water, within which grow flowers made of various kinds of jewels. Atop the flowers are hundreds of thousands of transformation buddhas and numerous transformation bodhisattvas. They each radiate light from the white tuft of hair between their eyebrows, and the light illuminates the fires, turning them into golden dragons. Seeing this, the practitioner becomes happy.

He should then imagine placing the vase beneath the fires, with the stigmas of the flowers reaching up toward the buddhas. When he touches the vase, his hands feel cool and refreshed. Throwing his entire body down before the vase, he prostrates to the buddhas and immediately sees the transformation buddhas emit light from between their eyebrows. It falls gently upon each part of his body as a shower of ambrosia. Each place it touches transforms into beryl, and the ambrosia flows into his large intestine. When it is filled with ambrosia, the fires gradually go out and are replaced with jeweled flowers glowing red and white.

He should then imagine the god Maheśvara, who approaches the practitioner riding a golden bull and carrying a jeweled water pitcher. Within the water is a medicine named "poison destroyer," which he gives to the practitioner. Maheśvara then places a pearl named Candramāni (which in Chinese means "moon essence") on the crown of the practitioner's head.[36] Medicines drip from the pearl into his ears, eyes, and nose. As soon as the practitioner sees these things, he will be cured.

Maheśvara, a great bodhisattva who constantly disports himself in the *samādhi* of the heroic stride, then emits a bright light from between his eyebrows that becomes an image of the Buddha surrounded by five hundred transcendent beings. He then preaches for the practitioner an ambrosial healing method.

The Buddha said to Śāriputra: "You must remember this teaching. Do not forget it."

When Śāriputra and Ānanda heard what the Buddha said, they joyfully undertook to carry it out.

[14] The Method for Curing Insanity Caused by the Terror of Seeing Inauspicious Things upon Entering the Earth-Element Samādhi.

Further, Śāriputra, upon entering the earth-element *samādhi* a practitioner may see dark mountains in all directions, within whose crags are innumerable *kumbhāṇḍa*-demons, squatting on piles of dirt, with forked penises and extremely ugly. Numerous *yakṣa*-demons charge forward to seize control of five of the mountains, causing the *kumbhāṇḍa*-demons to become dreadfully afraid. Crying out horribly they approach the practitioner. He now sees demons with disheveled hair wielding great iron clubs tipped with boulders.

They too approach. He further sees *yakṣa*-demons dancing about with boulders lifted high above their heads. Female *rākṣasa*-demons wielding trees as weapons approach the *yakṣa*-demons and fight with them angrily. There are also *piśāca*-demons who carry black boulders above their heads and hold dead tigers in their mouths.

Seeing these things, the practitioner becomes alarmed and gets goose bumps. Because of his fear, the *rākṣasa*-demons become more aggressive in their battle with the *yakṣa*-demons. When the *rākṣasas* gain the advantage, they decapitate the *yakṣas*, slice off the hands and feet of the *piśācas*, wearing them as garlands, and the penises of the *kumbhāṇḍas*, which they use as decorative head ornaments. Dancing wildly before the practitioner, their fangs point upward like the branches of sword trees. Hail rains from their eyes and lightning flashes.

Then the *yakṣas* gain the upper hand. They capture the *rākṣasas*, tear the skin from their faces, and gouge out their vulvas. They cut off the penises of the *kumbhāṇḍas* and the hands and feet of the *piśācas*, turning them into decorative head ornaments, earrings, or neck-piercings. Dancing wildly before the practitioner, they shake their bodies, shout loudly, and produce a medley of horrible, frightening sounds.

The practitioner then sees the goddess Vimalatī, mother of the gods of the four great oceans, lying on her back upon the ocean. She has one thousand heads and two thousand hands and feet. She stretches her body across the four directions, exposing her vulva, which stands tall and foreboding like a blood-smeared mountain with many terrible sword-tree hairs. Within it grows a tree resembling a thicket of blade mountains, and from it stream innumerable demons with donkey ears, bull heads, lion mouths, horse hooves, wolf tails, and *kumbhāṇḍa* penises.

He also sees a great dragon emerging from it several tens of miles long, with hundreds of thousands of heads. He sees a bestial demon emerging with the body of a lion and ten thousand feet, within the claws of which are hundreds of thousands of poisonous snakes. He further sees emerge hungry ghosts, their bodies tens of millions of miles tall, vomiting forth poison and fire and carrying boulders above their shoulders. He further sees emerge a thousand wolves sharing a single tail but with separate bodies, whose teeth are like stone spikes. He further sees emerge a thousand tigers whose tails bear heads. Their bodies pressed together closely, they walk with heads bowed down. He further sees emerge a dragon-woman adorned with garlands and extremely beautiful who is then eaten by the *yakṣas*. He further sees emerge from it all manners of evil, wild beasts such as cats, rats, apes, jackals, and evil fox spirits, as well as the spirits of the Whirlpool-Burner mountain of the Avīci hell,[37] the spirits of the eighteen hells, nine million bull-headed hell guardians, eighty million hungry ghosts, a thousand million dung beetles, and five hundred million parasitic worms.

Some of these many horrible demons in this frightening scene hold blade mountains, some hold sword trees, some shake Mt. Sumeru, some shake the Yugaṃdhara or Encircling Iron Mountains.[38] The practitioner then sees his own body filling the earth, his three hundred thirty-six bones as tall as mountains, reaching up to the formless realms. Water emerges from his navel, with the poisonous snakes of the four elements sporting within it. Fire emerges from his mouth with ten evil *rākṣasa*s scurrying within it. Wind emerges from his ears and anus, blowing upon the mountains. All these demons and gods approach him, glaring hatefully with bulging eyes. At this, the practitioner becomes afraid and is likely to go mad.

If the practitioner sees such things, he must quickly be cured.

The method for curing this is as follows. He must first imagine a sun together with a sun god who rides in his palace made of the four precious substances and plays hundreds of thousands of kinds of beautiful music. The sun shines down from above the dark mountains, making them gradually brighter. Having imagined one sun, the practitioner should next imagine two suns. Imagining two suns, he must next contemplate the three hundred thirty-six white bones of his body, as white as the snow-covered mountains upon which the suns shine. Then, above his head, he imagines the moon god accompanied by hundreds of thousands of attendants in his palace made of the four precious substances. The moon god places a moon pearl on the practitioner's head.

When this meditation is complete, he imagines a third sun above the mountains, exactly the same as those described above. When he has seen this sun, he next imagines the bone at the crown of his head, and rising over the snow white mountain [of his bones] appears another moon. Seeing this moon, he must imagine a fourth sun above the mountains, which shines upon the dark mountains. Seeing this sun, he must imagine the mountain of the three hundred thirty-six white bones of his own body, each corner facing another (the four corners [of each bone] positioned directly across from one another), and in the space between each corner there are moon gods radiating moonlight who grasp the two pearls [of the facing bone corners] and hold them together. In this manner, at each joint the practitioner should fix his mind on the space between the corners of each of the bones for ten inhalations and exhalations, carefully contemplating and making it very clear. He sees the twenty-eight asterisms on each bone. The bones are bright and lovely, like pearls made of the seven precious substances.

When this meditation is complete, the practitioner next imagines a royal golden-winged bird that wears a wish-fulfilling pearl atop its head. It chases after the four panicked snakes and six dragons, while the demons and spirits of the mountains run about frantically.

If [the sun and moon] appear dark in color, this is retribution for the violation of the precepts in a past life. The practitioner must then diligently repent in order to purify his precepts. When his precepts have been purified, the light of the sun and moon will become ever brighter.

If he thinks evil thoughts, speaks evil words, or commits even a minor offense, then black dirt will rain upon the wish-fulfilling pearl. The sun and moon will become obscured with dust, and Jupiter will no longer follow its course. The king of the titans will suddenly appear, with his nine hundred ninety-nine hands and one thousand heads, shading the sun and moon and obscuring Jupiter.

This is called backsliding. The bandits of transgression have robbed the practitioner with the sword of evil thoughts and the fire of evil speech. If he wishes to take the excellent, ambrosial medicine, he must first maintain the precepts and be pure in all minor matters of conduct, repenting his karmic obstructions and evil sins.

Then he must concentrate his mind, sit upright without moving, count his inhalations and exhalations, seal his breath within, and contemplate his three hundred thirty-six bones as before. He must make the corners of the bones face one another, and [see therein] all those things associated with the asterisms and the moon explained previously.

His mind then becomes increasingly perspicacious, and within each joint he sees moonlight, like a piece of cloth, and starlight, like thread, stitching [the bones] together.

He then sees a fourth sun appear, [whose heat] reduces the waters of the four oceans by two-thirds. He sees a fifth sun appear, which melts away Mount Sumeru itself and dries up the oceans. He sees a sixth sun appear, and he imagines all the mountains gradually melting away. He sees a seventh sun appear, which incinerates the entire earth. All the demons and *rākṣasas* fly into the air, but the pillars of flame follow behind them all the way to the heavens of the realm of desire, and then further to the heavens of the realm of form. They try to keep going to the formless realm, but they are engulfed by the mass of fire, their hands and feet twisting and burning and their dreadful shrieking shaking the earth. (When one enters this *samādhi,* the earth shakes slightly, like a spinning carriage wheel.)

With all due haste the practitioner must hold his mind firm and imagine his three hundred thirty-six bones as an adamantine mountain, beautiful in form, surpassing even Mount Sumeru, unmoved by earth, water, fire, or wind. He sees only the four snakes [of the four elements], holding wish-fulfilling jewels in their mouths and dwelling within the mountain of his skeleton.[39]

He must then imagine the emanations of the buddhas.[40] He sees, at the adamantine nadir, an adamantine pillar topped with a *maṇi*-jewel mirror within which appear the emanations of the seven buddhas of the past. He must carefully contemplate the white tuft of hair between the eyebrows of these buddhas Vipaśyin, Śikhin, Viśva,[41] Krakucchanda, Kanakamuni, Kāśyapa, and Śākyamuni. When he sees the white tuft of hair between their eyebrows, it is as if pure crystalline water were cleansing his bones. Bathed by this water from the white tufts of hair, his three hundred thirty-six bones become brilliantly white, pure and sparkling as a mirror, beyond all compare.

Because of this, he now sees five adamantine wheels mounted atop pillars made from the seven precious substances. They emerge from below, spinning in the air and preaching the teaching of the four truths. Though he sees and hears all this, he keeps his mind fixed in its contemplation of his mountain-like skeleton. He will then see the buddha Śākyamuni pour a pitcher of water over his head, and so too the other six buddhas.

The buddha Śākyamuni then addresses him: "O Dharma child, you must carefully contemplate that matter, sensations, perceptions, volitional formations, and consciousness are painful, empty, impermanent, and devoid of self."

Śākyamuni then further explains the teachings of emptiness, signlessness, non-doing, and non-wishing. He explains that the body is empty and quiescent, that the four elements have no master, that in the five *skandha*s there is nowhere to make one's home, that they are ultimately quiescent and extinguished, the same as empty space.

As a result, the practitioner immediately awakens to the impermanence and fragility of the world.

He now contemplates the four truths. During the space of five breaths, he smashes through the raging defilements of twenty million rebirths and becomes a stream-enterer. In the space of the next ten breaths, he escapes from the flood of desire and becomes a once-returner. In the space of the next ten breaths, he cuts off the gross defilements, the defilements of the sphere of desire,[42] and the roots of all these defilements, and becomes a non-returner, one who will never again return to the realm of desire.

In the space of the next ten breaths, he disports himself in emptiness and, his mind free of any entanglement, dwells in the thirty-fourth mental moment where he attains a non-diminishing, indestructible deliverance from the ten root-defilements,[43] thereby smashing the mountain of the ninety-eight defilements.

The Dharma banners of the light of wisdom of the valiant general then arrive from the four directions. Precious adamantine seats emerge from below and in knocking against each other expound the teachings of emptiness. The five adamantine wheels come to rest beside the practitioner's left knee, where they spontaneously expound the teachings of the nine moments of the immediately successive path and the eight moments of the path of liberation.[44] Voice-hearers from the past, immersed in the beryl *samādhi,* appear before the practitioner. Then the buddha Śākyamuni expounds for him the meaning and character of the confirmatory visions of the adamantine *samādhi.*[45]

With this, the practitioner becomes tranquil. No longer aware of his own body or mind, he enters the adamantine *samādhi.* He emerges from the adamantine *samādhi* as a great arhat, having obliterated the mountain of the defilements, having severed the roots of affliction, having dried up the river of ignorance, having eradicated death, old age, and despair, having brought to a definitive end his allotted time within the cycle of rebirth, having fully established his holy practice, having become like purified gold, having put an end to all desire, and having accomplished what is to be accomplished.

Those who aspire to the awakening of a buddha, when first seeing the light from the white tuft of hair of the seven buddhas, will [instead] see that light split into ten separate rays that turn into jeweled flowers, ten jeweled trees, and ten jeweled terraces, all arrayed in the air. The buddhas of the ten directions too will then emit glowing water that cleanses all the practitioner's bones, as described previously. And from within the buddhas' white tuft of hair emerges the growing sound of the preaching of the eighteen practices of love, the eighteen practices of great compassion, the eighteen practices of great joy, and the eighteen practices of great equanimity.[46]

Having received these instructions, the practitioner cultivates these four measureless minds [of love, compassion, joy, and equanimity]. Becoming fully possessed of the four measureless minds, he is then taught the ten kinds of clear mind. Coming to possess these, he is then taught that "form itself is emptiness; it is not that emptiness occurs with the destruction of form." Contemplating emptiness in this way, he is then taught the six methods of the bodhisattva. Practicing the six methods, he then cultivates the six remembrances and brings to mind the Dharma body of the buddhas. Bringing to mind the Dharma body of the buddhas, he then arouses the mind of the dedication of merit. After dedicating merit, he takes the four universal vows in order not to forsake living beings. With the four vows established, he acquires the bodhisattva precepts. With the bodhisattva precepts completely acquired, he begins practice of the approximate perfection of giving.[47] When the approximate perfection of giving has been obtained, he begins cultivation of the remainder of the ten approximate perfections.

When this meditation is complete, he contemplates emptiness both inwardly and outwardly. He sees before him hundreds of thousands of innumerable buddhas who anoint his head with water, tie pieces of silk cloth around his neck, and preach for him the teaching of emptiness. He now understands emptiness and enters the ranks of the bodhisattvas.

This is called the first confirmatory vision of the bodhisattva path, that of the stage of nature.[48] In this method, many give rise to pride. One must be aware of this. These are the features of the first confirmatory vision for those who have given rise to the aspiration for the awakening of a buddha.

The Buddha then said to Śāriputra: "This is called the method for curing problems arising from the earth *samādhi,* and for destroying the frightful signs of ignorance, mother of the three poisons. You must remember it. Do not forget it."

When Śāriputra and Ānanda heard what the Buddha said, they joyfully undertook to carry it out.

[15] THE METHOD FOR CURING THE WIND ELEMENT

Further, Śāriputra, while in the wind *samādhi* a practitioner may see five kinds of wind emerge from the nine openings of his body, as if they were deep gorges. He may also see, from each of the three hundred thirty-six bones of his body white as a snow-covered mountain, a wind blows forth various zombies. The zombies hold iron clubs and wear garlands made from a thousand skulls. They come before the practitioner together with ninety-eight species of dragons and demons. When he sees these creatures, the practitioner becomes alarmed and his hairs stand on end. He goes mad as a result or else contracts eczema. This must quickly be cured.

The method for curing this is as follows. He should first contemplate the four transcendents of Fragrance Mountain in the Himalayas, who are great bodhisattvas. He must imagine them and their sixteen-foot golden bodies. In one hand they hold flowers, in the other hand golden wheels, and in their mouth they hold fragrant medicines. They shield the practitioner with their bodies to prevent any winds from arising. Using flowers, they cast a spell over a vessel of water, from which a dragon appears and sucks up all the wind. The dragon's body swells to an enormous size and then lies down on the ground in a deep sleep. The practitioner must contemplate this dragon. It is wrapped in layer upon layer of skin like the leaves of the trunk of a plantain tree, unable to breathe out any air.

The World-honored One then spoke a spell:

> NAMOFOTUO NAMODAMO NAMOSENGJIA NAMOMOHELISHI PISHELUOSHE AIDUOTUODATUO SUOMANDA BASHELUOCHI TUOLUOJUETUSHITU SHULISHULI MOHESHULIHUMOLIHUMOLECHI XIDANPIYANPI AYANPILI JIUJUJUCHI PUSATUOLUONICHI ASHANTIMOJUMOJULI YINGYIXUMIXUMIXUMOXU MOSAGUOHE.

When the World-honored One had spoken this spell, he said to Śāriputra: This magic spell that I have now spoken was previously spoken by innumerable past buddhas. In the future, Maitreya and the other bodhisattvas of this fortunate eon will also preach it. This magic spell has as much power as the god Maheśvara. It can purify the minds of evil monks living during the five hundred years of the later age and harmonize excesses and deficiencies in the four elements of their bodies. It can also cure the four hundred four illnesses of the heart, the visions produced by [disturbances of] the four hundred four channels, the ninety-eight defilements, and the seeds of sexual desire. It can also cure the evils of both karmic obstructions and transgressions of the precepts, permanently eliminating them without remainder. It is known as the spell that cures the sorrow of the seventy-two sicknesses. It is also known as the spell that extirpates the roots of the five kind of ignorance. It is also called "presently seeing all the buddhas and voice-hearers who preach the true teaching that destroys all defilements."

The World-honored One then spoke the following verse:

> The nature of all things is without ultimate ground,
> and in this way emptiness should be contemplated.
> If you can contemplate the four elements [as empty],
> you will not be harmed by the defilements.
> If you take medicine, practice meditation,
> recite this spell,
> and single-mindedly bring all buddhas to mind,
> then the defilements will never again arise.
> The ocean of affliction will be drained forever
> and the river of attachment will run dry.
> With nothing left to cause desire,
> you can declare yourself liberated.
> Free of trouble, the mind at peace,
> you playfully wield the six magic powers
> and also teach this
> spell to others.

When the World-honored One finished speaking this verse, he said to Śāriputra: "Know that after I have passed into nirvana, a monk, nun, layman, or laywoman who manages to hear this profound secret method for the purification of their precepts and this spell of the victory banner of the king of radiant light, which is a medicine for the illnesses that arise while practicing meditation, can be known to have planted good roots under not merely one, two, three, four, or five buddhas, but to have cultivated the aspiration for one of the three kinds of awakening in the presence of innumerable hundreds of thousands of buddhas.[49] Know that all such persons, upon hearing this profound secret method and cultivating it properly, are in their last rebirth and will soon attain, like a quickly flowing stream, the four holy fruits or the bodhisattva practices."

When the Buddha had spoken, the five hundred Śākya monks progressed even further and completed their attainment of all six supernormal powers [and became arhats].[50] Upon hearing the Buddha's teachings, one thousand members of the laborer class from Śrāvasti, who in their past lives had gone mad while practicing trance, immediately experienced great happiness and became stream-enterers. Eighty million gods were able to cure their bodily illnesses and with their bodies and minds free of trouble, they immediately gave rise to the aspiration for the supreme path of buddhahood and rained heavenly flowers upon the Buddha and the great assembly. When the eight groups of nonhumans consisting of the gods, dragons, and others heard what the Buddha had said, they proclaimed in unison: "The Tathāgata appears in the world to cure maddened, demonic practitioners who hold heretical views, making them regain their original minds and become beautiful flower pillars. How extremely pleasing and delightful. Excellent, O World-honored One! You are as precious as the *udumbara* flower which appears but once in each age."

Then the great assembly spoke the following verse of praise:

O prince of the solar lineage,
descendant of the Sugarcane King,
maternal nephew of Starlight Moon,
son of Lady Maya.[51]
At birth you took seven steps,
each step shaking the cosmos,
and the gods of the ten directions came in greeting
to you, who have auspicious marks thirty-two in number.
Casting aside your throne as if it were spittle,
you sat beneath the tree of enlightenment.
There, at the auspicious adamantine seat of awakening,
you defeated innumerable demons,
attained the path of awakening,
your face pure like the full moon,
mental stains eliminated forever.
We now bow down to you with all our hearts,
O most excellent of the Śākyas,
who, possessed of supreme compassion,
helps all living beings
to escape forever from the suffering of birth and death.

When the World-honored One heard the fourfold assembly speak these verses, to encourage them yet further he extended his golden hands and touched the heads of Śāriputra and Ānanda to entrust them with this teaching.

When Śāriputra, Ānanda, and the rest of the assembly heard what the Buddha said, they joyfully undertook to carry it out.

Notes

1. For details, see Greene (2021b, 76–82).
2. Unschuld (1985/2010, 141–142). The four-element disease theory had a certain amount of influence in medieval Chinese medical thinking (Salguero 2010, 63n103).
3. Of some interest in this regard is a passage in the larger meditation treatise of which *Methods for Curing* is a part that mentions five bodily power centers that are clearly a version of the *cakra* system (Greene 2021b, 186n363).
4. *Taishō Tripiṭaka* no. 620, 15: 333a7–337c18 (hereafter, *T*). The translation below has been excerpted from Greene (2021b, 249–300) and reprinted here, with minor stylistic modifications, with permission from the University of Hawai'i Press. The translation follows the text-critical emendations to the Chinese text that are discussed there. In addition to containing the full text of both sutras, Greene (2021b) also provides more extensive notes to the content, which interested readers are invited to consult; in this version only those notes deemed necessary for understanding the text are retained.
5. What this number "seventy-two" refers to is not clear, as the total number of sicknesses and methods given in the ensuing text are far fewer than this.
6. This subtitle claims that the ensuing text is part of the *Connected Discourses* (*Za ahan-jing*), one of the major collections of early Buddhist sutras. No known version of that collection, however, contains anything resembling *Methods for Curing.*
7. Virūḍhaka is remembered in Buddhist literature above all for having spearheaded an invasion of the Buddha's home city of Kapilavastu and his massacre of the Buddha's entire clan, a story that here finds a vague echo in the way that Virūḍhaka's actions bring harm to five hundred Śākya monks (that is, monks who originally belonged to the Buddha's extended family). On the legends surrounding Virūḍhaka, see Pu (2013).
8. "Bad reputation" could be a euphemism for violation of the precepts.
9. This may be a play on the word *sheng,* "sound" but also "reputation."
10. The classical Indian god Brahmā, who in Buddhist cosmology is the ruler of only one set of heavens.
11. This presumably means that he sews the flowers onto the heart.
12. In the understanding of this text, the "large" intestine precedes the "small" intestine in the order of digestion.

13. Indian Buddhist literature, when discussing the impurity of the body, often describes various species of "worms" (*krimi*) that live within it. Some of these descriptions, and the names assigned to the worms, overlap with accounts from Indian medical literature (Kritzer 2023).
14. Literally, regains his "original mind." This idea is also mentioned below in § 15. The notion of recovering one's original mind may also invoke the idea of awakening and liberation.
15. This formulaic phrase normally describes the magic power of moving through solid objects as freely as if they were water. The idea may be to suggest that these famous arhats have been able to enter the impenetrable caves by virtue of their magical power (recalling, perhaps, the legend in which Mahākāśyapa, after the Buddha's death, entered the solid rock of a mountain to remain there until the appearance of Maitreya).
16. The meaning of this expression is unclear.
17. The "adamantine seat" (*vajrāsana*) is where the Buddha sat at the moment of his awakening.
18. "Adamantine wheels" are mentioned below in § 14.
19. This presumably refers to Śāriputra, Maudgalyāyana, Kāśyapa, and Kātyāyana, mentioned above in § 4.
20. The "lung point" (*feishu*) is an anatomical term drawn from Chinese medicine and refers to the acupuncture or moxibustion point associated with the lungs; see Greene (2021b, 65n41).
21. This passage seemingly alludes to trepanation (surgically opening the skull), which was practiced in ancient India (Zysk 1994, 67–68).
22. As noted by Salguero (2014, 85–86), this is a clear reference to acupuncture.
23. What "upward" and "downward" mean here is not entirely clear. I assume it has something to do with regulating the competing energies of the four elements, with fire and wind tending to go upward, while earth and water tend to go downward.
24. "Six organs" (*liugen*) seems to point here to the entirety of the physical body, not the "six sense organs" in the usual Buddhist sense. See, similarly, Greene (2021b, 230n556).
25. These are the four *brahma-vihāras* (*apramāṇas*), associated with rebirth in the brahma heavens.
26. "Blockage" (*yi*) is the name of a condition that early Chinese medical texts describe as involving difficulty of digestion (*Zhongyi dacidian*, 1688).
27. Lake Anavatapta is the source of the four great rivers in Indian Buddhist cosmography.
28. Jīvaka is a famous physician mentioned in many Buddhist scriptures (Salguero 2009).
29. *Abaddha* is *Apotuo* in the Chinese. This word is unattested elsewhere, but *potuo* is in another context explained in the *Dazhi dulun* as a transcription of the Sanskrit word *baddha*, "bound" (*Dazhi dulun*, *T* no. 1509, 25: 408b25–26). *Apotuo* thus could be

abaddha, "unbound," an apt name for the medicine that both cures "blockage" and leads to liberation.

30. This refers to the thirty-seven factors of awakening.

31. "Diarrhea" here is, literally, "down-going" (*xia*), a common word for this condition in early Chinese medical texts (Tessenow and Unschuld 2008, 463–464).

32. "Golden winged bird" means the *garuḍa*, the roc-like bird of Indian mythology known for feasting on the *nāgas*.

33. The reconstruction of this name from the Chinese is tentative. "Uttaraga" could be taken as meaning "Upward-Goer," making this an apt choice of deity to cure the "down-going" of diarrhea.

34. The reconstruction of this name, unattested elsewhere, is tentative. The meaning of "Sahanaka" could be "maker of endurance," which again seems possibly tailored to the problem of diarrhea.

35. The "twelve gates of trance" (*shi'er men chan*) are a common topic of discussion in many early Chinese Buddhist meditation texts (Zacchetti 2003). They comprise the four *dhyānas*, the four *apramāṇas*, and the four formless meditations.

36. I use parentheses to indicate a note that is present in the *Taishō* text, as opposed to material I have introduced in the process of translation, which is placed in square brackets.

37. According to pre-Buddhist Chinese legends, Whirlpool Burner is a large rock far in the eastern ocean around which the seawaters swirl and then evaporate, preventing the ocean from overflowing. Some medieval Chinese Buddhist texts explain that the "Whirlpool Burner mountain" is the tip of a large mountain that reaches down into the Avīci hell, from whence comes its heat.

38. In Buddhist cosmology the Yugaṃdhara mountains are those that immediately surround Mount Sumeru (which sits at the center of the world), while the Encircling Iron Mountains form the outer boundary of the continents.

39. This image suggests that the four bodily elements have now been brought into a state of balance, curing the excess of earth with which this section began.

40. On the idea of the "emanations" (*ying*) of the buddhas, see Greene (2021b, 52–53).

41. The name of the third buddha of the past is normally Viśvabhū.

42. "Defilements of the sphere of desire" are probably what are usually called the five "lower" (*avarabhāgiyā*) defilements whose destruction is characteristic of the nonreturner.

43. This passage references the complex theories about the moment of awakening found in Sarvāstivāda-Vaibhāṣika scholasticism. Based on these, the "thirty-fourth mental moment" spoken of here should mean the final moment of the awakening process (arhatship).

44. This is another reference to doctrines about the moment of awakening found in Sarvāstivāda-Vaibhāṣika sources. For details, see Greene (2021b, 214n494).

45. According to Buddhist doctrine, the adamantine *samādhi* (*jin'gang ding; vajropama-samādhi*) is the meditative state in which arhatship is achieved.

46. Love, compassion, joy, and equanimity are the objects of the four *apramāṇa* meditations. I am unaware of any formal division of these into eighteen steps or methods.

47. The "approximate perfections" are preparatory steps to be fulfilled before the practice of the pure perfections (see *Dazhi dulun*, *T* no. 1509, 25: 139b1–6).

48. The "stage of nature" (*xingdi*), meaning the stage at which one first obtains the nature of a bodhisattva, is often said to be the *second* bodhisattva stage (*Dazhi dulun*, *T* no. 1509, 25: 421c8–12).

49. This presumably refers to the aspiration to become an arhat, a *pratyekabuddha*, or a buddha.

50. The six supernormal powers (*abhijñā*) can be completely attained only by arhats. This line seems to complete the promise made in § 3 above, where the five hundred Śākya monks, having attained stream-entry, were said to be assured of future arhatship.

51. The Buddha is often said to descend from the solar lineage (*sūryavaṃśa*) of King Ikṣvaku ("Sugarcane"), a standard genealogy for Indian sages (*Fo suo xing zan*, *T* no. 192, 4: 1a8). "Starlight Moon" must somehow point to Mahāprajāpatī, the Buddha's foster mother and maternal aunt.

Chapter 5

Demonic States Arising in Contemplation

Excerpt from the Śūraṃgama Sūtra

JAMES A. BENN

The *Lengyan jing,* also known as the *Śūraṃgama Sūtra,* is a Mahāyāna Buddhist scripture that was most likely composed in China in the early eighth century. Although it claims to be a translation of an Indian work, it is widely regarded as a Chinese creation. The scripture explores various topics related to the nature of reality, the mind, and the practice of meditation through a dialogue between the Buddha and his disciples, particularly his cousin and manservant Ānanda. It consists of ten chapters and includes a long magical spell intended to protect practitioners from evil influences.

The *Lengyan jing* has had a significant impact on Chinese Buddhism, particularly in the Chan (Zen) tradition. It has been praised for its profound insights, poetic language, and innovative teachings on topics such as the purity of the sense faculties and specific methods for attaining awakening. However, it has also faced criticism for its questionable authenticity and unconventional doctrines.

The scripture incorporates elements from Daoism, Confucianism, and indigenous Chinese beliefs into its worldview, reflecting the religious and philosophical context of its time. It responds to criticisms from non-Buddhist opponents and addresses doctrinal positions taken by contemporary Buddhist teachers. The *Lengyan jing* promotes a form of Mahāyāna asceticism that emphasizes the renunciation of worldly attachments and the cultivation of moral purity. It also emphasizes the protection and transmission of Buddhist teachings in a turbulent age.

The sutra can be divided into three main parts. The first part recounts how Ānanda was almost seduced by a young woman ("the Mātaṅgī girl") armed with a magic spell, but the Buddha saved him by reciting a powerful mantra (this long mantra is contained in the *Lengyan jing* itself).

In the second part of the scripture, Ānanda asks the Buddha which faculties of perception he should focus on in his practice. The Buddha refers the question to the audience that is gathered to hear the teaching, and twenty-five sages share their awakening stories. Seventeen of them describe practices involving one of the elements of perception, while the final speaker, Avalokiteśvara, describes a process of attaining awakening through hearing. The Buddha then asks the bodhisattva Mañjuśrī to recommend one of these "twenty-five Dharma gates" to Ānanda, and he endorses the practice described by Avalokiteśvara.

In part three, the scripture warns practitioners about fifty specific "demonic" states of mind that can arise during meditation. These states can hinder progress and lead to mental instability, hallucinations, or even demonic possession. They can also cause practitioners to deviate from the path and adopt heterodox teachings. The *Lengyan jing* provides detailed descriptions of the mental and physical phenomena associated with each of these fifty states. Ten states of mind/body/behavior are described for each of the five aggregates, or *skandhas*, the various aspects that make up a person's mental and [physical being:] form (*rūpa*), feeling (*vedanā*), perception (*saṃjñā*), impulse (*saṃskāra*), and consciousness (*vijñāna*). The development of meditation in this section progresses systematically through the five aggregates, with the instruction to master one aggregate before moving on to the next.

The meditative states described in the *Lengyan jing* are called "demonic" primarily because they can lead to misinterpretation, which can hinder a practitioner's progress toward awakening. While these states are referred to as "attainments" because they represent specific states of consciousness that the practitioner has achieved through effort, the text emphasizes that they should not be mistaken for true awakening. The "demonic" aspect lies in the potential for misinterpretation and the subsequent deviation from the path to awakening. For instance, the text describes various scenarios in which practitioners, upon experiencing certain phenomena during meditation, falsely conclude that they have achieved awakening. This misinterpretation, coupled with attachments to the experience, can lead to mental instability, hallucinations, or even susceptibility to demonic influence. Therefore, it is important to recognize that these states are not inherently "demonic" but become so when misconstrued and clung to. The scripture emphasizes the importance of recognizing these states for what they are—temporary experiences on the path—and not mistaking them for the ultimate goal. We should also note that the Buddha warns his audience that it is crucial to be on guard against assaults from actual demons who, motivated by anger, do intend to attack Buddhist meditators because of the spiritual power they generate. The demons can only cause harm via disruptions in the meditator's mind, so it is important to keep the mind pure and clear.

In the passages translated below, the *Lengyan jing* explains the potential consequences of falling under the influence of certain "demonic" states in the practice of meditation on the first two aggregates, form and feeling. It is important for meditators to be aware of these potential challenges and approach their practice with caution and discernment. The scripture emphasizes the need to protect practitioners from the influence of celestial demons and support them in achieving supreme awakening by warning them against the potential negative side effects of deep meditational states.

In my translation, I have used male pronouns since the setting of the *Lengyan jing* is the world of the male monastic, and there appear to be no nonmale members of the audience to whom the Buddha's advice is addressed. This is not to say that the warnings regarding the demonic states apply only to male meditators.

Further Reading

Benn, James A. 2008. "Another Look at the Pseudo-Śūraṃgama Sūtra." *Harvard Journal of Asiatic Studies* 68 (1): 57–89.

Benn, James A. 2024. "'Lengyan jing': Chinese Buddhist Apocryphon or Late Mahāyāna Sutra." *International Journal of Buddhist Thought & Culture* 34 (2): 81–117.

Hsüan Hua. 2009. *The 'Śūraṅgama Sūtra': A New Translation.* Translated by Buddhist Text Translation Society. Buddhist Text Translation Society.

Jia, Jinhua. "Translation and Interaction: A New Examination of the Controversy over the Translation and Authenticity of the *Śūraṃgama-sūtra.*" *Religions* 13 (2022): 474. https://doi.org/10.3390/rel13060474.

Luk, Charles (Lu Kuan Yü). 1966. *The 'Surangama Sūtra' (Leng Yen Ching).* Rider.

Excerpts from the *Śūraṃgama Sūtra*[1]

The Buddha spoke to Ānanda and the gathered assembly:

I want to explain something about life in our world. There are twelve different types of beings.[2] The most fundamental, enlightened, and brilliantly clear state of being is not really different from the buddhas we find in all directions. However, because of our confused thoughts and attachments, ignorance starts to spread, leading to widespread confusion. This is how emptiness comes into existence. Our confusion transforms into a never-ending cycle, creating entire worlds. It's like these tiny lands, scattered all around in the universe. They're not entirely pure because they are shaped by our misguided thoughts.

Now, think of your own mind. Inside it, emptiness arises, similar to a small cloud patch in a clear, vast sky. But what happens when someone like you attains true enlightenment? It's as if a ripple effect takes place, and the entire universe begins to shake. The empty lands in all directions dissolve as a result of your awakening. How can the universe remain unaffected? Your mind merges with the minds of bodhisattvas and awakened beings across the universe and with the minds of advanced individuals who've let go of all impurities. You'll be in a state of absolute clarity. The demon kings, ghosts, and regular deities will witness their homes mysteriously crumbling, the earth shaking and splitting, with water and land seeming to fly and soar. They'll be left in utter amazement and fear.

Ordinary folks, however, will remain in the dark, unaware of these incredible changes. These supernatural beings and demons have obtained extraordinary powers but are still tied to the troubles of our world, particularly the lingering effects of their past actions. They might not be thrilled about you shaking up their homes. That's why, during deep meditation, deities, demons, different heavenly beings, goblins, and spirits may come to bother you.

Think of these demons as beings who might be really angry, but they're stuck in the chaos of our world, while you, on the other hand, are in a state of wonderful awakening. They're kind of like wind trying to blow out a light or a knife slicing through water—completely ineffective. You, on the other hand, are like boiling water, and they're like solid ice. As your warm steam approaches, they'll start to melt. These demons mostly rely on their special powers and can't stick around for long. They can only bother you through your own mind's five components. If your mind is clear, they can't touch you.

When you're deep into meditation, fully awake and not confused, these demonic experiences won't stand a chance. Your five aggregates will dissolve, and you'll enter a state of clarity. These mischievous beings depend on darkness, but your light is powerful enough to defeat them. If they come close, they'll be destroyed. They wouldn't even dare to stay and disrupt your meditation.

However, if someone isn't awakened and gets lost in their own thoughts and feelings, they might become a disciple of these demons or even turn into a demon themselves. It's a bit like the Mātaṅgī girl who tricked you into breaking some Buddhist rules.[3] But here's the thing, Ānanda, you only broke one rule out of the eighty thousand good practices.[4] And because your mind was pure, you didn't fall into wrongdoing.

But if these demons ever manage to harm your precious state of awakening, it's like a government minister's family losing everything they have.[5] They'll be scattered and left with no one to help or comfort them.

[1. Aggregate of Form]

Ānanda, let me explain something to you. When you sit down to meditate and manage to clear your mind of all thoughts, a remarkable kind of wisdom, beyond the realm of thoughts, will remain untouched, still, and the boundaries between remembering and forgetting will blur into one. As you remain in this meditative state, it's akin to having crystal-clear vision in the middle of utter darkness. Your inner essence is truly wonderful and pure, but your mind has yet to be illuminated. This stage is known as "the realm of the form aggregate."

Now, when your inner vision becomes sharp and unobstructed, it's as if the entire universe opens up in all directions, and there's no more darkness left to obscure your view. We call this stage "the culmination of the form aggregate."[6] Achieving this allows you to transcend the turbidity of time. If you ponder how one attains this state, it's because the false illusion of solid matter forms the foundation of this aggregate.

Ānanda, when a meditator reaches this mental state, his focused contemplation might miraculously reveal that the four elements no longer bind him. In an instant, his body can move beyond any obstacles. We call this "essential awareness that extends into the realms before you." However, it's essential to understand that this is a temporary attainment and doesn't signify achieving sagehood. As long as one doesn't mistakenly believe they've become a sage, we can call it a wholesome state. But if someone misinterprets it as full liberation into sagehood, they could find themselves grappling with various misaligned influences.

Moreover, in this mental state a dedicated meditator's contemplation might remarkably allow them to peer inside his own body. Suddenly, this person might find the ability to remove worms and parasites from his body, leaving his body appearing unharmed and undamaged. We call this "essential awareness pervading the physical body." However, remember, this is a temporary achievement and doesn't signify sagehood. As long as one doesn't misinterpret this as achieving sagehood, we can consider it a wholesome state. Yet misinterpretation could lead to encounters with various misguided influences.

Additionally, in this mental state the meditator may diligently investigate within and around themselves. During this time, his souls, will, and spirit, no longer bound to the physical body, may harmoniously converge or disengage, exchanging roles.[7] Suddenly, in the vast emptiness, he might hear the sound of someone expounding the Dharma or hear voices all around, conveying identical secret teachings. We call this "the harmonious interaction of essence and spirit." However, it's vital to understand that this, too, is a temporary attainment and doesn't mean he has achieved sagehood. As long as one doesn't misinterpret this as full liberation into sagehood, we can label it as a wholesome state.

But misconstruing it could lead to encounters with various misguided influences.

Furthermore, in this state of mind, vivid and translucent, the meditator emits an inner radiance that illuminates all directions. It transforms everything into the colors of the rose-apple tree, and all living beings become like buddhas. During this moment, they might suddenly behold Vairocana Buddha seated on a radiant throne in the sky, surrounded by thousands of other buddhas who simultaneously manifest within lotus flowers across countless lands. We refer to this as "the awakening of the mind and spirit, with its light illuminating and permeating all the worlds." However, it's crucial to remember that this, too, is a temporary state of being and doesn't signify sagehood. As long as one doesn't misinterpret this as complete sagehood, we can consider it a wholesome state. But misinterpretation might lead to encounters with various misguided influences.

Moreover, in this state of mind, as the meditator earnestly focuses on the wondrous brightness, he might find it challenging to interrupt his contemplations. He attempts to control and manage these experiences, preventing them from becoming overwhelming. Then, suddenly, the empty space in every direction transforms into an array of colors akin to precious jewels, perhaps even an entire spectrum of hues. These colors fill space entirely without clashing with each other. The meditator perceives pure shades of blue, yellow, red, and white. We term this "restraining the overpowering force." However, it's important to recognize that this, too, is a temporary achievement and doesn't imply sagehood. As long as one doesn't mistake it for full sagehood, we can consider it a beneficial state. Misinterpreting it, though, may lead to encounters with various misguided influences.

Additionally, in this state of mind, as the meditator investigates with clarity, the essential light remains undisturbed. Suddenly, even in the dark of night or within a dimly lit room, they see things as if it were broad daylight. Nothing remains hidden in the shadows. We call this "the refined and clear vision of the mind, capable of perceiving what's concealed in darkness." Yet remember that this, too, is a temporary state of being and doesn't signify sagehood. As long as one doesn't consider it full sagehood, we can categorize it as a beneficial state. Misinterpreting it, however, may lead to encounters with various misguided influences.

Moreover, in this state of mind the meditator may completely enter a sense of nothingness. Suddenly, his four limbs might feel as if they were as insensate as grass or wood. Even if subjected to fire or a blade's edge, they remain oblivious to pain. Notably, flames fail to scorch him, and when his flesh is cut, it's like cutting through wood. We term this "the sense objects merging with the four elements and transcending them simultaneously." Nonetheless, this is only a temporary state and doesn't signify sagehood. So long as one doesn't mistake it for full sagehood, we can consider it a beneficial state. Misinterpreting it, however, may lead to encounters with various misguided influences.

Additionally, in this state of mind the meditator may attain a state of purity and clarity. As the powers of his pure mind reach their peak, he might suddenly witness the lands, mountains, and rivers of the entire vast Earth transforming into splendid Buddha realms. These realms radiate with the complete splendor of precious jewels, casting brilliant light in every direction. Countless buddhas, as numerous as the grains of sand in the River Ganges, manifest as Thus-Come Ones, completely filling the boundless expanse. They reside in resplendent palaces and heavenly structures. Gazing below, he can witness the realms of suffering, and looking up, celestial abodes come into view, unhindered by any obstacles. We refer to this as "when deep-seated everyday thoughts and feelings of preference and aversion gradually transform." Yet bear in mind that this is only a temporary state and doesn't signify sagehood. So long as one doesn't interpret it as full sagehood, we can categorize it as a beneficial state. Misinterpreting it, however, may lead to encounters with various misguided influences.

Moreover, in this state of mind, as the meditator delves deeper into contemplation, suddenly, during the darkest hours of the night, he may witness distant city streets, winding alleyways, and gatherings of friends and family. He might even overhear conversations. We refer to this as "pushing the boundaries of the mind to an extreme, compelling it to explore and encounter various visions." It's crucial to remember that this is a temporary experience and doesn't signify sagehood. As long as one refrains from mistaking it for sagehood, we can consider it a beneficial state. However, misinterpreting it may lead to encounters with various misguided influences.

Furthermore, in this mental state, as the meditator engages in exceptionally subtle scrutiny, he may perceive the physical forms of virtuous teachers undergoing transformations, with various changes that seem to have no apparent cause. We label this as "the mind being influenced by deceptive forces." On occasion, a celestial demon might enter the mind, prompting the practitioner to inexplicably preach the Dharma, feeling as if they have uncovered profound truths. Yet it's important to emphasize that the practitioner has not yet reached sagehood. If they refrain from regarding this experience as the mind of a sage, the influence of demonic forces will dissipate. However, interpreting it as sagehood may lead to encounters with various misguided influences.

Ānanda, it is important to understand that these various meditative states and their corresponding experiences arise from the interaction between the physical and mental aspects of our existence. These manifestations naturally occur due to this relationship. Unfortunately, many individuals, lacking self-awareness and insight, encounter these states and become ensnared in delusion. They mistakenly believe they have reached a state of sagehood. This fundamental misunderstanding leads them down a perilous path, ultimately culminating in the Hell of No Intermission.[8]

As you find yourselves in the age following the Buddha's passing, it is your duty to disseminate this teaching. By doing so, you can prevent celestial demons from exploiting these states. Instead, you should aim to protect and guide practitioners on their journey toward supreme awakening.

[2. Aggregate of Feeling]

Ānanda, when a virtuous individual cultivates meditative absorption and, in the profound stillness of his practice, delves into the aggregate of feeling, he may experience profound insights. It's as if he can clearly perceive the awakened wisdom of the buddhas, much like seeing his own reflection in a polished mirror. However, even if he attains such insight, it can be challenging to apply it effectively. It may feel like finding oneself in a waking nightmare, where one's senses are unobstructed, but an unsettling influence seems to control the mind, rendering the person immobile. This state is referred to as "the realm of the aggregate of feeling."

If this nightmarish sensation dissipates, the person's consciousness separates from his physical form. He can observe his own face and move freely without hindrance. This represents "the culmination of the aggregate of feeling." A person who reaches this stage can transcend the confusion associated with ordinary emotions. Upon closer examination, they recognize that this aggregate of feeling is deeply rooted in illusions and deluded thoughts.

Ānanda, that virtuous individual, while exploring the realm of the aggregate of feeling, may experience a profound inner radiance. His mind shines brilliantly, and if he overly restrains it, he might suddenly be overwhelmed by boundless compassion. In this state he sees even mosquitoes and flies as tenderly as he would newborn babies. His heart brims with pity and empathy, sometimes even leading to unexplained tears. This is referred to as "excessive suppression of exertion." Achieving this realization is not a fault, but it does not signify sagehood. If he understands this and remains undeluded, this condition will naturally fade away. However, if he mistakenly believes he has reached sagehood, the demon of excessive compassion could enter his mind. He might feel profound sorrow when seeing others, weeping continuously and eventually losing his correct meditative state.

Furthermore, during deep meditation, when the virtuous individual experiences the fading of the aggregate of form and the vibrant qualities of the aggregate of feeling, he might become extremely excited. Suddenly, he feels an immense surge of courage. His thinking becomes clear, and he starts to have grandiose ideas, aligning their aspirations with those of the buddhas. He may believe that in a single thought he can accomplish what would typically take three endless eons. We call this "being overly eager in one's efforts." It's not a problem to reach this understanding, but it doesn't mean he has become a sage. If he understands this and avoids getting carried away, this state will naturally fade away. However, if he mistakenly believes he has attained the wisdom of a sage, he might become overly proud, with arrogance taking over. When interacting with others, he may brag and become excessively full of himself. This state can progress to the point where he no longer sees the buddhas above or regular people below, leading him to lose his meditative clarity, and he will inevitably return to his previous state.

Furthermore, during deep meditation that virtuous individual, upon noticing the diminishing of the form aggregate and the clarity of the feeling aggregate, may begin to believe that there's nothing new to achieve. In his attempt to return to his previous state, he loses his former clarity. His intellectual abilities decline, and he falls into a deep lethargy, unable to perceive anything. Suddenly, a strong and intense thirst emerges in his mind, and he remains continuously absorbed in remembrance, believing this to be a sign of diligent effort. This is what we call "cultivating the mind without wisdom, resulting in loss of self." If he reaches this realization, it's not a problem, but it doesn't imply he has achieved sagehood. However, if he mistakenly thinks he's reached the awakening of a sage, he risks the demon of memory entering his mind. Day and night, he'll cling to his memories, fixating on them in one place. He will lose the meditative clarity he has correctly attained and will inevitably fall from this level.

Furthermore, during deep meditation that virtuous individual, upon noticing the diminishing of the form aggregate and the clarity of the feeling aggregate, might start to feel incredibly confident. He could even think he's reached a level of wisdom that goes beyond his meditative practice. With this newfound confidence, he might wrongly believe he's become Vairocana Buddha. He might even consider his modest achievements to be something extraordinary. This state is referred to as "losing the ability to objectively assess oneself and falling into misconceptions due to an inflated ego." There's no problem in experiencing this realization, but it doesn't mean he's achieved sagehood. The issue arises when he convinces himself that he's attained the wisdom of a sage. That's when the demon of self-satisfaction with shallow understanding can enter his mind. In the presence of others, he might boldly declare, "I've achieved the ultimate and unsurpassed awakening." However, this misplaced confidence will lead to the loss of his proper meditative focus, and he will inevitably regress from this advanced state.

Furthermore, during deep meditation that virtuous individual, upon noticing the diminishing of the form aggregate and the clarity of the feeling aggregate, even though he hasn't achieved a new level of understanding, might feel like his previous mental state has vanished. He goes through intense phases of experiencing existence and nonexistence, experiencing pain and suffering. Suddenly, he is overwhelmed by immense anguish, as if he were sitting on a burning bed of iron or had consumed poison. He no longer has a desire for life and constantly seeks out others that could harm him, hoping for a quick escape. This state is referred to as "losing the ability to practice with wisdom." There's nothing wrong with experiencing this realization, but it doesn't signify that he's reached sagehood. The issue arises when he mistakenly believes he's attained the wisdom of a sage. This is when the demon of unending sorrow can enter his mental space. He may even resort to self-harm with a knife or sword, deriving pleasure from giving up his life. Alternatively, he may be perpetually sorrowful, seeking solace in remote areas like mountains and forests, unable to face people. In the end, he'll lose the meditative focus he had properly attained and inevitably regress from this advanced state.

Furthermore, during deep meditation that virtuous individual, upon noticing the diminishing of the form aggregate and the clarity of the feeling aggregate, may find himself in a state of pure inner calm. Suddenly, an immense joy wells up within him, and his mind overflows with delight that can't be contained. This is described as "indulging in happiness without the wisdom to control it." Achieving this state isn't a problem, but it doesn't mean he's reached sagehood. The issue arises when he mistakenly believes he's attained the wisdom of a sage, which can invite the demon of excessive joy into his mental realm. In the presence of others, he might burst into laughter, sing and dance in the streets by himself, declaring that he has already achieved complete and unhindered liberation. Consequently, he'll lose the meditative focus he had properly attained and inevitably regress from this advanced state.

Moreover, during deep meditation that virtuous individual, upon noticing the diminishing of the form aggregate and the clarity of the feeling aggregate, might start to believe that he's achieved everything he needs. Suddenly, he is overwhelmed by groundless and intense pride. This pride can escalate into arrogance as he begins to view himself as equal or only slightly inferior to those he once considered far above him. These feelings all surge simultaneously. He may even look down on the Thus-Come Ones from all directions, not to mention the followers of the lesser teaching and solitary awakened individuals. This is what we mean by "feeling superior without the wisdom to hold it back."

Achieving this realization isn't an issue in itself, but it doesn't signify attaining sagehood. The problem arises when he mistakenly believes he's reached the wisdom of a sage, allowing the demon of excessive pride to infiltrate his mental realm. He may disrespect stupas and temples, even desecrate scriptures and sacred images. He might tell donors, "These are mere objects made of various materials, like gold, bronze, clay, or wood, and scriptures are just paper or cloth. The physical body is the only truth, and you fail to honor it. Revering wood and clay is truly misguided." Those who deeply believe these words may destroy these sacred objects, leading to suffering for countless beings. In the end, these believers and those who misled them will fall into the Hell of No Intermission, abandoning the meditative state they had rightly achieved.

Furthermore, during deep meditation that virtuous individual, upon noticing the diminishing of the form aggregate and the clarity of the feeling aggregate, might reach a state of great clarity and awakening to fundamental principles. He feels profound ease and suddenly experiences boundless tranquility and comfort. In his joy, he might proclaim that he's achieved perfect sagehood and complete self-mastery. We call this "attaining clarity and lightness through wisdom, but without a true grasp of the sacred." Achieving this state isn't inherently a problem, but it doesn't mean he's reached sagehood. The issue arises when he mistakenly believes he's attained the wisdom of a sage, allowing the demon of complacency to infiltrate his mental realm. He becomes content and stops seeking further progress. Such individuals can mislead others, similar to the ignorant monk [who confused the fourth level of trance with attaining arhatship], leading to suffering in the Hell of No Intermission.[9] In the end, he will lose the correct meditative state he had attained.

Furthermore, during deep meditation that virtuous individual, upon noticing the diminishing of the form aggregate and the clarity of the feeling aggregate, might reach a profound understanding characterized by emptiness. Suddenly, he may start thinking that there's a state of eternal extinction and abandon the notions of cause and effect. He completely immerses himself in emptiness, believing that liberation comes through severance and annihilation. Achieving this state isn't a problem in itself, but it doesn't mean he's reached sagehood. The issue arises when he mistakenly believes he's attained the wisdom of a sage, allowing the demon of emptiness to infiltrate his mental realm. He may criticize the practice of upholding precepts, claiming it belongs to the Lesser Vehicle.[10] He questions why bodhisattvas need to observe precepts when they are already awakened to emptiness. In front of his devoted followers, he might engage in unwholesome behaviors like drinking alcohol, eating meat, and indulging in sexual misconduct. Using his demonic influence, he manipulates his followers into blind obedience. Over time, these demonic thoughts can lead him to even consume feces, urine, alcohol, and meat, seeing them all as equally empty. This goes against the Buddha's teachings and leads others into sinful actions. He will lose the correct meditative state he had attained and will certainly fall from this level.

Furthermore, during deep meditation that virtuous individual, upon noticing the diminishing of the form aggregate and the clarity of the feeling aggregate, might find himself deeply immersed in a profound clarity that penetrates his mind. Suddenly, an overwhelming affection arises, intensifying into madness, leading him into the realm of intense desire. This is called "when meditative tranquility is infiltrated by attachment, lacking the wisdom to guide one and falling into various desires." Attaining this state isn't a problem in itself, but it doesn't mean he's reached sagehood. The issue arises when he mistakenly believes he's attained the wisdom of a sage, allowing the demon of desire to infiltrate his mental realm. He may promote desire as the path to awakening, teaching laypeople the practice of indiscriminate desire. He may claim that those who engage in sexual misconduct should be called "upholders of the Dharma." Due to the influence of demons and spirits in the latter age, he will subdue ordinary and ignorant people, amassing large numbers of followers, ranging from a hundred to several hundred, or even five to six hundred, and sometimes even tens of millions. But as these demonic thoughts wane, he will lose their power and virtues, facing challenges from the king. He misleads and deceives beings, leading them into the Hell of No Intermission. He will lose the meditative state he had correctly attained and will certainly fall from this level.

Ānanda, these ten meditative states and their associated experiences all result from the interplay of the feeling aggregate with the active mind. Because beings are stubborn and deluded, they do not introspect. When they encounter these causes and conditions, they become deluded without self-awareness, mistakenly believing they have attained sagehood. They engage in gross falsehoods, leading to a descent into the Hell of No Intermission.

Therefore, all of you should transmit the teachings of the Thus-Come One after my *parinirvāṇa* during the time of the decline of the teaching, so as to cause beings to awaken to this truth. Do not allow the celestial demons to have their way. Protect practitioners and support them so that they can achieve supreme awakening.

Notes

1. Translated from *Taishō Tripiṭaka* no. 945, 19: 147b4–149b15 (hereafter, *T*).
2. The *Lengyan jing* has a unique list of twelve types of beings that are said to exist in *saṃsāra*. The first four types correspond to the familiar Buddhist categories of forms of

birth: *taisheng* (Skt. *jarāyuja*) birth from the womb (this applies to humans and animals); *luansheng* (Skt. *aṇḍaja*) birth from an egg (birds); *shisheng* (Skt. *saṃsvedaja*) birth from moisture (insects); and *huasheng* (Skt. *upapāduja*) birth by transformation (dwellers in the heavens and hells). The following six categories are described as "beings that have form, beings without form, beings that have thought, beings without thought, beings that neither have form nor are without form, beings that neither have thought nor are without thought" (*T* no. 945, 19: 138b28–c1). In typical Mahāyāna fashion, these last two categories are then inverted to give us the eleventh and twelfth categories: "beings that are without form yet that have form" and "beings without thought yet that have thought." To the best of my knowledge, this twelvefold categorization is not attested in any genuine sutra. Some of the examples given of beings representative of some of these latter types of rebirth betray a distinctly Chinese conception of the natural order, as I have previously noted elsewhere (Benn 2008).

3. The reference is to the outcaste young woman who attempts to seduce Ānanda with the help of a magic spell, as recounted in the opening scene of the *Lengyan jing*. The Mātaṅgī girl is an intriguing character in the *Lengyan jing,* and her story has captured the attention of Chinese Buddhists throughout history. In the scripture, she is initially portrayed as an outcaste who attempts to seduce Ānanda. However, through the Buddha's intervention, she eventually joins the Sangha and attains awakening. Interestingly, the *Lengyan jing*'s portrayal of the Mātaṅgī girl's story is highly condensed, suggesting that the authors assumed readers were already familiar with her tale from other sources. These sources, such as the *Mātaṅgī-sūtra* (Ch. *Modengqie jing; T* 21, no. 1300) and the *Sutra of Prince Sardulakarna and the Twenty-Eight Nakṣatras* (Ch. *Shetoujian taizi ershibaxiu jing; T* 21, no. 1301), provide a more detailed account of her story, including her desire to marry Ānanda and their past lives connection. Despite the condensed narrative in the *Lengyan jing,* the Mātaṅgī girl's transformation from an outcast to an awakened being remains a significant aspect of the sutra. Her story serves as a testament to the transformative power of the Buddha's teachings and the possibility of enlightenment for all beings, regardless of their background.
4. This refers to the vast number of rules and guidelines for Buddhist practitioners, encompassing both monastic and bodhisattva precepts.
5. The specific reference to the family of a government minister is difficult to explain in the context of the scripture. I have suggested that it refers to some specific circumstances around the life of one of the alleged translators of the *Lengyan jing,* an exiled high official. See Benn (2008).
6. This phrase marks a specific stage in the *Lengyan jing*'s meditation system. The scripture lays out a detailed map of fifty demonic states, ten for each of the five aggregates, and this phrase signals the completion of the first stage. The *Lengyan jing* proposes mastering each aggregate sequentially, which is not typical for Chinese Buddhist meditation systems.
7. The *Lengyan jing* assumes here that multiple souls reside within the body, as was conventional in Chinese soul theory of the time. Buddhist texts from India generally assumed that there was no soul (Lo 2008; Yü 1987).

8. The Hell of No Intermission, which is mentioned repeatedly in these passages, is the most severe hell in Buddhist cosmology, reserved for those who commit the gravest offenses. This destination helps us to understand the severity of the consequences that can arise from meditative errors, according to the *Lengyan jing*. This severe karmic punishment is in line with the scripture's conservative stance on moral behavior and its concern with upholding monastic discipline.
9. This references a figure the Buddha had mentioned earlier in the scripture, an improperly trained monk who attained the fourth level of trance and falsely claimed that he had attained arhatship. When his celestial reward for this attainment had run its karmic course and the signs of decay appeared on his divine body, he slandered the arhats and in a later lifetime fell into Avīci hell.
10. Unusually for a Mahāyāna sutra, the *Lengyan jing* devotes little attention to critiques of the so-called Lesser Vehicle and takes a fundamentalist position on the necessity of upholding the monastic precepts. See Benn (2024).

Part II

Historical Texts

Chapter 6

Healing Disease with Meditation

"Contemplating the Objects of Disease" from Zhiyi's Great Treatise

PAUL L. SWANSON

The esteemed Tiantai master Zhiyi (538–597), considered by many as the greatest philosopher and paramount interpreter of Buddhist teachings and practices in East Asia, contributed many discussions on disease and how to control it through meditation or contemplation. While he composed several treatises on this subject, the translation below is his most comprehensive and mature presentation. This is a section of his magnum opus on the theory and practice of Buddhist contemplation, the *Great [Treatise on] Cessation and Contemplation,* or *Great [Treatise on] Śamatha and Vipaśyanā.* Zhiyi uses the Chinese terms "stopping" (*zhi*) and "insightful seeing" (*guan*) for *śamatha* and *vipaśyanā,* emphasizing meditation that calms one's feelings and thoughts to achieve an insightful contemplation, as calm waters allow mud to settle so that one can see clearly to the bottom of a pond. Zhiyi promotes such a meditative regimen as the best way to control and heal both physical and mental disease.

The section translated below is part of the third section of Zhiyi's analysis of "Ten Objects of Contemplation," which take up the bulk of *Great Cessation and Contemplation.* It is preceded by a detailed discussion of the contemplation of "sense fields" (coming first since our sense experiences are the most accessible objects for contemplation) and "passionate afflictions," and it is followed by sections on "karma," "demonic forces," "meditative concentration," and "mistaken views." (The final three sections on "arrogance," "the two vehicles," and "bodhisattvas" were left unfinished.) Each of these themes is analyzed and then interpreted in terms of "ten modes of contemplation": (1) contemplating objects as inconceivable, (2) arousing compassion, (3) skillful means for a peaceful mind, (4) a universal deconstruction of phenomena, (5) knowing what penetrates and what obstructs contemplation, (6) cultivating the steps on the path, (7) controlling and healing through auxiliary means, (8) knowing the stages of attainment, (9) resting in patient forbearance, and (10) avoiding passionate attachments.

In the earlier, introductory section of *Great Cessation and Contemplation,* the most widely read section of this text, Zhiyi summarizes all forms of Buddhist practice in what he called the "four *samādhis,*" or four categories of meditative concentration: (1) constantly sitting, (2) constantly walking, (3) both sitting and walking, and (4) neither just sitting or walking (or, cultivating contemplation in any and all aspects of daily life). These categories do not concern us here, except for indicating that Zhiyi is known for his comprehensive analysis and his attempt to organize and incorporate all the complicated (and at times seemingly contradictory) aspects of Buddhist teachings and practices that had been introduced haphazardly to China over the previous centuries, as well as apply what he saw as the beneficial aspects of Indigenous Chinese traditions. In this section on healing disease, he discusses both Buddhist and local Chinese medical analyses of disease, such as the features of disease in terms of the five viscera or the four basic elements, as well as various types of breathing and qi.[1] Zhiyi uses these elements to summarize the causes and conditions that give rise to disease: (1) an imbalance of the four elements, (2) intemperance in drinking and eating, (3) unregulated sitting in meditation, (4) demons and spirits, (5) demonic activity of Māra (the tempter and lord of demons), and (6) karmic activity. He then looks at ways to heal or control disease, again in six parts: (1) calming (or the clear focusing of thoughts), (2) qi, (3) counting one's breaths, (4) using "conventional" methods, (5) contemplation of the mind, and (6) divination techniques. The final section of the chapter, "Clarification of Losses and Benefits," introduces a number of contemplations on disease that can provide insight and deepen one's practice. That section has not been included here because it pertains to illness more generally and not specifically to those that arise in meditation.

Not surprisingly, Zhiyi recommends the careful application of calming and insight as the best way to overcome disease, while warning against unregulated meditation that can cause mental and physical problems such as "pain like the piercing of needles; or acuteness like being pulled with ropes; or itching like being bit by bugs; or cold like being doused with water; or hot like being broiled with fire," or being subject to demonic temptations. Whether such meditative contemplation can indeed heal any and all disease is open to debate, but Zhiyi provides an insightful analysis of the medical expertise of his times, along with a careful warning about some negative conditions that may be involved in practicing meditative contemplation.

Further Reading

Hurvitz, Leon. [1962] 1980. *Chih-i (538–597): An Introduction to the Life and Ideas of a Chinese Buddhist Monk*. Institute Belge des Hautes Études Chinoises.

Salguero, C. Pierce. 2017. "Healing with Meditation: 'Treating Illness' from Zhiyi's '*Shorter Treatise on Śamatha and Vipaśyanā*.'" In *Buddhism and Medicine: An Anthology of Premodern Sources*, edited by C. Pierce Salguero. Columbia University Press.

Stevenson, Daniel B., and Neal Donner. 1993. *The Great Calming and Contemplation: A Study and Annotated Translation of Chih-i's "Mo-ho chih-kuan."* University of Hawai'i Press.

Swanson, Paul L. 2018. *Clear Serenity, Quiet Insight: Chih-i's "Mo-ho chih-kuan."* 3 vols. University of Hawai'i Press.

"Contemplating the Objects of Disease," the Third of the Ten Objects of Contemplation in the *Great* [*Treatise on*] *Cessation and Contemplation*[2]

The third of the ten objects of contemplation is contemplating the objects of disease. Those who have physical bodies will suffer from disease. The four snakes (i.e., the four elements of earth, water, fire, and wind) differ in their natures; for example, water and fire are mutually opposed so they are like kites and owls sharing a nest, or a python and rat sharing a hole. The physical body is a poisonous vessel, a heavy burden, and a swamp of suffering. The four elements are like four neighboring countries always invading and attacking each other; if there is a balance of power there may be some peace for a while, but as soon as there is a sign of weakness they try to swallow up the other. You should know that the vagaries of the four elements [and thus our physical bodies] are like these analogies. A standard greeting among the Buddhas is "May you have little disease and little suffering," which shows that the Buddhas are the same (in suffering such illness) as other people. People will suffer disease; even if temporarily it may seem that you are without (disease), it just means that it is only "less" (than others and not apparent).

There are two meanings to "disease": the first is "real" disease from causes, and the second is "provisional" disease [such as the example of the layman Vimalakīrti who,] while in repose at Vaiśālī, took the opportunity of his illness to teach (the Buddha Dharma). Through (the manifestation of) physical illness he was able to clarify the teachings for ordinary, mundane people, rejecting the Hinayana and rebuking the (inadequate) Mahayana (interpretations). Along with Mañjuśrī he broadly clarified the causes of illness and the three types of regulating and overcoming them, and also broadly clarified the results of illness and the four types of healing. Again, when the Tathāgata approached his physical extinction (by death), he expounded [in the *Great Nirvana Sutra*] on what is constant, and of (ten) powers regarding disease. These all refer to provisional and skillful use of disease for the sake of teaching the Dharma and guiding people concerning disease and suffering. These kinds of "provisional disease" are not what are to be contemplated now.

What is to be contemplated now is the physical body that is the result of retributive karmic actions. When the four snakes (i.e., the four elements) are active and produce (disease), you abandon cultivating the noble path. If you are able to thoroughly contemplate (the disease), you will gradually benefit from this mental discipline. People of sharp faculties with superior wisdom understand the "resting in forbearance" [as explained previously in the *Mohe zhiguan*] and have penetrating insight regarding the objects of disease, so (for them) I would not complicate matters with repeated explanations. But for those who do not yet understand I will now make some further distinctions. As felling a great tree requires ten thousand swings of an axe before it falls, and as sculpting a great stone requires a million bores, I will repeat my explanations.

A long disease and traveling afar are both great hindrances to meditation. If your body is stained with illness and you have lost the benefits of cultivating the path, you may arouse immeasurable offenses. A sutra tells of breaking the floating bag (of the precepts that keeps you afloat) and removing the beams of a bridge [of patience] so that your true concentration is forgotten and lost. Breaking the precepts because of disease is like the bursting of the floating bag (that keeps one afloat), and breaking meditation (through loss of patience) is like removing the beams of a bridge. Arousing a deviant and perverted mind, holding dear a pus-filled and bloody body, and destroying the pure Dharma body are the result of losing your true concentration. For these reasons you should contemplate the objects of diseases.

Again, there are people who leisurely loiter and are lazy when they are healthy, but when they suddenly become sick have a change of heart and are able to accomplish many things. Again, the capabilities are not the same (for all people), and some are awakened because they become sick. Thus, the four methods of instruction should be used in accordance with causes and conditions to contemplate the objects of diseases.[3]

The subject of "contemplating disease" has five sections: [I] clarification of the features of disease; [II] the causes and conditions that give rise to disease; [III] clarification of the methods for healing disease; [IV] clarification of losses and benefits; and [V] clarification of the practice of calming and insight (apropos disease). [The latter two are not translated here.]

I. The Features of Disease

First are the features of disease. If you have good medical techniques and skillful knowledge of the four elements, a superior doctor will listen to the voice (of the patient), a middling doctor will observe the features of the color (of the patient's face or body), and an inferior doctor will examine the pulse. It is not necessary now to make fine distinctions regarding such medical methods, but I will provide some summary information.

The method of examining the pulse is a matter for medical specialists, so I should not speak in detail about it. Instead, I will summarize the features of disease in terms of the five viscera (i.e., lungs, heart, liver, kidneys, and spleen). If the pulse is like a deluge and direct, this is a mark of the disease of the liver; if light and floating, this is a mark of the disease of the heart; if acute and sharp, this is a mark of the disease of the lungs; if like a string of jewels, this is a mark of the disease of the kidneys; if heavy and slow, this is a mark of the disease of the spleen. The details are as explained by specialists in healing the body.

If the physical body is suffering and heavy, stiff with many aches and pains, withered and numb and feeble, these are marks of disease of the element of earth. If swollen and bloated, these are marks of the disease of the element of water. If the whole body is feverish and the bone joints have hardened so that breathing has become labored, these are marks of disease of the element of fire. If the mind becomes anxious or suddenly ecstatic, or anguished and forgetful, these are marks of disease of the element of wind.

Again, if the face has no shine and the hands and feet are (dry) without sweat; these are marks of disease of the liver. If the face is pale and swollen these are marks of disease of the heart. If the face is yellowish-black, these are marks of disease of the lung. If the body is listless and lacking in energy, these are marks of disease of the kidney. If the body is astringent like barley bran, these are marks of disease of the spleen.

If there is some white matter on top of the liver, this will cause a reddishness in the pupils of the eye, the pulse will be extended and you will suffer from leukoma, or the pupils will burst, or there will be boils above and below (the eyes), or tears will flow when (the eyes are) struck by the wind, or there will be itching or a sharp pain, or the pupils will sink in, so that when you come in contact with something you become angry. These are diseases that arise when the lung is harmed by the liver. They should be healed by using the HE breath.[4]

If the heart is inflamed, and the hands and feet in contrast are cool, and the heart is in agony and weak, the lips and mouth dry and chapped, and below the navel there is an obstruction of the bowels so that you cannot eat hot food, yet you feel an aversion to cold food, you are dizzy and distressed and like to sleep, you become forgetful and the heart is swollen, the head gets dizzy, the mouth stutters, the shoulder-blades become stiff, the four limbs often ache, the heart is fatigued and the body inflamed, you are suffering from malaria, or have an obstruction of the bowels, or incontinent bladder, or eyes with cataracts or nearsighted; these are caused by the kidney harming the heart, and should be healed through breathing exercises.

If the lungs swell and the chest is constricted, there is pain in both underarms, the shoulder blades hurt as if carrying a heavy weight, the head and nape of the neck feel pinched, the breath is gasping and labored so that you can exhale but not inhale, sores appear all over the body, the throat itches as if infested by insects or worms but unable to cough them out, sores appear in the throat and the jaw is affected, or sneezing bloody mucus from out of the nose, the eyes are dark and the nostrils painful, there are meaty growths in the nose so that the air cannot pass through and you cannot distinguish between good scents and bad smells; these are caused by the heart harming the lung, and you should drink cold water and eat hot food. Coming in contact with these marks causes disease, and these should be healed through the use of slow breathing qi.

If the hundred pulses are not flowing and the joints are painful, the body is swollen, the ears deaf, the nose obstructed, the lower back in pain, the back stretched, the heart and belly swollen, the upper air in the chest obstructed, the four limbs heavy, the face black and thin, the bladder in acute pain and agony, the urinary tract either just dripping or not working, the feet and knees feeling cold; these are caused by the spleen harming the kidney. Again, the demon of this disease is like the lord of the hearth; without a head or a face, appearing suddenly and covering people. These should be healed through the use of the XI breath qi.[5]

If there are measle-like spots appearing here and there on the body and on the face so that the whole body agonizingly itches, these are caused by the kidney harming the spleen. If the color (of the face or the body) is (yellow) like a basket or a bucket, or you feel like a small child pounding on their crib, or like a tornado churning things around, these (symptoms) should be healed through the use of the SI breath qi.

Again, [1] if you are sorely confused, this means that there is no soul in the liver. [2] If you are frequently forgetful of what is before or after, this means that there is no spirit in the heart. [3] If you are full of fear and the afflicted with dementia, this means that there is no soul in the lungs. [4] If you vacillate between sadness and laughter, this means that there is no will in the kidneys. [5] If you are tossed around and perplexed by delusions, this means that there is no ambition in the spleen. [6] If there is much despair and discontent, this means that there is no vitality in the body and mind. These are called the six psychological marks of disease.

II. The Causes and Conditions That Give Rise to Disease

Second is the clarification of the causes and conditions that give rise to disease. There are six categories: [1] disease caused by an imbalance of the four elements; [2] disease caused by intemperance in drinking and eating; [3] disease caused by unregulated sitting in meditation; [4] disease caused by demons and spirits; [5] disease caused by (the evil demonic activity of) Māra; and [6] disease caused by the results of karmic activity.[6]

1. DISEASE CAUSED BY AN IMBALANCE OF THE FOUR ELEMENTS

Disease caused by an imbalance of the four elements refers to when your practices are irregular, you have taken on too strong a burden, and do not take care for cold or heat. Outer heat assists the element of fire; if the element of fire becomes strong, water is destroyed; an increase in this leads to diseases of fire. Outer cold assists the element of water, and an increase in water harms fire; this leads to diseases of water. Outer wind assists qi; qi blows out fire and fire moves water, which leads to diseases of wind. Or three elements (of fire, water, and wind) harm the element of earth; this is called diseases with equal elements. Or if the body increases and harms the three elements, these are also diseases with equal elements but belong to the diseases of the earth. In this way the four elements are in motion and through this competitiveness give rise to various sufferings.

2. DISEASE CAUSED BY INTEMPERANCE IN DRINKING AND EATING

Second, intemperance in drinking and eating can also cause disease. Ginger, cinnamon, and other spicy foods cause an increase in the element of fire. Sweets like sugar and honey are cool and cause an increase in the element of water. Pears cause an increase in wind, greasy fat causes an increase in earth, and cucumbers lead to feverish diseases. Since these are (diseases brought about by) foods with an unstable taste, those who eat them should be careful to make distinctions concerning their nature. If you eat them, after they are eaten they enter your stomach and are digested, the crude materials become feces and urine, and the fine materials are digested, and from the three orifices at the waist they drip into the four limbs. The pure materials change into blood and enrich the whole body, like dust when it is watered. If the body does not have enough blood, it withers and loses weight. The turbid materials change into oily fats, the old roots decrease and become dirt, and the new roots coagulate and become meat.

Again, if the fire in the body is in the lower part, it promotes digestion by the organs, so that food and drink are digested and distributed throughout the body. A worldly proverb says, "If you wish to attain long life, you should heat your feet and cool your neck." If the fire of the body is in the upper regions and you eat food that is unsettling to the body, you will be troubled by disease.

Next, if you eat of the five flavors (i.e., acidic, bitter, spicy, salty, and sweet), your organs will increase or take a loss accordingly. Acidic flavors cause an increase in the liver and a loss in the spleen. Bitter flavors cause an increase in the heart and a loss in the lungs. Spicy flavors cause an increase in the lungs and a loss in the liver. Salty flavors cause an increase in the kidneys and a loss in the heart. Sweet flavors cause an increase in the spleen and a loss in the kidneys. If you know about the hindrances to the five viscera, you will avoid those that are harmful (and cause a loss), and consume those that are healthy (and cause an increase), and act appropriately to the situation.

3. DISEASE CAUSED BY UNREGULATED SITTING IN MEDITATION

Third is disease caused by unregulated sitting in meditation, for example, relying (inappropriately) on a wall or a pillar or clothing, or lying down when the multitude of people have not yet left [and are still practicing meditation]. This reveals an arrogant and lazy mind, which is taken advantage of by (the demon king) Māra so that the human body, especially the back and the joints, will suffer pain.[7] This is called a disease of (the inability to control) the "flow" (of the mind), which is most difficult to heal.

The eight tactile sensations and counting breaths. Next is unregulated counting of breaths, which often leads people to suffer from chronic intermittent fever and contraction of the tendons. If the eight tactile sensations (of heavy, light, cold, hot, rough, smooth, soft, and coarse) are aroused, and your breathing is inappropriate to the tactile sensations, this can cause disease. The eight tactile sensations are as follows: the mind and the four elements merge to form the four proper physical tactile sensations and also the four dependent tactile sensations; together these are the eight tactile sensations. "Heavy" is like sinking down. "Light" is like rising up. "Cold" is like being in an ice house. "Hot" is like in an oven. "Rough" is like resisting [or "pulling against" the natural flow of things]. "Smooth" is like grinding fat. "Soft" is like being boneless. "Coarse" is like husky flesh. Of these eight tactile sensations, four go upward and four go downward. Breathing in, in accordance with the element of earth, is "heavy." Breathing out, in accordance with the element of wind, is "light." Again, breathing in, in accordance with the element of water, is "cold." Breathing out, in accordance with the element of fire, is "hot." Again, breathing in, in accordance with the element of earth, is "rough." Breathing out, in accordance with the element of wind, is "smooth." Again, breathing in, in accordance with the element of water, is "soft." Breathing out, in accordance with the element of fire, is "coarse." If, for example, the tactile sensation of "heavy" arises, and you count the breaths as you exhale but they are not in alignment with the tactile sensations, this will cause disease to arise. The other combinations should be known in the same way.

Calming. Again, if you use only the methods of calming (*śamatha*) for meditation without other means, this will cause disease. If you constantly stop your thoughts in the lower regions, often diseases of earth will be aroused. If you constantly stop your thoughts in the upper regions, often diseases of wind will be aroused. If you constantly stop your thoughts too quickly, often diseases of fire will be aroused. If you constantly stop your thoughts too slowly, often the diseases of water will be aroused.

Contemplation. Next, if the use of contemplation (*vipaśyanā*) is unregulated and one-sided, this can cause disease. When you are first entrusted to the womb (as a fetus), conceptions and thoughts arise and (the fetus) is moved and calls out to its mother, and the mother thinks of the five sensations of color, sound, smell, taste, and touch. A trifle of qi is activated and becomes water, water becomes blood, blood becomes flesh, and flesh becomes the five sense organs and the five viscera. Now, a person who sits in meditation who does too much conceptualizing during contemplation damages the five viscera and arouses disease. If there are many conditions of "color," the liver is affected. If there are many conditions of "sound," the kidneys are affected. If there are many conditions of "smell," the lungs are affected. If there are many conditions of "taste," the heart is affected. If there are many conditions of "touch," the spleen is affected.

Again, next for the eye, if there are many conditions of blue-green, this affects the liver. If there are many conditions of red, this affects the heart. If there are many conditions of white, this affects the lungs. If there are many conditions of black, this affects the kidneys. If there are many conditions of yellow, this affects the spleen.

For the ear, if there are many conditions of calling out, this affects the liver. If there are many conditions of verbiage, this affects the heart. If there are many conditions of crying out, this affects the lungs. If there are many conditions of muttering, this affects the kidneys. If there are many conditions of singing, this affects the spleen.

For the nose, if there are many conditions of rancid smells, this affects the liver. If there are many conditions of scorched smells, this affects the heart. If there are many conditions of fishy smells, this affects the lungs. If there are many conditions of stinky smells, this affects the kidneys. If there are many conditions of fragrant smells, this affects the spleen.

For the tongue, if there are many conditions of sour tastes, this affects the liver. If there are many conditions of bitter tastes, this affects the heart. If there are many conditions of spicy tastes, this affects the lungs. If there are many conditions of salty tastes, this affects the kidneys. If there are many conditions of sweet tastes, this affects the spleen.

For the body, if there are many conditions of hardness, this affects the liver. If there are many conditions of warmth, this affects the heart. If there are many conditions of lightness, this affects the lungs. If there are many conditions of coldness, this affects the kidneys. If there are many conditions of heaviness, this affects the spleen.

In this way the five viscera arise mutually, and if conditions are excessive (and imbalanced), this gives rise to disease.

What if these interact adversely? If there are many conditions of white color, this subdues the liver. If there are many conditions of black, this subdues the heart. If there are many conditions of red, this subdues the lungs. If there are many conditions of yellow, this subdues the kidneys. If there are many conditions of blue-green, this subdues the spleen. The other items such as sound and so forth should be known as explained above [i.e., following this same pattern].

If the diseases of the five viscera are hidden and difficult to know, they can be prognosticated through sitting in meditation and in dreams. If during meditation or in a dream there are many sights of the color blue-green, or pale blue-green people, or beasts like lions, tigers, or wolves, and you are filled with fear, these are diseases of the liver. If during meditation or in a dream there are many sights of the color red, fire burning, red people or beasts, red (bloody) battles with swords, red (erotic scenes of) young men and women embracing intimately, or of father, mother, brothers and so forth giving rise to joy or fear; these are diseases of the heart. The other items can be known in accordance with the various colors [following this same pattern].

Again, an imbalance in contemplation can affect the four elements. If the objects of contemplation are unsettled, with these conditions or those conditions so that the mind is quarrelsome, and because of this conflict a wild wind arises, resulting in diseases of wind. In such cases you should take a walk with steps like a little child, and let it be. If you rush and try to solve it quickly, you will become sick.

Again, if you focus solely on one object and arouse a hopeful mind, but the winds of retribution and powerful heat (of passionate afflictions) are not extinguished, the result is diseases of "heat."

When you are contemplating objects and thoughts are arising, but you think they are perishing, or when they are perishing you think they are arising, so that your thoughts and the marks (of disease) are in opposition, this leads to painful itching and results in diseases of earth.

Again, if you cannot "taste" the objects of your contemplation but you force yourself (to continue anyway), the element of water will increase and result in diseases of water.

4. DISEASE CAUSED BY DEMONS AND SPIRITS

Fourth, diseases caused by demons are as follows: The four elements and five viscera are not demons, and demons are not the four elements and five viscera. If they enter the four elements and five viscera, this is called the diseases caused by demons. You may say that there are no diseases caused by demons, but there are times when evil sorcerers succeed in controlling demons. You may say that there are no diseases caused by (disharmony among) the four elements, but there are times when medical specialists succeed in healing them with liquid medicine. There was once a ruler of a country who suffered from a disease of demons that dwelt in his orifices, who repeatedly used acupuncture to kill them. The king of demons himself came and dwelt above his heart, so that the acupuncturist had to submit (and could not continue treatment). Therefore, it should be known that diseases caused by demons do exist [and therefore exorcistic methods may sometimes be required]. But demons are not rampant in making people diseased. Rather, it is because people arouse perverse thoughts regarding various matters or seek to know about sorcery. The five-colored demon Dou Xiluo [or Helmeted Hidda] causes many changes, so that if colors such as blue-green and yellow enter the body from the five sense organs, the consciousness will make mistaken interpretations about good and bad fortune, or matters of good or bad fortune of one body, or one family, or one village, or one country. These are not to be considered "noble knowledge." If these diseases are not healed and they continue for a long time, it will kill the person.

5. DISEASE CAUSED BY THE DEMON KING MĀRA

Fifth is diseases caused by Māra. These are different from those caused by demons (in general). Demons merely cause diseases of the body; Māra destroys the contemplative mind, destroys the vital wisdom of the Dharma body, arouses deviant thoughts, and robs people of their virtues, so this is different from (the effects of) demons. Again, depending on those who are practicing sitting in meditation, if they have evil thoughts of personal profit Māra will appear (and offer) various clothing, drink and food, the seven jewels, and other material things, and people will accept them and rejoice. Thus, (Māra) enters the mind and causes disease. These diseases are difficult to heal; I will explain the way of healing (these matters) below [in the next section on "Contemplating Demonic Matters"].[8]

6. DISEASE CAUSED BY KARMIC ACTIVITY

Sixth is disease caused by karmic activity (in the past). Sometimes it is only the karmic activity from previous lives, or sometimes it is from breaking the precepts in your current life which affects the karma from previous lives, and this karmic power causes disease. You should know about these offenses (that cause bad karmic effects) in terms of the five sense organs.

If you commit the karmic action of the offense of taking life, this leads to diseases of the liver and the eyes. The karmic actions of the offense of drinking intoxicating beverages lead to diseases of the heart and mouth. Karmic actions of the offenses of illicit lust lead to diseases of the kidneys and ears. Karmic actions of offenses of deluded speech lead to diseases of the spleen and tongue. Karmic actions of the offenses of stealing lead to diseases of the lungs and nose. Karmic actions of breaking all (of these) five precepts arouse diseases of the five viscera and the five sense organs, and if these karmic actions decline, (their effects) will go away.

If in your current life you keep the precepts, this can also affect the karma and cause disease. Therefore, it is said that if you have committed a grave offense, a headache may remove it, and grave offenses for which you should fall into hell may be lightly recompensed during your lifetime as a human being. These are karmic actions that you wish would disappear but cause disease. There are many types of diseases caused by karmic action: tumors, congestion, jaundice, and depletion. Any and all manner of diseases should be minutely and closely examined. Knowing the root causes of diseases can later lead to healing them.

III. Clarification of the Methods for Healing Disease

Third is clarifying the methods for healing disease. These should be appropriate to the situation and are not the same (for everyone). If your work or eating and drinking leads to sickness, this should be treated with medicine, and with regulated care this disease will end. If sitting in meditation is unregulated and this leads to sickness, this should in turn require further sitting in meditation. Well-regulated contemplation of breaths should make this (sickness) end. Liquid medicine (i.e., conventional medicine) is not appropriate in this case. As for the two types of diseases caused by demons and Māra, these should be treated with the power of the practice of deep contemplation and the use of great spells, and you can make them end. As for diseases caused by karma, you should internally use the power of contemplation, and externally make confession and repentance, and these will come to an end. All of these methods of healing are not the same (for everyone and every situation), and you should be aware of this meaning. You should not (inappropriately) take up a knife or wield a blade and thus hurt yourself.

Now, in terms of sitting in meditation, in sum there are six ways of healing disease: [1] calming, [2] qi, [3] breathing, [4] conventional conceptualization, [5] contemplation of the mind, and [6] divination techniques.

1. USING CALMING

First, using the practice of calming (*śamatha*) to heal disease: Master Wen says,[9] "Link your mind and concentrate on your navel as if it were a large bean, unfasten your robe and clearly apprehend your posture, then close your eyes and arrange your mouth and teeth, lift your tongue toward the palate, and regulate and calm your breathing (or qi). If your mind runs wild and wanders to external matters, contain it and make it return. If your thoughts become imperceptible, rearrange your robe and look at [your navel to regain your concentration] and carefully apprehend your posture, and repeat as before." This practice is able to heal various diseases, and also is able to arouse various meditative concentrations. When this contemplation is performed, it has immeasurable characteristics. At times there is pain like the piercing of needles; or acuteness like being pulled with ropes; or itching like being bitten by bugs; or cold like being doused with water; or hot like being broiled with fire. In this way, when various tactile sensations arise, diligently continue your practice single-mindedly, without retreating or giving up. If you can be free of these tactile sensations, you will be able to arouse various meditative concentrations; if your psychological condition is quiescent, this is the mark of lightning-like concentration. Through this you are able to attain meditative concentrations; how can you not heal diseases?

The reason you "link the mind to the navel" is that (in meditation) the breath goes out through the navel and then enters from the navel, and the going out and coming in (of the qi-breath) is limited to the navel, which makes it easy to realize (the truth of) transiency.

Again, when you are entrusted to the womb (as a fetus) and your conscious spirit first coalesces with blood, the navel cord forms a connection and the link (to the mother) is through the navel. Again, this (navel) is the source of the stomach and intestines, so if you investigate the source you are able to perceive the impurity (of the physical body) and are able to stop covetous desires. In terms of the four mindfulnesses,[10] contemplating the navel is the "mindfulness of (the impurity of) the body." In terms of the "six sublime gates,"[11] (concentrating on the navel) is the gate of calming. Both of these practices enable you to enter the path and are therefore used often.

A proper use of these practices for healing disease also involves the *dantian*, which is a sea of qi that is able to lock up and contain all diseases. If you "stop" (and focus) the mind on the *dantian*, your qi/breathing is regulated and calm, and thus you will be able to heal disease. This is the meaning here.

Again, a certain master said, "An excess of upper qi; congestion in the chest; pain on both flanks of the body; pressure on the spine and back; pain in the shoulders; vexing heat in the heart; troublesome pain that cause loss of appetite; swelling of the heart; chill in the lower abdomen; heat in the upper and cold in the lower (parts of the body); a disharmony of yin and yang; coughing: these twelve types of disease should all be dealt with by focusing on the *dantian*.[12] The *dantian* is two-and-a-half inches below the navel. Or, if the pain is acute, shift your attention to focus on three inches (below the navel). If the pain is not removed, shift to focus on the (acupuncture) point at the side of the nails on the big toes of both feet, and try to put an end to it.

If you have a headache and your eyes itch and are red, your lips and mouth are hot, pimples form around the nose, there are sudden pains in the abdomen, both ears become deaf, and the neck is tight: for these six diseases, you should make the area between your legs the object of your focus and link your thoughts to it. If you suddenly suffer acute pain from abdominal edema, just single-mindedly focus on this area. If the mind is troubled you should take short breaths, and if possible, arise and repeat the previous practices. If you experience a little relief, you should continue to use these methods for healing. If these practices cause acute pain in the waist and/or legs, imagine and conceive of a ten-foot chasm below your feet and shift the focus of your attention to the bottom of this pit, and focus your thoughts primarily on this until (the pain) naturally comes to an end. This must be done in a quiet room.

Again, by constantly stopping (and focusing) your thoughts on your feet, you are able to heal all manners of disease. Why is this so? The five consciousnesses (of sight, sound, scent, taste, and touch) are in the head, and the mind thus often has connections with this upper region, so the mind follows (the element of) wind, wind affects fire, fire melts water, and water moistens the body. Therefore, even if the upper region is regulated, if the lower regions are disturbed this will lead to various diseases, such as chronic swelling of the legs and feet, and so forth. Again, the five viscera are like lotus blossoms that bloom extravagantly but face downward, but since consciousness usually has connections to the upper region, if the qi is strong in pressing against the bowels, this can in turn be destructive and cause disease. If the mind has connections to the lower region, fire will blow and slide to the lower region, drink and food will be digested (properly), and the five viscera will be in balance. Stopping and focusing on the feet is thus the best for healing disease. So now there will be profound benefit if you constantly and repeatedly use this method. Through this you can heal others, as has already been tested (and proven) many times over. Jiang [Tianwen], Wu [Mingche], and Mou [Xi] are examples of such people (who have verified these medical methods).[13]

Again, if in accordance with the place of the disease you clarify the mind and stop and focus on this place; before three days have passed, surely conditions will have improved and you can put an end (to the disease). Why is this so? As the wind will blow through when a gate is opened, or be still when a fan is closed, the mind responds to the conditions of external objects like the opening of a gate. If the mind stops and focuses on the place where there is pain, this is like the closing of a fan. This is just the way things naturally are. Again, the mind is like a king, and diseases are like bandits; if the mind is calm, the bandits will disperse and be destroyed.

Again, you do not necessarily and exclusively stop and focus the mind on the physical place which is diseased. The *Secret Methods of the Emperor* says, "The two qi from heaven and earth merge, and each has the five phases, thus producing metal, wood, water, fire, and earth. These circulate and thus metal is transformed and water arises, water flows and wood grows, wood moves and fire is lit, fire burns and earth is chaste; thus do they mutually arise. Fire meeting water means an extinction of light; water meeting earth becomes immobile; earth planting wood produces tumors; wood meeting metal brings about wounds; thus do they interact adversely."[14] As metal overcomes wood, if the lungs are strong and the liver weak, you should stop and focus the mind on the lungs and gather white qi, and the disease of the liver will end. The other four organs should be understood in the same way.

Again, using "stopping" (or "calming") to heal the diseases of the four elements is as follows: a quick stopping heals the diseases of water; slowly stopping heals the diseases of fire; stopping (and focusing) on the head heals the diseases of earth; stopping (and focusing) on the feet heals the diseases of wind (and so forth).

2. USING QI

Second is using qi to heal diseases, that is, (the Six Breaths exercise using the syllables) CHUI, HU, XI, HE, XU, and SI. All of these are formed by the lips and mouth, converted by the teeth and tongue, and carefully applied in the mind and conceptualized, thus producing the breaths. When cold use CHUI, as in exhaling fire. When hot use HU. When the hundred joints itch and are painful, use XI and heal the diseases of wind. If there is troublesome swelling and the upper air/qi (in the chest is obstructed), use HE. If there is too much mucus, use XU. If exhausted, use SI.

The Six Breaths for healing diseases of the five viscera are as follows. HE heals the liver, HU and CHUI heals the heart, XU heals the lungs, XI heals the kidneys, SI heals the spleen. Again, the Six Breaths together heal one organ. If the organ is cold, use CHUI. If hot, use HU. If painful, use XI. If troubled by swelling, use HE. If there is mucus, use XU. If weary and lacking (energy), use SI. It is the same for the other four internal organs.

Again, by exhaling with the mouth you get rid of a chill, and exhaling through the nose removes internal heat. Inhale calmly and carefully so that there is no clashing [between the breaths or energies]. Once you are seated (for meditation), repeat (this cycle of breathing) seven times, then calm your mind, and after calming your mind for a little while, again utilize the breaths. This is what it means to use (qi) for healing diseases. Usually, it is enough to spew out defilements (through exhaling the breath) once or twice. Inhaling through the mouth gets rid of heat; inhaling through the nose brings pure and cool (air) inside.

XI [breathing] through the mouth gets rid of pain by removing the element of wind, through the nose brings internal peace.

HE through the mouth gets rid of annoyances, and qi in the lower regions of the body disperses mucus. As for mucus in the chest, that in the upper regions should be spit out through the mouth, and that of the lower regions smoothed out through breathing. Therefore, it is not necessary to supplement [by blowing with] the nose.

XU helps get rid of swelling and lets in calm assurance through the nose.

SI gets rid of fatigue and lets in harmonious supplements (of qi) through the nose. Carefully inhale and exhale without doing so in excess. If this is done with discretion, with increases and decreases appropriate to the situation, you will not only be able to heal your own diseases, but also help save others.

3. COUNTING THE BREATHS

Third is using (counting of) the breaths to heal disease. The body and mind are mutually dependent when involved in breathing, like firewood and fire rely on each other to produce smoke. By observing the purity or turgidity of the smoke, you can know the rancidness or dampness of the firewood; so, by examining the strength or weakness of the breaths, you can verify the health or disease of the (human) body. If the element of wind blows in the body as it pleases, then pain and itching will give rise to disease; you should not be unhurried in attending to it but should quickly heal it. First you should be conscious of your breathing as having four associations. [1] If (the breath) makes a sound, this is called wind; if you follow this, your thoughts will be dispersed. [2] If (the breath is) stagnant, this is called qi; if you follow this your thoughts will be obstructed. [3] If the inhaling and exhaling is not exhausted, this is called "gasping"; if you follow this you will be fatigued. [4] If the breathing neither makes a sound nor is stagnant, and the inhaling and exhaling are both exhausted, this is called (proper, correct) breathing; if you follow this you will attain concentration.

You should seek a quiet place, sit in the lotus position, and straighten your body and be calm. Let the body relax, spread out the four limbs and stretch the bones and muscles. You should see to it that the joints are in harmony, neither leaning (unbalanced) nor bent. Loosen your belt, lean to the side, and turn the body to adjust it (into a comfortable position). Place your left hand on the top (palm) of your right hand, and lightly touch the tips of the thumbs. Make your cheeks vertical, open the mouth slightly, and exhale deeply four or five times. Next, gradually straighten the head and slowly close your eyes. Do not close your eyelids with great haste, but always (shut out the light) as in a cage, and then use your breathing.

Using your breathing to heal disease through being in accordance with and in opposition to the eight tactile sensations is as follows. If the sensation of "heavy" is the cause and this gives rise to the great diseases of the earth element, mostly use the exhaling of breath to heal it. If the sensation of "lightness" is aroused and gives rise to diseases of wind, mostly use the inhaling of breath to heal it. If the sensation of "cold" is aroused and gives rise to diseases of water, mostly use the exhaling of breath to heal it. If the sensation of "heat" is aroused and gives rise to the diseases of fire, mostly use the inhaling of breath to heal it. The others should be understood in the same way. If you attain regulated harmony and equanimity, follow the workings of your mind to put this to use. Constantly count your breaths, and do not produce other kinds of breaths.

Next are distinctions concerning the application of twelve types of breathing, that is, [1] upper, [2] lower, [3] scorched, [4] full, [5] increasing and growing, [6] decreasing and extinguishing, [7] cold, [8] hot, [9] rushed, [10] maintained, [11] harmonious, and [12] supplemental. These twelve types of breathing outline the thoughts of temporary conceptions. What does this mean? When there is the first thought (of the fetus) upon entering the womb, there are (already) the (natural, inborn) breaths from karmic recompense. [At first the breaths are] in accordance with the qi-breaths of the mother; the child gradually grows, the wind passages become smooth, and the inhaling and exhaling of the child is no longer in accordance with that of the mother. It is born and becomes apart from (the mother), so that each have their own (separate) breaths. This is called "breaths from karmic recompense." "Dependent breathing" refers to that which relies on the mind to arise; for example, at a time of anger or desire, the breathing becomes aroused. This is called "dependent breathing." The six qi (breathing methods) discussed above are (of the type) of "breaths from karmic recompense" and involve conceptualization. These twelve types of breathing belong to "dependent breathing" and involve conceptualization, and therefore they are not the same as the previous. The previous (types of breathing) were explained in terms of the five colors and their relation to the diseases of the five viscera. These depend on the organs to arouse disease, and therefore you should now use "dependent breathing" to heal them. [1] Upper breathing heals the sinking and heavy diseases of earth. [2] Lower breathing heals the empty suspended diseases of wind. [3] Scorched breathing heals pressure from swelling. [4] Full breathing heals withered emaciation. [5] Increasing and growing breathing is able to give rise to the growth of the four elements. Non-Buddhist ways for applying qi-breathing merely use the application of these (kinds of) growing and increasing of qi or breathing. [6] Decreasing and extinguishing breathing dissipates diseases of the heart membrane. [7] Cold breathing heals fever. [8] Hot breathing heals the chills. [9] Rushed breathing heals bowel obstructions and swelling from poison. [10] Maintained breathing heals the shakes and instability. [11] Supplemental breathing heals whatever is lacking. [12] Harmonious breathing blends the four elements.

When producing these kinds of breaths, each is accompanied by conceptual thoughts that bring them to fruition. Know the diseases in detail, using the various types of breathing, and do not err in their application.

4. HEALING BY CONVENTIONAL CONCEPTIONS

Fourth, healing diseases through conventional conceptions: the previous sections on qi and breathing methods involved using conceptualizations, but now I refer to methods that use only conventional conceptualizations, such as the "debate masters" who have methods for (getting rid of) warts, such as (acupuncturists) using needles for people suffering from sickness, such as using warm resuscitative techniques for relieving fatigue like that found in the *Āgamas*, such as the method of "swallowing snakes," and so forth.[15]

5. HEALING BY CONTEMPLATION OF THE MIND

Healing disease by contemplation does not involve conventional conceptions nor breathing techniques but is a direct contemplation of the mind. Whether you seek it internally or externally, the "mind" cannot be obtained, so even if disease comes, who does it afflict, and who experiences this disease? [That is, it should be contemplated that there is no "self" that experiences disease.]

6. HEALING BY DIVINATION TECHNIQUES

Sixth is healing disease by divination techniques. These techniques may seem distant if you do not know of them, but if you know of them, they are quite close to home, such as methods for healing hiccups, methods for fixing toothaches, healing the liver by twisting the thumbs, and so forth. These techniques are shallow and common, and are often based on illusions. They should not be used by home-departed ones (i.e., the Buddhist sangha). Basically, they need not be studied, and if they have been studied, should be quickly rejected. If you cultivate the four *samādhis,*[16] the physical body that is weak like a water bubble has uncertain increases and decreases. If (these divination techniques) can be borrowed and used to heal diseases, it may make it easier to stay on the path (of practice to awakening), so you should not despise them. However, if they are used to invite fame or to gain profit, and thus provoke or stir up the worldly people of the times, this is a delusion and farce of Māra and should be quickly rejected, (I repeat,) quickly rejected.

When the thirty-six types of beasts surround a person,[17] you should chant these spells three times:

> BO-TI-TUO. PI-YE-DUO, NA-MO-NA, JI-LI-BO, A-WEI-PO, TUI-MO-TUO, NAN-TUO-LUO, YOU-TUO-MO, JI-LI-MO, PI-LI-JI. ZHE-TUO-MO.

At first be carefully attentive, and when you come in contact with outside objects [e.g., troubling spirits] the mind will be alarmed, and because of this qi will increase and the stomach will feel full, the chest will be troubled, the head ache, and the heart feel oppressed. Six mental conditions parade through the entire body, causing surprise and a loss of your guard. Externally there will be evil spirits that enter the body and snatch away your place of abode, thus guiding you in this way. The method to heal this is to close your mouth and plug your nose and do not let your qi or breath escape. Maintain the qi or breath until it permeates your body, and then release the qi or breath long and far away. Conceptualize its expulsion throughout the body, from your head to the feet. Pull until it is exhausted. Do this three times, and then chant these spells:

> ZHI-BO-ZHOU, WU-SU-BO-ZHOU, FU-LIU-BO-ZHOU, QIAN-QI-BO-ZHOU.

After chanting these three times, then regulate the breath and from one to ten command the exhaling and inhaling of breaths, saying, "A-NA-BO-NA, A-ZHOU-BO-ZHOU," and the diseases will come to an end. If you suffer from dysentery or white diarrhea, sudden bad health or "apoplexy," a pale face, "reversal of the eyes," blackening of the lips, and are not able to distinguish between people, (then you should) twist the *dantian* with your hand until it hurts, and surely these diseases will end. Again, in accordance with the place on your body that hurts, hit the diseased place with a staff in your hand until it hurts, up to forty or fifty times. What is the meaning of this? Just this: diseases are products of the mind [literally, "There is nothing that is not produced by the mind"]; the mind has thoughts of depressing misery, and thus introduces perverse qi. Now if you attack it with pain, there is no room for extraneous conceptions, so the perverse qi will go away, and the disease will be removed.

Notes

1. The Chinese concept of qi is complicated and difficult to translate. It can refer simply to the breath, the atmosphere, or to a mysterious energy that pervades the body, so my translation of this term varies by context. See Stanley-Baker (2022).
2. *Taishō Tripiṭaka* no. 1911, 46: 1–140 (hereafter, *T*). A previous version of this translation was published as part of Swanson (2018) and is reproduced here with permission from the University of Hawai'i Press. Below, I use parentheses when the meaning is implied but not explicit in the Chinese and square brackets when I am adding information or an interpretation that is not implicit in the Chinese and may possibly be interpreted in a different way.
3. The "four methods of instruction" are discussed in detail earlier in the *Mohe zhiguan*. In Tiantai parlance they refer to the four methods a buddha uses to present the Dharma teachings to an audience: (1) the worldly method, in ways understandable to a worldly audience, (2) the individual method, tailored to each individual listener, (3) the therapeutic method, applying teachings according to the disease, as one would prescribe medicine, and (4) the supreme method of teaching the Buddha Dharma directly.
4. "HE breath" is a reference to one of the Six Breaths (*liuqi*), introduced in more detail below. On this practice, see Despeux (2006).
5. XI breath, and also *si* breath, are additional references to the Six Breaths.
6. This list of six categories is quoted by Paul Unschuld (1985/2010, 143). Although not identifying Zhiyi or the *Mohe zhiguan* and relying on an essay by Paul Demiéville in the *Hōbōgirin* (1929), Unschuld identifies this list as one that combined and summarized previous developments in Chinese medicine, especially among the Buddhists. Thus, this analysis by Zhiyi shows his talent for synthesizing vast amounts of teachings and ideas.
7. Māra is the king of demons and the ruler of the demonic realm. Such references can be to an external demon or to internal demonic forces that obstruct meditation. See the discussion in chapter 3.
8. For an annotated translation of this and other sections of the *Mohe zhiguan,* see Swanson (2018).
9. The identity of Master Wen is not known, though Zhiyi refers to him in a number of his works.

10. The "four mindfulnesses" refer to mindfulness concerning four objects—that is, to be mindful of and have insight that (1) the body is impure, (2) sensations involve suffering, (3) the mind and thoughts are impermanent, and (4) phenomena are without substantial reality. These are the first four practices or levels of practice in the Buddhist "thirty-seven steps on the path."
11. The six sublime gates of meditation—that is, counting your breaths, following after your breaths, *śamatha, vipaśyanā,* reflection, and purity.
12. The *dantian,* literally "cinnabar field," also translated as "elixir field," are important focal points throughout the body for internal meditative techniques. In Chinese medicine and also martial arts, the navel area is particularly important as the focal point for breathing techniques. In Buddhist meditation, focusing on the navel, or the *dantian* in the lower-abdominal area ("two-and-a-half inches below the navel"), helps to control thoughts and emotions and is an important step to attaining insightful concentration.
13. These are three historical military figures from Zhiyi's time: Jiang Tianwen (fl. sixth century), Wu Mingche (512–578), and Mou Xi (516–587).
14. A quote from a commentary on *Questions on the Classic of the Yellow Emperor* and the related *Eighty-One Questions of the Yellow Emperor,* compiled in the mid- to late Han (239 CE). For details, see Unschuld (1986b).
15. See, for example, the passage in the *Miscellaneous Āgama* (*T* no. 99, 2: 319b27–c12), which tells of using a full bowl of curd, a bottle of oil, and a bottle of honey, along with some warm water, to relieve back pain. The sutra says that the oil was rubbed on the Buddha's back, then washed with warm water, and he drank the curds and honey; thus, the Buddha was relieved of his back pain.
16. The "four *samādhis*" refer to Zhiyi's classification, explained in detail in the *Mohe zhiguan,* of all Buddhist practices of concentrated meditation into four types, consisting of constantly sitting, constantly walking, both sitting and walking, and neither just sitting or walking.
17. The "thirty-six beasts" are the animals associated with the various times of the day, with three animals for each of the twelve periods of two hours each.

Chapter 7

The Perils of Deviant Meditative Absorption

Zhiyi's Sequential Gate to Meditation

DAVID CARPENTER

The text by Zhiyi (538–597) translated in chapter 6 is concerned primarily with physical illnesses that may be brought on by improper meditative practice. But Zhiyi also discusses various "deviations" that can arise in the course of the practice of meditation that include what we today would probably think of as mental illness. While these are mentioned briefly in his *Shorter* and *Great Treatises* (*Xiao zhiguan* and *Mohe zhiguan*),[1] we find a more extensive discussion of them in an earlier work by Zhiyi—namely, his *Explanation of the Method of the Sequential Practice of the Perfection of Meditation* (*Shi chan boluomi cidi famen*), popularly known as the *Sequential Gate to Meditation.* This lesser-known work is in fact the source of much of the material found in the *Shorter Treatise,* the chapter on illness in the latter being taken with only minimal changes from the earlier text.

Meditation as laid out in the *Sequential Gate to Meditation* is an intense practice that can lead to intense experiences, with the potential to create mental disturbances. After extensive preparation one typically begins with the preliminary practice of calming meditation (*śamatha*). If all goes well, when the mind becomes sufficiently concentrated, the meditator will enter a state of deep concentration known as access concentration and suddenly begin to experience a variety of subtle sensations that mark the entry into a deep meditative absorption known as the first *dhyāna* (Pāli *jhāna*), the first of the four progressively deeper meditative states frequently mentioned in the earliest Buddhist scriptures. These sensations are presented as subtle or "non-ordinary" and are contrasted with the kinds of ordinary sensations that may arise for the meditator while in a still-unconcentrated state. These subtle sensations arise within and gradually suffuse the body, making it feel "cloud-like." They are explained as resulting from the contact of the meditator's coarse material body (the "desire realm body") with the subtle matter of the realm of form, a fine material realm of experience made accessible by these deeply concentrated states.[2] The subtle sensations that arise from such contact should ideally be attended by one or more of an array of virtuous qualities, indications that the meditator's state is wholesome. But this is not always the case.

The process of calming the mind and entering meditative absorption opens up the deeper strata of the meditator's mind, revealing whatever positive qualities may already be present as a result of one's previous practice (especially in earlier lives), as well as the karmic obstacles that can prevent one's further success as a meditator. Zhiyi emphasizes that the proper discernment of such qualities and the signs that manifest them is of vital importance for understanding how to progress on the meditative path. On the one hand, they allow students, typically aided by a teacher, to identify which practices are best suited to their own karmic disposition. They also serve the important function of identifying the obstacles and pitfalls that may await an unwary practitioner on the path. Zhiyi accordingly devotes a great deal of attention to a kind of phenomenology of such qualities and the signs that signify their presence.

Of particular interest is Zhiyi's instructions on the signs of "deviant" meditative states to avoid, along with vivid descriptions of the consequences of failing to do so—meditation gone wrong, as it were. In these states the subtle sensations are attended not by virtuous qualities but by deviant ones, qualities that Zhiyi describes in detail. Here we are presented with an expanded understanding of "meditation sickness," reaching beyond physical illness into the areas of mental and even social health. Although the *Shorter Treatise* also contains a parallel discussion of such deviant states, the discussion in the *Sequential Gate to Meditation* is much more developed, and thus it merits translation in full. Contemporary meditators may not conceptualize such disturbances in terms of past-life karma and demonic influence but rather think, for instance, of the influence of early life trauma. Nevertheless, Zhiyi's cautions, particularly concerning the kinds of inflation and grandiosity that powerful meditative experiences can sometimes elicit, retain their relevance today.

Further Reading

Gunaratana, Henepola. 1985. *The Path of Serenity and Insight: An Explanation of the Buddhist Jhānas.* Motilal Banarsidass.

Meyers, Karin. 2012. "The Pleasant Way: The Dhyāna-s, Insight and the Path According to the Abhidharmakośa." In *Buddhist Philosophy and Meditation Practice, Academic Papers Presented at the 2nd International Association of Buddhist Universities Conference.* International Association of Buddhist Universities.

Stevenson, Daniel B. 1986. "The Four Kinds of Samādhi in Early T'ien-t'ai Buddhism." In *Traditions of Meditation in Chinese Buddhism,* edited by Peter Gregory. University of Hawai'i Press.

Wang, Huei-hsin. 2001. "Zhiyi's Interpretation of the Concept 'Dhyāna' in His 'Shi Chan Boluomi Tsidi Famen.'" PhD diss., University of Arizona.

Signs of Deviant Practice[3]

When the sensations manifest in the [four] fundamental absorptions, following the manifestation of a single sensation [for example the sensation of movement], if there are deviant qualities present there will be signs of deviation. Deviant qualities are many. Now in terms of a single sensation we can briefly set out ten pairs of deviant qualities in order to clarify the signs of deviation. First, [the quality of] an increase or decrease of bodily sensations; second, [the quality of] being either concentrated or scattered; third, empty or existent; fourth, light or dark; fifth, worried or joyful; sixth, suffering or happy; seventh, good or bad; eighth, ignorant or wise; ninth, bound or free; tenth, a strong or weak mind. These ten pairs clarify the signs of deviation. The [signs] can all be distinguished in terms of whether or not these [qualities] occur.

First, the increase and decrease of bodily sensations. Perhaps when there is the manifestation of the sensation of movement, either the body moves, the hands rise, or the feet also [move] accordingly. A person [observing from] the outside sees the meditator motionless, as if asleep. Or perhaps if one encounters a demon the body and hands move repeatedly. Or perhaps while sitting one sees all kinds of different objects: These are all signs of increase. Decrease: When movement first starts to manifest, whether at the top or at the bottom [of the body], not to mention all over the body, it is gradually extinguished or subsides, and thus perceptual objects are completely lost; when sitting one is dull, with no way of controlling the body. These are the signs of decrease.

Second, concentrated or scattered. Concentrated: When the sensation of movement first manifests, the knowing mind as well as the body are bound because of the concentration, unable to be free, and for this reason one easily enters a deviant concentration and doesn't come out for as much as seven days. Scattered: When the sensation of movement manifests, the mind is scattered and agitated and doesn't remain on its [meditative] object.

Third, empty or existent. Empty: When the sensations manifest, one does not see the body at all, and one [mistakenly] calls this the realization of a formless absorption. Existent: When the sensations manifest, one experiences the body as solid and hard, just like wood or rock.

Fourth, light or dark. When the sensations manifest, one sees externally all kinds of luminous appearances, even the sun, moon, and stars, and all kinds of lights, green, yellow, red, and white. Dark: When the sensations manifest, the body and mind are dark and dim, as if entering a dark room.

Fifth, worried or joyful. Worried: When sensations manifest, one's mind is afflicted with worry, weary and despondent, without happiness. Joyful: When sensations manifest, the mind is greatly joyful. There is an upwelling of movement, and one is not able to calm oneself.

Sixth, suffering or happiness. Suffering: When sensation manifests, the body and mind are everywhere afflicted with pain. Happiness: When sensation manifests, there is great happiness. Craving and attachment bind and entangle one.

Seventh, good or bad. Good: When sensations manifest, thoughts are scattered outside and [even] wholesome thought and reflection destroy *samādhi*. Bad: When sensations manifest, then all bad mental states arise, such as having neither conscience nor shame.

Eighth, ignorant or wise. Ignorant: When sensations manifest, the knowing mind is ignorant and deluded, lost, muddled, inverted. Wise: When sensations manifest, there is the acute affliction of knowing the [five mistaken] views, and the mind produces evil thoughts and destroys *samādhi*.

Ninth, bound or free. Bound: When sensations manifest, the five hindrances and all the afflictions obscure the knowing mind. Free: When the sensations manifest, it is [falsely] regarded as the realization of emptiness, the concentration without signs, attaining the path, attaining the fruit, breaking the fetters and [attaining] liberation, and one becomes arrogant hating one's superiors.

Tenth, a strong or weak mind. Strong: When sensations manifest, one's mind is unyielding and strong; going in and out one does not attain freedom. Just like tiles and stones it is hard to change, and one doesn't conform to the good path. Weak: When sensations manifest, the mind and the will are weak and can easily be defeated and destroyed, just like soft mud cannot be made into a vessel.

In this way twenty kinds of bad sensations disturb and confuse both the sitting and the mind, destroy the absorptive concentration and make the mind deviate. These are the signs of the manifestation of deviant concentration. Furthermore, the twenty deviant qualities accompany whatever manifests. If one does not discern what is deviant and false and the mind gives rise to strong attachment, the result is a scattered mind that is frenetic and unrestrained, and one either sings or cries, either smiles or sobs, sometimes runs about everywhere restive and deranged, or sometimes falls ill. Sometimes this results in death. Sometimes one wants to throw oneself from a cliff, or immolate, strangle, or maim oneself. Thus, the hindrances and afflictions are numerous. Furthermore, following the manifestation of one of the deviant qualities among the twenty kinds of deviations, if it is associated with one of the demonic teachings that are among the teachings of the ninety-six [heterodox] paths,[4] one who is unaware of this will then think of that path and practice that teaching. By following these thoughts, the demons will easily enter among the [deviant] qualities that have been attained, and therefore one will become caught up in a demonic teaching. The demon adds its power, and perhaps profound but evil concentrations manifest, as well as the eloquence of wisdom, worldly knowledge of fortune and misfortune, strange supernormal powers, and the display of unusual things. These affect all living beings and widely effect deviant transformations and are able to do great evil and destroy peoples' good roots or perhaps accord with good deeds but falsify and confuse what is done.

Worldly people lack wisdom, and in vain they see these extraordinary people and call them wise. With all their heart they believe and submit to them. But because these people are inwardly misguided, exclusively practicing a demonic method and constantly teaching people by means of it, those who believe in them and practice their method then destroy the correct precepts, destroy right view, destroy proper decorum, and destroy right livelihood. Sometimes they eat excrement and shamelessly expose their bodies. They do not respect the Three Honored Ones [Buddha, Dharma, Sangha], parents, and teachers. Or they destroy the scriptures, images and stupas, committing all heinous crimes, eradicating good roots. Signs equivalent to these appear. Sometimes they praise themselves saying that what they do is equal [to the Dharma]. Therefore, being themselves on the wrong path, they without hindrance or impediment denigrate others who are doing good, saying that they are not on the correct path. Sometimes they teach that there is no cause and no effect, or they teach a heterodox cause and a heterodox effect, and thus the heretical teachings confusedly corrupt the correct Dharma.

As for those who hear and accept them, the heretical teachings pollute their minds, and they inwardly realize the deviant meditative absorptions, *samādhis,* and wisdom that cut off merit and virtue. Themselves outside the various gates of the Dharma, they are limitlessly eloquent, and with an air of importance they convert beings and thereby acquire the benefit of fame, followers, offerings, respect, praise, etc. This is described in the *Scripture on the Ninety-Six Kinds of [Heterodox] Paths:*[5] In order to teach the Dharma these people are aided by demons, and then all their hearers cannot help but believe and accept them. All who see them give rise to love and respect. By means of such things people become wholeheartedly attached and cannot turn back. The perversions of heterodox practices are various and many.

Notes

1. The former is translated in Salguero (2017), the latter in chapter 6 of the current volume.
2. Zhiyi is here drawing upon the traditional Buddhist cosmology of the three realms: the coarse material realm, the subtle realm of fine materiality, and the formless realm. For the correlation of these realms with meditative states of consciousness, see Gethin (1997).
3. *Taishō Tripiṭaka* no. 1916, 46: 496c20–497b20 (hereafter *T*).
4. The heterodox views of the ninety-six non-Buddhist groups mentioned in the *Saṃyuktāgama, T* no. 100, 2: 390b28. See Bingenheimer (2011, 237–243).
5. Zhiyi cites this scripture four times in the *Sequential Gate to Meditation* and it appears in a number of Chinese catalogues as a work of one or two fascicles, but is no longer extant.

Chapter 8

Winds in the Heart

Tibetan Geksel *Practices for Healing Insecurity and Anxiety*

MICHAEL R. SHEEHY

By the eleventh century, during the formative period of the Tibetan Renaissance when new Buddhist orders were institutionalized in Tibet, contemplatives on the plateau were experimenting with meditation. In monasteries and retreat huts, meditators practiced contemplative techniques introduced from Indian Buddhism, recorded their contemplative experiences, and cultivated new contemplative lives and culture in Tibet. They read the Indic source texts in translation that prescribed different contemplative practices—from observing the mind to performing scripted visualizations, engaging in rigorous physical exercises, and fostering conditions for endogenous visions. Amid their experimentation, challenging experiences and maladies inevitably emerged, and in response practitioners innovated contemplative interventions to prevent and counteract such adversities. Among these were practices designed to dispel obstructions to well-being (*geksel*) and practices to enhance meditative performance (*bogdön*).[1]

These dispelling and enhancing practices complemented the main meditative practices of the "generation stage" (*kyérim*) contemplations of simulating oneself as a sublime deity and the somatic yogas of the completion stage (*dzokrim*). For both preventive measures and as remedies, meditators wrote down prescriptions and compiled handbooks that circulated among their fellow practitioner communities. Most often, these prescriptions were synthetic compositions drawn from different genres with varied styles and vocabularies. Authors drew from available Buddhist yogic and tantric texts, meditation instructions, medical diagnostic literature, and their own experimental first-person trial and error. Their writings shared affiliations with existing Tibetan literature, including liturgies to protect against disease, evil spirits, and obstacles;

instructions for increasing positivity and purifying negativity; medical texts on symptomatology and methods of treatment; instructions for "taking attractions and aversions onto the path" (i.e., integrating thoughts, emotions, external adversities, pain, sickness, and the dying process into the continuity of the waking contemplative life); and guides on how to indicate signs and measures of meditative progress or regress.

Manuals that prescribed contemplative interventions developed considerably in scope, proportion, and sophistication from the eleventh through the thirteenth centuries, likely due to the circulation of these texts among networks of practice communities throughout south and central Tibet. Based on extant historical Tibetan sources, these manuals were circulated most widely within networks of meditators who practiced in the Sakya Lamdré, Sixfold Yoga of the Kālacakra, Six Teachings of Niguma, Six Teachings of Nāropa, and early Kagyü Mahāmudrā and Nyingma Dzogchen traditions. Each of these contemplative systems customized practices as treatments and countermeasures specific to emergent cognitive, affective, and somatic effects. Written procedural instructions became integral to a contemplative life and were included in larger anthologies and guidebooks on how to conduct a meditation retreat in the mountains. Consequently, a significant body of Tibetan contemplative literature describes and prescribes practices to alleviate specific challenges or adverse meditative experiences.

This chapter presents select practices for remedying a category of ills associated with the psycho-emotional turbulence caused by "wind energies" (*lung*) from two important Tibetan language anthologies, *The Great Anthology of Practices for Dispelling Obstructions* (*Geksel Chenmo*) by Jikten Gönpo Rinchen Pel (1143–1217) and *Garland of Gems: Direct Instructions for Dispelling Obstructions* (*Norbü Trengwa*) by Minyak Drakpa Dorjé (d. 1491). Jikten Gönpo was the founder of the Drikung Kagyü order and Minyak Drakpa Dorjé was a scholar of the Sakya order, and their respective anthologies compile various practices to dispel obstructions in these two traditions. Jikten Gönpo authored several handbooks that contain remedial and enhancement practices, which are scattered throughout his *Collected Works.* Minyak Drakpa Dorjé's *Garland of Gems* is among the most eclectic and comprehensive anthologies of remedial practices and includes taxonomical enumerations of obstructions to well-being along with practical instructions on how to directly relieve these obstructions via contemplative techniques.

Employing the well-known Buddhist analogy that the Buddha is like a doctor and his Dharma teachings are like medicine, these practices are applied as medicine to counteract an ailment diagnosed within the practitioner. This analogy is extended to literally entwine Tibetan medical knowledge and methods with these preventive and remedial practices through the application of antidotes to alleviate a pathology, either primary or symptomatic. Such pathologies include mental and bodily pains and disorders as well as social or external adversarial forces, circumstances, and malfunctions. Practices can be prescribed by an experienced meditation teacher or self-medicated to counteract emergent impediments or adjust contemplative techniques based upon experiences. Preventive practices are prescribed to maintain health and well-being so that more exertive practices, especially the somatic yogas, can be performed with minimized health risks. Remedial practices treat both adverse effects derived directly from meditative experiences and disorders inhibitive of meditation. These contemplative interventions are applied to a broad spectrum of ailments, including indigestion, edema, depression, fever, dysentery, swelling of the throat, toothache, headache, bloody nose, worm infections, diarrhea, dehydration, and gout, to name a few.[2]

This chapter includes interventions selected to exemplify practices to prevent, diagnose, and remedy the mental health disorders associated with the turbulent fluctuations of internal winds that circulate throughout the human body and affect the mind.[3] Buddhist tantric physiology understands that the body is not limited to the biological organism but rather includes the flows and mechanisms of a subtler visceral body that can be manipulated via interoceptive techniques.[4] The anatomy of the subtle body includes tube-like channels that run vertically, vitality centers in the shape of wheels along the central axis of the body, vital winds that flow and circulate up and down the channels, and essences that resemble the shape of liquid drops. The Tibetan term for wind is *lung,* which is a translation of two distinct Sanskrit technical terms, *vāyu* and *prāṇa.* While the term *vāyu* refers to the breath that is inhaled and exhaled throughout the respiratory system, the term *prāṇa* refers to the energy that courses through the body. When Tibetans historically translated these two Sanskrit terms, they chose the single word *lung* to capture the differences and synergies. In the context of *geksel* practices to dispel obstructions, wind sickness is psycho-emotional turbulence that emerges from imbalances in the energetic flows of the body. These can be caused by disturbances in respiration as well as stress or nervous frenetic motion within the mind-body complex.

In particular, "winds in the heart" or "heart-winds" (*nying lung*) is a disorder that denotes melancholy, sadness, or depression, it also includes a spectrum of anxiety, psychosis, and pre–heart attack experiences. The heart in this context is not always the physical organ but is also associated with one's emotional center. Tibetan medicine characterizes heart-winds as a kind of psychosomatic wind sickness with telltale diagnostic signs of neurotic flightiness, a heavy feeling in the torso, pains in the lower body, mindlessness or forgetfulness, and a persistent feeling of being tired or burned out. If heart-winds increase, it can make one crazy. In the *Garland of Gems,* practices for alleviating heart-winds are categorized along with tumors, indigestion, and insecurity. (The Tibetan term for insecurity literally means to lack certainty, and while its antidote is self-confidence or feeling certain, the practices prescribed closely resemble those for heart-winds.)

Many of the practices selected here share three distinct contemplative techniques, namely (1) the visualization of a sublime body,[5] (2) the imagery of light, and (3) sonic meditations. Visualizations can take the shape of buddhas, deities, or, as is the case of these practices (§ 1.1, 1.2, 2.2), one's personal meditation teacher in a manner resonant with Tibetan *guru yoga* practices. One practice from *The Great Anthology* (§ 1.2) bears a striking resemblance to the beloved seven-line prayer to Padmasambhava, the Lotus-Born Guru, who is indelibly connected with the founding of Buddhism in Tibet.[6] The well-known supplication uses motifs and language descriptively to invoke the presence of one's teacher within the pistils, stamen, and petals of a lotus flower.

In the *Garland of Gems,* one practice (§ 2.2) leverages the sublime body of one's teacher to suffuse the practitioner's body image with light to heal. The practice elicits an imagined sense of an intrinsic radiance permeating the body of one's teacher, and as light rays emanate from their body, the practitioner is bathed in this naturally glowing white light. Light and color are evoked repeatedly, including the image of a white light that encircles the practitioner's heart "like a white silk enclosing a tent." A visualization of the three colors of white, red, and lapis blue is used to imagine all sickness seeping out of the body (§ 2.3, 2.5). Along with these visualizations, the syllable HA is prescribed for the practitioner to recite in the selected practices to cure heart-winds. Immersion in this self-generated sound is understood in these contemplative traditions to elicit a vibrational pattern with healing and restorative powers. The use of sonic meditation coupled with mental imagery infused with light intentionally induces a multisensory synesthesia, a heightened experience of sensemaking.

Further Reading

Duckworth, Douglas. 2017. "Rangjung Dorjé's Key to the Essential Points of Wind and Mind." In *Buddhism and Medicine: An Anthology of Premodern Sources,* edited by C. Pierce Salguero. Columbia University Press.

Gyalwa Yangönpa. 2015. *Secret Map of the Subtle Body: Visions of the Human Energy Structure.* Translated by Elio Guarisco. Shang Shung.

Marek, Todd P., and Charles Jamyang Oliphant of Rossie. "Treating Disorders of the Subtle Winds in Tibetan Buddhism." In *Buddhism and Medicine: An Anthology of Premodern Sources,* edited by C. Pierce Salguero. Columbia University Press.

Rangjung, Dorjé. 2015. *The Profound Inner Principles.* Translated by Elizabeth Callahan. Shambhala.

1. *The Great Anthology of Practices for Dispelling Obstructions*[7]

[1.1] Practice for Wind Sickness

These practices include techniques to reverse the winds, causes for reversing winds, and signs of emergence. To begin, there are two practical causes, divided into distal causes and proximal causes:

As for distal causes: Even for adept meditators who have arrived at a crucial point in their meditative stabilization, challenges can emerge from previous negative actions. As it reads in the *Amoghapāśa Tantra:*[8]

> At the very moment when meditative powers arise,
> there is subsequently a reversal of previous actions.

This is how it's explained.

As for proximal causes: These occur during advanced practices, including inelegantly bending the torso while performing physical exercises. Consequently, awareness will tighten, which will prevent you from rising above discursive thoughts, and as you proceed, distractions can become increasingly acute.

As for signs of emergence: These include unstable awareness, thirst, ardently fidgeting, flights of mind, and light sleep at night. Without a spiritual practice, you could have visions of serpentine and noxious spirits performing great miracles. With a spiritual practice, you could see buddhas and bodhisattvas even with the various ebb and flow of experience.

When these meditative experiences emerge, find a secluded place and sit relaxedly with your legs crossed on a comfortable mat. Comfortably rest your hands on your thighs with your palms downward. Totally straighten your lower back and open up your torso. With your eyes either open or closed, look directly at the essential point of whatever is your meditative experience.

Then, meditate on the third preliminary practice of renunciation along the path and so forth.[9] For the main practice, imagine the body of your sublime teacher about the size of a thumb sitting below your navel. From that, a thick but subtle nine-pronged gold *vajra* scepter emerges about the size of a barley grain along your lower back and descends, falling below your waistline downward into the underground. As it falls lower, visualize it moving with the sound of wind into the infinite regress of subterranean space. Meditate on that without distraction for as long as you can.

Furthermore, focus your awareness on the intermediary spaces where discursive thoughts do not arise. While lucid, rest in that lucid continuum without attending to meditative experiences in your body.

Next, visualize the fire of pristine wisdom emerging from the body of your teacher and like before, imagine that descending underground. Without being distracted, focus intently on the tips of the flames below.

When you feel tired or weary, prop yourself up with a pillow in your bed and sense the lethargy throughout your body.[10] Afterward, lie down on your back, extend your legs to stretch outward, and comfortably rest your hands down beside your thighs. As before, concentrate on the meditative experience.

Rub very nutritious substances including aged butter, fat, and so forth on the soles of your feet. From about three armlengths underground, find and heat a flat stone that is about four inches in size and about four inches thick.[11] For food, keep to what's most nutritious, including all kinds of cooked foods. Abstain from spoiled and rotten meat, medicinal plants, bitter foods, and so forth.

[1.2] Practice for Heart-Winds

To treat sickness of winds in the heart: Be impartial to warm or cool foods and drinks and instead be attentive to what is most nutritious. Remain mindful![12]

> [Imagine] by stretching a string from the heart,
> it extends from your anus to a valve at the tip of your heart.
> There, meditate on an eight-petaled red lotus.
> In its anthers, meditate on your sublime teacher.
> Say words to attune yourself with harmonizable friends.
> Then, you'll be freed from sickness of winds in the heart.[13]

[1.3] Diagnosing Signs of Heart-Winds

> When flights of the mind fill your torso, winds reside in your heart.
> Pain will consume your entire lower body, and you can become mindless and faint.
> When you feel worn out by the uncontrived, you can become crazy with heart-winds.[14]
> [Heart-winds are] marked by nerve disorders in six or seven joints.
> When the disorder is mature, if the secret wind [points] is pressed, you will groan or whistle the sound HA.[15]
> These are the measurable signs of having winds sickness.[16]

2. *Garland of Gems: Direct Instructions for Dispelling Obstructions*[17]

[2.1] Healing Heart-Winds

When you are irritated, restless, and so forth,
feel your heart ravish and your heart break.
Imagine your heart being encircled by whiteness like white silk enclosing a tent.

In that state, gaze at the many spaces in between your pores.
While you recite HA,
imagine from within those pores, immeasurable white light rays emit and disperse as pale light.
Continue to recite HA.

[2.2] Healing Heart-Winds

[Imagine] your heart is inflated like a balloon, empty and clear;[18]
gaze at the many spaces in between your pores.

Rest in the nature of light and the light rays of your teacher's body, white in color, the size of a thumb. From every facet of their body, light rays shine forth and radiate outwards from their pores as every light ray descends into your body.
As you imagine yourself suffused [with light],
recite HA.

In that state of light, you possess the natural light of your teacher's body.
That's the shining of light rays!

[2.3] Healing Heart-Winds

Tilt your head downward to face your heart.
Imagine in four, eight, or sixteen portions,
all sicknesses ooze out at the edges [of your body] as the three colors of white, red, and lapis blue.
Imagine that all the pus, blood, and serum are emitted,
recite HA.

[2.4] Healing Heart-Winds

With all your heart,
[Imagine] your sickness being dispersed upward into whatever is there.
Continue to recite HA, just as before.

[2.5] Healing Heart-Winds

Gaze at the many spaces in between your pores,
both on the front and back side in the areas of your heart and mouth.

Expelling the sound HA,
all sicknesses become the three colors of white, red, and lapis blue.
Imagine that all the pus, blood, and serum are emitted,
recite HA.

[2.6] A Preventative Care Routine

In this way, the signs of sickness and challenges that can be produced if you are totally healthy include: various frightful appearances that manifest as signs of challenge by malevolent forces, sickness of the channels that can come about from a tear in the knots of your channels, and wind sickness that emerges from over-exertive forceful breathing.[19] Without distaste for any of these, spontaneously practice to recognize meditative concentration.

Regarding this, there are five meditations:

Recognize all images to be empty appearances. Recite HA.
Recognize all sounds to be empty audibles. Recite HA.
Recognize all smells to be empty sensations. Recite HA.
Recognize all tastes to be empty experiences. Recite HA.
Recognize all touch to be empty tactility. Recite HA.

By alleviating sickness, your body will be radiant with good complexion. When it is time to get up, you will be lustrously clear. By alleviating malevolent forces, you won't be afraid of anything. In this way, you will take command of all the malevolent forces![20]

Notes

1. Practices to dispel obstructions (*gegs sel*) and enhance meditative performance (*bogs 'don*).
2. See similarities with Lindhal et al. (2020, 8); Lambert et al. (2021, 1115–1119).
3. Gerke (2013, 90–94).
4. Gerke (2013, 83–88).
5. The "sublime body" (*lha sku*) denotes the sacred form of a body, typically the body of a deity or an adept meditator, which is distinct from the "subtle body" (*lus phra ba*) that refers to the energetic constituents of a body.
6. Jamgon Mipham (2015, 29–31).
7. 'Jig rten mgon po (2008). The date when the work was completed is uncertain.

8. A reference to the Amoghapāśakalparāja, the Sovereign Ritual of Amoghapāśa. This early *Kriyā Tantra* is a large compendium of rites associated with Amoghapāśa, a principal emanation of the deity of compassion, Avalokiteśvara.
9. The four typical preliminary practices are contemplating (1) the rare and precious human life, (2) certainty of death, (3) moral causality, and (4) pains of cyclic existence. This refers to the contemplation of moral causality, how one's actions affect one's mind and well-being.
10. The text reads *byin,* which I am reading as *bying,* meaning drowsiness or lethargy.
11. A flat, heated stone (*rdo dugs*) is used as a medical treatment to induce warmth.
12. In this context, the practitioner is being instructed to recall the practice instructions.
13. 'Jig rten mgon po (2008, 44–45).
14. These signs are also associated with disorders of the nervous system. 'Jig rten mgon po Rin chen dpal (2008, 93–94); Loizzo (2016, 2–6).
15. "Secret wind points" is a reference to moxibustion points associated with disorders that affect numerous joints in the body and that run through the central nervous system from the back of the head (*gtsug rgyab*) down the spinal cord (*sgal tshigs*) and are engaged therapeutically to treat anxiety and related ills.
16. 'Jig rten mgon po (2008, 93).
17. Mi nyag Grags pa rdo rje 2008. Completed in the year 1486 at Dar Drongmoché Monastery, a satellite monastery of Sakya Monastery in south central Tibet.
18. The Tibetan phrase *phru ma phub btab pa lta bu* literally means "blown up like an inflated bladder."
19. These are references to the abnormal health conditions that may result from overexertion of the somatic yogas during the completion stage. Sickness of the channels (*rtsa zug*) and knots in the channels (*rtsa mdud*) are common descriptions of emergent ailments in tantric literature.
20. Mi nyag Grags pa rdo rje (2008, 342).

Chapter 9

The Soft Butter Method

Hakuin's (1686–1769) Method for Curing the Maladies of Meditation

JUHN Y. AHN

Zen master Hakuin Ekaku (1686–1769) is commonly regarded as the reviver of Rinzai Zen. Inspired and alarmed by the growing influence of the Ōbaku Zen sect, Hakuin actively engaged in efforts to broadly reform Zen monastic training and kōan practice. He sought to restore what he believed to be the authentic Zen traditions of the monasteries Daitokuji and Myōshinji. Through these efforts Hakuin was able to turn his temple, Shōinji, into an active center of Zen monastic training. Talented monks such as his chief disciple Tōrei Enji (1721–1792) flocked to Hakuin's temple in Hara and later disseminated his teachings to other areas of Japan. Hakuin's spiritual descendants became so successful during the Meiji period (1868–1912) that virtually all Zen masters of the Rinzai Zen sect today trace their lineages back to him. It is also common to attribute the kōan system currently in use within the Rinzai Zen sect to Hakuin.

Hakuin left behind a large body of writings, but arguably no work has received more attention than his *Idle Talk on a Night Boat* (*Yasenkanna*), a story about Hakuin's encounter with the hermit Hakuyū published in 1757. Hoping to find a remedy for his "meditation sickness" or "Zen illness" (*zenbyō*), Hakuin widely searched for and eventually found the hermit, who provided him with several different remedies.

Unlike Chan or Zen masters of the past, Hakuin offered relatively detailed descriptions of the mental and physical symptoms that accompany the malady. As Hakuin explains in the translation of *Idle Talk on a Night Boat* below, meditation sickness is accompanied by parched lungs, cold feet, fear, depression, ringing in the ears, constant perspiration, and hallucinations. Hakuin's explanation of these symptoms, as I have demonstrated elsewhere, seem to have had in mind the growing interest in printed medical literature imported from China and certain passages in Tiantai Zhiyi's (538–597) magnum opus *Great [Treatise on] Śamatha and Vipaśyanā Meditation* (*Mohe zhiguan;* see excerpt in chapter 6).[1] Following Zhiyi's example, Hakuin's work focuses more on traditional concerns about poor breathing and the misuse of *śamatha* (calming) and *vipaśyanā* (contemplation) found in earlier Buddhist treatises on meditation.

After its first appearance as part of *Sendai's Comments on Hanshan's Poems* (*Kanzanshi sendai kimon*) published in 1746, the story of Hakuin's encounter with Hakuyū appeared regularly in Hakuin's other writings. Hakuin's fondness for this story had much to do with his continued interest in post-*satori,* or post-awakening, training. This, Hakuin believed, was what set authentic Zen apart from Ōbaku. Hakuin believed that failure to engage in post-*satori* training would result in the appearance of a gap between theory and practice, phenomena and principle, or the quietude of meditation and the activity of everyday life.

In giving advice on how to cure meditation sickness in the translation below, Hakuin focuses on remedies such as inner contemplation (*naikan*) and something called the "soft butter method" (*nanso no hō*). The latter, related to visualization practices found in *Secret Essential Methods for Curing Meditation Sickness* (*Zhi chanbing miyao fa;* see chapter 4), has been frequently cited in Western Buddhist media as a treatment for various maladies of meditation.

The partial translation of Hakuin's *Idle Talk on the Night Boat* below is based on the critical edition of the text published in volume 4 of *The Complete Collection of the Dharma Talks of Zen Master Hakuin* edited by Yoshizawa Katsuhiro.[2]

Further Reading

Ahn, Juhn. 2008. "Zen and the Art of Nourishing Life: Labor, Exhaustion, and the Malady of Meditation." *Japanese Journal of Religious Studies* 35 (2): 177–229.

Ahn, Juhn. 2021. "Meditation Sickness." In *The Oxford Handbook of Meditation,* edited by Miguel Farias, David Brazier, and Mansur Lalljee. Oxford University Press.

Mohr, Michel. 2006. "Imagining Indian Zen: Tōrei's Commentary on the 'Ta-Mo-to-Lo Ch'an Ching' and the Rediscovery of Early Meditation Techniques During the Tokugawa Era." In *Zen Classics: Formative Texts in the History of Zen Buddhism,* edited by Steven Heine and Dale S. Wright. Oxford University Press.

Waddell, Norman. 2010. *Wild Ivy: The Spiritual Autobiography of Zen Master Hakuin.* Shambhala.

Williams, Duncan Ryūken. 2004. *The Other Side of Zen: A Social History of Soto Zen Buddhism in Tokugawa Japan.* Princeton University Press.

Excerpt from *Idle Talk on a Night Boat*[3]

The day I first began Zen learning I made a vow to muster up the fearless mind of faith and kindle the steadfast spirit to [pursue] the Way. Two or three years of painstaking self-refinement had already passed and then suddenly one night I instantly lost myself.[4] The various doubts of the past melted away from the roots and the karmic roots of countless rebirths thoroughly dissolved like bubbles in water. I thought to myself, "The Way is truly not far from people. The ancients [practicing] for twenty or thirty years—what kind of made-up outlandish story is this?"[5] Out of pure joy I danced mindlessly for several months.

Afterwards, reflecting upon my daily behavior [I noticed] that the two realms of activity and quietude were completely out of balance and that my movements were not completely unconstrained. I thought to myself, "Without fear I will make effort and once again throw my life into this endeavor." I clenched my teeth and opened my eyes wide. I gave up sleep and food. Before long, in less than a month, the Heart-Fire rose up against its natural course and parched the Lung-Metal. Both legs [felt] as if they were immersed in ice and snow and in both ears it seemed as if I were walking between a mountain stream. The Liver and Gall [i.e., the source of courage] grew timid and weak on account of which I became fearful in my actions; mind and spirit were troubled and tired, and hence asleep or awake I had visions of various objects. Both armpits persistently sweat, and both eyes were continuously filled with tears. At this point I tried visiting wise teachers all over and looking for famous physicians, but all the medicine [in the world] had no effect. . . .

[Hakuin makes an arduous trek to find the reclusive master Hakuyū and begs him for help managing his symptoms.]

At that point Hakuyū gently took my hand and carefully examined my Five Zang Viscera and read my nine pulses. His fingernails were half an inch long. He furrowed his brows in pity and said, "Alas! The method of your contemplation went beyond measure and the advancement in practice lost regulation; this grave illness has thereby come about; truly, what is difficult to cure medically is your meditation sickness. If you tried to cure it with the three methods of acupuncture, moxibustion, and medicine, then later, even if you desire to save yourself from this, [the venerated physicians of antiquity] Bian Que, Cang Gong, and Hua Tuo could try to do their best, but their efforts would be in vain.[6] You have been harmed by contemplation. If you do not diligently accumulate the power of inner contemplation, then you will never be able to get better. As it is said, "what is lowered by the earth must be raised by the earth."[7]

I said, "I wish to hear the secret essentials of inner contemplation. I will practice it as I learn it." Hakuyū respectfully changed his face and quietly said, "Ah. You are an inquisitive gentleman. I can tell you what I heard a long time ago. This is a secret formula for nourishing life. Very few people are aware of it. If you practice it diligently it will be effective, and you can also expect to live a long life. The great Way is divided into two principles. Yin and yang harmonize to produce people and things. A primordial energy endowed naturally by Heaven circulates silently within [the body], furnishing it with the Five Viscera and moving along its channels. Blood and qi are active, each rising, falling, and circulating [the body] fifty times each day and night. The Lung-Metal is a female viscera that floats above the diaphragm. The Liver-Wood is a male viscera that sinks below the diaphragm. The Heart-Fire is Great Yang and is located in the upper body. The Kidney-Water is Great Yin and is located in the lower body. The Five Viscera house the seven spirits.[8] The Spleen and the Kidneys each contain two spirits. Exhalation comes out of the Heart and Lungs. Inhalation enters the Kidneys and Liver.

With each exhalation, [blood and qi] move three inches in the channel. With each inhalation they move three inches in the channel. Each day and night we take thirteen thousand five hundred breaths, [so blood and qi] make fifty circuits through the entire body. Fire is light and always likes to rise upwards. Water is heavy and always tries to flow downwards. If a person is not aware of this and his contemplation loses regulation or his determination becomes excessive, then the Heart-Fire will flare up and scorch the Lung-Metal. When the Metal-mother is suffering, then the Water-child will become weak. Mother and child will injure each other and exhaust the Five Zang Viscera and attack the Six Fu Viscera. The Four Great Elements will increase and decrease and give rise to a hundred and one illnesses. You will reach that point where all the medicine [in the world] will have no effect and all the physicians fold their arms without being able to say anything." . . .

I said, "May I inquire about the technique that makes use of butter?" Hakuyū said, "If the practitioner realizes that the Four Great Elements are not in sync and both his mind and body are exhausted, then he ought to gather himself and construct the following thought:

Picture soft butter clear and pure in color and aroma. It, an object the size of a duck egg, appears suddenly on the crown of the head. It, extremely sublime in texture, moistens the head all over and continues to permeate and moisten as it melts downward. It flows gradually down from the two shoulders, both elbows, and two breasts into the space between the chest and the diaphragm, lungs, liver, stomach, intestines, spine and hip bones. At that moment, the illness of stagnation of the Five Zang Viscera and the Six Fu Viscera in the chest will follow the mind and descend.[9] There will be a clear sound that resembles that of flowing water. After circulating the entire body, it will drench both legs, reach the soles of the feet, and then stop.

The practitioner ought to repeat this visualization. The streams that permeate and moisten as they flow downward fill up and inundate the area below the navel, soaking it with warmth. It is just like a skilled worldly physician who gathers various herbs of sublime aroma, fills a bathtub with them, and soaks the area below our navel. When practicing this visualization, since all things are manifestation of the mind, the nose will suddenly smell a rare fragrance and the body will unexpectedly feel a sublime sensation. Mind and body will be far more in balance than they were in one's twenties and thirties. At this moment, the Viscera will be harmonized, stomach and intestines will be in sync, and the skin will, unbeknownst to oneself, glow.

If one is diligent and not lazy, what illness could not be cured, what power could not be acquired, what transcendence could not be attained, and what Way could not be accomplished? How quickly this visualization proves to be efficacious depends only on the practitioner's efforts to practice it.

Notes

1. See Ahn (2008).
2. Yoshizawa (2000). For a complete, annotated translation of *Idle Talk on the Night Boat,* see Waddell (2002).
3. Translated from Yoshizawa (2000). A portion of this translation was previously published in Salguero (2017) and is reproduced and expanded here with permission from Columbia University Press.
4. Here, the word "lost" (Jp. *rakusetsu*), as Yoshizawa Katsuhiro points out, was more commonly used to refer to loss in profit; see Yoshizawa (2000, 98n2).
5. This is a reference to a passage in *Doctrine of the Mean* (*Zhongyong*), chap. 13; see Legge (2013, 393).
6. Bian Que, Cang Gong, and Hua Tuo are legendary Chinese physicians of the Han and pre-Han era.
7. This seems to be an allusion to a verse uttered by Upagupta (the Fourth Patriarch) found in fascicle 1 of the *Jingde Era Record of the Transmission of the Lamp:* "If the earth causes you to fall, the earth must [also] cause you to rise. To try to rise without ground [to stand on] is ultimately untenable" (*Taishō Tripiṭaka* no. 2076, 51: 207b16–17); noted in Yoshizawa (2000, 109n12).
8. As Yoshizawa points out, the heart is said to house the spirit (*shen*), the lungs house the earthly spirit (*po*), the liver houses the cloud spirit (*hun*), the spleen houses intention

(*yi*) and wisdom (*zhi*), and the kidneys house essence (*jing*) and will (*zhi*); see Yoshizawa (2000, 112n15).

9. Hakuin here refers to the illness of "stagnation and lump pain." The word "stagnation" (*senheki* or *sen*), according to Manase Dōsan's (1507–1594) *Collection of Inspirational Writings* (*Keitekishū*), refers to a sharp pain in the testicles and small intestines caused by the prolonged stagnation of damp heat. The physician Ashikawa Keishū's (date unknown) medical dictionary *Explanation of the Names and Terminology of Illnesses* (*Byōmei ikai*) defines this illness as a pain in the small intestine caused by the depletion and weakening of blood and vital energy and the consequent accumulation of yin and cold energy in the body. "Lumps" are also explained as instances of accumulation (*shaku*). See Ahn (2008, 192–193).

Chapter 10

Treating Meditators' Ailments

Translations from the Chinese Medical Literature by Zhang Lu (1617–1699) and Xinchan (fl. 1890)

LESLIE E. DE VRIES AND LEO W. LOK

Here we present two passages from Chinese medical texts that deal with disorders caused by meditative practices. Both texts date from the Qing dynasty (1644–1911), fairly late in Chinese medical history. We concur with Zhang Lu, the author of the first text translated below, that earlier medical literature has little to offer about conditions like meditation sickness.[1] We can think of several reasons why this might have been the case. The medical community might have considered meditation to be an innocent practice with no real threats to physical and mental health. From other contributions to this volume, however, we know that this was not how authors from within meditating communities thought. Another explanation might be that literate doctors, who left the written traces we as historians can dig into, did not come across too many patients with disorders caused by meditation. A third possibility is that when meditation went wrong, problems were dealt with within the specific social contexts in which meditation was learned and practiced.

Zhang Lu completed his *Medical Virtuosity According to Doctor Zhang* (*Zhang-shi yitong*) in 1695 when he was seventy-nine years old. In a chapter on "Psycho-Emotional Topics," he included a section on "Entering the Demonic State and Losing Control of the Fire." This section title consists of, in reverse order, the two parts of the phrase "losing control of the fire and entering a demonic state" (*zouhuorumo*), which is now commonly used for qigong-induced mental disorders (see chapter 17).[2] Although "losing control of the fire" and "entering a demonic state" feature separately in earlier literature, Zhang Lu was probably the first to combine both expressions.[3] In his text, Zhang reserves "entering a demonic state" for Buddhist and "losing control of the fire" for Daoist practices.[4] Even though Zhang treats both groups of practitioners using herbal decoctions, he attributes different primary causes for disorders caused by their respective practices. For Buddhists, the primary causes are a lack of morality and overuse of the mind. For Daoists, the primary causes are overapplication of techniques and a lack of knowledge of how to let the inner alchemical process unfold naturally by itself without intervening erroneously and unnecessarily. Although Zhang Lu does not reveal himself as a meditator, his discussion is based on a rich exposure to patients suffering from meditation sickness.

Xinchan, the author of the second text translated below, was an ordained Buddhist monk and practicing physician active in the Buddhist temples on Mount Putuo and in the intellectual circles of the Hangzhou area.[5] In "Experience of Treating Damage to Yang and Spitting Blood Caused by Sitting Meditation," a case record contained in his *Collection of Occasional Understandings* (*Yide ji*, 1890), Xinchan recounts how he treated a Buddhist monk who developed serious conditions of emaciation and coughing up blood after prolonged, nightly sessions of sitting meditation. Xinchan discusses the clinical processes underlying his patient's condition and cures him with an herbal decoction. He warns his patient about mistaken approaches to meditation from both medical and Buddhist perspectives. He argues against Daoist-inclined instructions that motivated his patient to meditate for a prolonged period without sleep, which caused his patient's disease. Xinchan further points out that sitting meditation is a means to reach a spiritual goal and should not be the goal itself. Still, Monk Xinchan considers meditation to be an important part of Buddhist practice, as long as spiritual practices (*xiuyang*) are done in accordance with principles of nourishing life (*yangsheng*) and especially the dictum that rest and action should be in moderation, as outlined in the first chapter of the *Inner Canon of the Yellow Emperor* (*Huangdi neijing*).

Zhang Lu and Monk Xinchan both approach meditation sickness from a clinical perspective, based on pulse diagnosis; understood in terms of qi and blood, heat and phlegm, and yin and yang; and treated with the repertoire of Chinese materia medica and medicinal formulas. They share the concern that if the heart/mind (*xin*) becomes exhausted and loses control, all kinds of problems may arise. Zhang Lu adds thoughts about situations in which a doctor cannot bring relief, such as, for instance, when Buddhists suffer ills caused by "unsavory karmic seeds and evil roots" (*yezhong mogen*), or when Daoists show conditions that appear to be pathological but are part of the normal alchemical process. Yet if diseases affect the materiality of the body, both Zhang and Xinchan are confident that doctors have their role to play. Moreover, Zhang underscores the Buddhist values informing his medical ethics. "Physicians," he says, "should, as guardians of human life, embody the heart of the Dharma King."

While both doctors are convinced that wrong approaches to meditation do more harm than good, they do not discourage the practice. Beyond treating disorders caused by meditation, doctors can medically assist meditators. Thanks to Xinchan's prescription, for instance, his patient's health improved to such an extent that he could meditate without experiencing any further distress.

Further Reading

Hinrichs, T. J., and Linda L. Barnes, eds. 2013. *Chinese Medicine and Healing: An Illustrated History.* Belknap Press.

Lo, Vivienne, Michael Stanley-Baker, and Dolly Yang, eds. *Routledge Handbook of Chinese Medicine.* Routledge.

Scheid, Volker. 2020. "The Neglected Role of Buddhism in the Development of Medicine in Late Imperial China Viewed Through the Life and Work of Yu Chang (1585–1664)." *Bulletin of the History of Medicine* 94 (1): 1–28.

Unschuld, Paul U. 2003. *Huang Di nei jing su wen: Nature, Knowledge, Imagery in an Ancient Medical Text.* University of California Press.

1. "Entering the Demonic State and Losing Control of the Fire" by Zhang Lu[6]

Within the realms of humans and heaven, the Three Teachings [i.e., Buddhism, Daoism, and Confucianism] are of the same origin. Yet the paths toward transcendence differ in emphasis. The physician guards human lives and embodies the heart of the Dharma King. The sufferings due to illnesses from people of all strata in society converge in him.[7] He should master the principles [of medicine] so thoroughly that there is no chance of suffering the pitfall of self-deception.

I have heard that the treatment for nuns and widows is different than for normal people.[8] But what about Buddhist monks who enter demonic states during meditation retreats,[9] or Daoist alchemists who lose control of the fire while moving qi during sitting meditation? Are they any different from normal people?

Even though I am not that intelligent, I have devoted myself to the study of these practices. I have combed through the medical books, and yet I was unable to find relevant discussions on this topic. Whenever I observe dull-minded cultivators who could not see their own true nature, they tend to frequently get into demonic states. They might lose control of their own faculties and become puppetlike, or they might also cry, laugh, and act crazy, as if possessed by spirits. In actuality this is due to the overuse of their mind. The heart spirit vacated its place, and it is now occupied by phlegm fire instead.[10] If we were to analyze these types of cases carefully, they are not that different from the state of despondence people feel when they are unable to realize their ambition in life. Except in this scenario, it is frequently accompanied by the fire of the five emotions.

Although the presenting symptoms and pulses may appear vacuous, the various medicinals that are warm supplementing, boost the yang, and astringe the essence should not be administered. I have seen many cases that did not respond to the strategy of phlegm clearing and mind calming but were instead cured by consumption of Sole Ginseng Decoction.[11] There were those cases that did not respond to the strategy of mind calming and qi tonifying but instead were cured by consumption of the Six Ingredient Rehmannia and Kidney Nourishing pills.[12] There were those cases that did not respond to the strategy of phlegm clearing and fire downbearing but instead were cured by long-term consumption of Heavenly King Heart Supplementing Pills for several years in a row.[13] Even then, these are people of low spiritual caliber. Clinging to their confusion without discernment, they allow their attachments to flow into their consciousness.

Moreover, there are those who have unsavory karmic seeds and evil roots. Via improper channels, they become associated with their famous teachers, using this as a means for hiding from their past in repentance. They are usually fiercely diligent in the beginning. As such, they draw encouragement from their spiritual friends upon displaying their insights. Not realizing that the advancement that comes quickly also dissipates rapidly. Not long after, their previous nature is rekindled. Wanton behaviors, greed, and gluttony start to show up in the extremes. Arrogance, ignorance, and abject cruelty; not one is left unexpressed. This is the karma from one's past. Not even the buddhas can transmute it, let alone medicinals!

As for those [Daoist] meditators who cultivate the true and refine their qi, they do not follow the principle of naturalness. They are obsessively focused on the mechanics of breathing out and breathing in. This causes qi to become chaotic on the inside and fire to flare up on the outside, thus resulting in problems of palpitations, counterflows, agitations, lack of calmness, etc. In this case, one must take care not to use medicinals that consume the qi and release the exterior. The harm from such an approach is unfathomable. Furthermore, there are those who are unable to consolidate their essence and concentrate their mind. Their true qi is unable to fortify the exterior and supplement the interior. This results in the body being invaded by cold and wind and compromised by food and drinks. In this case, only Astragalus Supplementing the Middle and Unripe Bitter Orange Supplementing the Middle [formulas] are the proper treatments.[14] As for the rest of the situations caused by the seven emotions and six climatic factors, [physicians] should use their own discernment. In the case of vacuous fire due to injury to the center caused by overdosing, use Sole Ginseng Decoction in a huge dosage to subdue it.

Even for those who are skilled, during the time when the true qi has first been regulated, the yin-qi throughout the whole body will be purged. There will be abdominal pain and rumblings in the intestines. Worms and filth will come out of the anus. After which the true qi can then truly abide within. Only then is the forming of the [alchemical] embryo possible.[15] Only then is fasting advisable. When it comes to this juncture, it is paramount to not mistake the process as an illness and to treat it with medicinals, which can in turn lead to exhaustion of the true qi. Not only will this undo all the previous efforts of cultivation, but it can even result in death.

There is also the problem due to improper placement [of the fire]. If there is an inability to control the fire and unsettled embryonic breath, then take Nourishing the Proper Pills with Sole Ginseng Decoction.[16] This is to take advantage of the resonance between cinnabar and lead-mercury, who naturally seek out each other.[17] This will result in the calming of the embryonic breath.[18] If the physician is unaware of this nuance, he will mistake this flaming heat and steaming as an external invasion and attempt to disperse the exterior. This will most certainly result in the burning down of Kun Lun and incinerations of both jade and ore.[19] Not only is the dispersing of the exterior prohibited, all the following medicinals should be avoided: acrid medicinals that are dispersing and qi moving, cold and bitter medicinals that injure the yang, and yin-assisting medicinals that sink and subdue [the yang].

In general, when it comes to the principle of qi cultivation, one's yang is regarded as the most precious. When one is filled with pure yang, one becomes an immortal. When one is filled with pure yin, one becomes a ghost.[20] This is the most obvious principle. One who administers medicinals should not be ignorant of this. Nowadays, the medical skills among physicians are quite low. Medicinals are no longer efficacious. As such, there are many instances where one resorts to the method of sitting meditation to eradicate illnesses. If the dull-minded ones could not be decisive during the moment when it is needed to cut off erroneous thinking and pierce through the critical juncture, it will cause vigorous fire to flare up, resulting in a red face and a hot head. These symptoms, in tandem with palpitations, a stifled diaphragm, shortness of breath, and profuse sweating, are all signs that point to a syndrome of Upper Desertion.

There is also the case of dissipation of yin-qi, resulting in prolonged erection and inability to consolidate essence and marrow. Together with symptoms of urinary and bowel incontinence, these are signs that point to Lower Desertion. Right when the desertion is about to happen but has not yet occurred, use a high dosage of Numinous Cinnabar Pill and Protect the Original Pill in order to rescue Upper Desertion. Take Black Tin Pill with Six Ingredients Decoction repeatedly to secure Lower Desertion.[21] I have used this method to achieve miraculous results in a short amount of time. The readers should know that the fluids and blood of the body are controlled by the spirit-qi (*shenqi*).

Looking at the practices of the Three Teachings, even though they have different emphasis, the cause of diseases is not divorced from the physical body. There are those who have not investigated thoroughly such a causative principle and then profess to be able to treat people without deceit. I do not dare to believe such claims as a matter of fact.

2. "Experience of Treating Damage to Yang and Spitting Blood Caused by Sitting Meditation" by Monk Xinchan[22]

Someone conveyed the following about sitting meditation to the venerable Xingzhi: "If you practice for a long time, your spirit and qi will become completely full, and they will rise up to Niwan. When you start to be able to leave and enter states of meditation, you will free yourself from the Sea of Sufferings from Life and Death."[23] Thereupon, he forced himself not to sleep and sat like a withered tree for the whole night.[24] After two months, his body gradually became emaciated. Each time he coughed, blood was sent up, of which he spat out two cupped handfuls.

Then, he came to see me for a consultation. His pulses were vacuous, large and without force, and it was the same at all three locations [of taking the pulses]. I said:

"According to the *Inner Canon,* 'If being active and at rest are balanced and you do not labor in vain, you can fully maintain body and spirit and complete the years [allocated to you] by heaven. You will pass away after having lived one hundred years.'[25] This is how the ancient sages taught the people the way of nourishing life. Why would this not be relevant for [Buddhist and Daoist] spiritual practices? How would forced sitting like a withered tree allow you to become a Daoist Immortal or a Buddha? The ancient saying 'How can you make a mirror by polishing a brick? How can you become a Buddha through sitting meditation?' makes a lot of sense.[26] Moreover, making the spirit return and refining qi refer to Daoist practices. In Buddhism, seeing one's nature with an enlightened mind is regarded as superior. Although sitting meditation is indeed important for seeing one's nature, there are more exquisite ways to examine [the truth]. The *Platform Sutra of the Sixth Patriarch* (*Liuzu tanjing*) says: 'When alive you sit and do not lie down; upon death you lie down and do not sit.'[27] Here understood, the state of life and death does not rely on sitting or not sitting. This is something further you should reflect on by yourself, Venerable, as it cannot be clearly explained by words!

As for sitting timed by joss sticks in the meditation hall, after you sit for the time of one joss stick, you stroll for the time of one joss stick.[28] First you walk at a slow pace, and then you speed up your steps. As such, qi and blood of the whole body will flow unimpededly up and down, which prevents stagnation. After 11 p.m.,[29] you should go to sleep. Actually, if you do not sleep between 11 p.m. and 1 a.m.,[30] blood will not return to the channels, which will definitely cause symptoms like spitting blood and nose bleedings.

Once, Monk Zhigong lectured day and night on the scriptures. Heavenly King Deng felt compassion for his exertion and composed and offered him [Heavenly King] Heart Supplementing Pill.[31] You should know that the human body is a microcosm. It is with the qi you inhale and exhale that you interpenetrate with [heaven and earth]. If you do not make use of this proficiently, you will most definitely experience immediate setbacks. Compare with the grains that are the root of nourishing life. If you are already full and force yourself to eat [more], you will only damage your own health. [Or,] compare with the material belongings that are the source upon which you build your livelihood. If you already acquired [enough] but still take without permission [things that others could make use of], it will only harm justice in society.

I am not saying that sitting meditation does not have any benefits. But if you overexert yourself, you will for sure enter the demonic way. In this case, contrary to what should be the purpose, the mind cannot act for itself anymore. Chan Master Damei said: 'The mind is the Buddha.'[32] This is the gist of Chan practice. [If] you can abide by this principle, then you will not be misled by the side doors and other bodies [of teachings] when you are starting out. When the mind knows the material appearances, you should consider who it is that knows the material appearances. When the mind is troubled by hindrances, you should consider who it is that knows the hindrances. Contemplation without thoughts is true contemplation. Walking, standing, sitting, and lying down, [in every state] you should apply the effort in such a manner. Then, in one sudden flash of open and wide understanding, you really do not know why it is so, but it is so. An ancient verse says: 'The armored horse knocks the green stone gate open; the jade chicken pecks and breaks the golden shell.'[33]

Venerable, when you retreat and sit with this piece of information in quiet contemplation, you should be able to obtain it yourself. To sum up, perfect yourself from your own nature. This is the daily practice of the Chan Gate. In darkness, brightness can be perfected. In heterodoxy, orthodoxy can be perfected. In evil, goodness can be perfected. Wisdom perfects ignorance. Generosity perfects stinginess and greed. Clear tranquility perfects hindrance. These are called the Six Perfections. Through the Six Perfections, you will arrive at Buddha's Dharma World.[34]

Now, Venerable, someone has misled you. If you sit like a withered tree without sleeping, the pivot of yin and yang cannot alternate. As a result, yang drifts up to the outside, and yin is not guarded inside. Who would not become ill in such a case? As a method to make yang sink down and to solidify yin, use raw and prepared rehmannia,[35] ophiopogon root and asparagus root,[36] dendrobium,[37] big scrophularia root,[38] apricot kernel,[39] scutellaria root,[40] donkey-hide gelatin,[41] aster root,[42] turtle shell,[43] and oyster shell.[44] After decocting, add half a jug of human milk. Make sure you take twenty doses. There is no need to alter the formula."

The Venerable prostrated respectfully and left. After more than twenty days, he came back. According to what he said, he stopped spitting blood after only two doses. And now, because his vigor became stronger day by day, I removed apricot kernel and aster root from the earlier formula and added Chinese angelica,[45] peony root,[46] and wolfberry.[47] After taking this, he was stronger and healthier than ever before. Afterward, he sat in meditation without any further hardships.

Notes

1. An earlier criticism on meditation practices from a Confucian perspective can be found in the Ming dynasty text *Introduction to Medicine* (*Yixue rumen*). See Li (2006, 53–54).
2. See, for instance, Chen (2003).
3. A variation on this phrase, "losing control of the fire and entering a demonic state while sitting in quiet meditation" (*zuochan ji zuohuo ruxiemo*), occurs in the title of chapter 87 of Cao Xueqin's (1710–1765) *Dream of the Red Chamber* (*Honglou meng*, eighteenth century). Yet another variation of the phrase appears as *zoumo ruhuo* in the text of this chapter. Chapter 87 tells the story of Miaoyu, one of the twelve beauties of Jinling, who is afflicted by delusion and delirium after trying to forcibly suppress her sexual desire by engaging in Chan meditation practice. See also Zhou (2011, 287).
4. A search of the CBETA Online Reader at https://cbetaonline.dila.edu.tw/zh/ reveals that there are no fewer than one hundred references in the Buddhist literature on "entering the demonic state" (*rumo*) during the Tang dynasty alone and hundreds more in the Ming and Qing Buddhist literature. We have found fifty-nine references on "losing

control of the fire" (*zouhuo*) by a search in the digitalized *Daoist Canon* (*Daozang*) through http://www.xueheng.net/dz.html. Yet, none of it was related to meditation. Nonetheless, Zhang Lu clearly uses *zouhuo* for the loss of control or a mishap during inner alchemical meditation practices, as is clear from his repeated references to the control of fire in his exposition on the etiology of sickness in Daoist practitioners. In Daoist literature, it is common to observe the mention of the need for nuanced control of fire during the practice of alchemy. See, for instance, Pregadio (1995, 161–162).

5. The famous scholar Yu Yue (1821–1907) wrote a preface to Xin Chan's medical text *Collection of Occasional Understandings* (*Yide ji*, 1890). For the publication history of *Collection of Occasional Understandings*, see Zhao and Zhong (2021, 227).

6. *Medical Virtuosity According to Doctor Zhang* (*Zhang-shi yitong*, 1695, 6.163a–165b). Facsimile of the Baohan Lou edition from the Kangxi period, contained in *Collected Books from Professor Zhuang Zhaoxiang's Study* (*Zhuang Zhaoxiang jiaoshou zhizu shushi*), Chinese University of Hong Kong Library website, accessed November 22, 2023, https://repository.lib.cuhk.edu.hk/tc/item/cuhk-372000, p. 221.

7. "The Three Teachings and Nine Streams" is an idiomatic expression that refers to the various strata of people in premodern Chinese society.

8. Referring to Chu Cheng, the fifth-century doctor Tao Hongjing pointed out that the medical treatment of nuns and widows differs from that of wives and concubines. See Unschuld (1986a, 38) and Furth (1999, 91).

9. *Da qi* are meditation retreats in the Chan tradition done in multiples of seven-day intervals. See, for instance, *The Recorded Sayings of the Ancient Master Xuezhe* (*Gu Xuezhe chanshi yulu*), in *Jiaxing Tripiṭaka* no. B208, 28: 321a19–20.

10. Phlegm invasion of the heart causing psycho-emotional disturbance is a common etiology in Chinese medicine. As Simonis points out, "By the 14th century, most doctors whose writings have survived understood insanity as caused by mucus and inner 'fire,' and treated it with purgatives and emetics. This attribution of insane and possession-like behavior to mucus then became a culturally ubiquitous way of explaining the failures of human acts and perceptions" (Simonis 2015, 603).

11. *Dushen tang.*

12. *Liuwei dihuang wan* and *zishen wan.*

13. *Tianwang buxin dan.*

14. *Huangqi jianzhong* and *zhishi jianzhong.*

15. The goal of inner alchemy (*neidan*) is to realize an inner state derived "from generating and nourishing the perfected or realized one's (*zhenren*) 'holy embryo' (*shengtai*)." See Pregadio and Skar (2000, 481).

16. *Yangzhen dan* and *dushen tang.*

17. Cinnabar, lead, and mercury are key products in the Daoist alchemical process. In internal alchemical practices, lead refers to true yang and mercury to true yin.

18. The term *taixi,* here translated as "embryonic breath," has a double meaning. *Tai* can translate in English to both "embryo" and "womb," Despeux (2015, 163).

19. This is an idiomatic expression referring to the complete and indiscriminate destruction of all and the Chinese equivalent of "throwing the baby out with the bathwater." Legge translates it as "When the fire blazes over the ridge of Kun, gems and stones are burned together."

20. This expression features in Wu Wu's *Record of a Chance Encounter in a Fishing Village* (*Yuzhuang xiehou lu,* twelfth century), *Daoist Canon of the Zhengtong Reign* (*Zhengtong daozang* 1086, 3b).

21. *Lingsha dan, baoyuan tang, heixin dan,* and *liuwei* (*dihuang*) *tang.*

22. *Collection of Occasional Understandings* (*Yide ji* 1890, 3.41–42). Facsimile of the 1936 Shanghai edition, contained in Qiu Jisheng, comp., *Collection of Rare Medical Books* (*Zhenben yishu jicheng*), vol. 14 (repr., Shanghai kexue jishu chubanshe, 1986). The same case record is included by Qin Bowei's *Selected Medical Records of Famous Qing Physician* (*Qing-dai mingyi yihua jinghua*), first published in 1929. Qin Bowei attributes this case to Xu Shanlin, however. Qin (2007, 332–333).

23. In Buddhist contexts, *niwan* can be a transliteration of "nirvana." From a Daoist perspective, however, the translation of *niwan* as "Mudball" would be more logical. "Mudball" refers to a location inside the skull, often equated with the brain. Sea of Sufferings from Life and Death (Shengsi Kuhai) can refer to the water regions in the lower part of the body but also allude to Buddhist doctrine of *saṃsāra* as well. For Daoist body charts with these terms, see Despeux (2019, 27–33) and Huang (2012, 78–85).

24. The term "withered-tree sitting" (*kuzuo*) first appears in *The Extensive Records of Chan Master Hongzhi* (*Hongzhi chanshi guanglu*), *Taishō Tripiṭaka* no. 2001, 48: 79b28 (hereafter, *T*). In this text, Hongzhi Zhengjue (1091–1157) uses the metaphor of a withered-tree sitting to emphasize the importance of sitting meditation in the Caodong tradition of Chan Buddhism. See Byrne (2019, 185–192). Xinchan belonged to the Linji branch. Linji monks countered this view and use the term "withered-tree sitting" pejoratively. The Japanese monk Hakuin Ekaku (1686–1769) famously uses the term "withered-tree sitting" to criticize Ming dynasty Chinese monk Yunqi Zhuhong's (1535–1615) misunderstanding of the *Platform Sutra* (*Tanjing*). See Ahn (2008, 209).

25. This is a passage from the first chapter of the *Inner Canon of the Yellow Emperor: Basic Questions* (*Huangdi neijing suwen*). For an alternative translation, see Unschuld and Tessenow (2011, 31–32).

26. "Polishing a brick to make a mirror" is an idiomatic expression commonly used in the Chan tradition for something impossible to achieve. The earliest version of this saying appears in *Anthology of the Patriarchal Hall* (*Zutang ji*) transcribed in 952; see *Buddhist Canon: Supplementary Sections* (*Dazang jing bubian*) no. 144, 25: 370a14–b3.

The saying "polishing a brick to make a mirror" also plays a prominent role in Mazu Daoyi's (709–188) enlightenment account as told in Nanyue Huairang's (677–744) entry in the *Jingde Record of the Transmission of the Lamp* (*Jingde chuandeng lu*); *T* no. 2076, 51: 240c07–241a26. As McRae points out, Mazu Daoyi's enlightenment account "echoes the *Vimalakirti Sutra* and the *Platform Sutra* in downgrading purificative and gradualist practices instead of direct insight into the Buddha-nature" (2003, 80–83).

27. Huineng's *Dharma Treasury Platform Sutra of the Sixth Patriarch* (*Liuzu dashi fabao tanjing*), *T* no. 2008, 48: 358b24. For an alternative translation: "You can sit [in meditation] without lying down from the day you're born, / But when you die you will lie down and not sit up." McRae (2000, 73).

28. We read *gui* (to kneel) as *pao* (to stroll). *Pao* is often used in this context and makes more sense in relation to the following sentence. Compare also with Qin (2007, 234), where *pao* is used.

29. Literally, the second drumbeat. This refers to the second night watch, from 11:00 p.m. to 1:00 a.m.

30. Literally, the *zi* hour, and the preferred time for meditation in Daoist contexts.

31. [*Tianwang*] *buxin dan*. The story of Zhigong (Baozhi, 418–514) and Heavenly King Deng also appears in Zhang Jiebin's (1563–1640) *Jingyue's Complete Writings* (*Jingyue quanshu*). See Zhang (1999, 1616). Although Zhang Jiebin refers to the *Daoist Canon* for the origin of this story, we were unable to trace it in the *Daoist Canon*. Despeux suggests that this formula, which first appears in the Chinese scholarly medical literature in Wei Yilin's Yuan-dynasty *Efficacious Formulas of a Hereditary Medical Family* (*Shiyi dexiao fang*), goes back the formula *buxin wanfang* recorded in the Dunhuang text S. 5598. This Dunhuang text explains that the monk Daoxuan (596–667) received this pill from the Heavenly King Vaiśravaṇa. See Despeux (2020, 142).

32. Damei Fachang (752–839) was a disciple of Mazu Daoyi. See case 30 in Wumen Huikai's (1183–1260) *Gateless Barrier* (*Wumen guan*); *T* no. 2005, 48: 296c27–28.

33. This expression features in Zhongfeng Mingben's (1263–1323) *The Extensive Records of the Monk Tianmu Zhongfeng* (*Tianmu Zhongfeng heshang guanglu*); *Buddhist Canon: Supplementary Sections* no. 145, 25: 775a13–14. For a study of this text, see Broughton (2023).

34. The list given here does not match the common list of Six Perfections (*ṣaṭ-pāramitā*) in Mahāyāna texts: generosity (*dāna*), morality (*śīla*), patience (*kṣānti*), vigor (*vīrya*), concentration (*dhyāna*), and wisdom (*prajñā*). For discussions on the Six Perfections, see Aitken (1994) and Wright (2009).

35. Literally, "the two *di*," i.e., *shu dihuang* and *sheng dihuang*.

36. Literally, "the two *dong*," i.e., *maimendong* and *tianmendong*.

37. *Shihu*.

38. *Jing yuanshen*.

39. *Xingren.*
40. [*Huang*]*qin.*
41. [*E*]*jiao.*
42. *Ziwan.*
43. *Guiban.*
44. *Muli.*
45. [*Dang*]*gui.*
46. [*Shao*]*yao.*
47. *Gouqi.*

Chapter 11

Vicissitudes of *Vipassanā* Practice

Four Excerpts from the Oral Dharma Discourses of Sayagyi U Ba Khin (1899–1971)

SWE SWE MON AND DANIEL M. STUART

The translations presented here are drawn from the oral teachings of one of the most important popularizers of Burmese lay insight meditation (*vipassanā*) in the twentieth century, Sayagyi U Ba Khin (1899–1971). U Ba Khin was one among a small number of Buddhist lay meditation teachers in late colonial and early postcolonial Burma who came to prominence at a defining moment of global social and religious change. U Ba Khin was particularly influential in contributing to the internationalization of insight meditation in the early years of Burma's independence.[1]

One reason that U Ba Khin became influential was that he played a consequential role in Burma's fledgling postcolonial government as the first accountant general of independent Burma. He was, therefore, at the center of the political and social life of Burma's capital, Rangoon, in the early years of Burmese independence. He was a close confidant of the first prime minister of independent Burma, U Nu (1907–1995), and he began his career as an insight meditation teacher by teaching meditation to his employees in the office of the accountant general, many of whom were not of Burmese ethnicity and were also not Buddhist. This context was central to the formation of a tradition of Burmese insight meditation that was both lay focused and nonsectarian.

Beyond Burma, U Ba Khin is perhaps best known as the teacher of the even more influential insight meditation guru, S. N. Goenka. Goenka took U Ba Khin's teachings out of Burma and built a global noncommercial insight meditation franchise that has become the single most influential lineage of global insight meditation in the twentieth and twenty-first centuries. Goenka is well-known for repackaging U Ba Khin's teachings, streamlining one particular mode of U Ba Khin's practice model, framing it as nonsectarian, and teaching it to large groups of people, first in India in the 1960s and 1970s and then globally from the 1980s onward. In the process of this repackaging, however, some of the local particularities of U Ba Khin's teachings were downplayed. As a result, very little is known about the on-the-ground details of his theoretical approach to insight meditation and his teaching and practice methods.

The selection of excerpts translated here is drawn from talks U Ba Khin gave to his Burmese students in the early 1960s. These materials have not been previously translated, and they provide insight into the local particulars of his teaching methods and the somewhat forceful approach to meditation that he employed. They also offer a glimpse into the ways in which U Ba Khin's talks were performative: He used stories about his students' meditative experiences to teach, illustrate, entertain, and impress.

In the first excerpt, U Ba Khin details his general theoretical understanding of why it was very common for people at his meditation center to run into serious difficulties in the process of meditation. He draws on a classical narrative in the Buddhist disciplinary literature about suicide among the Sangha (included in this book in chapter 2), interpreting the story in order to explain how imbalances caused by meditation are ultimately the result of karmic effects from past lives. According to U Ba Khin, the process of insight meditation was primarily a process of burning off past karma. Seeing "the truth as it is" catalyzes the arousal of latent karmic forces that reside within the body-mind continuum and allows one to release them. The final three excerpts present teaching anecdotes that instantiate U Ba Khin's theory in descriptions of meditation-teaching and meditation-healing modalities.

Further Reading

Braun, Eric. 2013. *The Birth of Insight: Meditation, Modern Buddhism, and the Burmese Monk Ledi Sayadaw*. University of Chicago.

Houtman, Gustaaf. 1997. "The Biography of Modern Burmese Buddhist Meditation Master U Ba Khin: Life Before the Cradle and Past the Grave." In *Sacred Biography in the Buddhist Traditions of South and Southeast Asia,* edited by Juliane Schober. University of Hawai'i Press.

Stuart, Daniel M. 2020. *S. N. Goenka: Emissary of Insight*. Shambhala.

Stuart, Daniel M. 2024a. "Local Cure, Global Chant: Performing Theravadic Awakening in the Footsteps of the Ledi Sayadaw." *Numen* 71 (2–3): 256–302.

Stuart, Daniel M. 2024b. *Insight in Perspective: S. N. Goenka and the Emergence of Global Insight Meditation and Mindfulness*. Projekt Verlag.

1. On the Third Monastic Rule Entailing Expulsion[2]

At the time of the Buddha, a training rule entailing expulsion from the monastic community (*pārājika sikkhāpada*)—not to kill human beings—was laid down. Have you ever heard about it? Monks are not allowed to kill human beings. If they do, they violate a *pārājika sikkhāpada.* If he violates it, like a toddy tree that cannot grow anymore when it is cut from the middle of its trunk, a monk falls away from monkhood.

There is a background story about the promulgation of this training rule. Five hundred monks came to the Buddha to practice meditation. Here, in this center, if such monks come, I will not let them in. But the Buddha has great compassion for beings. Right? And the Buddha could not tell them not to come to him and meditate. If a person wants to meditate in a monastery, will monks tell him to go back home? But here, we tell such a person to go back home because this is a private center. To accept [someone] or not is up to us. I have to see and check the people who come here to meditate. If they appear to be troublesome people, I wisely don't allow them. Now, in this audience there is no troublesome person. But there are still people who can give a little trouble. But that's okay. I can bear it.

Well, five hundred monks came to the Buddha. The Buddha gave them the meditation object of "the impure" (*asubha kammaṭṭhān'*). Then, by practicing that, the power of Dharma entered into them. Because of this power, the impure forces (*dhāt'*) inside of their bodies were aroused, and they all became deranged.[3] The Buddha foresaw such an event, and he thought about whether he could save them. And he came to know that it was out of his reach. He saw their bad past karma. So, after giving them the meditation subject, the Buddha decided to enter [retreat, meditating in] the absorption of the fruition state (*phalasamāpatti*). Only a monk who had to offer alms could go and see the Buddha. No other monks were allowed to go and see the Buddha. The Buddha set it up like this.

The five hundred monks practiced meditation. During their meditation, they encountered the quality of coolness. Such nature fought the nature of heat from inside [their bodies]. Have you ever seen a bonfire? If right now we put big wood into the fire, such a fire can burn until ten or eleven o'clock at night. When you pour water on it, what will happen? Doesn't it make a loud sound, revolting from inside? Don't fumes come out? Likewise, when the qualities of cold and hot meet inside of you, fumes come out. How about if we pour ice instead of water? Does it become stronger than pouring normal water?

When [those] five hundred monks meditated, the pure and peaceful force of the true Dharma met intensely with the unwholesome stuff (*dhamma*) inside their bodies. It depends on the amount of unwholesome stuff inside the body. At that time, the unwholesome stuff inside became frightening. They thought that life was too much suffering, immense suffering. It was better to end such suffering. With such a desire, they thought that committing suicide by cutting their throats was the best way to end the suffering.

Here [in Myanmar], some meditation centers have had such experiences. At first those monks killed one another. But later, they felt tired and went to a courageous monk. They offered their robes and alms bowls to that monk and requested [him] to kill them. That monk did as they requested, accepting the robes and alms-bowls. I forget the name of that monk. You can find it in the text. In this way, many monks were killed by him, but not all. Nearly all.

At that time, the Buddha got up from the absorption of the fruition state. While engrossed in that state, the Buddha did not know anything of the mundane matters happening outside. It was very peaceful. Then he checked on the monks and found out that only a few of them were left. He asked the reason for it. The monks explained to the Buddha what had happened. Because of their bad past karma, even the Buddha could not save them. Do you think meditation is good? Don't think it is good. You can become deranged like them. Take note of it. Some people can be relieved [from such impurities], but not all. If you just sit and are sleepy in the meditation cell without meditation, how will the disease be cured?

2. Healing Through Intensive Meditation[4]

Recently, an old man came here. I told him, "You did not come here to be comfortable. Here I teach [you] to realize the truth of suffering. By realizing the truth of suffering, you can see the true quality [of reality]." [*Audience laughing*] Well, I [also] amuse you [in my talk].

So I instructed him to meditate on impermanence (*anicca*). During his mediation, like Pho Htaung, forces (*dhāt'*) inside his body were aroused because these forces could not withstand [the power of] impermanence. So I carefully watched over him. At night I got an idea that I should give him the meditation of strong determination (*adhiṭṭhān'*) early the next morning. After changing into *vipassanā* meditation, we have the meditation of strong determination. It is meditating without moving any part of the body for one hour. . . . He sat in the front row during the meditation of strong determination. . . .

I told him: "Well, you should take a bowl in case you need it." In the past we had lots of bowls, as most of the meditators vomited during meditation practice. He said that in his lifetime he never vomited. But I took a bowl for him [anyway]. Then they meditated, and I spent the time talking with Sayāmā.[5] At

8 a.m., I did not even announce the end of the strong-determination session. Ko Chit Shein ran out of the room and called me. "What happened?" I asked. Ko Chit Shein responded: "I don't know what's wrong with him. A bowl is filled with his mucus, and he breathes very loudly, making a sound like *huuu, huuu.*" . . . I went to them. A bowl was filled with mucus, like foam. I found that old man with a red face and his expression was like this. [Probably U Ba Khin is making a facial expression to the audience]. Well, I saw the facial expression of a *nāga* in him.[6]

The forces of ignorance (*avijjādhāt'*) cannot exist within a body that the forces of wisdom (*vijjādhāt'*) are going to occupy.[7] They must leave. I said: "Rejoice in my merits!" That person was like half human, half animal. . . . Suddenly, he flipped his body over with his legs upright. In this manner, he crawled to me. Though I wanted to leave, I just stayed quietly [meditating] with "impermanence, impermanence, impermanence." Then, he rested his head on my thigh, shaking it and looking tired. I touched his back with my hand to comfort him by sharing loving-kindness (*mettā*) and my merits with him.[8] Finally, he asked for water. Sayāmā gave him a cup of water. After drinking two cups of water, he became normal. His face also turned back to normal. When I asked him, "What happened to you?" he replied that he did not know. Then, I told him to continue his meditation. This animal [inside of him] caused him to get high blood pressure. Now, he is a very healthy man.

3. Removing Coarse Defilements in the Early Stages of Meditation[9]

How many [of the defilements that are the] causes of suffering do we have to eradicate?[10] There are three levels [of cause].[11] The level of physical and verbal transgression is coarse. When the coarse unwholesome forces [of physical and verbal transgression] come into contact with the wisdom of impermanence during insight meditation, we call it an eruption of forces. When water is poured onto fire, there is a loud noise. Right? Pho Htaung, will you scream again? We don't know who is next [to scream because of the striking of forces inside the body]. I ask you not to hold back if you want to scream. [Unwholesome] forces from inside the body rise up and run away screaming.

Well, how do you run away when you are followed by enemies? Will you run away silently, smiling? No, you run away screaming. Each person has more or less unwholesome and impure forces. When unwholesome and impure forces strike against the force of deep meditative absorption or the force of nirvāṇa, unwholesome and impure forces can no longer stand to stay inside the body. They run away screaming. . . .

Do you know Ma Khin Ei? She came here and meditated in a building over there. She sobbed while meditating, shouting that she wanted to return home. I went and checked on her. I loudly said: "Who wants to go back? Okay, go go go, back to your home!" Then, she stopped crying and smiled. She asked: "What happened to me?" Well, [the one] who wanted to go back home returned home because of my shouting, and Ma Khin Ei was left. I may shout like this. Don't be afraid. I will not allow anyone to stay here who does not want to meditate. Well, we have to experience such things when we practice meditation.

This is the destruction of defilements related to physical and verbal transgression, which are coarse [forms of] defilement. Everyone has unwholesome karma that can send them to hell. Do you think you don't have such karma? How many times have you experienced anger?

[Audience:] Frequently.

The Buddha said that karma formed by hatred (*dosa*) will result in rebirth in hell. So, your debit balance is in hell. Well, we can destroy such unwholesome karma by [meditating on] impermanence during meditation. If all unwholesome karma is destroyed, isn't it good? I have seen people who can destroy all their unwholesome karma.

Have you ever seen a greedy person who has unbridled greed? As I am an accountant, I have seen such people. Amazing! Some people sell the thing that is worth only one kyat for five kyats. They are greedy people. What will happen to them? They will be reborn in the animal abode. They will be dull and stupid. When you feel dizzy during your meditation, it shows that forces imbued with greed erupt and get expelled. At that time, I will say: "Well done" (literally, *sādhu, sādhu, sādhu*). Without practicing meditation, you may not feel dizzy. Do you not? As you are practicing meditation, forces imbued with greed erupt and get expelled when they meet with the forces of the Dharma (*tarādhāt'*). The quality [of greed] emerges. In the case of meditators who are possessed by hungry ghosts (*peta*) or demons (*sabhak'*), their body will shake and tremble.

Mr. Robert Hover is a mechanical engineer and a research specialist in the spacecraft industry from California. His job was making rockets. He is a master of science.[12] As he is a master of science, he may be connected with demonic deities (*nat'bhīlū"*) who are very crude. Because he was making missiles that can destroy at least a city, good deities who are associated with the Dharma won't stay with him.[13] Even forces associated with greed and hatred and forces associated with the act of killing a[n individual] person won't stay with him. As he has worked on the project of killing millions of people, the forces [inside his body] are extremely coarse.

He came here to meditate. In the meditation room, he focused his mind at the nostrils with [the practice of] awareness of breathing to establish concentration. He worked hard, paying due respect. As soon as he got concentration, his body flipped over like an epileptic, and his legs raised upward. When the pure and clear nature of concentration met with his coarse forces, there was an eruption, a collision [of forces]. The next day also, the same thing happened. It was amazing. Finally, he overcame it. Among my followers, there is nobody who has greater veneration for me than him.

4. On Invasive Forces[14]

U Ba Aye, who is deputy commissioner of Taungoo, fell down from a car and had a stroke. He could not work for a year. . . . [During retreat], after shifting to insight meditation, I gave him the room in front of the *linlun* tree. He practiced very hard. His practice was also very good, and he felt his whole body continuously flush with subtle sensations. I wrote a notice that family members are not allowed to come here, but his wife came here to meet him on Thursday with some oranges and other things. U Ba Aye was inside [the meditation hall], as it was around 2 p.m. I was out at my office. She met with Daw Ohn Thein and told her that she came to meet with U Ba Aye. Daw Ohn Thein replied that she could not meet with him because of Sayagyi's order. Then Daw Ohn Thein explained that she came by bus in scorching weather and from far away. U Ba Aye liked oranges and he did not like to be alone. He wanted her to come and ask about him. Daw Ohn Thein replied: "I do not understand these things, but if you are willing to wait until Sayagyi comes back, you can wait. For some time now, nobody gets a chance to meet with meditators without permission." "What time can I see him?" [she asked]. "On Monday," [Daw Ohn Thein replied]. She became angry and left. She left some clothes and oranges for him.

I returned around 4:30 p.m., and I checked on U Ba Aye: "How is the mediation today, U Ba Aye?" [He replied:] "Sayagyi, my meditation has been good all the time. But I do not know what was wrong with me around 2 p.m. I lost my concentration and my mind became scattered." The forces from his wife had struck him. If these forces strike from afar, their velocity may be obstructed on the way. But in this case, she came inside of our compound and the force struck U Ba Aye. Therefore, U Ba Aye could not meditate well. The nature of forces is very strange!

Notes

The translations presented here were produced collaboratively. Swe Swe Mon made an initial transcription and rough translation of U Ba Khin's oral discourses. The translations were then refined collaboratively by Swe Swe Mon and Daniel M. Stuart. A final refinement was carried out by Daniel M. Stuart in the process of rendering the translated excerpts into a form of English suitable for a general audience. The introduction was written by Stuart.

1. For biographical information about U Ba Khin, see Chit Tin (1999); Vipassana Research Institute ([1991] 1994).
2. Ba Khin (n.d. [1960?], 2.1: 11:14–17:38). (This refers to the CD number and then the file number found on the CD, followed by the timestamp.)
3. There is an overlap in U Ba Khin's usage of the term *dhāt'* (Pāli/Skt. *dhātu*) to refer to elemental forces of the universe, the traditional eighteen elements of Buddhism—comprising the six sense faculties, their organs, and their objects—and supernormal agentive forces. It becomes clear from an assessment of U Ba Khin's teachings and teaching practices that his way of thinking about *dhāt'*, or "forces" as he often referred to them in English, should likely not be understood without reference to the broader context of Burmese esoteric traditions (*weizzā*) and a range of other local cult practices. On the contours of the esoteric *weizzā* traditions, see Patton (2014); Rozenberg (2010, 2015); Foxeus (2013).
4. Ba Khin (n.d. [1960?], 3.2–4.1, 28:06–2:40). This excerpt is a slightly revised version of a passage presented in Stuart (2024, 174n218).
5. Sayāmā, known to her students as Mother Sayāmā, was U Ba Khin's teaching assistant. She was known to possess supernormal powers that allowed her to see the past lives of her students and assess their karmic capacities for Buddhist liberation. On this aspect of U Ba Khin's teaching context, see Stuart (2020, chap. 3).
6. A *nāga* is a serpent-like being within Buddhist cosmology, understood to be generally invisible to most humans and to reside under the earth. They have control over the waters and the weather, and those who follow the Buddha work to support the Buddhist community and the Buddha's teachings. On the history of representations of *nāgas* in art, see Guy (2023). It is not entirely clear whether U Ba Khin is suggesting in this anecdote that his student had the karmic forces of a *nāga* within him from a past life or whether he was possessed by a *nāga*.
7. The term *vijjādhāt'*, pronounced in Burmese as *weizzādhāt'* and translated here as "forces of wisdom," has layered meanings in the Burmese context. It refers in the passage here to the wisdom of insight meditation, the wisdom of understanding global impermanence. At the same time, the term evokes associations with a range of Burmese esoteric traditions involving alchemy, mediumship, and the development of spiritual power oriented toward immortality and world conquest. For more on these *weizzā* traditions, see the references in note 5.
8. The Burmese term translated here as "loving-kindness" or *khyam'"sā* literally means "peace" or "nonhostility." It is sometimes used as a gloss for *mettā* or "loving kindness."
9. Ba Khin (n.d. [1960?], 3.1: 9:53–16:05).
10. We have translated the term *samudayasacca* here as "the causes of suffering," which in this context refers to the inner defilements of a practitioner. The term literally means

"the truth of [the] arising [of suffering]." This is the second Noble Truth of Buddhism and, in its normative doctrinal formation, refers to the idea that desire is the fundamental cause of suffering.

11. The Theravāda tradition outlines three levels (*bhūmi*) of defilement: that related to physical and verbal transgression (*vītikkamakilesabhūmi*), that related to hindrances that possess one when working to concentrate the mind (*pariyuṭṭhāna*), and that related to latent karmic tendencies (*anusayakilesabhūmi*).
12. The phrase "a master of science" is a translation of the Burmese phrase *lokadhat' charākrī,* which literally means "a teacher/master of worldly forces," counterposed to one who is a teacher/master of supernormal forces, such as U Ba Khin.
13. In Burmese tradition, "good deities who are associated with the Dharma" (Sammādeva) are deities, many with extremely long lifespans, who have been awakened through the teachings of the historical Buddha or a past buddha and remain in the cosmos to support the teachings.
14. Ba Khin (n.d. [1960?], 6.2: 11:14–17:38).

Chapter 12

Meditation Sickness as a Blessing for Those Seeking Enlightenment

Excerpts from Kurata Hyakuzō's (1891–1943) Illness Memoirs

MELISSA ANNE-MARIE CURLEY

The passages translated below are selected from two memoirs by Kurata Hyakuzō—the first titled *The Mind's Power to Accept and Endure and the Overcoming of Pain* (*Seishin no ninjuryoku to kunō no kokufuku*) and the second, *A Heaven for the Anxious: My Experience of Being Cured Without Being Cured* (*Shinkeishitsusha no tengoku: Narazu ni naotta watashi no taiken*)—collected and published as a single volume in 1932. Kurata had been an enormously influential essayist and fiction writer before his career was abruptly interrupted in 1926 by the onset of an anxiety disorder, characterized particularly by recurrent struggles with obsessive thinking. Both of the memoirs describe these struggles and their symptoms, the treatment he undertook, and his experience of cure.

What makes this reflection on obsessive thinking of interest to readers of this volume? Kurata had long been drawn to Japanese Buddhist thought and practice, although his engagement with traditional Buddhist sources was self-consciously and deliberately idiosyncratic. As we see in the material below, in making sense of his illness Kurata freely blends psychiatric, philosophical, and Buddhist vocabularies, asserting that the disease we now call obsessive thinking is the same one referred to as meditation sickness (*zenbyō*) and diagnosing his own issue as "contemplation sickness" (*kansō no sawari*) triggered by his passionate commitment to cultivating a life of the mind. In addition to offering us an instructive early example of an effort to think through the relationship between meditation sickness and modern disease concepts like anxiety disorder, Kurata's interpretation of why he became ill and how he got better also has some surprising implications in terms of how one might think about the significance of meditation sickness—and perhaps psychiatric illness too—more broadly.

Kurata often characterizes his condition using terms that, in Japanese, can mean disorder or dysfunction, as well as obstacle or hurdle (*sawari, shōgai*). This reflects his understanding of obsessive thinking as having driven him toward a seemingly impassable barrier in order to ultimately transcend it. Drawing on the language of Rinzai Zen, Kurata suggests that obsessive thinking in fact operates as a difficult-to-pass kōan (*nantō kōan*). In the Rinzai curriculum, the difficult-to-pass kōans are a set meant for advanced practitioners who have already attained a certain level of awakening—the "easy" transformation that turns an ordinary person into a sage—and who are, consequently, at risk of idling away the rest of their lives delighting in their own attainment, never returning to this world to help others. The difficult-to-pass kōans are thus "meant to cut the monk's attachment to his own awakening" by throwing him "back into crisis," enabling the difficult transformation of the sage into an ordinary person.[1] Interpreting his illness in this way allows Kurata to make a case for those suffering with certain psychological conditions—including and above all himself—as having already developed certain capacities and insights not readily available to those who do not experience such psychological distress. It also allows him to draw out a counterintuitive possibility present in Japanese Zen accounts of meditation sickness—namely, that meditation sickness itself may be a positive sign of one's advancement on the path of awakening, insofar as it represents an instance of the kind of crisis or crushing doubt that kōan practice is designed to produce.

In Kurata's case, passing the kōan of contemplation sickness enabled what he describes as a complete psychological transformation, turning him away from what he calls logical idealism (*gōriteki risōshugi*) toward dharmic naturalism (*hōteki shizenshugi*). For Kurata, "logical idealism" means to give primacy to the world constructed in the mind: a world of ideas and, consequently, an ideal world—the world as it should be, obedient to the laws of ethical reason. Logical idealists, observing the discrepancy between this ideal world conjured by the intellect and the material world, believe that they can make the material world accord with their ideals by exerting their willpower. In fact, Kurata tells us, this turns out to be impossible: The material world is, after all, not a world of ideas but a vibrant world of living things that are not under our control. Elsewhere, Kurata describes this situation in more concrete terms. In an ideal world, snakes would not eat frogs, sea bream would not eat sardines, and human beings would not eat sea bream. Saints and sages exhaust themselves in an effort to live according to such an ideal. But in the actual world, there can be no life without death—snakes must eat frogs, sea bream must eat sardines, and human beings must, by our nature, take the life of other living beings in order to live.[2] When we stop trying to be saints, we can recognize that we exist by the grace of the world around us and begin to live in a way that is obedient to the patterns that shape the vital life of the universe. Kurata describes this in terms borrowed from Japanese Pure Land thought, as abandoning calculation (*hakarai,* or the ego-driven effort to attain awakening relying on one's own power) and realizing naturalness (*shizen* or *jinen,* or relying completely on the power of Amida Buddha for salvation). Kurata's account of the turn from logical idealism to dharmic naturalism thus operates on two registers simultaneously. On one level it describes a shift from understanding the intellect as primary to understanding "life"—including the body and its affects—as primary. On another level it describes a conversion from the self-power path of saints and sages (represented by Zen, which, for Kurata, epitomizes Buddhist intellectualism) to the other-power path of faith (represented by Pure Land).

It is important to note that while Kurata borrows from Buddhism liberally, he uses those borrowed ideas in unorthodox ways. For example, he takes advantage of the double meaning of the term *shizen* as "natural" in the premodern sense of spontaneous or inborn and "natural" in the modern sense of biological or organic in order to recast Amida Buddha—the Buddha of infinite life—as a figure for the life force or the vital energy that surges within us as living creatures. Following this line of thinking, Kurata leads us to the conclusion that Buddhist liberation in fact describes the ability to freely access and express one's own unconscious impulses. In this way, while Kurata allows the traditional disease concept of meditation sickness to have an impact on the modern disease concept of anxiety, suggesting the liveliness of the traditional concept in the process, so, too, does he allow the modern concept to affect the traditional concept.

Further Reading

Curley, Melissa Anne-Marie. 2024. "A Cure for Mindfulness: Buddhism, Anxiety, and the Problem of Work in Modern Japan." In *Buddhism and Healing in the Modern World,* edited by C. Pierce Salguero, Kin Cheung, and Susannah Deane. University of Hawai'i Press.

Davis, Bret W. 2014. "Naturalness in Zen and Shin Buddhism: Before and Beyond Self- and Other-Power." *Contemporary Buddhism* 15 (2): 433–447. http://dx.doi.org/10.1080/14639947.2014.935258.

Harding, Christopher, Iwata Fumiaki, and Yoshinaga Shin'ichi, eds. 2015. *Religion and Psychotherapy in Modern Japan.* Routledge.

Obsessive Thinking as Meditation Sickness[3]

Since February 11th of last year, I have been doing battle with ceaseless, uninterrupted pain. It would not be an exaggeration to call it something close to torture. I've often felt as though it has exhausted both my energy and my willpower. . . . My pain comes from what is called obsessive thinking.[4] This pain is caused by conflicts that arise between the conscious mind and the unconscious mind. To put it another way, it is meditation sickness. . . . Obsessive thinking is, precisely speaking, a mental affliction—indeed, the quintessential form of mental affliction, as though created in a laboratory, boiled down and concentrated in order to show us what a mental affliction is. It is caused by attachments in the conscious mind. This one word, attachment, is actually quite complicated—being attached to the notion that one ought to be unattached to things, for example, is also a kind of attachment. . . . And being attached to being unattached to the notion that one ought to be unattached to things is a kind of attachment too. Attachment never ends. The way not to fixate is *just not to fixate.*[5] Everything else is a kind of attachment.

Since ancient times, obsessive thinking has been treated as incomparably difficult to overcome.[6] Once you've had the bad luck of being stricken by it, you'll never be able to cure it, and your symptoms will be an indescribable series of miseries. The origins of this illness, the ways in which it develops, and the way it is broken through are determined by the most subtle and profound causes—actually, we might well call obsessive thinking a religious problem. This is why, since ancient times, many have referred to this disorder as meditation sickness. Indeed, its impacts bear a striking resemblance to being given a Zen kōan and made to solve it.

What is the best way to behave in the face of such pain? What will come of this behavior? Is there a path that will deliver us from pain that seems otherwise inescapable? If you study these questions carefully, eventually you'll end up dealing with religion in its real sense—the world of meditation, calling the name of Amida Buddha, and so on. Recovering from the illness itself is just a side effect of this.

Onset: Obsessive Thinking Rooted in the Search for Enlightenment[7]

. . . What I want to make clear is that it was my own effort at seeking enlightenment that caused me to spiral into obsessive thinking. It happened because of my completely sincere attitude as a logical idealist: I had established an ideal realm that I felt needed to be achieved, and tried hard to move toward it, exhausting all my power in the process. . . . This was the tragedy of my fate.

Until I was stricken with obsessive thinking, I lived a life of contemplation. The life of contemplation is possible only after we have come quite far in the development of our inner lives—a life of contemplation is by no means a shallow one. Even some of the great men of old stopped at this stage. Had I not been stricken by obsessive thinking, and my life of contemplation not been shattered, perhaps I too would have stopped at this stage. The lives of Saigyō, Bashō, and, more recently, the poet Shimaki Akahiko are, I think, profound examples of such a life.[8] It is a life of unbroken tranquility—this is not consummate nirvana, but it has the power to intoxicate us, for it carries with it a sense of the infinity of nature and of human existence.

In my case, I arrived at a life of contemplation after having pursued various paths and peregrinations. From the time I was thirty-three or thirty-four years old, contemplation had become my center of gravity. My life no longer revolved around women and ambition but instead around the contemplation of nature and human existence. It had become the wellspring for my writing and not just that—for me, contemplation was incomparably luscious. Contemplating nature and human existence filled me with an infinite sense of arising, saturating me. It gave me so much happiness, it was almost debauched. Seeing the light spill onto the veranda put me in a state of rapture. I needed nothing else to be happy. Just seeing the sparrows, or the shadow of a cloud moving across the sky, filled me with contentment. A scrap of paper in the street, dust floating on the surface of a pond, a little dog cowering by the road, rice heaped in a bowl, the steam rising from it, the trace of a stain on a wall—anything and everything filled me with a boundless sense of beauty. . . . Because contemplation had come to be the center of gravity in my life, I felt I had to try to achieve the deepest depths of contemplation—it's only natural that I would have this feverish attitude. But in fact, this is what gave rise to tragedy. Cruel, isn't it? "What if I try to see the beauty in things, as much as I possibly can?" This was the problem set for me; this was what I felt I had to do; this was my duty. But to see the beauty in things is not just to see them as splendid, or pretty, or pleasing. To see the true beauty in a thing is to see it as it truly is—to see its real form.[9] It is to see a true image of nature or human existence. When you have insight into the real form of something, then you can write a good poem about it. But how does the real form become visible? You need to see things as they are[10]—what Bashō calls "being in emptiness while acting through form" or what in Zen is called giving rise to aspiration while not abiding in anything.[11] You need to see without seeing. As Takuan Zenji said, "If you put the mind nowhere, it can be everywhere."[12] You must release the mind and allow it to turn its radiance on the entirety of an object, and at the same time, you must concentrate your attention on every little nook and cranny. With this in mind, I tried hard to follow this path.

On first reflection, this all seems fine and natural but actually, it's terribly difficult—even dangerous. Takuan too says "become fixated and you will certainly go down the wrong path."[13] What is it to become fixated? For the logical idealist, fixation is a kind of fervor. When you establish what you feel you need to do (an ideal), and you're trying hard to achieve it, you would expect that the more fervent you are about it, the better. Back then, I did not yet recognize the flaw in the logical idealism that had been guiding me for twenty years, so I tried hard to single-mindedly cast off my attachments and to concentrate, trying to attain the deepest depths of contemplation. I worked at it constantly, morning and night. . . . But what was the result of my having devoted myself so to this conscious effort? What did I achieve? Did I see things as they truly were—their real form? Although I expected that I would, in reality, I lost the ability to pay attention in a natural way and became incapable of making sense of things. This is how my obsessive thinking began.

Early Symptoms: Insomnia and an Inability to Make Sense of Things[14]

On the evening of February 11th, 1926, I was standing in the corridor on the second floor of my home in Fujisawa, looking as I always did at the sun setting in the western sky. The clouds were aglow. Suddenly, I found myself in a strange state of mind. Although my eyes were trained on the clouds in front of me, they did not register in my mind as clouds. I could see colors and shapes, but I could not make sense of them.[15] I had no sense of seeing anything at all. Thinking this strange, I looked again, but it was just the same. Alarmed, I tried fixing my gaze, but then I could see even less. I could see but I couldn't *see.* Now much alarmed, I stopped fixing my gaze, trying instead to glimpse the clouds in an absentminded way—but just as before, I couldn't make sense of them. Though I tried looking in various ways and tried taking up various attitudes toward what I was seeing, I couldn't find a way out of this predicament. This was how my contemplation sickness began—it was a strange and totally unexpected experience. I was terribly afraid.

Here I want to beg the reader's attention. Many readers will think it seems strange now, but I believed that controlling my own mind through an effort of will was entirely possible, and that being unable to do so was nothing but weakness of will—this was something I took to be self-evident. This belief was rooted in my zeal for idealism. But now a perfectly humdrum thing like seeing the clouds in front of me—not seeing them as beautiful, particularly, just seeing them in an ordinary way—had become impossible, however hard I tried or didn't try. This completely upended my long-standing beliefs, destroying the foundation of my whole inner life. Even worse, it rendered me incapable of the contemplation that was essential to my work, to my leisure, to my life. I was alarmed and frightened. All at once, the life I had lived for twenty years—the life of an idealist—had crumbled. A complete transformation in the way I was to live my life was underway. This was, for me, a great crisis. Consumed by worry, I wondered how I would be able to sleep that night.

Nevertheless, out of habit, I applied the same principle to sleeping as I had to seeing. That is, I tried hard to fall asleep, thinking I could do it by quieting my mind. But trying hard to quiet my mind meant that I could not quiet my mind. And thus, I could not fall asleep. A sense that you should be able to fall asleep easily and trying hard to do so never brings on sleep—on the contrary, it ensures that you won't sleep. Here too my idealism and the efforts it inspired were breaking down. Naturally, I became an insomniac.

I have to make it clear here that for the ten years prior, I had been a sound sleeper—the ideal sleeper. My sleep was not disordered in the slightest. I could get into bed, fall straight to sleep, and sleep until dawn almost uninterrupted. If I wanted to, I could fall asleep in the middle of the day as well, whenever I liked. But now, somehow, I could not sleep. Even the night before, I had had a deep sleep, but now I could not so much as doze off. From that moment forward, for a long time and to an extreme degree, insomnia and the inability to make sense of things came to torment me. Both were forms of obsessive thinking.

Ordinary people just gaze at the clouds without paying them any mind; ordinary people just fall asleep without paying it any mind. Once we become conscious of these things—once we begin to try hard to gaze at the clouds or try hard to fall asleep—already we have begun to fall into unnaturalness, or *calculation.* Consider the case of contemplation. In ordinary circumstances, you'd just look at an object; you wouldn't get hung up on it. But once we begin to pay attention to the object in a conscious way, we start to understand how complex the mind with which we perceive phenomena is, don't we? Ordinarily, we act without any self-consciousness of the mind's complex operations. Hence, no contemplation sickness. But once we become conscious of these operations, we become concerned with all the choices we have—ideas about different possibilities overwhelm us and conflicts arise within us. It's as if a centipede began to wonder which foot it should move first in order to be good at walking. Just so, in order to be good at contemplation, one can't think about what one should be paying attention to. . . .

Readers will be astonished at my saying such things—"It's because he's become too attached to the object," they'll think. "It would be better if he let go of the object and let himself vaguely intuit the whole. It would be better if he relaxed about trying in vain to see the object and let himself just calmly get a hint of it." I had that thought myself a thousand times—I tried to do exactly that. But to no avail: unconsciousness isn't something that can be consciously manufactured. Trying hard, consciously, to let go of an object only gets you more and more tangled up with it. Working hard to forget something is not other than to remember it. In Zen, they compare this to a donkey tied to a hitching post. If you hitch a donkey to a post, it will run around in circles, wanting to escape. But as it circles the post, the rope will get shorter and shorter—the more the donkey struggles, the less able it will be to move. The Third Patriarch said, "Using the mind to rule the mind—what grosser error is there than this?"[16] Indeed, this was what was causing my pain. For me, not being able to control my mind signaled the collapse of the logical idealist methodology that I had lived by for twenty years. This left me without a single pleasure in life, and incapable of working as an artist. Although I had two healthier-than-average eyes, I couldn't see a thing. I wanted to recover an ordinary person's unremarkable ability to make sense of things, even if it meant surrendering all the skill that I had acquired at sinking deep into the life of contemplation in my training up to this point. With this in mind, I contrived to take up a certain attitude. But my contrivances only made my disorder worse. . . .

My sickness got steadily worse. But there was no way to escape it. Because of my inability to make sense of things, I had lost my only pleasure in life. I could no longer hope to receive creative inspiration from the contemplation of nature and human existence. I had gone blind, I thought, and as a blind artist, like Milton, all that was left was what could be born out of the power of imagination that welled determinedly within me. On the one hand, because of my insomnia, this too quickly broke down. But so long as my body persisted, I had no choice but to go on working. . . .

It was as though I was a madman who was still self-aware. Madmen are not aware that they are mad, but I was distinctly aware of my mental abnormality. And I knew, too, that I was beyond curing. What cruel torture. I felt my fate had been designed to torture me—I even thought perhaps I had been possessed by something. . . .

Although there are people struck by a similar fate, in cases where that blow hits from the outside, one can easily fight it by focusing the power of one's mind. But when one is being devoured by the internal functioning of the mind itself, that is something that truly saps one's courage. There is no easy way through this. It's an inescapable fate imposed upon you—but though this is so, by resigning yourself to it coldly, as something to be accepted and endured absolutely, you become capable of getting through it. Accepting and enduring is the highest virtue—one can't but call it divine.

In this way, resigned to the bodily breakdown caused by my insomnia and giving up the joys of contemplation, I resolved to go back to work, thinking of myself as having become a blind man.

But things did not end there. Now if I happened to look at an object, I felt as though it was moving. If, thinking something oughtn't be moving, I stopped and paid attention, it would gradually, clearly begin to move. If I tried to stop it moving, it began to move all the more, starting to spin round and round. . . . And then, suddenly, what was spinning was not the object but my eyes themselves—"How is this happening?" I thought. And then, naturally, a dreadful thought floated through my head: "How is it that my eyes can see themselves?" I was horrified. In an instant, I made the following deduction: "In order for us to sleep, we have to close our eyes. If we did not have eyelids, the eyes couldn't help but keep looking at things willy-nilly. Why then don't the eyes look at the eyelids?"

And then, even though I closed my eyes, my eyelids were visible to me. Though I tried not to look, I couldn't help but see them. There was no way to escape. I had always to be looking at something, endlessly. Because when I tried [to close my eyes in order] not to look, I was still looking. Thus, I could not sleep.

Ordinary people can sleep because they are completely unaware of being able to see their eyelids. In my case, by contrast, all I did was become aware of being able to see my eyelids. But this one moment of *becoming aware* seemed to become somehow a dreadful obstacle.

My eyes would never be able to rest! The idea that my eyes would stay fixed, open, that I would never be able to close them—just to imagine it filled me with an eerie dread. Now it had become my reality, manifesting in my body. Even if I were to try to accept and endure this, what would be the result? It goes without saying: I would die. . . .

Did I have to lose my entire life simply because I had *become aware*? Why had I become aware in this way? All of a sudden, I had become aware. This was my misfortune. It was coincidence, just as though I had been riding aboard a train that flipped over. Such a cruel coincidence! But in fact, in this world, there are these kinds of coincidences, and there was nothing I could do about it. Before Adam and Eve became aware of good and evil, they lived in paradise. When they became aware of good and evil, it cost them heaven. But once having become aware, they could no longer forget. For this reason, they had to restore the heaven they had lost in some other way. Namely, they had to transcend good and evil. One can know good and evil and despite this, transcend them.

In my case, I had to find a way to see the inside of my eyes without it being a hindrance for me. But this was not easy—in becoming able to do this, I first had to go through indescribable torment. I don't use the word "suffering" lightly—obsessive thinking can only be properly described as *suffering*. Indeed, I exhausted myself with desperate efforts a hundred times over, a thousand times over, and the despair when those efforts crumbled, the despair when it seemed there was nothing left for me to try—there is nothing I can compare it to.

They say that if you call the name of Amida Buddha a million times, you'll be saved; truly, I couldn't help but feel as though I had despaired a million times. I tried and failed, tried and failed again, returning to try again over and over—not like someone returning to a game, but with the seriousness appropriate to matters of life and death. This was pain beyond description. Had I not been stricken by obsessive thinking, I wouldn't understand. It's subjective pain, of course, but pleasure and pain are essentially subjective things. As far as pain goes, whether that pain is caused by organic illness or not doesn't change a thing.

Treatment: Exhausting Calculation[17]

As I see it, my experiences over the last several years have been about becoming acquainted, in practice, with the process of being rid of calculation. This was the real meaning of my struggles. The result was absolute life, and with it, casting off my sickness. This calculation is not something I could get rid of myself—I could only be rid of it. The state of being without calculation is called *letting things be as they are*. What we call according with reality, or real form, or the original face is none other than this.

The method of Dr. Morita Shōma, who discovered an original psychotherapeutic treatment for nervous anxiety is as follows: bedrest in a locked room, cut off from anything that would distract one from pain—meetings, reading, conversation, snacking, smoking. Looking through the window at the garden outside is prohibited, as is looking at the clock. This method forces you to face your pain in the present moment, single-mindedly, immersing yourself within it.

Over the course of a week, my suffering reached an extreme. . . . All that was left was the *calculation* of trying to sleep, and the *calculation* of trying to stop paying attention to the inside of my eyelids. Even knowing that this *calculation* would be to no avail, there was nothing else for me to do. . . . So long as the karmic momentum of *calculation* kept accumulating, I wasn't able to stop calculating.

In this way, even as I kept working hard not to calculate, I kept on calculating, more and more. I was gradually falling into a pit that I could not find my way out of. I was just like the donkey tied to the hitching post. In the end, I couldn't doze off for even a second, trapped in the predicament of not being able to stop looking at the inside of my eyes for even an instant. I had no choice but to remain as I was—I was hemmed in on all sides. Now there was no longer even a way to calculate. Not sleeping for a moment, I just stared, frozen, at the inside of my eyes—there was nothing else I could do. I reached an absolute limit.

I was in despair. But that night, strangely, I slept deeply—that is, I was able to sleep deeply while still looking at the inside of my eyelids. This is not something I could have imagined. But the facts are the facts. For all that I tried to sleep, I couldn't sleep, but when I lost all hope that I would ever sleep again, I was able to sleep deeply.

This strange experience gave me confidence. I could not conceive of a more profound, more straightforward situation of insomnia. Yet even so, I was able to sleep deeply. . . .

Since that night, I have acquired a strange calmness of mind in terms of sleeping. And to this very day, I have been completely unaffected by insomnia. Even now, of course, when I become aware of the inside of my eyelids, they're visible to me. But even as I look at them, I can fall asleep, and so forget about them, as is usual. This is, however, not a matter of being able to forget by trying to forget. This is a mentality of *transcendence* that enables freedom or liberation in every situation; it is the thread running throughout all of my obsessive thinking and now, similarly, throughout my attitude to my life as a whole.

What did I learn from insomnia and overcoming it? That you yourself cannot eliminate *calculation,* regardless of how well you understand the origins of this curse intellectually and regardless of how much you exert your will in trying to bring it to a halt. Only when you reach a place in which there is no room left for calculation will you attain the kind of awakening in which calculation ceases on its own.

How can I describe the essence of what I have come to know as a result of this experience? It is, in short, that however well you understand calculation intellectually, and however hard you exert your will, calculation will never stop until its karma is exhausted. When calculation stops, that in itself is the concrete realization of what it means to accept and endure. And while there will still be pain, as there was before, that pain will not hurt you—you will have been released.

There is in fact profound meaning in the fact that you can do nothing with your intellectual understanding and your efforts of will—that is the reality of this world. Being *trapped* by an obstacle,[18] *calculating* ways to escape, calculation ending and things being allowed to be as they are: all of it is necessary. It's not the case that we can pick and choose. Faith is submitting to what is necessary.

Though it's easy to speak of accepting and enduring things as they are, in practice, in order to achieve this state of mind, it's not enough to develop one's powers of will and determination; one in fact must return over and over to those points of coagulation and resistance—they must be smashed to pieces and made level. All that is arrived at by way of willful determination and intellectual perception is child's play, like breaking up a clod of dug-up earth with the end of a hoe until it's fine and soft. Getting rid of *calculation,* exhausting the karma of *calculation*—both its internal and external causes and the circumstances in which it can arise? That's never achieved through the power of will. Still less is it achieved by rallying some sentimental, heroic feeling of desperate necessity. In practice, this state of mind opens up on its own, as a result of our having come to a dead end. Coming to a dead end is painful, of course. And yet, without coming to a dead end, it is not possible to open up a path. There is no way for you to do it without suffering. This is as it should be. Seeking enlightenment and attaining liberation are inherently things that arise out of *necessity.* When you seek something that is not a necessity, it will not be delivered to you. Nature does not allow for such profligacy. In order for things to be generated, for things to be developed, for the creation of a new world, coming to a dead end is a necessity.

Before he actualized the way, Daitō Kokushi lamented,[19] "Though I gnaw up and down, left and right, I cannot get through." Daie Zenji too said,[20] "As one approaches the end of the path, one will pant breathlessly, and one's heart will burn with anguish. This is good news!" Only if there is first a dead end can there be no more dead ends.

The True Significance of Sickness and Suffering[21]

If I have come to know myself as truly a seeker of enlightenment, and take pride in being such, if anything I ought to feel grateful for having been stricken with obsessive thinking. It was by means of this [illness] that I was branded by fate as a seeker of enlightenment. I was made ready to seek enlightenment. Fate tempered me by giving me this affliction, so that I could know for myself that to be a true seeker isn't easy, that since ancient times, genuine seekers of enlightenment have suffered in earnestly seeking the way. This was fate calculating on my behalf, so that there would be nothing dishonest left in me. Fate made me an authentic seeker of enlightenment. If I had not been stricken with obsessive thinking, I would have sought awakening as though it were easy, idling my life away unknowingly, unable to test whether or not my awakening was the real thing. But now, I have no choice—my life is on the line. I have to gamble my entire fate on this one thing. I can't escape it, down to my absolute last breath. Even were I to try to be idle, to try to take it easy, I wouldn't be able to—I'm in a situation in which I can't do that. And whether or not my awakening is the real thing will be proven by the clear fact of whether or not I've been able to break through this barrier. Thinking about it this way, in fact, I see that it's a fate tailor-made for me.

My experience of obsessive thinking taught me so many important things. My whole mental life was changed because of it. I made a complete turnabout, from logical idealism to dharmic naturalism. And now my way of living is to live what I would call absolute life. I have come, I think, to understand—not merely theoretically but in practice—the relationship between calculation and naturalness, between can and must, between emptiness and form. I have been tempered, body and mind, in the cauldron of obsessive thinking. And now both my body and my heart-mind are resilient. Penetrating weakness, I have become strong.

I cannot but think of the profound meaning of Shinran's verses: "The cloud of light is unhindered, like open sky,"[22] "Beneath mist and cloud there is brightness, not dark."[23] The important thing here is that the clouds indeed exist. Yet while there are clouds, they pose no impediment—they are as emptiness. While there is mist and cloud, underneath them, it is bright. That is to say, there are abhorrent things that exist for us always, that we can't get away from, but what lies on the other side has real existence. Clouds and mist are a difficult hindrance in the sky of the heart-mind, forever causing pain, sadness, corruption. Who would not hate an endless ringing in the ears, staring at things without interruption, seeing things constantly rotating?[24] Though it was happening for the sake of my search for enlightenment, I scarcely felt grateful for it—I just kept wishing for it to stop. But I couldn't make it stop—there was nothing to do but accept and endure it. Now, having come to the point at which it is possible to bear it, for the first time I look back and can think about the profound significance of that suffering in my life, the gift it has given me.

Cure: Attaining an Absolute Way of Living[25]

The logical idealist approach to life applies only to the conscious world; it has no power in the unconscious world, which is the true domain of vital being itself—so I can no longer bring myself to live according to such an approach. The role of intellect and will should be to work on behalf of the desires of the original mind, not to have the privilege of determining what those desires are.

Let us live according to the desires of the original mind, using intellect and will as tools: this is the dharmic naturalism approach to life. "Dharmic" here means religious—the original mind is something absolute, that should be affirmed as it is, that is the essence of value, thus it is called dharmic.

Absolute life is difficult to explain in words but surely it exists as that way of living we speak of as "to live unconditionally" or "just to live." It isn't living for some particular reason or another—because to live is good or because to live is enjoyable—but because you're straightforwardly, immediately alive. Just to live, whether you're enjoying it or you're suffering. You do what has to be done. You live by *really* affirming your own life, *as it is.* While dizzy with vertigo, while tallying numbers, you live.[26] As for suffering, there's some suffering you'll avoid and some that can't be avoided, so while you're suffering, just as you are, you do what has to be done. Because no matter how much you refuse it, you can't do anything about it.

This absolute life, because it is the real religious life, is a straightforward, immediate affirmation of vital being. It is to *really* live life *as it is.* This is the religious heart-mind just as it is, in a way more direct, more serious, than something like praying to the gods for happiness.

When you wake up to absolute consciousness of this vital being, it is as though a fire has been kindled in your vital being—a life withered by suffering lifts itself up again, as though it's been beautifully starched. And with courage like that of a warrior making a charge, taking up a position with his back to the water, as if he's unafraid of the bullets flying around him, it will be as though you have been able to bring yourself back to life. It will be as though you are able to live sincerely and single-mindedly. Even as I think of the pain I was made to carry around like a carapace, its teeth sunk deep in my life, and even as I grieve the hollow corpses of the many hardships I struggled with as a result, I cannot but do my utmost to be all the more vitally alive now.

From the moment I fell ill, I was able to predict that if I broke through this illness of obsessive thinking, a certain liberated state of mind would open up for me, like a Zen monk solving a kōan, seeing his Buddha nature, and becoming a buddha. Thus, concentrating all of my mind and all of my power, I worked single-mindedly—literally—to break through this obstacle. Speaking of that hard work, it's not the kind of work spurred straight ahead by ordinary idealism. It is a stratagem that leaps crosswise,[27] crossing along a path without a path, through a gateless barrier. . . . [28] It is "not crossing by crossing," "crossing by not crossing." And more than this, this paradoxical way of crossing is itself a religious method—the marrow of faith. The secrets of Zen and Pure Land faith are contained within this method. By means of this method, I crossed completely beyond obsessive thinking; by applying it to the whole of my life, just as it is—to every aspect of my everyday life—I got beyond long-standing physical ailments . . . and came at last to be born anew. Nowadays, nobody sees me as an invalid. Nobody even cautions me to take care of myself.

I have no interest in speaking here simply about a technique for battling illness. I do believe, however, that you can undergo a fundamental psychological transformation in terms of how you make use of your mind that thoroughly reshapes your approach to living, and you can begin to live in a way that is fully absolute—a way of living that has been brought into perfect tension, as if you're walking a tightrope, or walking on water, or in the state we call "no horse beneath the saddle."[29] In short, you can begin a life of faith. And when you do that, the condition of the body changes completely, and miracles can be had: miracles like a long-standing illness "being cured without being cured."

To get our hands on such an absolute way of living is, I think, salvation for every person, and the ultimate instinct of every living creature. Indeed, by realizing this way of living myself, I have both come to be at peace by establishing my life in reality-as-it-is and escaped dying an invalid. More than this, I have been granted a dauntless heart-mind that acts as it pleases amidst the shame and filth of the ordinary world. It is the dauntless heart-mind that lives without fear, recklessly, like a seabird dallying on the shore. This is the very pinnacle of Pure Land faith. It is the *heart-mind* of Shinran.

Notes

1. Hori (2003, 139).
2. Kurata (2013, 36).
3. Kurata (1932, i, 8, 111–112).
4. *Kyōhaku kannen:* literally, "obsessive ideation" or "compulsive ideation." This term refers to the same disease concept identified in English as "obsessive-compulsive disorder." The connection that Kurata makes between his obsessive thinking and meditation sickness may be informed in part by the word *kannen,* or ideation, which is also used in Buddhist contexts to refer specifically to meditative recollection or contemplation (Sk. *anusmṛti*). See Charles Muller, "*Kannen*" *Digital Dictionary of Buddhism,* accessed June 24, 2025, http://www.buddhism-dict.net.
5. The emphasis here is Kurata's, as are the other instances of emphasis that follow in this text.
6. *Nantō,* literally, "difficult to pass." Readers may take note here of Kurata's presentation of himself as someone who had traveled far on the road of contemplation before being confronted with the "barrier" of obsessive thinking.

7. Kurata (1932, 10–13, 125–127).
8. Saigyō (1118–1190) was a medieval Buddhist renunciant and poet, well known for his use of images drawn from nature. Bashō (1644–1694) was an early modern poet, recognized now as the greatest master of the haiku form and known also for his travel diaries. Shimaki Akahiko (1876–1926) was a contemporary of Kurata's and a central member of the Araragi poetry circle, which sought to modernize Japanese poetry.
9. *Jissō:* reality, the real aspect of a thing; synonymous with suchness (*shinnyo*), the absolute reality that at once transcends and gives rise to phenomenal existence.
10. *Arugamama:* as it is, undisguised, honest. *Arugamama* is a key concept in Morita therapy, describing a state in which patients are able to accept reality—including both the facts of the external social world and their own emotions—as it is; in doing so, paradoxically, patients unblock their own vital power and become able to undertake constructive action in the world. David Reynolds glosses *arugamama* as "accepting one's self, one's symptoms, and reality as they are." See Reynolds (1982, 22).
11. Here Kurata is referencing a passage from the *Diamond Sutra* in which the Buddha describes how bodhisattvas and *mahāsattvas* arouse aspiration for enlightenment without clinging to phenomena: "They should give rise to the aspiration while not abiding in anything." See Muller (2013, verse 10). A nonabiding mind is also a key concept in Morita therapy, where it describes the healthy functioning of a mind free from fixations or preoccupations. See Morita (1998, 31).
12. Takuan Sōhō (1573–1645) was a Rinzai Zen master. See Haskel (2013, 41).
13. This phrase in fact appears to come from Jianzhi Sengcan's (529–613) "Inscription on Trust in the Mind" (*Xinxinming*). Burton Watson translates the Chinese original as "Sticklers always miss the proper measure, certain to set off on wrong roads." For Watson's translation and others, see "Jianzhi Sengcan (529–613): *Xinxinming*," accessed August 2, 2024, https://terebess.hu/english/hsin.html.
14. Kurata (1932, 14–22, 34–40).
15. The term I translate as "making sense of things" is, more technically, "apperception" (*tōkaku*)—the conscious perception of a sensory impression or the process by which perceptions are incorporated into existing frameworks of knowledge or experience, allowing them to be assigned meaning and value.
16. This phrase comes from "Inscription on Trust in the Mind." Burton Watson translates the Chinese original as "Using mind to stir up more mind—what grosser error than this?" In his gloss of the Chinese, Kurata replaces the character meaning "to use" with one meaning "to control or to regulate." See "Jianzhi Sengcan (529–613): *Xinxinming*," https://terebess.hu/english/hsin.html.
17. Kurata (1932, 31, 46–49, 65, 96–97).
18. *Sawari ni kakaru.* This expression can also be read as being stricken with illness.
19. Daitō Kokushi (1283–1338) was the second patriarch of the Ōtōkan lineage of Rinzai Zen in Japan.

20. Daie is the Japanese name for Dahui (1089–1163), the twelfth-generation Chan patriarch; his emphasis on the necessary relation between doubt and awakening had a decisive influence on Japanese Zen thought.

21. Kurata (1932, 26, 78–79, 123–124).

22. This phrase appears in Shinran's *Hymns of the Pure Land* (*Jōdo wasan*); the translation is taken from Hirota (1997, 326).

23. This phrase appears in Shinran's *Passages on the Pure Land Way* (*Jōdo monrui jusho*); the translation is taken from Hirota (1997, 305).

24. The examples Kurata offers here are taken from the list of symptoms he earlier described experiencing himself.

25. Kurata (1932, i–iii, 50, 99–100).

26. Again, taken from the list of Kurata's own symptoms.

27. *Ōchōteki kufū*. Here Kurata is invoking Shinran's understanding that the moment in which one realizes oneself to be the evil person, wholly incapable of any practice, is also the moment in which one realizes one is grasped by Amida, never to be abandoned. In his *Kyōgyōshinshō*, Shinran writes, "'Transcending crosswise' refers to being mindful of the Primal Vow and becoming free of the mind of self-power; this is termed 'Other Power of transcending crosswise.' It is the single within the single, the sudden within the sudden, the true within the true, the One Vehicle within the [One] Vehicle. It is the true essence [of the Pure Land way]." See Hirota (1997, 223).

28. Here Kurata is invoking the thirteenth-century kōan collection *The Gateless Barrier* (*Mumonkan*).

29. This phrase is associated with Takuan, who is said to have described the key to horsemanship as, in Peter Haskel's (2013) translation, "only that there must be no man on top of the saddle and no horse under the saddle" (122).

Chapter 13

Meditation Sickness in East Asia

Selections from Modern Chan Teachers

DIXUAN CHEN, FRANCISCO FIGUEROA MEDINA, AND TRANG T. D. NGUYEN

Originating in medieval China, the Chan tradition was transmitted throughout East Asia, becoming known as Seon in Korea, Zen in Japan, and Thiền in Vietnam. Today, across this region, the contemporary inheritors of Chan lineages across cultures consistently warn their students about the potential dangers of meditation practice. Given the tradition's historical focus on intensive practice, no doubt many of these warnings are informed by the personal experience of senior Chan teachers. At the same time, it is possible to hear in these contemporary discourses the echoes of the influential historical sutras and commentaries that appear in parts I and II of this volume. This chapter presents a sample of contemporary Chan teachings on meditation sickness (Ch. *chanbing*), including translations of excerpts from two books and a YouTube video. The reader's attention is drawn to how these discourses utilize themes from *Secret Essential Methods for Curing Meditation Sickness* (chapter 4) and the *Śūraṃgama Sūtra* (chapter 5), as well as the writings of Zhiyi (chapters 6–7) when it comes to the symptoms, prevention, and treatment of meditation sickness. This chapter thus demonstrates the ongoing relevance of these historical treatments of the dangers of meditation in present-day East Asian Buddhism.

The first selection in this chapter is a translation of a text by Yamada Mumon (1900–1988), a priest of the Japanese Rinzai Zen School. He was the president of Hanazono University from 1949 to 1978 and the *rōshi* overseeing Shōfuku-ji from 1953 to 1977. He also founded the Institute for Zen Studies in 1964 and was the chief abbot of Myōshin-ji from 1978 to 1982. In 1953 he gave a series of ritualized talks addressed to novice monks on *Principles of Zazen,* the oldest extant meditation manual of the Chan/Zen tradition. These talks were recorded, typed, and published in 1956 by Shinjinkai, a lay *zazen* group affiliated with Shōfuku-ji temple. In 1974 the Institute for Zen Studies included a revised and edited version in the quarterly *Zen Culture*. The issue was so well received that in that same year, the editor decided to publish it as a separate volume titled *The Path to Zazen* (*Zazen he no michi*). In 1982 this volume was republished with a new title, *Recommendations for Zazen* (*Zazen no susume*). In the editors' afterword, we read: "We hope this volume is useful as reference material for the more than five hundred *zazen* groups around the country. We also hope that it allows people already doing *zazen* to avoid getting tired of it, and that it inspires those who have not seated yet to sit at least once."[1]

In his works, Yamada promotes *zazen* as "the gate to the Buddhist teachings of peace and joy" and insinuates that if someone gets sick by doing *zazen*, it is because he is not being cautious enough. *Zazen* is to settle the body, the breath, and the mind. To settle the body is to assume a well-balanced posture with eyes open, to settle the breath is to practice abdominal (*tanden*) breathing, and to settle the mind is to repeat the main point of a kōan in one's mind so that it matches with one's breath.[2] The goal of these practices is not only for the practitioner to attain *samādhi* but also to realize that his true nature is emptiness. Having understood that emptiness cannot get sick, the practitioner's body will be healthy and his spirit vigorous. However, as his practice improves many obstacles known as demonic realms will appear.[3] The antidote to these obstacles is right mindfulness and clear understanding: to persist with the abovementioned practices, with a heart that has vowed to save all living beings, until the end. If the practitioner keeps right mindfulness and clear understanding before his eyes, "before long, he will arrive at the place of eternal dharma." There, he will be able to die sitting or standing, like the monks of old.

The second selection below translates the conversations between practitioners and Venerable Sheng Yen (a.k.a. Shengyan, 1931–2009), a Chinese Buddhist monk who integrated the lineages of both Caodong and Linji (Jp. Sōtō and Rinzai) transmissions.[4] Sheng Yen emerged as a meditation master in Taiwan and the United States during the mid-1970s and 1980s, actively promoting Chinese Buddhist traditions. He was the founder of Dharma Drum Mountain, one of the most influential Buddhist institutions in Taiwan.[5]

The excerpt includes Sheng Yen's response to questions about the adverse effects of meditation from his lay and monastic disciples. It was initially published by *Chan Magazine*, a quarterly publication that features the lectures delivered by Sheng Yen. It has been revised several times, and the current version is excerpted from the Chinese book *Chan Wisdom: Conversations with Master Sheng Yen* (*Chan de zhihui: Yu Shengyan fashi xinling duihua*).[6] The book aims to address modern readers' inquiries on how to correctly understand

Buddhist teachings and effectively integrate meditation into contemporary life. It highlights the potential adverse outcomes linked to meditation, which Shen Yen repeatedly calls "meditation sickness" (Ch. *chanbing*).[7] His repetition of this term signifies that it is a frequently discussed topic, reflecting the apprehensions of modern practitioners and the significance of the subject matter. Sheng Yen's response assures that the chances of harmful effects arising from meditation are low. Even if such negative effects do occur, they are manageable and treatable. While this stance indicates his acknowledgment of the possibility of issues, it also reflects his awareness of the need to avert unnecessary panic and anxiety among his audience.

In the current excerpt, Sheng Yen's references to scriptural sources are not discernible. However, in another sermon from 1985 he explicitly mentioned *Secret Methods for Curing Meditation Sickness* and Zhiyi's *Greater* [*Treatise on*] *Śamatha and Vipaśyanā*. His 1985 talk aligns with the excerpt presented here, with the only difference being the direct inclusion of some of Zhiyi's commentary on the Four Elements.[8] In the 1985 sermon, Sheng Yen pointed out four methods to avert the problems related to the Four Elements and Five Viscera: (1) establishing a suitable goal, (2) identifying appropriate meditation techniques, (3) maintaining balanced nutrition, and (4) harmonizing energetic and sedentary activities.[9]

The third and final translation included in this chapter is a recorded conversation between Venerable Thích Nhật Từ and a laywoman during his Dharma talk to a crowd in a Buddhist temple. It was later published as a nearly eleven-minute video on his official YouTube channel (Thích Nhật Từ Official). The conversation takes the form of a question-and-answer session and is part of a series on the channel about various topics related to Buddhist life.

Ven. Thích Nhật Từ is a well-known Buddhist reformer monk in Vietnam.[10] He was ordained in the Linji lineage but has strongly promoted the *Four Foundations of Mindfulness* (*Satipaṭṭhāna Sutta*), one of the primary meditation texts in Theravada Buddhism. Besides delivering many Dharma talks to Vietnamese and Vietnamese diasporic communities worldwide, he is an author, translator, editor, coauthor, and coeditor of 146 works in Vietnamese and English between 2000 and 2019, mainly focusing on applied Buddhism. Additionally, he holds roles as the founder and editor in chief of the popular Buddhism Today series (Đạo Phật Ngày nay), which includes books, Dharma talks, and songs (many of which he wrote himself). He is also the editorial director of the important printed collection *Three Divine Canons for Vietnamese Buddhism* (*Tam Tạng thánh điển phật giáo Việt Nam*) and the audiobook series *Great Vietnamese Buddhist Sutras* (*Đại Tạng kinh Việt Nam*).

Moreover, Thích Nhật Từ has been actively involved in many national and international Buddhist institutes and associations, such as the Vietnam Buddhist

University in Ho Chi Minh City, where he holds the position of standing vice rector, and the International Alliance for Buddhist Cultural Exchange, where he serves as the vice president. Thích Nhật Từ's efforts have been recognized by forty-six national and international awards and recognitions, thanks to his active participation in numerous Buddhist conferences in Asia and his various cultural and charitable activities. At the same time, he has become a controversial figure for criticizing Christianity and some famous Buddhists who he believed harmed Vietnamese Buddhism's reputation with their wrong views and acts.

Further Reading

Borup, Jørn. 2008. *Japanese Rinzai Zen Buddhism: Myōshinji, a Living Religion.* Brill.

Davis, Bret W. 2022. *Zen Pathways: An Introduction to the Philosophy and Practice of Zen Buddhism.* Oxford University Press.

Eifring, Halvor, ed. 2016. *Asian Traditions of Meditation.* University of Hawai'i Press.

Thiên Dô. 1999. "Quest for Enlightenment and Cultural Identity: Buddhism in Contemporary Vietnam." In *Buddhism and Politics in Twentieth Century Asia,* edited by Ian Harris. Continuum.

Yu, Jimmy. 2021. *Reimagining Chan Buddhism: Sheng Yen and the Creation of the Dharma Drum Lineage of Chan.* Routledge.

Excerpts from Yamada Mumon's *Lectures on Principles of Zazen*[11]

"Upon careful consideration, *zazen* is the gate to the Buddha's teaching of peace and joy." *Zazen* is to settle the body, the breath, and the mind, to bring them, just as they are, back to their natural condition: a state of mind of great contentment and ease, liberated from all earthly desires. . . .

While this splendid *zazen* is the practice of great peace and joy, it is possible that some people will get sick, but that is because they do not have enough caution. Or it is because somewhere there is something unnatural. *Zazen* is "to unify mind and body, without distinction between movement and stillness." If the mind is emptiness, the body must be emptiness too. Emptiness cannot get sick. Therefore, people who do *zazen* should not get sick. If one settles the body, it is naturally healthy; if one settles the breath, one's life span extends naturally; if one settles the mind, one must spend every day, from morning to evening, in religious exultation. The elderly priests, by doing *zazen* for fifty years, have not had such an illness as to have had to see a doctor, not even once. If one does *zazen,* one must not get sick. This is the elderly priests' faith.

Accordingly, if one reads carefully this *Principles of Zazen* and does *zazen* properly, "the Four Elements [that comprise the body] will be light and relaxed, and your spirit will be fresh and clear." The body will naturally be healthier and, the spirit, as the absolute clear source of all things, will become extremely refreshed and invigorated.

The Four Elements are Earth, Water, Fire, and Wind. In ancient science, it was thought that all things in nature were formed from these Four Elements. Consequently, the human body too is composed of these Four Elements. Solid things, like bones, teeth, and nails all belong to the Earth Element. Things like blood, saliva, gastric juice, which make up most of the body, belong to the Water Element. If it is alive, there is temperature in the body, this belongs to the Fire Element. The movement of the hands, the legs, and the eyes, is the power of the Wind Element. It was taught that, since each one of these Four Elements has one hundred and one diseases, human beings have four hundred four diseases.

However, if we do *zazen,* the Four Elements will constantly be in harmony, the body will naturally become healthier and diseases will disappear. Fire tends to ascend, while Water tends to descend. That is why people tend to have cold feet and hot heads. But, if we do *zazen* and manage to constantly gather strength in the lower abdomen, the Fire will come down, heating the legs, and the Water will go up, refreshing the head. In other words, reaching a condition where we keep the head cool and the feet warm, we will be able to keep our good health. Thereupon, our spirit always being fresh and vigorous, we will always wear a smile.

There, the fog of delusions and wrong views having already vanished without a trace, a state of mind like a clear and cloudless sky becomes aware of itself. In other words, it is "right mindfulness and clear understanding." Without sadness or happiness, without getting angry, we will, without noticing it, embody the flavor of Zen or the flavor of the Buddha's teachings. This will make our spirit more and more agreeable, and we will begin to enter a beautiful place of "absolute calmness and pure joy." . . .

[A]s your practice emerges more and more, "as your path becomes worthy, demons will flourish." To the extent that we improve and become good at our practice, many obstacles appear. "Both unfavored and favored will appear" means that within the demons that hinder the Buddhist path, there are favored and unfavored demons.

The favored demons are those which hinder our path in a clever way, by conforming very well to our volition and emotions. The unfavored demons are those which disrupt our moral sense, by going against our volition and emotions. As one becomes a senior monk at the monastery, one is pampered here and praised there. And while everyone sees one as a promising monk who will become an eminent *rōshi* in the future, one turns out to be a monk who only learned how to drink alcohol and who gave up his practice. This is what is called favored [demons]. It is truly an unfortunate thing, but it cannot be helped.

There are also outstanding monks who have understood what I just said above; who, having a heart which has thoroughly vowed to become a Buddha and save all living beings, bend their legs and practice, but their body being weak, cannot stay in the monastery; or whose teacher has died and, while still young, must manage a temple; or who, because of the surrounding circumstances, must interrupt their training. This is what is called unfavored demons. "Light is usually followed by shadow." The more one can practice, many hindering demons, "both favored and unfavored" assail. It is a terrifying thing.

Therefore, it says, "But if you keep right mindfulness before your eyes." No matter what hindering demon appears, you should persist with kōan *samādhi,* you must persist with practice *samādhi,* until the end, without being caught by any of them. There is no other method than to continue with right mindfulness and clear understanding. If you have the heart which has vowed to save all living beings, if you continue with right mindfulness, those hindering demons will not be able to do anything. Before long, you will arrive at the place of eternal dharma. At the place of the determined heart which has vowed to save all living beings, at the place of right mindfulness and clear understanding, the hindering demons "will not be able to hinder your path."

Likewise, when we are doing *zazen* many misunderstandings and illusions known as demonic realms will appear but we should not be caught up in them. These include the favored and unfavored demons mentioned above, but they also include things like seeing the figure of a Buddha or a Bodhisattva, or feeling one has fallen to the bottom of an utterly dark hell, or that one is flying freely in the middle of the sky. Since all these things are demonic realms, one should not be impressed or anguished by any of them. One should keep kōan *samādhi* and right mindfulness before one's eyes until the end. . . .

If one reads such books as the *Śūraṃgama Sūtra,* the Tendai School's *Shikan* [i.e., Zhiyi's *Greater (Treatise on) Śamatha and Vipaśyanā*], and Keihō's *Shushōgi,* one would find gentle advice regarding these demons. I believe it would be good for those who are concerned about the worst-case scenario to read their advice beforehand.

2. Excerpts from *Chan Wisdom: Conversations with Master Sheng Yen*[12]

Question: I have heard that some practitioners, after long-term intensive practice, experience a state known as meditation sickness. What is that?

Answer: Firstly, sickness resulting from meditation is quite rare. In general, those who practice for one or two hours daily will not lead to these problems. Even if some individuals have an inappropriate mindset or an intense drive for achievement in a hasty manner, it is unlikely that they will encounter serious problems. Such issues may only occur while intensively and continuously practicing for a lengthy duration. However, in most cases, meditation sickness rarely happens. If someone is aware that they might experience weird or exceptional psychological hallucinations, it is better to avoid intensive practice.

There are four major causes of meditation sickness: (1) the physiological aspect, (2) the psychological aspect, (3) obstacles due to karmic consequences, and (4) external forces such as spirits and demons. Due to these various factors, meditation sickness manifests in different ways.

If the cause is physiological, issues will still occur even without practicing meditation. In reality, these problems might have existed before engaging in meditation, and the practice may simply bring them to the forefront. There are numerous reasons related to the physiological aspect of meditation sickness, one of which is having an incorrect attitude toward religious cultivation. For example, pursuing supernatural powers through meditation may result in trouble. Some practitioners may aim to rejuvenate their youth or enhance their sexual prowess through meditation. If such an attitude goes too extreme, it may bring about not only health issues but also psychological problems.

Other causes of physiological problems include inappropriate postures and unnatural breathing methods. Maintaining a hunched back while sitting in meditation can result in lower back pain, backache, and neck pain. Attempting to control the breath may result in a tight diaphragm. Inadequate nutrition, such as irregular food intake and unbalanced diet, may also lead to problems. Some people refrain from eating or drinking while engaging in prolonged meditation. When deeply immersed in a concentrated state, the perception of time can temporarily fade away. It is acceptable to skip nutritional intake for a while. However, if one remains conscious of time, it is not appropriate to neglect regular meals.

Lack of sleep can also give rise to meditation sickness. Some people believe that meditation can replace sleep, leading them to either completely forego sleep or shorten their sleep duration. This can bring about severe problems, especially neurological issues. In addition, sitting for a long period without adequate movement or exercise may cause blockages of energy channels in the body.

Some individuals may have heard that meditation can improve health, treat illnesses, and open blocked energy channels. While these benefits are possible, they require time. If one is in poor health before starting meditation, one should practice even greater caution. Attempting to achieve immediate results and dedicating excessive time to meditation without first building the essential capability can exacerbate one's physical condition.

The second type of meditation sickness derives from psychological issues, particularly an overwhelming desire to obtain immediate results from practice. Some practitioners may be eager to attain enlightenment or acquire supernatural powers. This sort of issue is rooted in afflictions, arising from excessive greed, anger, ignorance, arrogance, and doubt. These emotions and desires are common to all, and most people can manage them. Unless guided appropriately, such attachments can lead to meditation sickness. Being too hasty to achieve accomplishment from practice increases the likelihood of adverse mental states and physiological illnesses. If such issues arise, one should remind oneself, "I neither need nor want whatever arises; I neither like nor fear whatever manifests." Although it is difficult, this is the attitude that one should cultivate.

The third type of meditation sickness comes from karmic obstacles. Everything may seem fine when one is not actively engaged in practice, but issues arise as soon as earnest practice begins. One may experience headaches, chest tightness, awful hallucinations, or other symptoms. This type of meditation sickness is a result of negative karma accumulated in the past. Neither medical treatments nor psychotherapy can effectively deal with it. It would be more appropriate to cease intensive meditation. But there is no need to completely abandon meditation, one should adopt a more relaxed approach. It is recommended to recite the Repentance Verse before and after meditation.[13] If one sincerely practices repentance, meditation sickness may gradually alleviate. However, repentance alone is insufficient; it is necessary to take vows. While repentance aims to deal with past misdeeds, taking vows involves commitments for the future. The vow should be oriented not only towards individual concerns but also for the benefit of all sentient beings. . . .

The fourth type of meditation sickness derives from demonic disturbance, which is extremely rare. Demonic forces can refer to external sources or internal psychological states. When I mention demonic disturbances and demonic realms, I am primarily referring to things that originate within individuals' own minds. They come from unwholesome thoughts, misguided methods, and wrong views or attitudes. For most people, interference caused by external demonic forces rarely occurs. If such interference does happen, it is usually accompanied by one's wrongful thoughts. Practitioners on the right path, having a correct understanding of Buddhist teachings, and avoiding excessive eagerness or greed are not vulnerable to such external forces.

When external interference occurs, practitioners may or may not be aware of it. Being aware is better than being unaware. The former type of people may recognize that spirits, deities, bodhisattvas, or Buddhas are using their bodies, understanding that it is not under their control. The latter type, those who are unaware, are more vulnerable. They may assume that they have realized enlightenment. If anyone points out that their experiences and behaviors do not align with the teachings of the Buddha, they may be unwilling to accept it. These individuals are overconfident in themselves and often possess the ability to influence others, making them susceptible to falling into demonic realms.

A more crucial problem is that they believe they have achieved Buddhahood. This misperception is even worse than a mental disorder. When dealing with those who have mental disorders, at least we can identify the specific problem and provide proper assistance. However, individuals who mistakenly perceive themselves as attaining the status of being Buddhas or bodhisattvas not only refuse to acknowledge that they need help but may also influence others to enter the wrong path.

If the problem arises from external forces such as spirits, and seeking help from physicians or psychiatrists proves ineffective, it becomes essential to use alternative methods. One approach is to apply certain external forces, such as spells or talismans, to expel ghosts or spirits. However, this method is not entirely reliable. In the best-case scenario, the spell or talisman may be effective, but it can only temporarily drive away the spirits. In the worst-case scenario, it might attract even more malevolent beings. Another approach is to encourage these individuals to engage in repentance practices. If they are unable to do it themselves, others can repent on their behalf. However, such effectiveness turns out to be limited. The efficacy of repentance also depends on the severity of the situation. . . .

In conclusion, meditation sickness is a rare occurrence. Moreover, in most cases, it arises from human factors in the present life, including physiological, psychological, or karmic obstacles. If the issue is physiological, seeking medical assistance will be practical and effective. For these physiological problems, appropriate guidance from a professional therapist or instructor is necessary. More importantly, practitioners must develop confidence in pursuing these treatments. If the problem is psychological, correcting one's perspective can alleviate any issues related to meditation. Mild self-doubt, anxiety, or anger are not severe psychological problems.

If the issue is physiological, it may not be completely treatable.[14] However, it is crucial to recognize that I am highlighting severe and extraordinary situations, and most people will never encounter such problems. Leg pain or the blockage of energy channels are not severe physiological issues at all.

It also depends on individual circumstances to determine whether one can resume the practice after recovering from meditation sickness. If all symptoms have disappeared, continuing the practice is acceptable. However, if any symptoms persist, it is better to refrain from intensive practice until all symptoms have completely diminished.

Question: Is it possible that a person is viewed as mentally abnormal by society, but, in reality, that individual is deeply immersed in a meditative state?

Answer: It is possible. These individuals are neither mentally disturbed nor experiencing meditation sickness. Instead, their perceptions of the world differ from the norm during this period, leading to behaviors and expressions that may seem peculiar. While others might identify them as mentally abnormal, in reality, they are well. This stage is merely transient, and they will eventually return to behaviors considered normal by societal standards.

Question: If practitioners recognize the concept of "non-self" but lack proper guidance, could they experience meditation sickness?

Answer: It is possible. In the absence of an instructor, if a practitioner undergoes an experience of "emptiness," which may not be identical to enlightenment, it may give rise to psychological concerns or confusion. That is why the Chan tradition and Esoteric Buddhism emphasize the importance of having a qualified teacher and the necessity of master-disciple transmission. On the spiritual journey, one will go through a certain process. Exercise caution when self-proclaimed enlightened individuals, lacking a recognized lineage and without qualified training, offer to assist you.

Question: You once mentioned that when we experience anything extraordinary, we should ignore it. I find this suggestion very helpful. You also said that we should consider anyone or anything that helps us as a blessing. I treat anything that supports my practice as a blessing and anything that hinders my path as a demonic force. For me, everything is an integral part of the cultivation.

Answer: When practitioners encounter external interference—whether from people, circumstances, or other living beings—rather than being impeded, they intensify their commitment to diligent practice. In this regard, these should be considered as blessings.

3. Question and Answer with Ven. Thích Nhật Từ[15]

Laywoman: Namo Buddha Śakyamuni! Dear Venerable! I just participated in two meditation retreats, but I have a question, and please help me answer it. One time, after meditating at home—only observing my in-and-out breath flow from the shoulders to the rump in a sitting position for a while, I felt that the upper part of my body disappeared, but I still felt myself sitting and breathed normally. A short time after that, my breath was still normal, yet my body expanded larger and larger. It kept ballooning and ballooning endlessly. Then, I could not feel my breath anymore, and I flew up in the air and over mountains and forests. And when I did not feel my breath at all, I was scared and snapped out of that phenomenon. I did not dare to sit anymore because I thought I had incorrectly practiced meditation. Please explain the phenomenon and what I should do, Venerable!

Ven. Thích Nhật Từ: Let me ask you a question. Have you ever practiced "bio-energy meditation"?[16]

Laywoman: No, I have not.

Ven. Thích Nhật Từ: The phenomenon [you] mentioned is a hallucination caused by wrong contemplative imagining. The essence of observing breath while meditating is to "marry" body and mind. When the body is breathing in, the breath flow goes through the nostril, alar rim, windpipe, chest area, abdomen area, and *dantian* (Viet. *đan điền*). Then, from there, the flow of air goes out. So, the mind must follow the flow of the breath and feel the touch of the breath on each body part.

I usually remind you of the phrase "expand, expand, expand." Breathe in for six seconds and feel the breath coming in to expand the chest, abdomen, and *dantian*. Breathe out and the flow is coming out from *dantian*, abdomen, and chest. Bear that thought in mind! As a result, the mind presents together with inhalation and exhalation. And the mind touches every body part that the breath touches. It is called mindfulness of breathing. If you correctly follow this instruction, the mind cannot "travel" to location A or appear at destination B. Breathing in and seeing the upper part of the body flying up and the lower part heavily weighing down means your practices are wrong—wrong contemplative imagining.

What is the wrong contemplative imagining? It means applying subjective imagination to the process of breathing. If you count breaths, you know how many breaths there are, how fast breathing speed increases, and where the airflow is. That is breath counting, mindfulness of breathing. When you count your breaths and see yourself flying up, it is not correct. It has something to do with imagination.

People with a habit of imagining should not choose variable meditation objects for *samatha* (*thiền chỉ*) meditation. When one changes meditation objects from A to B to C, as a result, the imagining mind keeps "running" to follow meditation objects out of habit. Instead of imagining many scenes as before, one's mind now imagines meditation objects. As your mind runs too much, you cannot focus on *samādhi* (*định*). So, people with wild imaginations should remember this in their head: deeply breathing in, the body and the mind being together; deeply breathing out, the body and the mind being together. Take this technique as a basis to coalesce the body and the mind. They are "loyal" to each other, never separated, and always associated with each other. It is mindful breathing practice correctly. . . .

Perception connects with remembering, thinking, interpreting, assuming, and concluding—many things. Different individuals have different ways of imagining things. The nature of meditation practice is about stopping the process of imagining. *Vipassanā* (*thiền quán*) means seeing the real nature of things inside themselves; then, there is no perception. But because we cannot see through things clearly, we imagine things.

If we are aware of the breath flow inside the body, it is impossible to see the body flying up. Therefore, the body sitting on the ground must be on the ground. It is no way that the body can fly! We should implement a particular thing that fits a specific place and time. Do not be greedy to perform multiple tasks at the same time and place. That is the technique to attain mindfulness—"the right here and the right now," with breath.

Whoever created the "astral projection meditation" is incorrect and straying from what the Buddha taught.[17] They use the mechanism of imagination. When you are sitting, your mind exists with the sitting body. However, if you imagine that you are traveling to some destinations, you use the mechanism of imagination. When you imagine things, you lose mindfulness.

So, again, one more time, you focus on observing the breath flow through the nostril, alar rim, windpipe, chest area, abdomen area, and *dantian*. Six positions, only these six positions, are enough to pay attention to while doing the breath-counting meditation. You count from number one to eighteen for one cycle and then back to number one again. Following this, you surely do not see the body flying up or getting immersed in any strange phenomena, and you definitely feel healthy and peaceful. For people who feel nervous or scared with pounding heartbeat in front of a crowd, when they inhale deeply and exhale strongly and focus on the breath flow coming in and out through these six spots, their heartbeat becomes stable immediately. The brain is comfortable, nervousness and stress decline. It is the result of practicing the breath-counting meditation correctly.

So, take such results as a measurement of whether you meditate correctly or not. Even though you have meditated for a long time, it does not mean you have done it well. If you get into qigong deviation (*tẩu hỏa nhập ma,* see chapter 18),[18] such as seeing yourself flying up, you are doing wrong. You have to adjust back to the correct meditation. Many people do not have the routine of controlling attention. Instead of concentrating on point A, they think about point B. Instead of reciting "NAM MÔ A DI ĐÀ PHẬT" [homage to Amitābha Buddha], in their head, it turns into "NAM MÔ A DI ĐÀ LẠT" [Đà Lạt is a popular tourist city in Vietnam]. [*Laughter.*]

So, after all, this method of practicing mindfulness of breath-counting will bring good results.

Notes

1. Yamada et al. (1982/2008, 224).
2. Jp. *watō* (Ch. *huatou*). There is a debate around the origins of the *watō* practice, also known in Japanese as *kannazen,* which is the meditation of contemplating the main point from a Zen dialogue, or kōan. Some scholars attribute it to Dahui Zonggao (1089–1163), while others trace it back to his teachers Wuzu Fayan (1024–1104) and Yuanwu Keqin (1063–1135). See Broughton and Watanabe (2017). However, Yamada Mumon regards it as an inheritance of Dahui's practice of focusing on *mu* (Ch. *wu*).
3. Jp. *makyō.*
4. I use the name Sheng Yen instead of the Pinyin Shengyan because it is the officially accepted spelling in his community. The rest of my Chinese transliterations are in standard Hanyu Pinyin.
5. For a discussion of the institutional development of Dharma Drum Mountain within a broader context of Taiwanese Buddhism, see Madsen (2007, 85–103).
6. Sheng Yen (2003).
7. The term *chanbing* repeats nineteen times in the Chinese text.
8. Sheng Yen's writings and public speeches are compiled in *The Complete Collection of Dharma Drum,* 2020, http://ddc.shengyen.org. His 1985 talk can be found at https://ddc.shengyen.org/?doc=04-05-022, accessed November 30, 2023. On Zhiyi's description of the Four Elements and Five Viscera, see chapters 6 and 7 of this book.
9. "Treating Meditation-Induced Sickness," *The Complete Collection of Dharma Drum,* 2020, accessed November 30, 2023, https://ddc.shengyen.org/?doc=04-05-022.
10. Đạo Phật ngày nay, "Vài nét về thầy Thích Nhật Từ," *Đạo Phật ngày nay,* n.d., accessed May 28, 2023, https://daophatngaynay.com/vn/thichnhattu.html.
11. In Yamada et al. (2008, 1–48), translated by Francisco Figueroa Medina with permission from the Institute for Zen Studies. The version translated here is from the eighth edition of 2008. This edition includes the same texts as the first edition of 1982, minus a text on preparatory gymnastics.

12. Translated by Dixuan Chen. Dharma Drum Mountain provided the Chinese source, and I extend my appreciation to Dharma Drum Publications and the Chan Meditation Center for granting permission.
13. Sheng Yen often cited the Repentance Verse during meditation retreats, which reads: "The evil deeds I did in the past all originated from beginningless desire, hatred, and ignorance. From actions, words, and thoughts they arose. Now, in front of the Buddha, I seek repentance." See "The Stages of Practicing Buddhist Teachings," *The Complete Collection of Dharma Drum,* 2020, accessed November 30, 2023, https://ddc.shengyen.org/?doc=04-17-019.
14. This statement appears to contradict the previous argument. We are uncertain whether Sheng Yen intended to convey this or if it was an unintended sentence during the conversation.
15. "Vấn đáp: Ảo giác trong khi ngồi thiền," *Thích Nhật Từ official,* YouTube video, 2019, accessed July 21, 2023, https://www.youtube.com/watch?v=oSE_GvAOvIk. Translated by T. D. Nguyen and included here with permission from Ven. Thích Nhật Từ.
16. According to Ven. Thích Nhật Từ, half of the practitioners following the non-Buddhist meditation technique of bioenergy meditation (*thiền trường sinh học*) suffer from hallucinations because they apply the mechanism of imagination in practice (see "Vấn đáp: Lạm dụng cơ chế tưởng trong khi ngồi thiền | Thích Nhật Từ," *Thích Nhật Từ Official,* YouTube video, 2019, accessed July 21, 2023, https://www.youtube.com/watch?v=GqkjcXEtM9w). One popular website promoting bioenergy meditation claims that the method is inconceivably helpful in treating many kinds of illnesses and healing or improving physical and mental health through absorbing positive energy from the universe as well as opening seven chakras inside the body (see "Thiền trường sinh học là gì và ngồi tập thiền như thế nào cho đúng?," *Kim tự tháp,* accessed July 21, 2023, https://kimtuthap.vn/thien-truong-sinh-hoc-la-gi-va-ngoi-tap-thien-nhu-nao-cho-dung).
17. Literally "soul-separated-from-body meditation" (*thiền xuất hồn*), this is a practice associated with the new religion Pháp Lý Vô Vi, founded around the 1940s by a Vietnamese who claims to have learned this spiritual path directly from the Buddha (see "Tiểu sử đức tổ sư Đỗ Thuần Hậu," *Suối đạo vô vi,* accessed July 21, 2023, https://www.suoidaovovi.org/sdvv/tieu-su-duc-to-su-do-thuan-hau/).
18. "Qigong deviation" (Ch. *zouhourumo;* Vn. *tẩu hỏa nhập ma*) is a Chinese concept referring to the state of mental disorders as well as physical illnesses caused by incorrect spiritual or martial art training.

Part III

Contemporary Accounts

Chapter 14

Meditation Madness in Buddhist Myanmar

Ethnographic Notes from Rakhine State

CÉLINE CODEREY

This contribution presents an episode of "meditation madness" I witnessed during fieldwork I conducted in southern Rakhine State, Myanmar, in 2007. Before presenting the case study through a transcript of my fieldwork notes and interview notes, I wish to describe the geopolitical context in which the case took place and to explain the position mental illness has within the local etiological and healing system and its relation to meditation practice. The case presented here was chosen less for its representativity—it is indeed rare to encounter a case of such intensity and seriousness—than for its heuristic interest. Indeed, it displays the plurality of interpretations and medical resorts local people may rely on when confronted with madness and allows us to understand how meditation madness fits into this broader field. It also allows us to see how suffering often carries the traces of a context of sociopolitical marginalization and of social and gender power relations.

Rakhine is one of the seven states of Myanmar, situated on the southwest side of the country bordering India, Bangladesh, and the Bay of Bengal. It is the second-poorest state after the Chin, and the local population mainly lives off fishing and farming. Like all peripheral states, it has historically suffered from the politics of centralization, oppression, and neglect implemented by the Burman central government toward minority ethnic groups. Health care services are highly lacking, especially in specialized sectors like mental health. Before being conquered by the Burmese King Bodawhpaya (1781–1819) and annexed to the rest of the country in 1784, Rakhine (then Arakan) was an independent kingdom, strongly influenced by India. Historians affirm that Rakhine received Buddhism in its different forms directly from India at different times.[1] Rakhine people often claim to hold a version of Buddhism that is purer and less "contaminated" by spirit (*nat*) cults and other "nonorthodox" beliefs than that practiced by Burmans.

Rakhine Buddhists understand health and illness as the expression of order and disorder in the relation between the person and the world, in compliance with the Dhamma, the Buddhist cosmic law.[2] In the local etiological system, mental illness (*seik yawga*) or madness (*a yu*) is defined as an abnormal condition of the mind (*seik*), whereby the mind or the nerves (*ayon gyaw*) are "broken" (*pyet de-*) or "work backward" (*pauk pyan de*). Mental illness is considered a form of *yawga,* a natural disorder produced by an imbalance among the four elements (*dat*) of the body: earth (*pahtawi*), water (*apaw*), fire (*tayzaw*), and wind (*wayaw*).[3] *Yawga* can manifest itself through physiological signs (fever, headache, etc.) or, in the case of a mental disorder, through psychological and behavioral signs (worries, obsessions, shouts, aggressive actions, obscene acts).

The ultimate cause of illness is known to be the imbalance between the four main body elements. The elements are naturally unstable, and yet they tend to veer further out of balance in certain periods of one's life—notably, during childhood, old age, pregnancy, menstruation, and menopause. Besides those conditions, other factors can lead to an imbalance of the body elements: karma, the mind, climate, and diet. These factors are said to act either alone or in combination, reinforcing or neutralizing each other.

Women are considered more vulnerable to mental disorders than men because, supposedly, they are more emotional and because of the significant stress they face as the main person in charge of their family's well-being. Moreover, the menstrual cycle, pregnancy, and giving birth all put them at risk because the impurity of the blood at such times might travel to the brain and poison it.[4]

Mental disorders represent a very special category of illness because of the stigma attached to them. This is, I assume, partly because the symptoms are the exact reverse of qualities highly valued in Buddhism: self-awareness and self-control. They are often seen as an irreversible, incurable condition that, like other incurable conditions, is attributed to a very negative karmic remainder from one's previous lives.

If most people see mental illness as a natural disorder, they also acknowledge that madness-like symptoms are engendered by *payawga* (external disturbance), a category that includes aggressions from witches, sorcerers, or spirits. *Payawga* represents the second main category of illness besides *yawga.* These symptoms are usually behavioral deviance (shouting, crying), mental confusion, or a specific physiological symptom (heavy head, sensation of bloated stomach, blurred vision). Aggressions from witches (*son*) and sorcerers (*auklan hsaya,* "masters of the lower path") can engender symptoms like shouting, running around naked, intense and prolonged crying, and so forth. These usually appear in a sudden and violent way. Even though these symptoms are similar to those of a mental disorder resulting from an imbalance of the body elements, in this case they are not referred to as mental disorders because they lack physiological inscriptions—there is no imbalance of the body elements—and, in most cases, they are just temporary.

My informants agree that although in theory anybody can face a supernatural aggression, this happens only if the karma of the person is temporarily low. And for those who say that the aggression can happen regardless of the karmic condition, they admit that it can affect the person only if the karma is bad.

People agree that every person has a personal spirit (*kosaung nat*) protecting them, and yet this protection is effective only if the person protects one's karma and power (*hpon*) by displaying good moral conduct and staying away from polluting acts and places. When the karma or the power is reduced by the perpetration of an immoral action or through contact with an impure object, the personal *nat* withdraws its protection, leaving the individual exposed to aggressions. Another factor that increases the vulnerability to aggressions is the temporary departure of the soul or vital principle, locally known as "butterfly" (*leikpya*), caused by trauma and nightmares. Finally, mental and physical weakness generated by normal illness, *yawga,* also can make the person vulnerable to aggressions. Yet once again, it is only if the karma is low that an aggression can be effective.

Women are deemed to be more vulnerable to aggressions than men because their *leikpya* is more fragile, pure, and beautiful[5]—a great appeal to invisible forces—and their karma and power lower than men's. They are particularly susceptible to witchcraft as they easily provoke jealousy from other women, especially with regard to marital life. Women are also seen as more impulsive than men and thus more likely to provoke a rival's revenge.

Interestingly, my informants never mention meditation sickness when discussing the general etiology of mental illness. Instead, they speak of it when engaging in conversation about meditation. This form of mental illness partially overlaps and cuts across the categories of *yawga* and *payawga* I have described. People who are knowledgeable about meditation affirm that when a person (especially a layperson) meditates, they should respect their own limits and avoid trying to go further. In other words, they should stay in the "middle way" lest "their mind breaks." From my informants' descriptions, I understand that a person's limits are physiological but also karmic and that the madness that results from surpassing these limits is a sort of karmic retribution. This disorder is, like *yawga* madness, irreversible.

Meditation carries a second risk of madness, which is a form of *payawga.* It is common for meditators to be disturbed by evil spirits while they practice.

Spirits want to counter any attempt people implement to progress in their path toward nirvana because this path is antagonistic to them. Meditation indeed gives access to a superior mental state and extraordinary powers (*eikdi* or *zan*), including hearing voices inaudible to others, seeing invisible things, reading other people's minds, foreseeing the future, and communicating with superior beings.[6] Some meditators use these powers as well as the recitation of formulas, the sharing of loving-kindness, and the fabrication of amulets to counter evil forces. It is also not rare for meditators to sense the presence of evil spirits or even to see them. If one's capacity to control one's mind is too weak, the person might be frightened and attacked by the evil entities. This is particularly true for "masters of the upper path" (*ahtet lan hsaya*), or exorcists, whose main function is precisely to control and counter these forces.[7]

Madness caused by a natural cause can be treated either by traditional herbal medicine (*taingyin hsay*) or by Western medicine (*ingaleik hsay*). Traditional herbal medicine is based on a combination of Buddhist medical knowledge, Ayurveda, and local knowledge. Though everyone in the region has a basic knowledge of this medicine and somehow practices it through the use of homemade remedies or dietary regimens, only traditional doctors who completed specific training have the know-how to cure more complex disorders.[8] In case of madness, hot or cold remedies are used depending on whether the symptoms suggest a hot or cold condition, the former characterized by agitated and violent behavior, shouting, and incoherent speech and the latter by stillness and apathy. In the Thandwe region, numerous traditional doctors are able to intervene for this kind of condition.

Scientific biomedicine treatments for mental health conditions are not available in the Thandwe region, where all medical facilities are highly deficient, and there are no psychiatrists or psychologists. In extreme cases that resist all other treatments, if the family has the means, the patient is brought to Yangon, the main city of the country, either to the psychiatric hospital or to a private psychiatrist.

However, if the condition is believed to have a supernatural cause, then exorcistic practices are the only solution. Most traditional healers (diviners, spirit mediums, monks, specialists in traditional medicine, and exorcists) are able to diagnose a supernatural aggression through their basic astrological knowledge or other divinatory techniques and to provide some basic treatments against it. For instance, they can prescribe astrological offerings (*yadaya*) to improve the karmic and planetary condition of the patient and culinary offerings to the supposed aggressor; some are also able to craft protective amulets as protection from further aggressions.[9] That being said, the diagnosis and treatment of the most powerful aggressions can be conducted only by specialists initiated to the "upper path." Only they possess the mastery of mantra, esoteric diagrams, alchemy, and concentration (*thamahta*) meditation and the ability to summon the *weikza*. *Weikza* are individuals who, through the very mastery of these techniques, have acquired extraordinary powers and succeeded in exiting samsara. These techniques encapsulate the highest Buddhist powers one needs to defeat the evil.[10]

Even monks, whom many see as representing the quintessence of Buddhism, cannot deal with the most difficult cases. It is less a question of power than of status. Monks are allowed to protect themselves and others from evil spirits by expressing loving-kindness and reciting Buddhist protective discourses and formulas, but according to the *Vinaya* they are not allowed to perform exorcisms. This is because an exorcism implies the manifestation of specific powers acquired through meditation and often resorts to supernatural forces, both practices proscribed for monks. Moreover, the neutralization of powerful aggressors often calls for the infliction of pain or even death upon them, irreconcilable with the premise that monks are to refrain from acts of violence.[11] Even though the "upper path" is theoretically forbidden to monks, many are those who have been initiated to this path and learned the *weikza* techniques. Among these is the monk of Watankwai, one of the villages at the core of my ethnography.

Further Reading

Coderey, Céline. Forthcoming 2026. *The Power of Remainder: Politics and Poetics of Healing in Buddhist Myanmar.* University of Hawai'i Press.

Skidmore, Monique. 2002. "Menstrual Madness: Women's Health and Well-Being in Urban Burma." In *Women's Health in Mainland Southeast Asia,* edited by A. Whittaker. Haworth Medical Press.

Spiro, Melford E. 1967. *Burmese Supernaturalism: A Study in the Explanation of Reduction of Suffering.* Prentice-Hall.

Spiro, Melford E. 1971. *Buddhism and Society: A Great Tradition and Its Burmese Vicissitudes.* George Allen and Unwin.

Tambiah, Stanley. 1970. *Buddhism and Spirit Cults in Northeast Thailand.* Cambridge University Press.

The Case of Hla La, Excerpted from my Ethnographic Notes[12]

Hla La is a woman native to Pago, a city in the south of Myanmar. At the time of the incident I describe here in 2007, she was in her mid-thirties. From 2002 to 2007, she lived in Lintha village in Rakhine State, working as a teacher in a tailoring school. Her employer allowed her to live in the school itself. Another woman, Aye Tan Shin, who was employed as a gardener for the same structure, shared the living space with her. For a few months in 2007, I also was living in that house as the owner kindly allowed me to do so. After the incident, Aung Tin Shwe reported to me that when Hla La welcomed me the first day with a cup of coffee she uttered some malefic words on the cup as she wanted to throw misfortune on me.

Hla La was deemed a gentle, generous, and friendly person and a very devout Buddhist, particularly because of her habit of staying up most of the night practicing concentration meditation through the recitation of Buddhist formulae. During my stay in the house, I was indeed always hearing her recitations. She used to start together with her students and then continued alone for a time that became longer each night. This form of meditation is especially common among women. They use it to calm one's mind, increase one's merits, and gain extraordinary powers but also to acquire a certain social recognition in a world where meditation—in its traditional, silent breathing form—is still more associated with (monastic) men. To recite for the entire night, however, is something rare, which might trigger some suspicions. For Aye Tan Shin and me, sleep became impossible. After a few days, we decided to kindly ask Hla La if she could soften her voice when she recited.

The following days, Aye Aye Pyone, a friend of mine, came to pick me up at home. Later, Aye Tan Shin told me that every time, after we left, Hla La ordered the girls to throw water on the stairs where we walked and to go up and down three times. When I later talked to the students, they denied washing the stairs and affirmed that Hla La did it herself. However, they admitted having followed the second order. These gestures were aimed at purifying the stairs from contact with people considered to be "evil spirits." To another villager who arrived at the house on a different occasion, Hla La shouted, "Go away evil spirit (*mekaungsowa*)!" and then threw water on the stairs. Another time, Aye Tan Shin told me that one day, when I was away, Hla La ordered the students to climb onto my bed and walk on it with bare feet. Feet being the lower part of the body—both physically and symbolically—this gesture was meant to "pollute" my bed and bring me misfortune as a consequence.

One evening, with her students gathered around her, she attempted to invoke the *weikza* Bo Ming Aung into her body, and acting as a medium, she offered the girls the chance to ask him questions through her. As a person who reached the highest spiritual level and who got released from samsara, the *weikza* Bo Ming Aung is almost omniscient and able to see people's futures. Most lay people and healers affirm that *weikza* do not possess but simply inspire via mental contact. They associate possession with territorial spirits (*nat*) and *nat* mediums, who they deem inferior. Anyway, two of the students addressed some questions to him about the results of their math exam, explaining that they felt they did poorly. First, Bo Ming Aung replied, "Of course you failed the exams; you are Rakhine and hence you are useless." Yet he then changed his words and stated, "Do not worry, you did pass your exams." It seems to me that Hla La, who is ethnically Burman, used the facade of Bo Ming Aung to express her negative thoughts and feelings toward Rakhine people. "Bo Ming Aung" then offered the students the chance to learn how to meditate, which they accepted. After a short session, the girls were sent back to bed, and Hla La continued her solitary recitation meditation. For three nights in a row, this scene was repeated: the invocation of Bo Ming Aung, answers to questions, meditation.

On the morning of the third day, I saw Hla La and the girls near the buddha altar facing a coconut with a lit candle on it. Hla La was talking about Bo Ming Aung in a strange and repetitive manner. Aung Tin Shwe called me in distress to show me her room: The door lock was broken, and water had been poured into the room. Again, a purifying act. That day, I went to Thandwe market as planned, yet inside I was feeling deeply concerned. From an interview I had with the students later, I learned that that day at eight o'clock, while the girls were cooking, Hla La called one of them to clean the buddha altar. The student then told the others that when she was accomplishing that, she felt strange, as if she were drunk, and began to mentally repeat Buddhist words. At that moment Hla La approached her and hit her on the leg. The two stared into each other's eyes. Hla La's eyes changed and became the eyes of a mad person. Sitting on her bed, hair down, she grabbed the girl and hit her head on the floor. Terrified and injured, the girl did not dare move from the ground or look her teacher in the eyes "because they were so frightening." The other girls, though, witnessing what was happening, were immobilized and unable to react.

Around 11 a.m., Hla La asked them to go out and buy bottles of water. They obeyed without realizing that they could take advantage of the opportunity to flee. When they returned, Hla La told them, "Two evil spirits have come to the house. Go away!" She then kicked the bottles the students had brought her and sent them back to buy new ones, handing them one thousand kyat to do so. When the students returned for the second time, Hla La put the new bottles on the buddha altar. She ordered them to prepare ten balls of rice and tea leaves to give to the other girl who was still in the room and to line them up in front of her. She then fed the girl three times with a spoon and touched her body with the spoon. At the end of the meal, Hla La started again to hit the girl, stopping only after four hours. At a certain point in the afternoon, Hla La announced to the girls that there would be a wedding, a wedding between Hla La and a man. She specified that she was not Hla La but Bo Ming Aung and claimed that a certain student was Hla La and another the groom. Then she ordered the other students to recite a Buddhist formula (*gatha*) fifty times in front of the so-called Hla La; she tied the hands of the spouses with a turban. Then, with a parasol, a ruler, and scissors in her hands, she left the room and asked the girls to follow her.

This episode is quite exceptional; I have never encountered in my fieldwork or in the literature a wedding officiated by a *weikza* or by a medium incarnating one. Although, it is common for territorial spirits (*nat*) to marry people they fall in love with and turn them into their mediums.

At 4 p.m., Hla La told the girls that if they wanted, they could go home and take a shower and then come back. When they left the house, their minds were not normal; they did not realize what had just happened. But the moment an old lady they met on the street touched their arm, their minds "returned to normal." My field assistant commented that Hla La had probably been bewitched and that the same witch who had attacked her was controlling the students' mind, or else it was Hla La herself controlling their minds. Once the girls reached their home, they told their families what was happening at the school. The sister of the beaten girl ran to the school to help her sister. From outside the building, she begged Hla La, "Teacher, please, release my sister," but Hla La replied, "I am not the mistress; evil spirit go away!" She then asked her prisoner to remove the candles and incense from the altar, and while the student was doing so, she hit her with a stick. The girl's sister outside told her again to free her sister, but Hla La responded that her sister had already returned home. The girl asked her again not to hit the sister, to which Hla La replied that she was not Hla La but Aye Aye Pyone (the friend who often picked me up from the house). When the victim's entire family and other villagers arrived at the house, Hla La threatened them with scissors, saying "All of you, evil spirits, go away!" The victim's sister asked Hla La for the number of the school's manager, but Hla La refused to provide it. When the girl threatened to call the police, Hla La gave her the number. But when they called the manager, he was not available. The girl then called the police, begging to come save her sister's life.

When the manager, informed of the fact, finally arrived, Aung Tin Shwe reported what was happening. The manager entered the house and ordered someone to take the scissors from Hla La's hands. Hla La came out of the house, her fingers injured by scissor cuts, threatening everyone around her; she then stopped a man on a motorbike, asking him to take her to the Aureum Hotel, a five-minute drive from her home. He agreed to do so, but along the way he realized something was not normal as Hla La was delirious and referred to him as her husband. He thus stopped in front of the Lintahr Oo

Hotel. There came the village chief, the police, and others. Together, they tried to contain her. In fact, she was walking around with her hair down, looking at people with fiery eyes and screaming. When the situation settled down, the villagers took Hla La back to her house. Yet that very evening she also hit Aye Tan Shin, who then had to go to the dispensary to have her wounds treated.

The Watankwai monk told me that the night of the accident, the sister of the girl who had been beaten came to see him. She explained the situation to the monk: Her sister was frightened and was not speaking to anyone. By listening to the girl's condition, the monk understood that something was abnormal. Yet when he calculated the girl's horoscope, he saw that she was in a lucky period, so the problem could only be minor. He suggested the sister make an offering (*khosa*) behind the house: a cup with two little balls, one of green tea leaf and one of rice. After the offering, the girl was fine. The monk explained to me that *khosa* is a traditional practice used in case a person is possessed or troubled by a spirit and that if the girl had a spirit in her body, this one would have left after eating the offering. It is commonly agreed that one can be possessed only if one's karma is temporary low, yet some people admit that the karma can suddenly drop if the person commits a mistake. To justify the monk's prescription, we can assume it was hypothesized that the girl had committed a mistake that caused her karma to drop, making her vulnerable to aggressions.

The same evening, after the victim's sister had left, the monk noticed that he had an insect on his neck; he thought that it was strange as those insects usually stayed on plants. So he threw it to the ground and with the wax of a candle he tried to kill it, but the insect survived and escaped. The monk thought that it was the *mekaungsowa* that had come out of the body of the girl and was coming to take revenge on him in the form of an insect. At midnight the brother of the beaten girl screamed out loud. His mind was not normal, and it was assumed that a foreign entity possessed him. Indeed, the boy said he wanted the monk to offer him five candles (the object with which the monk had tried to kill the evil spirit) and flowers and that only if the monk offered these things would he forgive him. The family brought the boy to the monastery, where the monk, without making any calculations, gave him the items required, and the boy recovered. The monk emphasized that it was not for the offering that the *mekaungsowa* left but because it was afraid of him as a monk.

For a month after these events, the school was closed, and the girls were sent home. Aye Tan Shin and I moved to another building. Hla La continued to live in the school, alone. For the first few days, some village women were with Hla La all the time. Then they came time to time, particularly to bring her food. Right in front of the school was a tea shop. In the days following the incident, people sat there, often looking toward the house, laughing and making fun of the fact that Hla La claimed to have Bo Ming Aung in her body.

According to some villagers, a few days after the incident a taxi driver, a friend of Hla La, took her to the doctor. The doctor asked her questions, but as other people were around, she refused to answer until they were asked to leave the room. After a little exchange, the doctor established that her mind was not normal as a consequence of her lack of sleep and excessive meditation practice. He prescribed her some medication, but she refused to take it. He then told her that if she did not take them, he would have to take her to Yangon (to the psychiatric hospital).

In the following days, Hla La alternated between moments of normality, where she did not remember what happened and calmly told people who asked that the school was closed because of the government, and moments of abnormality, where she would speak in a delirious way, mentioning Bo Ming Aung or Aye Aye Pione or send curses to passersby. For example, a few days after the event, seeing me and my assistant passing in front of the house, Hla La said to us, "Bad spirits go away!," "Here are two witches, Bo Ming Aung, chase them away!," and even "I wish you a car accident!"

Hla La's episode affected the entire village because of its seriousness, duration, and scale. In the weeks following the episode, several different hypotheses were formulated regarding the reason for Hla La's slippage, some relating to madness, others to a supernatural aggression by a territorial spirit (*nat*), an evil spirit (*meikhsa, makaungsowa*), or a witch.

The most widespread opinion as to what happened to Hla La was that she went mad (*a yu*). There were several hypotheses for this etiology. The majority of people believed that the reason for her madness was fatigue caused by the habit of spending the nights in meditation with little or no sleep. Such a habit is likely to weaken and destabilize the mind. Because of this, her mind was said to have become "not normal," "to have broken." A second hypothesis was that in her religious practice, she tried to follow a path "too high" for her. Several informants told me that "Buddha advised us to follow the middle path. On the other hand, some people aim to go higher than their abilities allow. Excessive meditation and recitations are only beneficial if you can control your mind; if you lose control, you get mad." A third hypothesis was that her madness originated from jealousy: "Living alone in a big house, without a husband, eager to become rich and famous, dissatisfied with her work, and jealous of others, her mind was always unstable and at some point broke down." Another hypothesis was that Hla La was entering menopause.

Interestingly, no one believed that Hla La was embodying Bo Ming Aung as she was claiming. First, people said that if Bo Ming Aung really was in her body, he would have done something good, not hit the girl or cursed Aye Aye Pione. Besides, everyone was of the opinion that even if beneficent entities (*bodaw*) like Bo Ming Aung established mental contact with women, they would never possess them.

When I interviewed the students about the incident, most of them were reluctant to speak at first. Although they had been victims of Hla La's violent behavior, they struggled to utter the word "madness" or "possession." This is likely because madness and possession are quite stigmatized in Rakhine society. Having such a condition strongly contrasts with the status of teachers, one of the highest and most respected professions in Rakhine and Burmese society. Moreover, it also seemed that the owner of the house and the employer of Hla La, a man of high reputation and authority, told the girls not to speak about the fact to others. He presumably wanted to protect his reputation.

After three weeks, Hla La's employer arranged for her to be brought to Yangon, where she had access to proper psychiatric treatment and slowly recovered. That said, the house remained haunted by the memory of this episode for quite some time.

Notes

1. See Bernot (1967, 129) and Gutman (2001, 26).
2. Local etiologies (not limited to mental illness) have been described extensively in my previous works. See in particular Coderey (2015, 267–269; 2017, 244–247; 2020, 9–12; 2023, 354–357; forthcoming 2026).
3. Mental disturbance caused by either natural or supernatural factors is described in my forthcoming book.
4. This association between the menstrual cycle and madness has been examined in detail by Skidmore (2002).
5. Spiro (1967, 147).
6. See also Coderey (2012, 190).
7. See also Coderey (Forthcoming 2026).
8. See also Coderey (2012, 187).
9. These practices are described in detail in Coderey (2012, 193; 2017).
10. The specificity of the *weikza* is described in detail in Coderey (2012, 204–205; 2015, 249–251).
11. Coderey (2012); Tambiah (1970, 322, 328, 334).
12. Notes written in 2007 while conducting fieldwork in Rakhine State, Myanmar.

Chapter 15

"Netflix Dilemma"

An Interview About Mindfulness Deviation with a Thai Bhikkhuni

DAPHNE WEBER

This piece is from an interview conducted with a Thai Theravada bhikkhuni (female monastic), during my seven-month stay at a bhikkhuni temple in Thailand. Luang Pi, the honorific used for most Thai monks, is the meditation teacher at this temple. Though Theravada bhikkhuni are not officially recognized by the overseeing institutions of Thai Buddhism, many women come to this temple to learn meditation from Luang Pi since she understands the impact of gender roles and how meditation can help provide understanding for womens' experiences.

Many practitioners recall having intense visual experiences during meditation when they are forced to sit in silence. Luang Pi refers to those visual phenomena, formally known as *nimita,* as "Netflix." The term "Netflix Dilemma" refers to the recollection of past experiences, such as a painful breakup or a parent scolding them in the past, through a series of such images that present themselves like a Netflix show. The meditator may continuously engage with the images, much like binge-watching a Netflix series. When continuous engagement with negative images entices people to change their worldview or daily habits, it presents a dilemma on how to move forward. Hence, the Netflix Dilemma. In such instances of intense visual experiences, Luang Pi tells meditators to simply acknowledge the presence of the images but to come back to the meditation. Luang Pi tells people to calm their *citta,* the body-mind-heart connection that is drawn into the dilemma, and to refocus it on the breath. The goal is *upekkha,* or equanimity toward all events and resulting reactions.

Though Luang Pi does not have many students who experience adverse reactions when practicing with her, she acknowledges the salience of what she calls "mindfulness deviation" for people who practice without a teacher. For example, if people learn how to meditate through YouTube, they cannot actively engage with a teacher when they experience images of distress. Without a teacher, novice meditators can take their Netflix images as real. For example, if a student sees a ghost lurking in the depths of their consciousness during meditation, they may think they are seeing an actual ghost and are being attacked. A teacher would likely tell the student that the ghost is not real, as Luang Pi does, but is perhaps a manifestation of the guilt provoked by the corresponding "Netflix show" (i.e., guilt felt about an event recalled during meditation). Without this insight, meditators might create routines in daily life to repel ghosts or protect themselves. While this might seem like a harmless reaction, it becomes detrimental when the meditator becomes all-consumed by these routines, even missing work and altering hygiene habits.

Therefore, a meditation teacher is the most effective way to prevent and remedy this particular variety of mindfulness deviation. According to Luang Pi, the lack of a meditation teacher to interpret a meditator's *nimitta* can ultimately lead to meditation sickness. When considering the male-centric leadership roles of Theravada Buddhism, especially in authoritative capacities, this interview with Luang Pi highlights how women may be more prone to meditation-related troubles because they lack official teachers who can take them on as students. Many women I interviewed recounted their struggle to find a teacher to instruct them in meditation, telling me that male monks are prohibited from taking on individual female students. Social and monastic regulations prohibit individual mentorship from male monks to female students.

It is important to note that, in Luang Pi's opinion, mindfulness deviation can also come from attachment to the euphoric feeling meditation sometimes induces. When people reach a certain level of consciousness, they may experience *piti,* a meditative state of euphoria. According to Luang Pi, *piti* can lead to problems as people become so attached to the sensation that their sole aim in future meditations is to cultivate that state. But the goal of meditation is not *piti:* The goal is to reach a state of *upekkha,* equanimity toward events that can provoke volatile emotions and generate bad karma. Ultimately, *upekkha* can lead to the end of rebirth and eventual enlightenment. If meditators are stuck on the feeling of euphoria, they are cultivating an attachment to happiness and comfort and derailing their path to *upekkha* and enlightenment.

Further Reading

Brown, Sid. 2001. *Journey of One Buddhist Nun: Even Against the Wind.* SUNY Press.

Cassaniti, Julia. 2015. *Living Buddhism: Mind, Self, and Emotion in a Thai Community.* Cornell University Press.

Cook, Joanna. 2010. *Meditation in Modern Buddhism: Renunciation and Change in Thai Monastic Life.* Cambridge University Press.

Lindberg-Falk, Monica. 2007. *Making Fields of Merit: Buddhist Female Ascetics and Gendered Orders in Thailand.* University of Washington Press.

Schedneck, Brooke. 2023. *Living Theravada: Demystifying the People, Places, and Practices of a Buddhist Tradition.* Shambhala.

Interview with Luang Pi: A Thai Bhikkhuni who Teaches Meditation[1]

DW: Sometimes, when people meditate, they might do it wrong and it can send them into mindfulness deviation (*sati piian bay*). Why do some people have that problem? What causes it and how do you get rid of it?

LP: Some people don't have that meditation deviance, because when you meditate, you should be mindful of what you're observing. I call that the mental object: your breath or some other object. Normally people's minds are jumping around, and they get used to that. So, when you sit in meditation, you have so many stories and movies in your head, like watching a movie. When it comes to meditation, you just train the mind in a different way. Bring it back to the true nature of the mind, which is just simply noting, or knowing; not interpreting, not criticizing, not giving value; just knowing in the present moment. So, when they start meditating, they learn. For example, they are told to focus on their breath at the tip of their nose.

It depends on the mind of these people. Some people, they have a very chaotic mind. So many thoughts come through their head. They might take quite a long time to come to a one-pointed state of mind. But those people who have been trained for a while, or those whose nature is not to have a chaotic mind, they can reach that one-pointed state of the mind in a shorter period.

DW: How do we know that we've reached that one-pointed state of mind?

LP: Normally, when you start, your breath is very rough. Then it becomes very soft and gentle. It might seem like you're not breathing at all. That's because the mind comes together with the body. The mind is anchored, so it wouldn't note something from the outside or something from inside like a mental formation.

These mental formations come from perception . . . Sometimes we call it *nimitta.*[2] *Nimitta* is not a dream, even though people call it that. It's just a sign. The sign comes through as pictures, sounds, smells, tears that you feel. *Nimitta* is simply the phenomena that happens at that particular moment. But those who are mindful, they don't stray from their anchor at the tip of nose.

They maintain their breath. That's why they don't experience *nimitta.* But those who do experience these mental formations sometimes mistake that image as something real. It looks so real and so scary at that particular moment that they take it as real and get shocked and feel out of sorts. But some people experience good *nimittas* and like the feeling.

Nimitta formation depends totally on their mental formation, and sometimes they mistake it as real.[3] So, if nobody tells them or helps them to get out of that state, they could possibly go mad. Sometimes the thought appears like a movie or like storytelling. That's why I always ask them to simply note that movie arising and come back to the breath again. That's how the *nimitta* goes away. Those who practice this way rarely sidetrack or deviate from the practice.

DW: It sounds like it's important to have a teacher to guide somebody through meditation.[4]

LP: Yes, exactly. That's why we interview our students about their meditations. That's how I heard about "Netflix" mental formations. The first time I heard that, I said "That's your mental formation! [*laughing*] You watch Netflix too much!" And some jump from this thought to that thought, and then they say this never comes to an end. It's because they don't know where the mental formation starts and ends. It keeps continuing with different stories that come to mind. They need to have intention and a plan for knowing when those mental formations start and stop. Make the plan for how to stop it so the mind doesn't keep wondering.

Actually, it's not the mind. The function of the mind is just simply nothing; not to think, but the thinking is there. But people nowadays, particularly this generation, are addicted to the thinking process. That's why they cannot get out of the loop where they keep thinking, thinking, thinking. So, they don't really know how the mind functions. Once that thinking process ceases completely, even for a moment, you will know the true function of the mind is just simply noting. For example, if you hear a bird during meditation, you should simply note the sound and stop there. But we tend to identify everything all the time. "Oh, that's the sound of the bird. Oh, that's this kind of bird" and keep going through that thinking process. Some people love the sound; others find it annoying. So your mind just swings, swings, swings back and forth. But you just simply need to sit and hear. There's just the sound. Just neutral.

DW: When people cling to those sounds or their Netflix images, they take it as good or bad, depending on their experiences. If they take that image or sound as real, as a threat, then what happens?

LP: They get so scared! Some people say they see a ghost or something like that. Something disgusting or whatever. It's because one technique for practice is contemplating on a dead body. Then, that becomes so real for them. They get scared. That's why they get out of control. The mind is out of control because it's so, so clear and real in their mind. Even our students, they keep saying "Oh, there are ghosts! I can hear them!" and then they work off of that information. But I just tell them come back to the breath. They don't need to observe that. It's just their mind that is lying to them.

DW: So, meditation sickness happens to the people who engage with the images?

LP: Yes. Some people are so scared of ghosts. One of our visitors said, "Oh, I'm so scared of ghosts. Would you put me in the room next to somebody else? I can't stay by myself because I'm so scared of the dark, and in the dark, there are ghosts." And I say "How do you know? You don't, because it's a mental formulation."

DW: But at a certain point it can make somebody mad (*baa*)?

LP: Yeah, usually when they are faced with something they are scared of they can go down the wrong path. But if it is something they like, they cling onto it. They say, "Oh, next time I want to see this," and I only ask them "is that true?"

So it's about mindfulness.[5] If you have strong mindfulness, you rarely experience meditation sickness. It's very rare. I don't know the rate . . . maybe one out of 1000. We don't have that scientific proof. I have heard of somebody who practices and then has very strange behavior. They say, "I can hear this very annoying sound in my ears" and keeps it in mind while meditating. And I say "No, just let go of that sound and come back to your breathing." Sometimes it can be physical sickness that causes ringing in the inner ears and that needs to get fixed. But sometimes it's just their mind clinging to the sound and lingering on it.

DW: Is it a weak *citta*[6] that attaches to the sounds or images?

LP: Yes. But if they are very mindful, they aren't scared of anything. They just know things as they are, and they know that's a causing effect of that. It's not like magic. [laughs]

DW: So, what did you do for the woman who heard the ringing?

LP: She took a silent retreat for five days. She told me during that time she made very good progress because the ringing was gone.

DW: How did she get rid of it?

LP: I asked her to focus on her breathing and not to pay attention to the sound.

DW: The other day, the abbess said a student might be experiencing meditation sickness because she keeps seeing blooming and dying lotuses during meditation. How have you helped her?

LP: I always tell her "Don't get sidetracked." Sometimes it's her preference to have these visions, but I gave her a warning. I told her "This is not the truth."[7] Sometimes, if we get too involved in those visions, we lose control and get out of sorts. So, we can just warn her, but whether she takes our advice is not up to us. We have done our part. . . .

I think meditation sickness is very rare, unless you don't have a teacher to give guidance. This is very dangerous nowadays because more people are meditating. They watch YouTube and then practice according to Teacher YouTube. But Teacher YouTube is not present with them. So, when the student experiences something they misunderstand and don't know how to approach, they get stuck on a wrong path that could be very harmful to them. When I look at YouTube, it's a double-edged sword. It's very dangerous. And most Teacher YouTubes don't teach according to the Buddha's teachings.

DW: Is it hard to bring people back from the wrong path? For example, if you have somebody who's been practicing wrong for five years and then they come to the temple, how do you fix them?

LP: It takes some time. I just ask them to empty their glass first, empty their previous knowledge about meditation. There are people who have practiced for more than ten years and say they are good at meditation. But when it comes to cultivating wisdom, they haven't done that much. So, they just maintain their happiness in concentration and say that's enough for them.

DW: Like the euphoric feeling some people get during meditation?

LP: Yeah, or even sometimes when you attain a particular state of mind and you feel joy. With this current group of students, some are very joyful. Tears come up to their eyes and I know they experience joy. Some people shake, their body shakes, swaying a little bit. It's a kind of *piti* [i.e., bliss-like energy] they experience, but they don't know it's *piti*. They think there is another cause for the tears or shaking. That's the wrong conception.

DW: Isn't *piti* a good thing, though? Isn't it a good feeling?

LP: [*Hesitant*] Yes, sometimes you feel goosebumps, tears come up to your eyes, swaying body, and you feel a good feeling throughout your body. You get really light, light body and mind. If they don't know about *piti*, some people get stuck there. So, I tell them just to observe the feeling, how it rises and falls. Once they have the right information, they can get through each step and make progress.

DW: But it could be hard for some people to accept that information, right?

LP: Yes, it can be hard for some people. One of my students said she got a headache and stiff body every time she meditated. She happened to meditate in front of me one day and I saw that the way she sat was too stiff and she was too focused. I said, "No wonder you got a headache! Now, let go of that posture. Don't lift your shoulder, even when you want to lift it. Keep the shoulders neutral and don't focus too much on your breath. Just feel the breath and observe." She followed my instructions, and the headache and stiffness were gone. Sometimes people experience blocks in meditation because of their physical posture. That's why I emphasize how to sit properly.

DW: What is the hand posture again? Left hand holds the right hand?

LP: . . . Yes, there is a small circle between our palms and thumbs. That is where the energy is kept. When you sit in meditation, the energy tries to scatter because it is very chaotic. But when you calm the mind, that energy gathers together like a beam. For example, a flashlight. If you're too far, the light is very dim and scattered. But when you hold it closer, the light is concentrated and more intense. In meditation, you are controlling that energy.

DW: So, your meditation pose becomes a conduit for the energy, which we keep contained and connected by enjoining our hands. Got it. In another meditation retreat, the teacher told me to manipulate my breath during meditation. Breathe fast and sharp, or long and slow. What does that do?

LP: You notice the difference between breaths. Then you know when your breath becomes slower, you tend to have more consciousness and more mindfulness. But if you start with a very light breath, you cannot notice the difference. It's the nature of the physical body to comfortably adjust the length of the breath. So, you know your state when it's shorter, but when you take a long breath, it's a new experience. The mind swings like that with the breath. When the breath is shorter, the mind becomes more focused, focused, focused. I ask my students to do body scanning, moving their *citta* consciousness through all thirty-two parts of the body. If they cannot keep their consciousness during the scan, they have to go faster. . . .

The trick of this technique is to see the truth of this yucky body. If you see the body is yucky, you can let go of it. But there can be side effects from this meditation practice. The Buddha came to a monastery and wondered why there were so few monks. He found out they were using this technique, discussing their disgust with their bodies, and killed themselves or asked someone else to kill them [see chapter 2].[8] That's the side effect.[9]

DW: So, this would be an example of what could lead to meditation sickness, right? Because they were not guided through their meditation?[10]

LP: Yes, that's the side effect. They did not go mad, like mentally crazy, but they felt sick of their body and didn't want their bodies anymore. That's why you just observe when you do the body scan. You shouldn't feel positive or negative towards this body or its parts. You should just know it as it is.

Notes

1. Luang Pi, interview by author, April 27, 2023, at a bhikkhuni temple (location withheld for interviewee's anonymity) through a combination of Thai and English.
2. Robert Buswell and Donald Lopez (2013) define *nimitta* as a sign or meditative image. Their definition is in line with Luang Pi's explanation. Importantly, Buswell and Lopez note that *nimitta* in a Theravada meditation context relates to an advanced mental state of concentration.
3. I argue in Weber (2024) that these reactions or mental formations come from early childhood training in socioemotional contexts. The *nimitta* that women experience may be interpreted as negative or positive, depending on their early childhood socioemotional training.
4. The importance of a meditation teacher becomes clear at the end of the translation, especially as it relates to gender. See note 10 for more detail.
5. For an overview of the many uses and implications of mindfulness in Asia, see Cassaniti (2018).
6. *Citta* generally refers to consciousness, but as a subject it takes on connotations of selfhood. I am partial to Jointu Chakma's (2016) definition of the *citta* as "the basic and fundamental bound of a person containing the physical and psychological strata of human body and mind" (95), as it shows the *citta*'s relationship between body and emotion. Broader discussions about rebirth also center on the clinging *citta* as the motivating force to find a new body (Rahula 1974, 33; Collins 1982, 214). So we might refer to the *citta* as the continuous identity in a cycle of rebirth and death.
7. "Truth" in Buddhism is often referred to within the dichotomy of "conventional" or "ultimate." In the context of Theravada bhikkhunis, Suwanna Satha-Anand's (1999) chapter offers a summary of the position.
8. The *Vinaya,* the monastic code of conduct, details a rule forbidding monks from suicide and murder. If a monk fails to follow this rule, they must disrobe.
9. It should be noted that Luang Pi is not referring to suicide or murder as a general side effect of meditation. Rather, what Luang Pi states is that without someone to interpret *nimitta* alongside life experiences, a meditator may spiral into a depression or mental breakdown to the point of self-harm, citing the *Vinaya* explanation as an example.
10. My future research will emphasize the importance of gendered mentorship in meditation practice to alleviate the negative effects of meditation, a topic that has generally been understudied in Buddhist studies. Implicit to this argument is the prevailing cultural belief of female rebirth as a karmic consequence and how these bhikkhunis' meditation techniques and explanations reconstitute gender roles in Buddhism.

Chapter 16

Shingon Perspectives on Troublesome States of Consciousness

An Interview with Asahi Seichō

NATHAN JISHIN MICHON

Asahi Seichō is a Shingon priest and abbot of Risō-in, a small temple in rural Hiroshima Prefecture, Japan. He previously served as an abbot of Shingon temples in Sacramento and Los Angeles and has taught numerous students on both sides of the Pacific. In Hiroshima, Risō-in is a *kitō* temple, which means that rather than leading a congregation of regular members who come for services like funerals and memorials, Asahi primarily conducts ritual ceremonies for those who come to the temple with specific needs and troubles.[1] His interview below often reflects such circumstances, and he refers to examples of people coming for such services numerous times. Related to the issues of difficult and challenging contemplative experiences, Asahi often speaks from the perspective of how he uses his own Shingon contemplative practices to help others going through such difficulties. However, he also provides some tools and frameworks that could be helpful to a practitioner dealing with such conditions. To better understand Asahi's many Shingon references, a brief introduction to some of the key people, practices, and terms would be beneficial.

Shingon Buddhism is a branch of Vajrayana Buddhism brought to Japan by Kūkai (779–835) during the early 800s. At the time, Kūkai helped rewrite the language of Japanese religiosity and ritual dynamics.[2] Shingon Buddhist practice is often said to center around the Three Mysteries of body, speech, and mind. Shingon practitioners try to purify these three aspects, respectively, through mudra (ritualized hand gestures), mantra, and visualization.[3]

One of the key tools that bring together many of the elements of these contemplative exercises is a set of two complex mandalas known as the Mandala of

Two Worlds (Ryōkai Mandara). These two, the Womb World Mandala and the Diamond (Vajra) World Mandala, respectively, are said to be like two sides of the same coin, representing the physical and spiritual realms. In the center of each is Mahāvairocana Buddha, whom Shingon teachings refer to as a personification of all the purity, light, and goodness of the universe rather than an actual historical buddha. The mandalas consist of many other buddhas, bodhisattvas, and other figures. Each of these figures can also be represented in the mandalas by a particular sacred object or Sanskrit letter, which symbolizes the figures' vibration in relation to the contemplative ritual practices.

The power of sound and its vibrations are connected to the Sanskrit letters themselves as well as the mantras produced by tying several of those sounds together.[4] Asahi's interview responses below also reflect his views of the power of sound through mantra, the way Sanskrit letters themselves are used in visualization as representations of particular vibrations and the ways different syllables can be used during Shingon's contemplative rituals.

When people become Shingon Buddhist priests, a central part of the training is an intensive four-part process called Four-Fold Training (Shidō-kegyō). This involves in-depth learning of various chants and central ritual aspects of the tradition focused around the Three Mysteries mentioned above. Each portion of the training focuses on one particular complex ritual. During the fourth section, Shingon priests learn a fire ritual called *goma* (Skt. *homa*).[5]

Although many *goma* ritual components come from Vedic Hindu origins, they have taken on Buddhist characteristics. The fire in Shingon represents the burning away of the defilements of greed, aversion, and ignorance, but it also serves to help invite or connect the practitioner to certain figures of the mandala. As Richard Payne notes, not only in Japan but across cultures that use the ritual, the ceremonial lead utilizes the fire of *goma* to convey offerings (such as leaves, beans, and water) to a deity in expectation of a quid pro quo, usually making requests or prayers in exchange.[6]

One of the primary figures that Shingon priests summon through the *goma* ritual is called Acala Vidyārāja (Fudō Myō-ō). Acala is often depicted as a fierce, fanged figure with fire behind him, holding a sword in one hand and a rope in the other. The ferocity of the image, however, is symbolic of what we might describe as "tough love." Shingon also views Acala as an alternate image of Mahāvairocana, the above-described central figure of the mandala, representing the purity and light of the universe. Whereas Mahāvairocana might be viewed as the gentle side of this purity and light, Acala is the wrathful side. For this reason, Acala can be an appropriate image for ritual contemplations focused on seeking out and eliminating problems.[7] Many forms of *goma* can be found in the Shingon tradition, depending on the issue someone might be dealing with, but they are all ultimately forms of the ritualized meditation and methods used and referenced by Asahi Seichō.

Further Reading

Oda, Ryuko. 1992. *Kaji: Empowerment and Healing in Esoteric Buddhism.* Mitsumonkai.

Payne, Richard K., and Michael Witzel, eds. 2015. *Homa Variations: The Study of Ritual Change Across the Longue Durée.* Oxford University Press.

Shinohara, Koichi. 2014. *Spells, Images, and Maṇdalas: Tracing the Evolution of Esoteric Buddhist Rituals.* Columbia University Press.

Unno, Mark. 2004. *Shingon Refractions: Myōe and the Mantra of Light.* Wisdom.

Winfield, Pamela. 2005. "Curing with Kaji: Healing and Esoteric Empowerment in Japan." *Japanese Journal of Religious Studies* 32 (1): 107–130.

Interview with Asahi Seichō[8]

NM: Meditation experiences are not always positive. What tools are in place within the Shingon tradition to help prevent people from having negative meditative experiences or to help them deal with such experiences that occur?

AS: Regarding tools, I think it is the Three Mysteries: body, speech, and mind. They can be good tools to find the problems, and also to lead us to freedom. If you examine those problems from your perspective and imagine that you are seeing from another's perspective who is with you, and also a third-person perspective [looking at yourself objectively], then you have three ways to see. Then, you can apply that to body through mudras, speech through mantra, and mind through visualization. So the Three Mysteries are tools. And without using those Three Mysteries, it is almost impossible to fully solve problems. If you leave any problem as it is, then it doesn't change. It doesn't do anything.

But, at the same time, those are the things that can create problems if used improperly. If you use them unskillfully, then you can double your anger. So it depends completely upon how you use those Three Mysteries. In terms of other tools, a mandala could be a tool, and *vajras,*[9] as well as icon images [of buddhas and other beings]. Anything could be a good tool to find out what the problem is and how to solve the problem. But without proper understanding, a picture is just a picture. It doesn't do anything. But if pictures have *both* proper understanding and skillful means, then it can work. It is just like a map. A map represents the earth. If you know how to read the map, and how to use it, you can choose the right or best path to your goal. But if you don't understand how to read a map, it doesn't help you at all. So from that perspective, anything can be a good tool: pictures, mandalas, *vajras,* bells. But you have to know how to use them. . . .

NM: What potential dangers can exist if people use these practices wrong or don't know how to use the practices?

AS: This Vajrayana ritual connects both with inner energy and outer energy and sometimes that is something you shouldn't connect to. For example, it is like a radio. You could enjoy listening to many stations. However, if you tune it wrong, then what you hear is just noise. Those things can happen.

NM: So people's practice can sometimes lead to getting aligned to a wrong frequency?

AS: Yes. And if you practice that way every day, then the "noise" [of a harmful frequency] becomes your focus. If an elegant melody [of beneficial practice] becomes your focus, then you can go into the melody. But if you focus on the noise, and you go into noise, then the result is totally different.

NM: So you're suggesting there is a way to change the "tune" of your meditative radio if necessary?

AS: Yes.

NM: And how does somebody realize that they should change their tune or frequency?

AS: You [the practitioner] have the key. You have the tuner. Each person has a tuner. Each person has the potential to set their own tune. That is why if you give a small kid a radio [*he laughs and makes gestures to jovially show a child making a radio tuner go quickly back-and-forth between many stations*]. But if you know a certain station, you can listen to classical music; another station is American pop music. If you understand the differences, you just set the tune to the proper channel. Setting it to the proper channel is the key.

NM: Can you describe what it is like for a practitioner to set that channel? How does somebody do that in practice?

AS: By using the Three Mysteries: body, speech, and mind. Mind is very important because you actually visualize. Even when the mantra [of the speech component] is wrong, if you have good visualization, you can reach a positive result. It might not be the best result, but it can still be a helpful result. It is best if you use those Three Mysteries together. But even if one is missing or wrong, you can still do something. To me, how you can produce a clear visualization is setting the tune. From my experience, the way body, speech, and mind function together are critical. Body is action. Speech, the right mantra, is like the key. Mind is visualization. To open a locked door, you need to have the right key. If you put the wrong key inside, it doesn't work. Then, some doors, you have to push open. Some slide. Some pull. There are many ways to open the door. That is action. Each door has a different way to open.

Then, when you go in, what is there? What if you open the door and there is a tiger? Woah! When a hungry tiger is on the other side, then it's stupid to open the door! So, what is in there? Why should I go in and what should I do? You have to have clear understanding and visualization before you take action. Even if you have the right key for voice and the right action, if you don't have this right visualization [*smiles and laughs*], who knows, your life could be in danger.

NM: So, just to clarify, the proper visualization is crucial to having a helpful meditation experience, but also unskillful visualization can be the cause of dangerous meditations?

AS: Yes, you can put yourself into very dangerous circumstances. Even if this time it is ok, there is no guarantee for the next time. So, to me, that is why visualization is so important. Clear and proper visualization is a key. You could tune in. You hear music, but is it enjoyable or not? You have to have a very clear understanding of what happens if you do this particular thing. If you have clear visualizations, ok. But if you do not have clear visualizations, you cannot enjoy it [*smiles with a little laugh*]. So that is why body, speech, and mind—you have to carefully choose all that.

NM: How do you ensure that you are making good, skillful choices?

AS: Finding a good teacher is the easiest way. And having a good, trusting relationship with them. For example, to be an Olympic athlete, you could practice on your own. But to compete with the best players, you should have a good coach. Otherwise, even if you have good skill, it might not be enough. But if you have a good coach, they really understand you. They understand what is the best way for you to get better and to lead you toward success. Some people say, "Oh, I could learn everything I need from books!" Yes, we could learn from books. But that's not the same as experience. "Oh, I read a book about how to operate and do a heart transplant." Sure, I understand more, but I better not do that operation! [*Laughs.*] It's similar to going to school. Why do we need to go to school? If we have books at home, we may think we never have to go to school. But we go to school because at school, we learn differently. We learn how to cooperate with others and we receive feedback. Self-study is just self-study. At school the learning is different.

I was taught by my teacher. He was taught by his teacher. He told me, "This is how Shingon Buddhism was handed down."[10] As a teacher, you should understand how your students are doing. You should even understand what kind of dreams your students are having. What kind of problems are your students feeling within? Without understanding that, it is impossible to guide them to success. As a teacher, you should understand everything about your students. That allows you to provide good lessons. Teachers should know you better than you know yourself. Otherwise, you cannot teach students [in the Shingon tradition]. Once I started teaching, I agreed. Everybody has their own speed. So, you adjust to different people depending on the conditions and circumstances.

NM: Do you find that there are negative experiences that are actually helpful?

AS: When you do sports training, you might do five reps [of an exercise]. Tomorrow, you do six. The next day, you do seven. Why? If you keep challenging yourself, it might be hard, but that's how you improve in any discipline. If you challenge yourself, the second session will be harder. The third and thereafter, even harder. You can build your skills that way. But knowing your limits is also very important. You can damage yourself. So that is why a good trainer or coach who has experience can say, "Ok, that is your limit for today. See you tomorrow." But without a coach, if you keep trying to do it more and more and more—you might exceed your capacity. You can damage yourself.

But also, if you have a proper understanding of problems, they might not be harmful. If you see something and you think it's a bad experience, but then you don't reflect upon it, you only have the bad experience. It doesn't help you in the future. But if you reflect upon it, and you think about how you can prevent yourself from doing the same mistakes again, then it will ultimately help. Everybody makes mistakes. Making a mistake is ok. But creating many mistakes is not ok—especially the same mistakes over and over [*laughs*]—that's awful! Everyone makes mistakes. Just reflect and think about how you can prevent that from happening again.

NM: Going back to these tools, are there certain buddhas, bodhisattvas, vidyārājas, or other figures that are more appropriate to treat or deal with certain meditation issues than others?

AS: I think so. We say "buddha," but in this way, buddha is more like a huge, immense life force. There are so many different energies in it. If I need some specific energy, I get that energy through the "source of life" (*seimei no kongen*) and through that particular channel. The differences of the buddhas are different channels. It's like using different cables to get that energy [*reaching over to pick up two different smartphone cables and holding them up*]. The names may be different, just like a different cable. This cable might be good up to ten thousand volts. Another cable might be good up to one hundred thousand volts.

The names are different: Vajrasattva, Medicine Buddha, Acala Vidyārāja, etcetera. But they are connected to the same source. Why are there four different types of beings in the mandalas? Because there are four different types of energies; four different ways to work toward that goal.

NM: Could you explain more about these four types of energy?

AS: There are four types of beings represented [in the primary Shingon mandalas]: Tathāgatas, bodhisattvas, vidyārājas, and devas. All of these can be called buddha or "source of life."

NM: So in Shingon, when you say "buddha" or "source of life" in this way, do you mean Mahāvairocana?

AS: Correct. Some people say these four classes of beings are different stages, but in this way, no. They are not stages. They work differently. The devas represent natural resources.[11] We need those natural resources. Without fire, we cannot survive. Without water, we cannot live. So they are included in the source of life. Other religions separate them all. God is God. God creates things for people. But in Buddhism, everything is ultimately the source of life. Everything is Mahāvairocana. We all come from that. Not only humans, but animals, bugs, trees, water, fire, and everything.

NM: Can you describe the differences in the types of energy of these different types of beings, or why one type of energy would be used rather than another in a given situation?

AS: Buddhas represent truth itself. Truth is included in the basis of life. We cannot see the truth. But we can understand it. We are part of truth. We are part of life. But we live independently. We may create differences between the truth and ourselves. For example, there is the physical body. Ideally, blood pressure should be in a certain range. If it is too high or too low, your life could be in danger. If our body or mind is out of balance, we might go over that limit. That means we are outside of truth. In those times, we ask what would be my best condition? Connecting with buddhas helps awaken us to these truths.

Bodhisattvas are more like an ideal human form. In baseball terms, it might be like Shohei Ohtani. He is the ideal. A small boy might look up to Ohtani if he wants to be a good baseball player: "Oh I want to be like him!" It is the same in Buddhism. Samantabhadra Bodhisattva. Avalokitesvara Bodhisattva. We ask what is the difference between that bodhisattva and myself? We use that bodhisattva to work toward an ideal. Vidyārājas are more like energies of emotion or instinct.

NM: So if you have too much emotion or unsettling emotions, then you use a vidyārāja?

AS: Yes, you use those channels. If you use the wrong channel, then you cannot reach them. If you use the right channel, then you can [then you can.]

NM: The last one is devas, which you said was natural resources. What does that mean in practice?

AS: Water is a natural resource. Most of our human bodies are water, so we need water. If you try to keep your water clean within, but if you get too angry or too emotional, you ruin the water inside. That water becomes sick or impure. How do we clean that water or fire energy within us? Water has a deva. Fire has a deva. Then you call on that energy you need.

NM: So those more specific elemental problems, each connect to a different deva energy?

AS: Yes, that is my understanding. Some people divide them as a category or division. But to me, they are all one thing. But they are different energies to call on and I have to choose the right one. There are also times when I want to call on a particular type of energy, but they don't come. . . .

Each person has a different energy and has different problems. Even if you do the ritual the same way, even if the amount of wood, and every part is the same, the fire is different. The color is different. The feeling is different. This is how I search for their issues. Finding the cause. Finding the influences. Then trying to find different results for them. I try to see which way to focus on them. Then, after the ritual, I talk to the person. . . .

NM: If troublesome emotions are arising in meditations, are there other ways Shingon has to deal with them?

AS: Negative input mostly comes from emotion. . . . But then, which part of emotion does it come from? We might just use one word to say "emotion" but that could be anger or hatred or sadness—there are many types of emotions. So we try to search where does the particular issue *actually* come from. How do we treat this? How do we deal with the actual problem and how do we solve this problem?

In Shingon meditation, first we try to focus on opening a pure space. Then, we try to bring the problem in the center [of our space of concentration]. Next, we try to see the problem from many perspectives. Then, we try to find where this came from and why it developed. We try to go in deep to examine that problem. Then we try to find a solution. It's almost like climbing a mountain. The top of the mountain is one place. But depending where you start climbing up, what you experience is different. What you see is different. What you think is different. The goal is one place, but there are many approaches. For us to reach the goal effectively, we need to basically do some research: Which path should we take? That type of approach is important in Shingon. That is why we try to see things first from many perspectives; not only one.

NM: Is that referring to problems or issues going on in one's own mind or another's mind or both?

AS: Both. If the problem is within, then you try to look at yourself as if you were another person, trying to see from both your own perspective and from other perspectives. If person A has a certain problem, then how would person B perceive or treat this? Look at it from many perspectives. By doing so, we get a clearer understanding. From my experience, that is the best way to face problems. If you take everything from your own viewpoint, then sometimes anger or another emotion wins. In other words, emotion is not bad. We sometimes need emotions to get through a situation. But other times, emotions can disrupt our lives. So then, we need to use knowledge, instinct, and wisdom to balance them out. When we get angry, the emotion portion becomes too big.

NM: So, this is about finding the balance between all these different dimensions?

AS: Yes, because we have those conditions within us. If you only see mind as one, without discerning its diverse dimensions, then it becomes hard to see where the problem comes from.

NM: So do you make use of the physical as well?

AS: Sometimes there is also a physical problem. I cannot always help them. One person was asking about pain in his left leg. I keep praying for it—but I told him I could not deal with his particular pain. I told him to go see a doctor and maybe ask the doctor for a painkiller [*laughs*]. "I can pray for you to get well, but I cannot treat your pain. Go to the doctor." There are some cases, where you must recognize that you cannot do the action in place of another person. If you are hungry, I cannot eat for you. I cannot take your pain away. I can wish that it is gone, but I cannot physically take it away. So pain is something that the individual person has to deal with.

What is pain? Pain is actually something we need. We want to get rid of pain, but if we have pain, we pay attention to it. Without pain, we don't pay attention to it. If we have a stomach pain, it tells us we have to do something about our stomach. If we don't know anything about it, but there is a serious problem, how else do we know to fix it? Pain helps tell us we have something wrong that we need to deal with. Otherwise, by the time we find some serious problem within us, it might be too late. [*Almost whispering in a careful but emphatic tone:*] Pain is not something bad. Pain is a warning. Pain is a signal.

NM: Do you think that notion can be applied to both physical issues and contemplative or spiritual issues?

AS: Yes, everybody tends to see pain as something bad. When I understood that pain is an important message from your body, then you need to listen and explore what is going on. Look for how to take care of it, how to deal with it. But many people just take a pill and look for the easiest way to deal with it without truly putting in the effort to understanding it.

So both physically and spiritually, pain is a signal. Either from your body or from your heart. We need to listen carefully and treat that aspect of ourselves better. Otherwise, when we realize something really bad, it might be too late. The earlier, the better!

For example, thirty years ago, finding cancer was bad. But now, the medical technology is really advanced. You can go see the doctor and find cancer at a much earlier stage—that's not bad! It's great! Because now you have the chance to cure it!

NM: So similarly, if someone is having a difficult contemplative experience, if noticing it early, then it is much easier to deal with it, right?

AS: Exactly. If you find out earlier before it develops, it is much easier to deal with. Their energies might be tangled. If it is very tangled, it is very difficult and it can take a lot of time to fix. But if it is just a couple little knots, then it is easy to solve the problem. So [*emphatically*], the earlier you can find out and recognize the problem, the better.

Everyone wants to live happily. But another issue is just that they don't see where the happiness is. But that's when they come here and we have to help them. But happiness is right there. They just don't see it. Happiness is in their life, but they just can't see it. Sometimes it is just a matter of perspective. Sometimes, they think they are facing a huge problem, but from another perspective, it's not much of a problem at all. I think, "Why are you worrying about that?" [*laughs*].

NM: So, sometimes it is also just helping people see that they can change their perspectives?

AS: Yes, look at it a different way. . . . We face problems, but we are only seeing one portion of the whole. But if you look from many different perspectives, it may not even be a problem at all. If you miss the train, you might have to take the next train. But then, what if the train hits a car and many people are injured. Then, missing the train was a good thing, right? It depends on the results and the different perspectives. What is good or what bad? It can be harder to say than what we think at first. We have a tendency to decide immediately. But many times, it is only just a different perspective and a different understanding. We simply need to step back and look at it another way.

There are no such things as problems. It just depends on how you see. It is either a learning experience or changing your perspective to look at it a different way. There is no precise right or wrong—just better or worse. We should stay away from two extremes. We all know that, but it's very difficult to do consistently in practice.

Notes

1. When the Japanese refer to a *kitō* temple, they mean a form of rituals also often called *kajikitō*. *Kaji* itself is a Japanese term commonly referenced in Shingon Buddhism and derives from the Sanskrit term *adhisthāna*, or "empowerment." *Kajikitō* are more specifically prayer-like rituals to help with a wide variety of both general and specific ailments and afflictions. The Shingon tradition has developed many compendiums of such rituals over the centuries, each one generally designed to treat a particular ailment. For the overarching theory and categorization of such rituals, see, for example, Mitsui (2016).
2. For a detailed discussion of Kūkai's impact on Japanese religion and culture, see Abe (1999).
3. I use the term "Vajrayana" here in the text for simplicity in a volume with other Vajrayana traditions, but traditions in Japan focused around these Three Mysteries primarily self-identify as *mikkyō*. Although it is regularly identified as Vajrayana, it is more frequently translated in English as "Esoteric Buddhism." Alternatively, others translate it as "Tantric Buddhism." Orzech et al. (2011) skillfully describe the various issues with representing this term and its traditions in English.
4. As Kūkai (2010) describes in his text *The Meaning of Sound, Letter, and Reality* (*Shōjijisōgi*), "The moment that the inner breath and the outer air begin to move, vibration inevitably arises. This is called *sound*. Vibration always relies on sound, thus sound is the source of vibration. Sound arises and is never meaningless." According to Kūkai, each of the Sanskrit letters has meaning associated with particular vibrations and sounds. Much of Shingon practice is based upon such ascribed meanings.
5. Several small variances occur in the Four-Fold Training that is taught to Shingon priests depending on the school. But each of them ends with the fire ceremony.
6. Payne (2015, 2).
7. A fairly comprehensive depiction of Shingon views of Acala Vidyārāja, along with his various manifestations and symbolism, can be found in Shimoizumi (2021).
8. Asahi Seichō, interview by the author, November 6 and 7, 2023. Interviews were conducted in both Japanese and English in person at Risō-in Temple in Akitakata, Hiroshima Prefecture, Japan.
9. *Vajras* are symmetrical ritual implements with an equal number of prongs or points on each end. Five-pronged *vajras* are common in both Tibetan and Japanese forms of Vajrayana Buddhism. Shingon also makes regular use of three- and one-pronged *vajras*.
10. Teacher-student relationships are considered incredibly important in Shingon, and they strongly emphasize that oral teachings passed on from teacher to student are prioritized over what is written in *shidai* (ritual manuals). For example, Thomas Eijo Dreitlein in the *Beginner's Handbook for the Shido Kegyō of Chūin-ryū* places the following statement in bold font: "The instructions of your teacher always take precedence

over what is given in the *shidai* and this handbook. Always follow the instructions of your teacher" (xviii; such statements are fairly common in messages to modern Shingon priests and in both modern and historical literature).

11. Asahi, in this case, used both the Pali *deva* and the Japanese *tengokujin* or *kami* as synonyms when discussing this same class of being. Traditionally, the Pali word *deva* literally refers to a being of light and is often translated as "heavenly being." It is one of six modes of rebirth often taught in Buddhism. Although Asahi does accept this explanation in certain contexts, the mandala usage emphasizes a different meaning in which such beings are understood more as "energies" or "vibrations" within the meditative rituals.

Chapter 17

"Losing Control of the Fire and Entering a Demonic State" (*Zouhuorumo*)

Interview with a Chinese American Buddhist Healer

KIN CHEUNG

The translation below is from an interview conducted with Cheung Seng Kan (Pinyin: Zhang Chenggen), a Cantonese-speaking Chinese American religious healer in the New York City area. He is a node of transnational religious healing, having studied martial arts, acupuncture, qigong, and Buddhist medical arts from four Chinese or Chinese American teachers. Cheung is also an autodidact who learns from Chinese-language popular books, radio and television programs, and online videos. In 2012 he became the center of an immigrant healing community consisting of over three dozen relatives, friends, students, and patients. Though he mainly engages those in the New York City area, he also teaches and heals people in Hong Kong and Guangzhou. He employs an eclectic repertoire of healing arts that includes qigong, Buddhist chants, reiki, acupuncture, and more.

In contemporary Chinese culture, "losing control of the fire and entering a demonic state" (*zouhuorumo*) describes deviation from proper self-cultivation or spiritual practices, a phenomenon that is also called "qigong deviation" (*qigong piancha; see also chapter 10*). This term applies to martial arts, qigong, and Buddhist and Daoist spiritual practices. *Zouhuorumo* is both a noun phrase and verb, and Cheung uses it in both ways in the discussion below.

In this interview, Cheung explains what he has learned and what he teaches to his community regarding *zouhuorumo*, qigong deviation, and meditation sickness (*chanbing*). Even though he speaks of these terms as separate issues at times, he also conflates the three. Cheung explains the various types of deviation and sickness, along with their causes and ways to avoid such maladies. He asserts that qigong originates from Daoist practices. His practice of Wisdom

Healing Qigong (Zhinengqigong) was invented by Pang Heming, who incorporated Buddhist, Daoist, and Yogic ideas into this form of qigong. Cheung explains that Pang created Wisdom Healing Qigong to obviate potential deviation by excising the use of intention to control the flow of qi, as it is the misapplication of intention that leads to deviation.

It is important to note that in his explanations Cheung interweaves Confucian (filial piety), Buddhist (*dukkha*), Daoist (effortless action, or *wuwei*), and popular Chinese religious (astrology) principles. Similar to how his explanations blur the demarcations that separate various Chinese religious, philosophical, and self-cultivation traditions, Cheung's repertoire crosses boundaries that separate China from the United States and religion from medicine. He identifies the sources of his knowledge to be books on Buddhism, qigong, yoga, and other self-cultivation practices. In addition, he draws from his own practices, personal experiences, and encounters with students. He emphasizes that there is much information we cannot find in books and that talking about qigong is like talking about swimming—it is useless if you do not actually practice.

In the context of ritual studies, deviation is one type of ritual failure, which is always a risk when conducting a ritual.[1] In the case of self-cultivation and spiritual practices, the possibility of *zouhuorumo* and the potentially very serious negative consequences legitimate ritual efficacy. In other words, the fact that *zouhuorumo* can lead to psychosis reinforces the power and potency of qigong or meditation when enacted properly and also reinforces the authority of a teacher who knows how to prevent or even cure such disorders.

The reader may be interested to learn that Cheung is my father. Elsewhere, I have written on the methodological issues of researching my father, proposing "filial ethnography" as a subset of autoethnography;[2] his own descriptions of his healing practice of *chan* tai chi (*chan-taiji*);[3] how his healing successes serve as examples of "natural miracles," thus introducing Buddhist and Chinese religious understandings of miraculous healing into the philosophy of religion;[4] a profile of Cheung's healing practice, more detail on his sources of knowledge, his role as a teacher and healer in his community, and an argument for how religion spreads through healing;[5] and his use of code-switching to oscillate among multiple medical languages and medical paradigms—that of qi, Chinese astrology and feng shui, Buddhist karmic healing, and biomedicine.[6]

Further Reading

Chen, Nancy N. 2003. *Breathing Spaces: Qigong, Psychiatry, and Healing in China.* Columbia University Press.

Cheung, Kin. 2022. "Miracle as Natural: A Contemporary Chinese American Religious Healer." In *Miracles: An Exercise in Comparative Philosophy of Religion,* edited by Karen R. Zwier, David L. Weddle, and Timothy D. Knepper. Comparative Philosophy of Religion Series 3. Springer International.

Cheung, Kin. 2023. "A Chinese American Religious Healer: Toward Filial Ethnography." In *The Familial Occult: Explorations at the Margins of Critical Autoethnography,* edited by Alexandra Coțofană. European Association of Social Anthropologists Series 47. Berghahn Books.

Cheung, Kin. 2024. "Buddhist Healing in the Community: A Chinese American Healer in New York City." In *Buddhism and Healing in the Modern World,* edited by C. Pierce Salguero, Kin Cheung, and Susannah Deane. University of Hawai'i Press.

Cheung, Kin, and C. Pierce Salguero. 2019. "Interview with a Contemporary Chinese American Healer." In *Buddhism and Medicine: An Anthology of Modern and Contemporary Sources,* edited by C. Pierce Salguero. Columbia University Press.

Interview with Cheung Seng Kan[7]

KC: Please speak on qigong deviation and *zouhuorumo.*

CSK: Qigong deviation and *zouhuorumo* are basically the same. The former is the term of qigong practitioners. It refers to straying from the proper path or channels. This means the proper path of qigong practice and appropriate channel of qi flow. Deviation leads to illness and that is the meaning of *zouhuorumo.*

There are many reasons for deviation. First is the inability to direct qi appropriately. For instance, needing to go left but ending up going right. Second, when a sudden disturbance frightens the practitioner during the practice of qigong. For instance, a loud noise from thunder or the wind blowing a door to slam shut. Fright can lead to improper direction. In both cases, we can imagine the problem arises like when we are driving and the car is going in the opposite direction of a one-way street. This can lead to a crash, and this is what is meant by *zouhuorumo,* which is not much different from qigong deviation.

KC: How are these issues portrayed in films and television?

CSK: Especially in films and television programs from Hong Kong, this has been shown for decades. The same stories are told over and over again. This is how Cantonese people understand *zouhuorumo.* The shows always need one person that *zouhuorumos.* The reason for this is that the martial arts the character pursues are of the highest caliber and their desire to master it is too intense.[8] There is no one else to blame here. It is a result of self-defeat. These stories are used to attract viewers. We have been watching these shows for decades and there inevitably is a villain in these shows that *zouhuorumos.* It is never the hero that *zouhuorumos,* but the villain who *zouhuorumos.* So now you understand.

It is important to learn more knowledge outside of what is being shown. First, there are many types of qigong. For instance, Orbit Circulation Qigong (Zhoutiangong) requires conscious direction of qi to circulate properly along major channels on the spine and torso.[9] The chances of *zouhuorumo* from this practice are relatively higher. Whereas Wisdom Healing Qigong (Zhinengqigong) has a lower risk because there is no need to consider when to inhale or exhale and the practice allows qi to flow more naturally, rather than consciously manipulating it. Hence, this is the safest practice. For instance, [*he points in the direction of a local market*] there is a giant flag outside the supermarket. Even if you do not know the directions or cannot follow directions well, as long as you head towards the flag, you will find the supermarket. Although you may take two extra turns to get there, you won't end up at the wrong destination. If instead, you were to look at a map, if you make a mistake, you could end up somewhere else. This is a clear example, right? Isn't it easy to understand with this analogy?

Now with qigong, if you have good master (*sifu*) or teacher to guide you, there will be no problem during normal conditions, if the practitioner does not have major problems such as mental illnesses.[10] There is a concern with mental illness because a person with mental illness cannot fully control themselves. For instance, someone with multiple personality disorder. This type of person will be the most susceptible to these problems. For example, if you drive, but have poor eyesight or poor hand eye coordination, you will have increased chances of accidents. Not only do you harm yourself, you harm others. This is a very straightforward line of reasoning.

KC: Please speak on meditation sickness.

CSK: There is meditation sickness of the mind and of the body. Right now I will speak on meditation sickness of the mind. Meditation practice is supposed to be effortless action (*qingjing wuwei*), the Daoist idea.[11] However, in daily life, people often have thoughts about today's work, making money, supporting the family, paying taxes, caring for children, parents are getting old. There is a lot of stress from life. But, they want to balance their body and health, which makes sense. Yet, there are too many of such stray thoughts. In meditation, we are aiming to be as peaceful and quiet as possible. It is never going to be absolutely perfect, but people may be seated and instead of aiming to clear their minds, they may dwell even more on such thoughts. This leads to meditation sickness of the mind. This is not to say you can never think these thoughts since your daily life requires this. This is why people who are serious about practice will go on retreat at a temple or on a mountain. Coming out of a seven-day meditation retreat, you will feel quite different. If you never have been on retreat, you will not be aware of the peace and quiet found from such experience. Coming out of the retreat, external noise will be unpleasant. This issue of dwelling on stray thoughts is meditation sickness of the mind.

There is also meditation sickness of the body. For instance, after seated meditation, one does not loosen or stretch one's legs and then goes directly to sleep. Doing this for a prolonged period will hurt the legs. That is why teachers say one has to massage and stretch all parts of the legs and feet afterward. There is also the practice of circumambulation around a Buddha statue. This helps clear up any blockages in qi circulation along the meridians. Normally, people circumambulate by doing this [*he walks at a normal pace around the room*], like this, this, this. However, I can teach you how to walk like this [*slow methodical steps to stretch the feet*]. Whenever there is disease, walking in the first way will cause pain. . . . This is meditation sickness of the body.

KC: What if it is difficult to find peace and quiet sitting at home?

CSK: You can still practice meditation at home. Make sure you keep the environment quiet and free from sudden interruption and disturbance, similar to how disturbances cause *zouhuorumo*. You can do this in a city too. There is too much noise in cities. I recommend beginners use ear plugs. So it depends on who is being taught. When teaching someone in Hong Kong, where space is limited and there is a lot of noise, then ear plugs are a must. This is a big help in reducing noise. There is also another method. If one has the opportunity, go near a river or brook. Why? Because of the continuous sound of the water. Listening to this sound will help you achieve peace and quiet. But how can one find this in the city? Well, people have aquariums where water can flow all day through a pump. The sound of this water works. This is a very good method. Very simple. So it depends on the environment. . . .

KC: Returning to *zouhuorumo,* how does one know they are in trouble or have deviated?

CSK: Speaking of *zouhuorumo,* if one practices qigong, if one feels worse after practice and does not find improvement from qigong, that is *zouhuorumo.* Yet, there is the issue of "illness from qi flushing" (*qichongbingzao*).[12] This is illness that is flushed out from qi flow. This is not deviation. If you do not know the difference, then you must consult a teacher. Sometimes you try to follow in others' steps, but you need to take a few extra turns before getting to the same destination. This is why meditation knowledge is important. This is why people look for a good master.

Same with meditation sickness. If you seek superhuman powers (*shentong;* Skt. *siddhi*), that will lead to meditation sickness.[13] Remember this.

Some people pursue superhuman powers. They do so continuously. Learning Buddhist practice will lead to superhuman powers for sure. But the proper attitude is when one achieves this one can be happy, and if not then one should be just as happy. For instance, when growing crops using water, the field will need a lot of water for rice. The main purpose is to cultivate rice. Now in this same field, sometimes we will find, for instance, shrimp, frogs, small fish. If people are seeking frogs and fish, this leads to deviation. This is the meaning of meditation sickness. Superhuman powers can come from meditation, but the purpose of meditation should be rice, not seeking shrimp or fish. This is a simple and clear example. This is very helpful, right? No one else uses this example, but I thought of this.

There is a story about someone who saw visions of Buddhas during meditation.[14] He asked his teacher if it was real, so the teacher said to chant the Buddhist spell OM MANI PADME HUM ("praise to the jewel in the lotus") and see if they chant back. On the second time he saw these visions during meditation, he chanted and the Buddhas chanted back, and he was very happy. During the third time this happen, when he chanted, demons came and he was scared. Even chanting did not help. He became crazy afterward. This is a fictional story used as a warning to not desire visions.[15]

Notes

1. On ritual failure, see Hüsken (2007).
2. Cheung (2023).
3. Cheung and Salguero (2019).
4. Cheung (2022).
5. Cheung (2024).
6. Cheung (forthcoming).
7. Cheung Seng Kan, interview by the author, September 10, 2023, in Cheung Seng Kan's New Jersey home. The interview was conducted in Cantonese, and all translations are my own. (However, I have used Hanyu Pinyin transliterations.) It has been edited and some sections moved for clarity, and some portions of the interview that do not relate directly to the theme of this volume have been omitted.
8. Chinese martial artists train to channel and strengthen qi. On the connection among qi and martial arts, including Buddhist forms such as Shaolin *gongfu* and Daoist forms such as Wudang, see Guangxi Wang (2012, 4–6).
9. On the circulation of qi, see Yasuo Yuasa (1993), especially chap. 3, "Ki and the Body in the Martial Arts and Meditation Methods."
10. On the term *sifu* and the "Kung Fu Family," see Partikova and Jennings (2018).

11. On *wuwei* and "notions of interdependent selfhood, including mutuality, relationality, interdependence, symbiosis, and responsiveness," see Lai (2007, 325).
12. "As they progressed, many Zhineng Qigong practitioners reported experiencing 'qi reactions' (*qichongbingzao*), which set in more frequently and more heavily as pathogenic and stagnant qi was believed to be transformed more rapidly. This often began with a discharge of body fluids such as sweat, mucous or diarrhea" (Winiger 2017, 135).
13. On superhuman powers and miracles in Chinese religions and Buddhist contexts, see Cheung (2022, 132–137).
14. The paragraph was shared with me on November 10, 2023, because Cheung wanted to add more information regarding this topic.
15. While Chan schools generally warn against the desire of visions, other Buddhist lineages, including Chinese ones, offer elaborate instructions on visualization exercises. See Greene (2016).

Chapter 18

Risk and Reward

Narratives of Practice-Caused Madness in Contemporary Amdo

SUSANNAH DEANE

This chapter presents edited excerpts from ethnographic interviews conducted with Tibetan religious and medical specialists, as well as lay Tibetans, living in the Tibetan region of Amdo in northwest China during 2018 and 2019.[1] These interviews were collected as part of a research project exploring Tibetan perspectives on madness more broadly and the Tibetan religious and medical notions of mind and body that underlie them.[2] During semistructured interviews, Amdo Tibetans described three key causes of madness: spirit affliction, heart illness, and tantric practice.[3] While this third factor only made up a portion of these conversations, in fact almost everyone I spoke to described someone in their community who had become mad this way. In addition, spirits and deities sometimes also played a role in these narratives of practice-related madness, as we will see below.

Key here is the Tibetan notion of "wind," which is understood to circulate in thousands of channels throughout the body. In the Tibetan medical tradition, wind is one of three energies (wind, bile, and phlegm), which have been adapted from the Indian Ayurvedic *tridoṣa.* In the Tibetan tantric tradition, the notion of wind has been adapted from the Indian tantric notion of *prāṇa*—usually translated as breath or life force. While in the Indian traditions these remain two separate concepts, in Tibet they have been conflated into a singular concept and term (*lung,* pronounced "loong"), which is key to both medical and religious understandings of mind-body structure and functioning and particularly relevant to the mind and consciousness.

In the Tibetan medical tradition, wind illnesses (*lung né*) are often related to particular dietary habits or specific behaviors (for example, spending too much time alone with one's thoughts) and mental activities (for example, worrying or overthinking). Such factors are understood to lead to unhealthy increases, decreases, or disturbances in the wind—all of which are described in the predominant medical text, the *Four Tantras* (Gyüzhi). Any such disruptions in the wind and its flow will affect the functioning of the mind-body, leading to psychological or physiological disturbances or both. Moreover, these causative factors become particularly relevant when we start to explore tantric practices. Not only are practitioners often spending significant time overexerting the mind in meditative practice but many of these practices specifically focus on the manipulation of wind within the body.

Often described as "high-risk, high-reward" activities, Tibetan tantric practices are viewed by adherents as the fastest way to attain realization. They are high-level practices, suitable only for knowledgeable and skilled practitioners and even then only after a considerable period of preliminary study and practice, overseen by a more experienced tantric teacher. Here, in what are known as channel-wind practices, complex manipulations of the wind through the bodily channels are used to influence the consciousness. As Kelsang Gyatso explains, "All pure dharma practitioners know how important it is to control the mind, but we cannot really control our mind without controlling our winds."[4] Key here, too, is the connection made between the drops (*thiglé;* Skt. *bindu*), which are understood to be carried through the body by the winds, and the notion of *bodhicitta* (the mind of enlightenment) that is so important in Mahāyāna and Vajrayāna Buddhist traditions. It is through manipulating these winds that the drops—and therefore the *bodhicitta*—can be directed toward realization.

With these winds also connected to the senses, their manipulation is understood to lead to both bodily and psychological effects. In a fifteenth-century commentary on the *Kālacakra Tantra,* for example, Khendro Norsang Gyatso describes how a particular channel-wind practice "should continue until the head begins to hurt, until the yogi sees his body encircled by light, or until the heart starts to jump."[5] Perhaps we can imagine how these kinds of intense sensations and experiences might cause concern or confusion for a meditator not properly instructed or prepared. As we shall see in some of the narratives here, this is often related to the notion of *namtok.*[6] A key concept in all Buddhist traditions, it translates as "conceptual thoughts"—that is, the thoughts of an unenlightened mind. However, in Amdo this term was frequently used (and translated, by those who knew English) to refer to feelings of doubt, suspicion, or fear, usually related to a practitioner being inadequately prepared for their high-level practices. Here, I heard examples that included a practitioner having undertaken insufficient preliminary practices (some of which may last months), an individual skipping ahead to more complex practices they had yet to be trained for, and someone struggling with high levels of practice after having failed to grasp the foundational Buddhist concept of emptiness.

Moreover, if conducted *incorrectly,* these kinds of channel-wind practices have the potential to cause significant harms—including madness—for meditators, related to the misdirection of wind in the body. This is often discussed in relation to the central energy channel(s) described in the two Tibetan traditions: the central channel (Tib. *tsa wuma*[7]) of the tantric tradition and the life channel (Tib. *sok tsa*[8]) of the medical tradition. Debates around whether these two central channels are one and the same date back centuries,[9] but multiple descriptions in the Tibetan Buddhist texts focus on the notion that life-wind illness can be caused by erroneous manipulation of the winds in tantric practice. Health problems and specific mental states may arise if wind becomes "imbalanced, traveling, or trapped in incorrect channels,"[10] and symptoms such as "insanity or seizures" may occur when wind currents and the mind erroneously enter the life channel.[11] Plus, with both of these central channels understood to be situated in the region of the heart—where the mind also resides—we also often hear "heart" or "heart-wind illness" discussed in this context.

Finally, in some of the narratives below we will also hear of madness resulting from practitioners' engagements with spirits and deities. In the tantric practice known as *chöd,*[12] for example, a practitioner envisions the dismemberment of their own body before inviting local spirits to feast upon it. In Amdo, narratives of practitioners experiencing fear related to local spirits and deities during this practice were often discussed in terms of *namtok.*[13] In addition, a practitioner may experience difficulties while conducting deity yoga practices aimed at transforming oneself into an enlightened Buddhist deity known as a *yidam.*[14]

The prevention of these kinds of madness and other conditions related to tantric practices is understood to lie in factors such as belief and faith in the Dharma teachings, practices, and teachers. These will both enable a practitioner to practice correctly and also prevent *namtok.* When these practices *do* lead to problems for practitioners, as we shall see here, treatment is often seen to encompass both religious and medical means, with Buddhist practices and Tibetan medical treatments both discussed by interviewees.

Further Reading

Ardussi, John, and Lawrence Epstein. 1978. "The Saintly Madman in Tibet." In *Himalayan Anthropology: The Indo-Tibetan Interface,* edited by James F. Fisher. Mouton.

Deane, Susannah. 2018. *Tibetan Medicine, Buddhism and Psychiatry: Mental Health and Healing in a Tibetan Exile Community.* Carolina Academic Press.

Deane, Susannah. 2025. *Illness and Enlightenment: Exploring Tibetan Perspectives on Madness in Text and Everyday Life*. Berghahn Books.

Epstein, Mark, and Sonam Topgay. 1982. "Mind and Mental Disorders in Tibetan Medicine." *ReVision: A Journal of Consciousness and Change* 9 (1): 67–79.

Marek, Todd P., and Charles Jamyang Oliphant. 2017. "Treating Disorders of the Subtle Winds in Tibetan Buddhism." In *Buddhism and Medicine: An Anthology of Premodern Sources,* edited by C. Salguero Pierce. Columbia University Press.

Namgyal, Aged Thirty-Two, Nyingma Buddhist Lama in Hainan[15]

The first cause of madness is the channels or the wind: If someone experiences some severe problems in their channels, then they may become mad. The second cause of madness is spirits. There are different kinds of symptoms of spirit-caused madness, but many patients will have problems with their memory, and their mind will not be calm—it will be conflicted, as if there is an inner fighting going on, causing the mind to go astray.

Life-wind illness is a kind of illness where our heart has become affected. Those lamas who focus their concentration too much on their studies or Buddhist teachings may experience life-wind illness. There are many lamas with life-wind illness; this is no different from lay people with madness related to life-wind—it is probably caused by studying too much, days and nights of studying: Those lamas have spent too much time on their studying, or too much concentration on their studies. Alongside that, maybe they have conducted the key tantric practices incorrectly. This second type of cause is when the meditation has gone wrong, or been conducted incorrectly, and then this has caused life-wind illness. Not all kinds of meditation will lead a person to go astray, or go wrong, but the methods for conducting the practices are important—if they are done incorrectly, then this may lead to some kinds of difficulties.

It is hard to say how common practice-caused illness is. We cannot say that *all* kinds of wrong meditation are caused by one factor—it's not like that. For example, maybe if a meditator has secluded themself to a remote place where there are no other people, and especially if they stay like this for a long time, and they don't have much external contact, this can cause problems.

There are different ways to treat different people with this condition. If someone has a severe life channel problem, then this may endure for their whole life, but if the problem is not serious, it can be cured by Tibetan Medicine—especially moxibustion. In the case of life-wind illness, it is also a state of mind: At that time, the person has no ability to control themself, so they probably get angry easily, and once they become angry, their body may tremble and shake. At that time, the essential thing they can do is to try to calm down, but for a case of a patient with a life-wind illness, normally when someone tries to talk to them to persuade them to calm down, it doesn't work very well, and even medicine and daily chanting is also not always effective. So really the patient has to calm themselves and make peace in their own mind. In addition, in the past I have used some religious tools and practices to treat people with this kind of madness—for example, conducting rituals for them.

Tsering, Aged Fifty-Seven, Bon Lama in Rebkong[16]

One kind of madness is caused by heart-wind illness. When heart-wind disturbance occurs, your senses become unclear, and then what you say, or what you do, doesn't make sense. Sometimes people may experience something like this in a religious context. I have seen this many times. For example, usually practitioners go and do tantric retreat in the mountains, but before you go for retreat in the mountains, your lama will give some teaching and guidance, including preliminary practices and things like that, to prepare you for the retreat. This preparation allows you to achieve the level of practice that you want to. But if someone doesn't have a teacher to give this guidance, and they go on retreat, then sometimes their heart may become uncontrolled. This can cause madness through heart-wind illness: If you cannot control your heart, then you cannot control your mind. This occurs in perhaps one out of every one hundred practitioners.

In addition, if the person has been to retreat in the mountains or visiting other places, there is also a possibility that they can get madness caused by *gyalpo* or *senmo* [spirits/local deities residing in the area]. Conducting *chöd* practice may also cause you to get madness. When you do *chöd,* you need a rinpoche's guidance, and permission to practice—proper initiation from your teacher—and you also need to perform preliminary practices before you can conduct *chöd.* Without this kind of initiation or permission, if you do it by yourself, sometimes it can cause you to become mad, and even kill you—maybe as a result of the spirits.

If this harm during practice is *not* caused by spirits, you can take medicine; if it is related to the life channel, you can take medicine. One way to treat this kind of madness is in hospital—taking Tibetan Medicine to treat the disordered wind. And when different people have this kind of heart-wind illness during retreat, there are many ways of treating this. For example, in the Tibetan sense, it can be treated by mixing roasted barley flour and butter and rubbing this on the body—this can ease the heart-wind. Another way to treat this is for the person to lie down with the sunshine on the lower half of the body. Also, if someone has heart-wind illness, you can bury an onion in [hot] ashes until it is half burnt, and then eat it. Most of this kind of knowledge is in the texts, but some of it comes from practitioners' own experience. In the Bonpo texts, they talk about madness and other illnesses, and how to treat madness through religious blessings or ritual. These texts talk about Tonpa Shenrab's teaching:[17] about this life—for example, when you get this kind of madness or this kind of illness, how it can be treated, and things like that—it's quite specific.

Another way of treating the heart-wind illness is by practicing the channel-wind practices. And another is to conduct ritual, such as a Bon exorcism/ransom ritual—there are 360 kinds of Bon exorcism/ransom rituals. Another method is to consult different kinds of rinpoches, lamas, or khenpos—the more powerful teachers. They can give you a drop of water to put on your face and head—special water that has been blessed by the teacher—these kinds of things can also treat this. Usually you need to get help from the lama or rinpoche for this condition, because while you are experiencing madness, your mind is unclear. People who have madness caused by spirits and things like this can only be treated through ritual. A *hon* [specific kind of ritual specialist] will usually conduct this kind of ritual, because if a practitioner doesn't have a really special ability in conducting this kind of ritual—if he is not skilled enough—it can sometimes harm the *hon* himself. All of this is described very specifically in the text.

Tsetan, Aged Thirty-Eight, Former Gelugpa Buddhist Monk in Rebkong[18]

It is possible for lamas to become mad from their practice, but it's not very common. The most common cause in these cases is that the person keeps practicing a lot—not relaxing or participating in any other activities. It is said in the tantric teachings that if you do not do the practice correctly, you can harm yourself. In tantric teachings, there are two different kinds of channels: the right and left channels, and the central channel.[19] One is about truth, and the other is *namtok*. So these are in parallel. The channels carry blood and wind, and also your consciousness. Channel-wind practices are a tool for different things. For example, if you do these practices to control your wind or channels, it can be for your bodily health, but they can also be practiced for spiritual purposes. For these kinds of practices, first you need to manipulate the wind, and at the end of the practice, there is a way to release it within the body. In addition, there are practices which you cannot conduct without conducting certain preliminary practices. And if you do not do the practices correctly, then you will get problems. For these kinds of things where the practitioner becomes mad, usually it's related to the person staying alone inside for a long time, conducting their practice alone.

I'm not sure how you treat this kind of madness or other problems from practice, but usually it depends on the person himself. Maybe he has to rest for a few days, and after a few days or a few weeks perhaps he will recover. I think probably moxibustion and acupuncture can help, and also bloodletting and herbal poultice—these could help, but I'm not really sure. For madness caused by mind or heart, there are treatments for the person himself to do, or for specialists to practice from certain texts. The problem of madness is related to psychology, so it does not only depend on rituals or offerings; it also depends on the person himself... Through the blessings from the [Buddhist] deities you can recover ... but it's mysterious! You must have faith in Buddha's teachings ... his knowledge. But his knowledge is also mysterious—you cannot know everything, but you must still have faith. Buddhist practices prevent *namtok:* The sense of good or bad ... clean or dirty ... beautiful or ugly—all of this results from *namtok.* So if you free yourself from *namtok,* then you will be ok.

Madness is also commonly caused by spirits, but most often, it is dependent on your mind, and we can say that if you do not have enough trust in what you are doing, or if you have *namtok,* then it is easier for the spirits to affect you. It's more common for lay people to be affected by spirits, because for the monks and other religious practitioners, they practice a lot of religion; and among lay people, people who often practice religion, they are less likely to be affected by spirits. But between lay people and monks, it's more likely for lay people to be affected.

With practices involving the *yidam* deities, problems can be caused by incomplete practice. For example, if you forget some steps in the practice, or if you mistakenly add something new, the *yidam* may become angry. So these kinds of rituals must be done step by step; if you miss a step, if you misuse or misplace the steps, then the *yidam* may become angry and harm the practitioner. But at the end of the ritual, there is always a section of the text asking for forgiveness, so at the end of the ritual, you must read this text asking for his forgiveness.

Aku Wangchuk, Aged Seventy-Two, *Ngakpa* and Tibetan Medicine Doctor in Rebkong[20]

The life channel is there at the beginning of life, and the basis of consciousness is located inside this. Then slowly, the life channel will disappear, but when we meditate, we can still focus on this. If we examine our bodies, we cannot see it, but we are able to meditate on it. Some people say that it is still there later in life and it's invisible, but this is not true—only the *function* of the life channel is there, located from the back of neck down to base of the spine. If tantric practice disturbs the life-wind here, it may cause madness. Most of these practitioners with madness did something wrong in their practice—this happens a lot. At the beginning of teaching, the teacher usually tells their students, "You have to be careful; you have to follow the instructions, otherwise the wind can go in the wrong way, and you can become mad"—usually they will give this speech.

These practices are related not only to wind—also to the channels and drops—so you have to work to control all of these. Otherwise, if you only focus on the wind, it is difficult. The drops are related to the dharmakaya [Dharma body]; you work with the channels for the nirmaṇakaya [transformation body]; and then wind for the sambhogakaya [enjoyment body]; and from the drops, the dharmakaya.[21] This is really complicated and very difficult—that's why many people make a mistake when they practice—that's why they go wrong—at *that* level—the level of these three. The explanation of wind in the life channel is quite general—this is how it is discussed in the medical texts. But there is another, very special, specific explanation from the perspective of Buddhism, but this is usually not allowed to be discussed openly, so there are some things I cannot talk about with you.

In addition, when you practice, if you have *namtok,* things will definitely go wrong. You need to totally eliminate *namtok,* but to do that, you have to understand *a lot*—for example, you need to understand the Buddhist concept of non-self. But if you can eliminate *namtok,* then you will have no problem.

People can rarely treat this kind of madness by themselves; some can, but this is rare. Often, people go to the doctor for treatment, also sometimes they will change their practice—that is also another way to treat this.

Tamdrin, Aged Twenty-Six, Teacher in Rebkong[22]

The Buddhist texts are very difficult to understand—for example, it is especially difficult to understand emptiness. So if a particular text is trying to explain emptiness, we might say that not everyone should be reading that book, because we vary from person to person—people are different. So sometimes, people say this book is good for you, but not good for me. For example, maybe a book is describing emptiness, and when a person reaches the meaning of this book, the knowledge is too big for them, and they can't understand the meaning of this. Maybe they will get *namtok*—sometimes experiencing *namtok,* sometimes trust. Between these, they lose their mind, and become mad. Then their behavior may become strange. For example, they may eat strange things, and eat things that are not food, or they may talk to themself . . . These are the usual symptoms.

I think it is possible to recover. First we have to do divination. Many Tibetans, they have a divination performed to decide which hospital they should go to, which lama they should visit, which medicine they should take.

One of my uncles was trying to reach a high level of tantric practice, and he became mad. Now he has recovered, but he was mad for almost twenty years. These days he is better—not completely, but he's better. He recovered by increasing his knowledge—through more study. There was a beggar here who was mad too. He was *really* mad—serious madness—and he died three years ago. He had been a monk, and he studied the high-level *yidam* deity practices, but he misunderstood some things. Trust and *namtok*—he was between these, and he lost his mind. We must go slowly, step by step, towards the Buddha.

Migmar, Aged Thirty, Buddhist Studies Master of Arts Student in Golok[23]

Maybe lamas don't become mad from tantric practice because they have a high level of knowledge, but perhaps this can happen *before* they become a lama. By the time they have received the title of lama, or the title of *ngakpa,* they will probably be conducting the practices in the right way, so they will not become mad. But those younger monks and *ngakpas,* when they're practicing, if they do it incorrectly, then maybe they will become mad.

If a practitioner conducts the meditation incorrectly, it will affect the wind. Also, if they have anxiety while they are practicing, then maybe this will lead to madness. For example, if someone is practicing [Buddhist deity] Yamāntaka meditation,[24] their appearance may change—maybe their face or body will change to become similar to Yamāntaka's face or body, and maybe all kinds of images of this buddha will arise—maybe, maybe not. If the practitioner gets confused by this, then it can cause a problem. In addition, when they are completing the practice, if the practitioner can't connect the visualized deity to their own Buddha nature, then it's like the wisdom and compassion can't connect together, and then they may make a mistake in the meditation. That might cause madness, or cause the person to become abnormal or something.

If the practitioner goes to get support from a higher-level teacher, then maybe the teacher can help them to calm their mind, and then tell them what they need to do, and maybe they will recover. But there are some practitioners who are arrogant, and they say, "I am the same as Yamāntaka!," or they don't go to consult their teacher for help—those practitioners' condition will get worse.

In *chöd* practice, the practitioner offers their body to the different kinds of spirits: In offering to those beings, they are practicing nonattachment. This is a high-level practice, and once you have really accomplished this practice correctly, you will understand that all sentient beings are equal, and you will develop compassion for *all* sentient beings. But when someone is performing *chöd* practice, if it goes wrong, and they become scared by something, then they may become mad. . . . While you are conducting *chöd* practice, if spirits or ghosts are near you, and you are saying, "I am offering my body to these beings," if you get scared by something, then maybe you will become *really* scared, and this may cause a problem. It depends on the practitioner: If they consult their teacher, and get advice on the practice, maybe they will be okay, but if not . . .

Notes

1. The Tibetan region of Amdo (one of the three major Tibetan regions) today composes the majority of the northwestern Chinese province of Qinghai, also taking in parts of Sichuan, Gansu, and the Tibet Autonomous Region. All of these interviews were conducted within Qinghai, specifically in the city of Xining and some smaller towns around the province.
2. Research for this chapter was conducted as part of my British Academy Postdoctoral Research Fellowship, which provided funding for the research at the University of Bristol. Additional thanks go to the Minzu University of China in Beijing, which hosted me as a visiting researcher for two semesters in 2018.
3. While the vast majority of my interviewees were Tibetan Buddhists (predominantly from the Gelug and Nyingma communities), one—a local Tibetan lama—was a member of the local Bon community. There is much debate over the history and classification of the various Tibetan traditions that come under the categorization of Bon (see, for example, Kvaerne 1995, 9), but in this context we are dealing with tantric practices within an "organized religion" usually referred to as Yung Drung Bon (Millard 2013, 145), which can be described as equivalent to their Buddhist counterparts.
4. Gyatso (1994, 147).
5. Kilty (2004, 502).
6. Tib. *rnam rtog*.
7. Tib. *rtsa dbu ma*.
8. Tib. *srog rtsa*.
9. Garrett and Adams (2008, 87).
10. Marek and Oliphant (2017, 418–419).
11. Yangönpa (2015, 46, 234).

12. Tib. *gcod.*

13. While "madness-causing spirits" are described in the Tibetan medical texts, in the context of Tantric practice they are more often discussed in terms of *namtok.*

14. Tib. *yi dam;* tutelary deity, meditational deity.

15. In-person interview conducted in Tibetan, October 2018.

16. In-person interview conducted in Tibetan, November 2018.

17. Tonpa Shenrab is understood to be an enlightened buddha and founder of the Bon tradition.

18. In-person interview conducted in Tibetan, November 2018.

19. These two "side channels" are related to the karmic winds (Tib. *las rlung*) of an unenlightened mind, with the central energy channel related to the wisdom wind (Tib. *ye shes rlung*) of the enlightened mind. As Guarisco explains, much channel-wind practice is focused on directing the winds from the side channels into the central energy channel (Guarsico in Yangönpa 2015, 72–74).

20. In-person interview conducted in Tibetan, November 2018.

21. This is the doctrine of *trikāya*—the three bodies of the Buddha—fundamental in Mahāyāna and Vajrayāna Buddhist traditions.

22. In-person interview conducted in English, October 2018.

23. In-person interview conducted in Tibetan, November 2019.

24. Dorjé Jikjé in Tibetan, this *yidam* was referred to by his Sanskrit name, Yamāntaka, by my Buddhist studies student interlocutor.

Chapter 19

Eliminating Obstacles and Protecting Practitioners

Interview with Tibetan Yogi Dr. Nida Chenagtsang

BEN P. JOFFE

The following transcript comes from a telephone conversation I had with Dr. Nida Chenagtsang about how the potential pitfalls and side effects of contemplative practices are understood and treated in Tibetan Buddhist and medical contexts. Dr. Nida, who was born in 1970 in a nomad community in Mahlo, northeastern Tibet, is a practitioner of Tibetan medicine, or Sowa Rigpa,[1] and a nonmonastic tantric Buddhist yogi (*ngakpa*).[2] After graduating from the Lhasa Mentsikhang and working for some years in Tibet as a doctor in a county hospital,[3] he relocated to Italy and now teaches Sowa Rigpa and Tibetan Buddhism to students around the world.[4] Dr. Nida is a lineage holder and prominent teacher of the Yuthok Nyingthig,[5] a collection of tantric Buddhist ritual and meditation practices transmitted in the twelfth century by Yuthok Yönten Gönpo the Younger, one of most important systematizers of Tibetan medicine.[6] These practices use the Medicine Buddha as a meditational deity (*yidam*) and are geared toward the needs and sensibilities of professional healers.

At the start of our conversation, Nida explains that the closest equivalent Tibetan concept to meditation sickness is *gek,* or "obstacle," a word used by Tibetans to refer to agents, conditions, or circumstances that prevent the successful accomplishment of virtuous, spiritual activities and meditation in particular (see also chapter 8). Although *gek* are often conceptualized as hostile spirit beings that disrupt Buddhist rituals and retreats, illnesses of the physical body, mental illnesses, blockages and imbalances of subtle energies, bad dreams, emotional disturbances, bad luck, accidents, unfavorable environmental and social conditions, doubt, loss of motivation, and crises of faith may all be identified as *gek* as well. Nida explains how obstacles to meditation can manifest in external circumstances, the physical body, the internal subtle body, or the more "secret" or private level of one's inner psychology. These varying levels of obstacles each have their own type of obstacle-elimination (*geksel*) procedures as well. These practices necessarily imply the Tibetan genre of Signs of the Path instructions (*lamtak*). Idealized road maps for proper meditative progress specific to particular lineages of teachings, these instructions help meditators to correctly identify obstacles and potential sidetracks (*golsa*) in their practice. While often preserved in writing, *lamtak* teachings highlight the long-standing reliance in Tibetan contexts on personalized, oral instruction and ongoing supervision from experienced teachers as safeguards against meditation problems.

In assessing symptoms experienced by meditators, Nida draws on humoral frameworks central to Sowa Rigpa and on the category of "wind disorders" in particular. He contrasts "dharmic" frameworks that use concepts like karma and merit to make sense of meditation sickness with Tibetan and Western medical approaches that interpret adverse effects through a less moral lens. While recognizing that Dharmic frameworks can be less stigmatizing and discouraging than pathologization in medical terms, Nida ultimately sees improved medical literacy for Buddhist teachers and organizers as a key factor in protecting students. He highlights the particular risks associated with lengthy, closed retreats and the dangers of engaging in tantric practices with untreated personality and anxiety disorders, or without proper preparation. He ultimately calls for flexible, individualized approaches to meditation training and increased familiarity between teachers and students as key forms of harm reduction.

While Nida glosses adverse reactions to meditation and "meditation sickness" as *gek*, his explanations show that *gek*—with its variously outer, inner, secret and bodily, energetic, and mental expressions—is a much broader concept than just "sickness arising from meditation." Equally, while certain types of wind disorder may be triggered through meditation, these are not exclusively associated with or caused by it. There is thus no single perfect Tibetan equivalent for the East Asian concept of *chanbing*. For Nida, meditation sickness is an inconsistent category with highly diverse causes, symptoms, and treatments. By contrast, through its threading together of so many different levels of experience, the concept of *gek* obliges practitioners to think carefully and honestly about their preparedness for meditation practice in an equivalently expansive way.

Further Reading

Chenagtsang, Nida. 2024. *Foundations of Sowa Rigpa: A Guide to the Root Tantra of Tibetan Medicine*. Sky Press.

Deane, Susannah. 2019. "Rlung, Mind, and Mental Health: The Notion of 'Wind' in Tibetan Conceptions of Mind and Mental Illness." *Journal of Religion and Health* 58 (3): 708–724. http://www.doi.org/10.1007/s10943-019-00775-0.

Gutschow, Kim. 2022. "A Case of Wind Disorder: The Interplay of Amchi Medicine and Ritual Treatments in Zangskar." In *Healing at the Periphery: Ethnographies of Tibetan Medicine in India,* edited by Laurent Pordié and Stephan Kloos. Duke University Press.

Lewis, Sara E. 2018. "Resilience, Agency, and Everyday *Lojong* in the Tibetan Diaspora." *Contemporary Buddhism* 19 (3): 1–20. https://doi.org/10.1080/14639947.2018.1480153.

Samuel, Geoffrey. 2019. "Unbalanced Flows in the Subtle Body: Tibetan Understandings of Psychiatric Illness and How to Deal with It." *Journal of Religion and Health,* 58 (3): 770–794. http://www.doi.org/10.1007/s10943-019-00774-1.

Interview with Dr. Nida Chenagtsang About Approaches to Meditation Sickness in Tibetan Medicine and Buddhism[7]

BPJ: Is there a concept of "meditation sickness" in Tibetan Buddhism and Tibetan medicine? Are there Tibetan terms for meditation sickness?

NC: Yeah, it's called *gek,* which means "obstacles." In Tibetan we say *dön gek*—obstacles caused by or manifesting as provoked spirits[8]—or *né gek*—obstacles connected with or manifesting as illness. *Gek* goes together with these.

BPJ: Okay. And so *gek* is something that's specifically associated with the practice of meditation, with people who are doing meditation retreat?

NC: Yes.

BPJ: It seems that this concept of *gek* operates on different levels—sometimes we hear about *gek* being more like physical disease, sometimes more like mental disease, sometimes more like spirits as you said. Can you explain a little bit more about these levels and how they are connected? How should we understand the relationship between these different kinds of obstacle?

NC: Yeah. In Tibetan we say *gek rik tongtrak gyebchu tsa zhi,* "the eighty-four thousand types of obstacle" or just *gek rik tongtrak gyebchu* for short.[9] So, *gek* can be understood in many different ways, but they really refer to any kind of obstacle. *Gek* has many different meanings. It can be a disease, it can be a kind of spirit attack, it can manifest in many different ways.[10] In Tibetan prayers we always ask for *gek* to be pacified—*gek* can refer to spirits, to physical disease or mental problems, or all these things together.

Then, as a solution, we talk about *geksel,* obstacle eliminating practices. *Geksel* also has different layers. There are practices for eliminating obstacles connected with the channels, the winds, and the drops (*tsa, lung,* and *thiglé*).[11] Obstacle eliminating practices for the channels are more connected with physical things. Wind obstacles can also be more physical and have to do with when the energy stops flowing, with energy blockages. And then the drops are more connected with the mind and blissful sexual practices. The chapter on obstacle eliminating practices in the Yuthok Nyingthig is mostly connected with physical disease. It includes treatments for various kinds of infections, inflammations, all these sorts of things.

BPJ: And that's the chapter on the outer level of *gek* elimination, right?

NC: Yes. The medical approach to obstacle elimination is really represented in the Yuthok Nyingthig.

BPJ: It seems like obstacle-elimination practices are often developed specifically for and by yogic practitioners. I remember you saying for example that *yukchö* therapy was maybe something that was developed by yogis and yoginis[12]—

NC: Yes. *Yukchö* and also some medicinal formulas like Bimala, developed by Vimalamitra.[13] It seems like originally it was used for protection of the meditator's mind, to treat mental imbalances that could arise in retreat, and then it became a general anti-anxiety medication for non-meditators as well. If you look at Vimalamitra's prophecy I think it says things about various spirit siblings who come and especially disturb the human mind. The Bimala formula was for expelling this kind of disturbance.

BPJ: There are often descriptions in Buddhist sources about spirits whose special job seems to be to disturb meditators, as if it's their favorite thing to do or their main activity. How should we understand these spirits?

NC: I think with these spirits you can start from the story of Māra, no? When Buddha was enlightened, the *māra* spirits were very unhappy. They attacked Buddha but didn't succeed so then they sent their daughters to distract him. They tried both ways: They attacked with men's anger first then with women's beauty and attraction. Even today, Dharma practitioners usually either get involved in fighting and are distracted by angry, proud spirits like the "king" spirits (*gyalpo*),[14] or they are more distracted by sex. So, it's better if we connect the kinds of spirits you're talking about with that original story, with Māra.

But then when we talk about channel, wind, and drop-related obstacles these sometimes have nothing to do with spirits. Your channels have problems because you are not moving enough in retreat. Your wind has problems, it gets stuck, or you don't take care of it, it's scattered, and so on. Then the drops can become a problem when you don't use them well. Texts like the Yuthok Nyingthig talk about "the pain caused by channels, wind-energy, and drops" and provide specific yoga exercises and visualization and breathing methods for eliminating these obstacles.

BPJ: I remember reading a text about the life story of Milarepa,[15] which talked about how all the spirit attacks and visions Milarepa experienced in retreat were connected with the movement of the winds in his channels—when a spirit appeared externally he knew that some change was happening in his *vajra body*. So, it seems like it's also possible for highly trained yogis and yoginis to understand spirit-related obstacles as happening on different levels, simultaneously?

NC: Yes, definitely. Then there are also visions connected with meditation. Sometimes you have visions which are signs of meditation progress or sometimes you receive Terma treasure revelations through visions. I think these are very natural, healthy visions. But then there are also unhealthy visions which are more like hallucinations. Sometimes people force themselves and do too much meditation. This results in pressure and stress which can lead to psychosis. But then maybe these meditators think to themselves, "Oh it's a vision!," a healthy sign. They are seeing and hearing things, so they think it must be a positive or significant sign but in reality they're super disturbed.

BPJ: In addition to *gek* obstacles, there's also the concept of *golsa*—

NC: *Golsa* are "sidetracks," points of deviation, yes. Going astray in your practice. You have delusional feelings and then you think that's the right path and then you get lost in your delusions. "Spiritual delusion symptoms" is one way to explain it.

BPJ: Like people think they're already enlightened after one meditative experience or something like that?

NC: Yeah. That they're enlightened or that they have received special signs proving that they're at a special level, that they're higher than Buddha, that sort of thing.

BPJ: And so, are the "sidetracks" one might experience specific to each kind of meditation practice or are they more specific to each kind of person or . . . ?

NC: I think that in general they are like delusional syndromes. *Golsa* can mean having feelings or sensations connected with meditation practice or can involve practitioners developing their own misleading beliefs. Sometimes these things arise and then they go away. But with these points of deviation there are deviations involving view—wrong view—then deviations involving meditation, and deviations involving behavior or ethics. Different levels.

BPJ: What methods would you use to avoid or to treat such deviations? Because, usually, if someone is delusional, they're not necessarily aware that they've gone astray, they think they're on the right path, right? So, how do you avoid getting sidetracked?

NC: To avoid this you need authentic, correct view, correct meditation, and correct behavior. You need to study and learn properly, all these things. If you search through Tibetan texts, I'm sure you'll be able to find different examples of *golsa.*

BPJ: On many occasions I've heard you speak about something that not many teachers talk about: the idea that students should adjust the type of meditation practices they do to their humoral, medical typology.[16] I suspect many people are not so familiar with this idea. Could you say a little about how the idea of medical typology fits with meditation?[17]

NC: Yeah. With typology, we see how *lung* or wind-humor type people experience troubles with meditation more easily. This is because wind-type people already have a predisposition to anxiety. And then *tripa* or bile-type people, they may be more at risk of anger issues, of pride, and these sorts of things. So, when they experience sidetracks, some people may become very spiritually narcissistic—that's like a type of sidetrack, right? They think they are in a safe place but they're actually in the wrong place; they're going down a dangerous path. I think another example of this is how sometimes when you do "calm abiding" meditation [Tib. *zhi-né;* Skt. *śamatha*], you become completely detached and dissociated. You can't feel anything, you just numb yourself, there is no mental clarity at all. They call this "dark" or "dark view" calm abiding in Tibetan.[18] These sorts of sidetrack problems are possible with calm abiding meditation too. Also, sometimes you'll talk about "concentration," but some people cannot concentrate and then they get a panic attack from forcing themselves to focus. Trying to concentrate and still their mind just increases their anxiety. On the other hand, if you're already able to meditate, you can work with this experience. Mingyur Rinpoche has often talked about his own fear, for example. What he describes is a typical panic attack-type response. We can see that as a kind of *gek* obstacle as well. But then he found a way to remove that obstacle with meditation. He knew how to remove it and did the necessary obstacle elimination or *geksel.*[19]

BPJ: Okay, so that brings up another question: Sometimes you hear about people doing meditation practices and they have various obstacles—they have these hallucinations or disturbing experiences and then you hear about these things becoming like the actual meditation practice itself, right? So, Mingyur Rinpoche has a panic attack but he's able to look at his fear and anxiety and he sort of brings it onto the path or makes it something he can work with or transform through meditation.

NC: Yeah, that's called *nyönmong lamkhyer,* "bringing afflictive mental-emotional states (i.e., Skt. *kleśa*) onto the path." You can do this if you are strong enough—otherwise, you become the victim of your afflictive states instead.

BPJ: Right. Because that's the thing—sometimes it seems like people have negative experiences while meditating and then other people tell them, "Oh no, it's okay, just carry on, do the practice more, work with it."

NC: I think the problem is that the teaching normally is that if you have good experiences while meditating you shouldn't be too happy and if you have bad experiences, you shouldn't feel too bad. If you follow this approach, you can kind of neutralize your experiences and balance them. Then it's okay. Normally, when something bad comes up for practitioners, many Tibetan teachers say, "Oh, it's your karma. You're purifying your karma." Maybe some teachers are not so interested in the medical aspect of practitioners' problems. So sometimes they just use that idea of karma as an excuse and then maybe they ignore that health aspect a little bit.

BPJ: Yeah. There could be some serious health issues for the student.

NC: Exactly. But they explain these things in terms of karma and merit, right?

BPJ: So do you think that that's just because those teachers don't know as much about the medical side of things?

NC: Yeah. Maybe they don't have much medical experience or maybe they just don't care much about that part.

BPJ: So, how do you know when it's time to stop? Sometimes you think, "Oh, well I'm feeling quite unstable or I'm having these negative reactions but maybe if I keep meditating it will pass." But then maybe if you keep meditating it will make the problem worse. How do you know when it's time to stop or when it's time to transform or work with the experience?

NC: Yeah, that's why you need a teacher. You should ask your teacher. Gampopa's style of Mahamudra meditation practice was like that:[20] Students would meditate for seven days and then afterwards they would go and talk about their experiences with their teacher. I think great meditators were very careful in that way. And then also, when you have strong faith, when you make heartfelt prayers and aspirations, you can overcome problems and obstacles. This is a more traditional way of doing it. But I think that as a doctor Yuthok really focused on medical healing and approaches.

It's interesting—if you read Jamgön Kongtrul Rinpoche's text on dark retreat, "The Sādhanā Through Which Buddhahood Is Realized in Seven Days," he says that for dark retreat you need an experienced teacher.[21] He says that otherwise you will have lots of potentially destabilizing meditative experiences or visions (*nyam*) and wind-related disorders. I think that's a very good point. Without a qualified teacher, students will have visions and so on and they won't understand what's happening. If their teacher is experienced, they will be able to say, "Okay, you need to come out of the dark, you need to take a particular medicine, you need a massage, you need to expose yourself to sunlight," and so on. They know what the student needs based on their own experience. If care isn't taken and a student spends too much time in the dark, they can go crazy too.

So that's why I think, generally speaking, every tantric text or teaching talks at least a little bit about obstacle-eliminating and enhancement practices.[22] But then, even so, some masters focus more on this topic and others don't focus on it at all. That's the difference. So that's why I think that the obstacle-eliminating chapter in the Yuthok Nyingthig is probably one of the best, because Yuthok was a doctor. He had already written medical books, so it was easy for him to put together that "Obstacle Eliminating Practices for Eliminating Elemental Disturbances of the Physical Body" chapter.[23] That part of the Yuthok Nyingthig is actually like a simplified version of the third tantra or volume of the *Four Medical Tantras.* The three humoral energies of wind (*lung*), bile (*tripa*), and phlegm (*beken*), all the basic things are there. I have a feeling that Yuthok included this in the Yuthok Nyingthig as a substitute for medical training, so that even if yogic practitioners and meditators didn't study medicine they would still know a lot of things, just by knowing that chapter, which is similar to the third "Oral Instructions" tantra, which is focused on pathology and treatments, categories and symptoms of disease, and so on.

BPJ: Yeah, it's like a crash course, a quick intensive training in medicine for yogis.

NC: Yes, he put everything in there: information about the symptoms and divisions of disorders and instructions for treatment via diet, lifestyle, medications, and external therapies.

Then there are sidetracks or deviations involving view, any kind of views, like the Dzokpa Chenpo[24] view, the view of Mahamudra, and so on. If you misunderstand them, that's a type of sidetrack and it is always potentially dangerous. Maybe you misunderstand the view of these teachings and then you say there's no such thing as karma, there's no good and no bad, I'm free to do anything without consequences, you know? "I don't care if I harm others because I'm free from dualism," blah blah, all these sorts of things. So that's "sidetrack in terms of view." "Sidetrack in terms of meditation" would be when practitioners meditate—probably especially when they're doing higher-level practices like Mahamudra, Ati Yoga, and so on, I think—and then the meditation produces more like a feeling of emptiness, or a kind of dissociative response.

BPJ: Like depersonalization-derealization, like you don't think anything's real?

NC: Yeah, like that, exactly.

BPJ: One often hears that wind disorders specifically are associated with meditation problems. Why is wind so connected with meditation?

NC: Panic attacks and anxiety are more connected with wind, and specifically excess or disordered wind in the heart (*nying lung*),[25] right? Practitioners start to worry, and then they don't get enough sleep and then wind increases and becomes imbalanced. Also, if you look at the symptoms of post-traumatic stress disorder [PTSD], many of them are wind symptoms. Psychosomatic symptoms are also connected with wind. You know, like some people who dream that a snake is biting some part of their body and then the next day when they wake up they feel very sick in that area and they are convinced that a snake-spirit, a naga or *lü,* is attacking them. All these kinds of more psychosomatic problems are mostly connected with wind.

BPJ: The subtle quality of wind.

NC: Yeah, exactly. I think we can say that wind-humor disorders relate with anxiety in the context of meditation problems. I think many people have anxiety like this. They do meditation but then start thinking they're not meditating enough, that they're not doing it the right way. There's so much fear involved with their meditation. And all these fears cause conditions like wind in the heart. In Tibetan medicine, anxiety is considered a wind disorder. And PTSD patients who cannot fall asleep—they have bad dreams and wake up repeatedly feeling bad. All these symptoms are mostly what we call *lungtruk,* wind disturbance.[26]

And then in some instances, meditation can cause psychosis—that's more like *soklung trukpa,* disturbance of the wind in the central life channel or aorta. Normally in Tibetan when we say somebody has "wind in the life channel" that means that someone has really gone crazy, like they're having hallucinations and that kind of thing.

BPJ: Like a full psychotic episode.

NC: Exactly, yes. So those things are explained as wind disease and doctors will give medicines and do massage, moxibustion, all the appropriate wind-balancing therapies. Of course, spiritual healing practices might be done as well, like exorcistic rituals to remove the obstacle (*gektrö*), ritual cleansings using blessed water (*chaptru*) or protective blessings rituals (*kargo*).[27] Since patients sometimes talk to spirits or invisible people when they get psychosis, people think that their condition is more spiritual and that spiritual healing is also necessary. The medical interpretation of some of these symptoms is more about wind disorder in the life channel, *soklung,* though. Instead of going down, wind-energy goes up, instead of going to the right side it goes to the left, and so on. That's why patients have these hallucinations and other symptoms—in medical terms, their energy is moving abnormally. In the

Dharma context, sometimes people will see someone having hallucinations and will say, "Oh, maybe that's provocations, that's possession, we'll do rituals," and so on, whereas from the perspective of Tibetan medicine, we might say, "Oh, that's wind in the life channel, we have to give them pills." It's possible to have different views sometimes.

"Wind in the life channel" is understood a bit differently in Sowa Rigpa compared to Dharma. In Tibetan medicine the *sokdzin lung* or the "life-sustaining" wind-energy is in the head or brain, but in Dharma it's in the heart or heart-chakra. Medically, disturbance of the *sokdzin lung* may not be associated with psychosis. It can be milder forms of sensory disturbance or confusion. In Dharma though, *soklung* is sometimes explained as a disturbance of wind in the *soktsa* or aorta. The *soktsa* or "life channel" is also thought of as the central channel of the subtle body in Buddhist contexts. So, in this case, *soklung* disorder can mean something wrong with the karmic winds which are partially connected with the central channel. I remember reading a text by Dudjom Rinpoche about Dorje Drolö wrathful deity yoga practice, where he says don't concentrate too much on the heart-chakra while meditating otherwise you'll get *soklung* and go crazy, something like that. There are quite a few tantric Buddhist texts where they talk like that. In medicine, *sokdzin lung* disturbance is more connected with diet and lifestyle, with stress, but in Dharma it's more connected with severe psychosis—with meditating too much or in the wrong way, spending too much time in retreat, and so on.[28] So, I think it's good to understand these differences.

BPJ: Could you describe some of the experiences you've had diagnosing, treating, or preventing meditation sickness in any of your students or patients? How did you determine that their symptoms were connected with meditation? Is there any type of treatment that's used generally for meditation sickness or is every case different?

NC: Every case is different. But when some people go into retreat they already enter with some kind of anxiety. They go in unprepared. So, I think there is that issue and then some people already have a base of anxiety, a predisposition towards it, as well. They stay alone in retreat and are deprived of many different things and then I think they have a base to develop these kinds of problems. Traditionally, meditation practice is very strict, and you have to do long, unbroken retreats. But I think that maybe today everybody should go into retreat with interviews, you know?

BPJ: You mean they should be screened before they enter retreat?

NC: Yeah, exactly. In Yachen nunnery[29] in Tibet they do this very strict "world renouncing" *chatrel*-type retreats, in these small huts, and so on. When I visited there once, I talked with this nun who was explaining how many nuns do this type of retreat and she was kind of proud. Then I asked her, "And do any nuns go crazy, do they get sick?" I think some of the people there thought I was quite strange for asking that! She looked at me and said "Ah, yes. Many of them!" If a doctor is present, they maybe try to take care of those people but if there's no doctor then they might just say, "Oh it's your karma" or "Your accumulation of merit is not good enough, you should do merit-accumulating practices" and so on. Sometimes you meditate and then become psychotic, but the good thing is that people don't necessarily treat you badly. Instead, they recognize that this happened to you during meditation, that it occurred after you meditated, and they don't stigmatize. I think that that is maybe kind of helpful, you know?

BPJ: Okay, yeah. So, there's a positive aspect to the idea of meditation sickness.

NC: Exactly. Let's say one of the nuns gets this kind of disease from doing Tummo, Dzogchen, or Mahamudra meditation, or whatever. Then their lama might say, "Okay, do practices to accumulate merit and to purify obscurations." Don't do these high-level meditations, do more low-level ones. So that means you return to the tantric preliminaries (*ngöndro*) and do prostrations, these very basic things.[30] I think that sometimes these things may actually work better than medical treatment too.

BPJ: Yes, it gives people more of a positive view, like, "Okay, I'm a little crazy, I'm a bit sick now, but if I keep working on this I can improve my merit and there's kind of a chance for recovery." Not just, "Now you're crazy. Oh, now we have to put you in the hospital."

NC: Yeah, exactly. If it's too much—if their symptoms are too severe—they send them to the doctor. But I think that many people may already have an underlying condition, like, something under the meditation sickness condition that arises. They might have personality disorders—maybe borderline or paranoic personality disorder. I think that practitioners with these kinds of conditions normally have more trouble in retreat and during meditation. It's not that everybody gets problems—I think that people with underlying conditions have to be more careful.

BPJ: So, as you said, it would help if there was more screening at different stages for people to understand these dangers. So then do you think that there are some personalities, some students who should never do any meditation, or is it more like they just need to find the right meditation or version of the meditation for them? Or should some people just never do calm abiding meditation, never do blissful heat (Tummo) meditation, and so on?

NC: I think everybody can find the right meditation. Maybe some people are not so good at concentration but are excellent at imagination or at focusing on the breath. Likewise, I think if people have a more paranoid nature, they should not learn or not do so many protector deity practices, because if they do, they'll get scared![31]

BPJ: So, just knowing the right medicine for the right person, I guess?

NC: Exactly, yeah.

BPJ: Are there any other stories or anecdotes you can think of about your own students or your own patients—obviously you don't have to share personal details—any other examples of how you've approached meditation side effects or meditation sickness in your own practice, with patients you've seen?

NC: One patient of mine did forty-nine days of dark retreat. After that he was completely "out," completely crazy. I thought that was kind of bad because why had he done forty-nine days of dark retreat if he was so unprepared or vulnerable? Later, I learned that he received instructions in this practice from an old Tibetan Bön[32] master. I know this Bön master—he is very open-minded. Whoever comes he just gives direct teachings. Sometimes people hear terms like "dark retreat meditation" and they really want to do it and really want to receive instructions and authorizations for it. So then they tell their teachers, "Oh, I'm a good practitioner, I've practiced for so many years, and so on, I want to do dark retreat, blah, blah." And then many teachers just give them the teaching without checking the person's condition. From what I could tell, this patient was already exhibiting some signs of psychosis before he went into forty-nine day retreat. I think this kind of thing is dangerous.[33] So, instead of flat-out saying, "Oh, you can't do dark retreat," I think it's maybe better to say something like, "You should do breathing exercises, or prostrations"—very basic, physical things. You should tell students that they are not ready, that they have to make their foundation. But then, I know there are some people who really want to do very specific retreats, and they are also very smart. They know how to ask for the teachings and permissions they want from teachers.

BPJ: To get what they want!

NC: Exactly. It's a bit like alcoholics—they can always find alcohol. Drug addicts can always find drugs.

BPJ: Even if it's negative for them, they still want it.

NC: Exactly! There's a reason we call Tantric Buddhism *sangngak,* "Secret Mantra," in Tibetan. We can definitely say it's not for everyone.

BPJ: And so, you treated this patient, after the forty-nine days. Was he able to return to some kind of normalcy?

NC: The problem with these kinds of people is that they think they are very advanced. They don't listen to you. He was already in very bad shape, and I told him that he should take pills and medicines and that he also then needed to have treatment with Western doctors but he said, "No, I don't like Western doctors! They know nothing—they use only chemicals!" He was really in denial and was very against Western doctors. But I suggested that he take some Tibetan pills and rest and all those sorts of things. But my feeling was, I was really left thinking, why did that teacher give such secret teachings as these to him? Because he was not ready. In a case like this, if the teaching was treated as "Secret Mantra," if it was kept hidden from this person then it would have been safer for him, right?

And another case: A guy did a few months of retreat for a very wrathful deity practice and afterwards he came back and was completely psychotic. This is one reason why visualizing or imagining deities[34] for too long can also be dangerous, I think. Practitioners do this and then they have visions. They see strange things and then think that they're "in the deity state." This man came back from retreat and then had lots of trouble with his family members.

BPJ: Did you also give him treatment or medicine?

NC: Yeah. I think that often the people who want to do long retreats, who really want to do these practices, are seeking something because they already have emotional traumas or problems, have already had visions, and so on. They are looking for some kind of solution. But then when they find a solution, they go after it and over-do it. They force themselves. Maybe they think, "Oh, this is what will resolve my problems!," and so on. But even if these Dharma practices are helpful, in the end, if you do too much, if you force things, you get stressed and then things get triggered and you just get worse.

BPJ: Mm. So, you mentioned before that one approach to prevent these kinds of problems from happening is to do more screening, more checking of students.

NC: Especially when sending them on long retreats, yeah.

BPJ: So shorter retreats are a safer option, maybe?

NC: Exactly, yes.

BPJ: And then you also mentioned this traditional idea of even if you're doing a longer retreat, you come out of the retreat and you have a sort of brief check-in with the teacher and you say, "These were my experiences."

NC: Yeah. You know with some of our more counseling-focused classes, we have a psychiatrist pre-screen and interview prospective students. Still, it's always possible that students will be accepted who still have issues. Sometimes there are students whose backgrounds I know better who pass the initial interview screening process. Because I know them, if they were to say to me that they want to do this training, I might have found another way and said, "Oh, you should train in another therapy, like simple physical yoga practices." Because

I would know this particular student can't handle counselor training, because they have this basis of anxiety, or a sensitivity to psychosis, and so on. But then even a professional psychiatrist might accept a student like this after interviewing them. And later they might have problems during their studies. It's a similar kind of thing with meditation. If you don't really know students, even if you do interviews, they can pass those interviews. And then in the middle of the course or retreat they run into problems. So that's why I think guiding students individually and understanding their individual conditions is always important.

BPJ: And you have to keep checking on people throughout the process, because you can't be sure how things are progressing.

NC: You can also have individual students in larger class groups who are completely "out" or psychotic but who do okay initially. And maybe they're very nice people, not disruptive or aggressive at all. But they can have more serious crises later on. Some people have these kind of issues—sensitivity to psychosis, trauma, anxiety, and so on—and that's partly why they want to learn about these things in the first place—about spirituality, healing, therapy, counseling, things like that. But sometimes they can't handle these topics, they can't digest them, and then they get triggered. That's why even if you do interviews, I'm sure some people really want to do a Tummo retreat so much and somehow they're able to convince you they can do it. So, when students are in a retreat I think that frequently interviewing them or you know, just checking on them is important.

BPJ: Like a "wellness check" to see how people are doing.

NC: Exactly.

BPJ: You mentioned the Sowa Rigpa counselor training program.[35] Did being involved with that and working with and co-teaching the course with a professional psychiatrist change your perspective at all, compared to before you were involved?

NC: Yeah. I especially like the personality disorder part of Western psychiatry. Because I think personality disorders are usually kind of hidden. Many people have these tendencies but they're not patients yet. Other people might just consider you a very "difficult" or "different" person, things like that. I think it is mostly people who have underlying conditions or these sorts of personality disorders who are triggered during long retreats and meditation. Yeah, I think that part of the counselor course helped my understanding a lot. Because in Tibetan tradition, we will talk about wind-humor types, bile types, and so on, but we are talking about typology, we are talking about the characters and characteristics of healthy people. We're talking about *personality,* right? There is a recognition that there are different base-line personalities, that some people are like this, some are like that. But I like this psychiatric focus on personality *disorder.* When you talk about "disorder," it's already a red flag, an indication of existing imbalance, a warning about potential problems. I think this red flag is very important in spiritual practice as well. With Dharma groups, even when sangha members aren't meditating, many times the persistent troublemakers, the type of people you see who fight with one sangha group then join another group and get into conflicts again, they tend to have personality issues. When there's a pattern of behavior like this, it becomes obvious that they really have these sorts of issues.

BPJ: Something I've thought a lot about is that Buddhism is about helping people who have problems, who are suffering, right? So, it's difficult to say, "Oh, you have a personality disorder" or "Oh, you're a troublemaker, no Dharma for you!" But it can also create so many problems in organizations or in Buddhist communities to just ignore these issues. So, what do you do with those sorts of people? You can't refuse them completely, because you have to be kind and help them if you can, but what kind of systems do you put in place to manage these issues? Sometimes it seems like some teachers are so generous, they just want to give teachings so freely and sometimes I think maybe there should be more screening. But personally, I'm never quite sure how open or how restrictive some things should be. What do you do?

NC: The number one issue for those sorts of people—you're thinking of borderline people, right?—is fear of being abandoned. So, if you say, "Okay, you cannot do this teaching, you cannot do this practice," that's exactly when they feel like they are not in the group, and so on. Normally, if we organize a group retreat, I think we should not make too many distinctions between participants. But if students need to do retreat individually then I think it's good to suggest that they really do light retreats, nothing that harsh. I think triggers mostly happen during the retreat or post-retreat if students do long retreats. But generally, if somebody in the group has a personality disorder, then it's a red flag. If everybody else knows, if the teacher knows, then I think that's already helpful, no?

BPJ: Yeah, some kind of awareness about patterns of behavior.

NC: Yes. We call it "a horse with ropes or reins." If a horse starts to cause trouble, you hold it firm from the reins to control it. This can protect the rider and the horse, will calm and stabilize them. Of course, some people might say, "Oh, this person is narcissistic, that person is this or that." We can definitely judge people too much and there's a chance we can get fixated on labels or on pathologizing people. In general though, I think knowing more about one's students, knowing in advance that somebody has a very difficult personality, I think that's always useful.

BPJ: So then that also suggests it would help if lamas and teachers know their students better and if they give instructions based on greater understanding of each individual student. Big group teachings are very popular these days. Nowadays with online teachings students don't even meet or spend time with the teacher in person and the teacher doesn't even meet them.

NC: Yes. I think the main thing is that most problems are connected with retreats. . . . That's why I really think meditation teachers need basic medical knowledge and training. That's very important.

It's also good that Tibetan doctors have a little bit of Western medical knowledge and training, or at least some respect for Western medicines and doctors. . . . At the very least, if somebody is having a mental health crisis and they need to take antidepressants or some other drugs, I think teachers should support this, instead of talking badly about Western medicine and saying, "No, don't take chemicals, chemicals will do this or that to you," and so on.

BPJ: Yeah. There's going to probably be a better outcome if the patient's spiritual guide is supporting their treatment.

NC: Exactly. Otherwise, if the guide says something else, of course patients will side with meditation, will choose the spiritual, right? But then when there's a medical crisis you cannot fix it with spiritual practices. If somebody has become completely psychotic and is in a severe condition, it's better we don't talk about meditation and things like that. We shouldn't talk about these things with them at all.

BPJ: Yeah, we have to bring them down to earth.

NC: Exactly. Once they're balanced again, we can bring up spiritual practices as a possibility. As I mentioned, there are suggestions in some tantric texts about what the practitioner should do if they experience hallucinations or this or that symptom. The text will prescribe specific meditations, medications, or treatments, or say you should do this or that practice. But if it's a severe case, I think it's better that we let a psychiatrist deal with the situation. Some meditation masters may think that if they abandon this person it means that their Bodhichitta—their altruistic intention—is deficient, that kind of thing. But genuine Bodhichitta has to go with *sherap,* intelligence. Compassion goes with intelligence, with wisdom. So, if you cultivate intelligence, you have to choose what is best for that person, right? Even if you yourself cannot help them, if you know of somebody else who can, you should let them do so.

BPJ: Do you have any simple advice for students who want to start meditating regularly? Maybe they have had some anxiety or other conditions in the past, but they want to start a regular meditation practice, or maybe they even want to do a retreat—what kind of things would you suggest to them to avoid any side effects or problems in the future?

NC: The key thing is stress. Stress associated with meditation—when you feel like you don't really understand the practice or like you're forcing yourself. Before you go into retreat, you have to know what you're going to do, how many practices you're going to do, for how long, and so on. I think everybody should know more or less, not what they *have* to do, not just the technical requirements of the meditation, but how much they are personally *capable* of doing. What you yourself can do—I think everybody should know that.

BPJ: So, everybody should know their personal limits, what's possible for them. A lot of people go into retreat with a feeling like, "Oh, now that I have this time, I *must* complete this many accumulations of practice or else I will not progress."

NC: In the past, I was strict with retreats. Now I tell students to do less retreat practice.

Notes

1. The "Science of Healing." While Sowa Rigpa is often treated as synonymous with Tibetan medicine (*bö men*), it includes knowledge and practices from Tibetan, Indian, Chinese, Nepali, Greco-Persian, Mongolian, and other sources and continues to be widely studied, practiced, and patronized in India, China, Mongolia, Nepal, India, and Russia. For more on Sowa Rigpa, see Chenagtsang (2024).
2. For more on *ngakpa,* see Joffe (2019b).
3. A medical college or university (literally, "house of medicine and astrology").
4. Dr. Nida is the founder and principal teacher of Sorig Khang International, an organization dedicated to teaching Tibetan medical and Buddhist practices that operates through a loose global network of student groups, clinics, and educational institutions. He is also the cofounder of the United States-based Sowa Rigpa Institute and the Ngakmang Research Institute based in Tibet, dedicated to preserving nonmonastic, noncelibate yogi and yogini traditions in his native Amdo and beyond.
5. "The Heart-Essence Teachings of Yuthok." My phoneticizations of "Yuthok" and "Nyingthig" follow existing standards used by Dr. Nida in his English publications. For other Tibetan terms, I have generally followed the system of Simplified Phonetic Transcription of Standard Tibetan developed by Germano and Tournadre (2010).
6. In addition to compiling and transmitting the teachings of the Yuthok Nyingthig, Yuthok the Younger is also widely regarded as the chief author or codifier of the *Gyü zhi,* or *Four Medical Tantras.* This four-volume textbook of Sowa Rigpa theory and practice still holds pride of place in Tibetan medical curricula around the world today. See Yuthok Yönten Gönpo (with Sumtön Yeshé Zung) (2023) for a recent edition of

the Yuthok Nyingthig put together by Dr. Nida, the Ngakmang Institute, and Sky Press.

7. Our approximately seventy-five-minute conversation took place in English in the early evening, while Dr. Joffe was in Porto, Portugal, and Dr. Nida was in Anzio, Italy. The transcript was edited for length, readability, and flow. Many Tibetan or Sanskrit terms used by Dr. Nida in the original conversation have been glossed in English.

8. *Dön* is a general term for invisible, nonhuman beings that harm humans and cause disease. Dr. Nida and other teachers sometimes translate *dön* as "provocation" to highlight the fact that such nonhuman attacks on humans are typically thought of as retaliative, as actions provoked by humans' misconduct in their current or former lifetimes.

9. The number eighty-four thousand is used in Buddhist contexts to mean "a vast number," "infinite," or "countless" in a way similar to the English emphatic "a gazillion."

10. In Tibetan medical theory, the "general distant cause" of all disease is ignorance (*ma rig pa*)—failure to realize selflessness and the true nature of reality. The "specific distant causes" of disease are the three root mental poisons that arise from ignorance—that is, desire-attachment, animosity-aversion, ignorance-confusion. The three humoral energies of wind, bile, and phlegm emerge subsequently from these poisons and are referred to as the three "near causes" of disease. The balance and flow of the three humoral energies help sustain the normal, healthy functioning of the body, speech energy, and mind. When these three humoral energies meet with specific secondary factors or adverse conditions (*kyen*), they are pushed into states of deficiency, excess, or disorder and ultimately manifest as explicit symptoms and full-blown disease. In Sowa Rigpa, spirit provocation is classified as one of four basic secondary factors for the development of disease, along with seasonal and time-related factors, diet, and lifestyle.

11. The "channels, winds, and drops," the primary components of the subtle Vajra body, play an important role in the theory and practice of Tibetan tantric yoga and the Dzokrim or Completion Stage of tantric Buddhist meditation. The flow of subtle wind energies through the channels and their nexuses, the chakras, correlates with specific physiological functions and states of consciousness. The drops are condensations of blissful energy, which exist on more and less subtle levels (Dr. Nida sometimes equates the more material level of *thiglé* in the body with hormones, for example, while subtler levels of *thiglé* have more to do with the innately blissful nature of embodied awareness); see Chenagtsang (2018, 147–153), for further discussion.

12. Stick therapy. In stick therapy, practitioners use pliable rods with wooden knobs or pouches of medicines attached to one end to tap on specific points on patients' bodies with varying intensity and pressure. This therapy is not taught in the *Four Medical Tantras* but was transmitted through the Terma or visionary revelation tradition. Stick therapy appears to have begun as a self-healing therapy for yogis and yoginis to treat imbalances of all three humoral energies that arose in retreat. See Joffe (2019a) for a translation of Dr. Nida's essay describing his research into this practice and his efforts to revitalize its use as both a self-healing therapy and a method for treating patients.

13. Bimala/Vimalamitra's Formula, also known as Dzāti Nyishu, Nutmeg 20 Formula, said to have been created by the eighth-century Indian Buddhist master Vimalamitra (Tibetans pronounce Vimala like Bimala). With a base of nutmeg supported by nineteen other ingredients, this formula is used to treat disorders of excess and disturbed wind and wind in the heart and life channel (*nyinglung, soklung*) more specifically.
14. Also known as *gyalgong,* these spirits are reincarnations of monks and lamas who were accomplished in tantric practice in their previous lives but who lapsed in their commitments and died with a great sense of self-importance and resentment. Sometimes propitiated as protector deities, they have a reputation for being particularly capricious and vindictive. Perhaps the most well-known and controversial *gyalpo* is Dorje Shugden, a protector deity associated with the Gelukpa school who has strongly divided Tibetan and Tibetan Buddhist communities since the 1970s.
15. The eleventh-century Tibetan yogi who is said to have achieved Buddhahood in a single lifetime by engaging in intensive meditation retreats and austerities in remote mountain caves over the course of several decades.
16. Typology encompasses various bodily, verbal-energetic, and mental tendencies. See Chenagtsang (2024) for more details.
17. Generally speaking, Dr. Nida recommends calm abiding meditation, breathing exercises, chanting, and mantra recitation for wind-dominant typologies; *vipaśyanā* and analytic, interpretive meditations as well as visualization and memory-intensive practices for bile-dominant typologies; and mindful walking, physical yoga practices, and prostrations for phlegm-dominant typologies. For a self-assessment exercise for determining one's typology and a fuller explanation of the logic of these meditation recommendations, see Chenagtsang (2024, 261–277).
18. *Münpa tawé zhi-né.* This sort of numb dullness may be associated with a predominance of *beken* or phlegm humor.
19. See Yongey Mingyur Rinpoche and Tworkov (2019) for extensive discussions on how Mingyur Rinpoche was able to "self-liberate" his panic attacks through meditation.
20. Gampopa Sönam Rinchen (1079–1153), a layman turned monk and great meditator who became one of the primary disciples of Milarepa, mentioned above. Mahamudra is the Great Seal, Chaggya Chenpo in Tibetan. Mahamudra teachings are regarded as the apex teachings of the New Translation (Sarma) schools of Tibetan Buddhism. They focus on the direct and unmediated realization of the nature of mind.
21. Jamgön Kongtrul Lodrö Tayé (1813–1899). Extended retreat in complete darkness is primarily associated with Dzogchen *tögal* practices, during which practitioners use the open-eyed hallucinations that arise through light deprivation and yogic practice to stabilize and expedite their realization of the nature of mind.
22. *Bokdön.* Contemplations, medications, and yogic exercises recommended for practitioners who fail to make sufficient meditative progress or to generate significant meditative experiences. Part of a triad of meditation supports along with "Signs of the Path" teachings and "Obstacle Elimination" practices.

23. See Yuthok Yönten Gönpo (2023, 483–517).

24. Also called Dzogchen, the highest level of teachings in the Old Translation (Nyingma) school of Tibetan Buddhism. Also called Ati Yoga.

25. The chapter on the treatment of wind disorders in the Oral Instructions Tantra of the *Four Medical Tantras* explains the symptoms of *nyinglung* as "trembling of the body; tightness and pressure in the upper body or chest (with associated hypertension); hallucinations; meaningless or incoherent speech or talking; dizziness; sleeping very little; sighing" (see Yuthok Yonten Gönpo [2017, 17], for an alternative translation). There is considerable overlap between *nyinglung* disorders and "wind in the aorta or central channel" (*soklung*) disorders.

26. Humoral disorders can be broadly categorized in terms of excess, deficiency, or disturbance of the humoral energy in question. Wind-disturbance disorders are characterized by a wide array of physical, energetic, or mental-emotional symptoms, which often present simultaneously. See Chenagtsang (2024); Dean (2019); Samuel (2019); and Yuthok Yönten Gönpo (2011, 115–116).

27. *Gektrö* rituals cast out obstructing spirits with the help of ritual fumigations, mantras, ritual gestures, and so on. With *kargo,* tantric meditational deities (*yidam*) or protector deities (*sungma*) are called upon to shield a patient from various kinds of harm and obstacles.

28. See Chui (2018) for examples of meditation techniques prescribed for *soklung* disorders caused by meditating.

29. Yachen Gar or, alternatively, Yachen Orgyen Samten Chöling. A nunnery or religious encampment (*gar*) located in what the Chinese state calls Gardze Tibetan Autonomous Prefecture in western Sichuan Province.

30. Contemplative practices that aim to provide practitioners with a sufficient foundation for engaging in more advanced tantric yogic and nonconceptual meditation practices. *Ngöndro* practices are typically repeated tens of thousands of times and are specific to particular cycles or lineages of tantric teachings. Tantric preliminaries proper, the so-called uncommon preliminaries, generally involve taking refuge and cultivating *bodhichitta,* doing prostrations, making mandala offerings, and engaging in guru yoga meditation.

31. Protector-deity propitiation is a common feature of Tibetan tantric Buddhist practice. Whether enlightened or unenlightened, protector deities are oath bound to protect Buddhist lineages, teachings, and initiates. They frequently manifest in gruesome and aggressive guises.

32. Often defined as Tibet's pre-Buddhist, Indigenous religion, Bön has nonetheless developed in close conversation with Buddhism in Tibet. Dzogchen dark retreat meditation is practiced in both Buddhism and Bön.

33. Nida retold this story in a joint interview he did for the *Guru Viking* podcast, along with Justin von Bujdoss, an American Buddhist teacher who has engaged in several dark retreats under Dr. Nida's supervision and whom Nida has authorized to teach the

Dzogchen practices of the Yuthok Nyingthig. Following this retelling, Nida and Justin discussed the importance of integrating and digesting meditative experiences post retreat and reintegrating into regular life more broadly, topics Nida and I did not discuss in our interview. See James (2023, 1:30.00–1.35.22).

34. Specifically, nondual tantric "deity yoga" (*lha yi nenjor*) practices in which practitioners imagine themselves as the deity.

35. A two-year training program offered through the Sowa Rigpa Institute combining insights from Western psychiatry, Tibetan Sowa Rigpa, and Tibetan Buddhism. See https://www.sowarigpainstitute.org/sowa-rigpa-programs for more information.

Chapter 20

A Psychiatrist's View from Contemporary India and Nepal

Interviews with Dr. Pawan Sharma

IRA HELDERMAN

The following are excerpts from a series of interviews conducted with the Nepali psychiatrist Pawan Sharma. Dr. Sharma, along with his Nepalese and Indian colleagues, has published on the topic of "meditation-related psychosis" in Anglophone medical journals. In our interviews, Sharma expands and clarifies his published findings drawn from clinical case studies of individuals presenting with psychotic symptoms seemingly associated with meditation practice. The semistructured interviews were conducted with Sharma over approximately five hours during four separate Zoom meetings from August through October 2022. The material has been consolidated, reorganized, and edited for the sake of flow and readability.

In the excerpts included below, Sharma discusses both his personal and professional history. Describing his religio-cultural background, he explains that in Nepal there is "not much delineation between Hindus and Buddhists." He notes that he grew up in what he calls a "meditation culture" in which certain meditation practices "for the attainment of salvation or Nirvana" were highly familiar to him. However, he has not meditated himself and rarely saw people close to him meditating during his childhood. Meanwhile, the place of meditation in the medical field has significantly changed over the course of his lifetime (he was thirty-six at the time of our interviews). Early in his medical training, he began to increasingly hear of new previously unfamiliar meditation practices (mindfulness and Transcendental Meditation) that were partially developed in the United States and promoted as therapeutic.

In our interviews, Sharma related the history of his research and clinical treatment of patients with meditation-related psychosis, beginning with his time as a training resident physician at the All-India Institute of Medical Sciences (AIIMS) in New Delhi and extending into his current psychiatric practice at Patan Academy of Health Sciences in Kathmandu, where he reports continuing to treat two to four such patients per year. He also engages with some of the core questions that currently surround the topic of challenging and distressing meditation experiences.

Dr. Sharma adds a uniquely valuable perspective to recent Anglophone conversations about meditation sickness. The interviews excerpted were initially conducted for my ongoing study of how psychotherapists have approached adverse meditation experiences throughout history. The vast majority of clinicians and psychological researchers currently publishing on adverse meditation effects have done so in the United States and Europe, studying and treating "meditators-in-distress" of European descent. In commentary on this topic, the cultural and racial backgrounds of these meditators can at times go almost completely ignored. Sharma, meanwhile, has treated Nepalese and Indian patients in a markedly different cultural context.

Listening to Sharma brings to light the importance of maintaining an awareness of cultural difference when considering meditators-in-distress from various backgrounds. Psychotherapists in the United States (predominantly white themselves) have increasingly stressed the need for this awareness when distinguishing psychopathology from religious experiences that might actually be common within certain cultures. Sharma, for example, describes a commonplace occurrence for him growing up, encountering "transient possession spells in the temples" (i.e., individuals who are temporarily possessed by a spirit). Because these experiences are socially normative, his team typically does not diagnose these meditators as experiencing a psychotic episode. This is despite the fact that they might appear to suffer from forms of dissociation depicted in biomedical diagnostic systems like the *Diagnostic and Statistical Manual of Mental Disorder* (*DSM*) and the *International Classification of Diseases* (*ICD*)—the former commonly used in the United States and the latter internationally, including in Nepal.[1]

At the same time, Sharma is resolutely biomedically minded in his assessment of meditation-related psychosis. He states in our interviews that, ultimately, "it's all neurochemicals." As a result, Sharma believes there are no differences between meditators from different cultural backgrounds in terms of what he calls the "core psychopathology" that he treats. He indicates that the particular delusions or hallucinations that meditators-in-distress might experience could be specific to their culture, but he would anticipate that the basic "cause and effect," the notion that certain approaches to meditation practice can trigger psychosis, would occur in the same way across cultures and "throughout the generations."

In terms of the clinical treatment of individuals experiencing meditation-related psychosis, Sharma consequently supports the use of antipsychotics regardless of the exact shape such psychosis may take. And yet Sharma also elucidates significant cultural differences between clinical treatment in Nepal and the United States. He notes that the symptoms of psychosis are often more intense than other forms of challenging and distressing meditation effects that might occur in the wider population. Further, psychiatrists in Nepal have tools that are unavailable to clinicians in the United States due to differing cultural views on individual "autonomy," as he refers to it. For example, in the United States involuntary hospitalization can only occur when a patient is at imminent risk of harming themselves or others. But in Nepal the role of the family is often centered and with the family's consent hospitalization and even "surreptitious medication" can be sanctioned.

Finally, Sharma also responds in our interviews to perspectives that might differ from his own on the etiology and treatment of meditation-related psychosis. He grants that some could have legitimate concerns about his approach but emphasizes that his views are markedly shaped by his location as a practicing clinician who sees upward of fifty or sixty patients a day.

Nonetheless, he also expresses an openness to resources that are typically classified as religious for responding to meditation difficulties. He states that biomedical and religious approaches are "not mutually exclusive" and "that the clinicians and the religious scholars should sit together" to best determine how to care for meditators-in-distress.

Further Reading

Charan, Deepak, Pawan Sharma, Gaurav Kachhawaha, Gurveen Kaur, and Snehil Gupta. 2021. "Meditation Practices and the Onset of Psychosis: A Case Series and Analysis of Possible Risk Factors." *Indian Journal of Psychological Medicine* 20:1–6.

Joshi, Sulochana, Anusha Manandhar, and Pawan Sharma. 2021. "Case Report: Meditation-Induced Psychosis: Trigger and Recurrence." *Case Reports in Psychiatry*, no. 1, https://doi.org/10.1155/2021/6615451.

Sharma, Pawan, Ananya Mahapatra, and Rishab Gupta. 2019. "Meditation-Induced Psychosis: A Narrative Review and Individual Patient Data Analysis." *Irish Journal of Psychological Medicine*, 39 (4): 1–7. http://www.doi.org/10.1017/ipm.2019.47.

Sharma, Pawan, S. Singh, S. Gnanavel, and N. Kumar. 2016. "Meditation—a Two Edged Sword for Psychosis: A Case Report." *Irish Journal of Psychological Medicine* 33:247–249.

Excerpts from Interviews with Pawan Sharma[2]

IH: Where did you grow up exactly?

PS: I grew up in the western part of Nepal; it's called Lumbini. I think you have heard of it as the birthplace of Lord Buddha. I grew up in that area, and then I studied up to my high school level in Kathmandu. And after I went to Kolkata for my undergraduate—that's in India, in West Bengal. I stayed in there for six years, and then after that I went to New Delhi, and then I completed my postgraduate. And I came back to Kathmandu, and after that I've been teaching [at the medical school].

IH: How would you describe your religious or spiritual background growing up? Would you say you grew up with any kind of religious affiliation or religious identity?

PS: We would identify ourselves as Hindus. And we would go to Buddhist monasteries as well. There is not much of delineation between Hindus and Buddhists here in Nepal. So we identify as Hindu but are not especially religious. We would observe whatever the general people would do. Religiously or culturally speaking, we were kind of more secular than religious people. We would visit temples occasionally or pujas (i.e., rituals) or something like that. And then there used to be pujas at home at some occasions, but not religiously or not regularly. And we didn't have much of that religious fanaticism or some such kind of thing; we were very open to everything. There were Muslim friends who used to visit my home, and we'd eat together. And then there was a Christian missionary hospital in my town, and we would visit there whenever we had some kind of illness or something. So we had that basic concept that we were Hindus, but then we wouldn't follow everything that the religion would demand us. We were very open. Our whole community was that way.

IH: Is there anything else that you feel would be important to share about your religious background?

PS: Well, the openness that we have regarding religion, that might have contributed to me going into this area [of research on meditation-associated psychosis]. I do not believe that spirituality is always good; I do not believe that religion is always right. My growing up might have led me to have this kind of open mind. That could be one reason.

IH: What was your experience with meditation practices growing up?

PS: I didn't myself practice meditation at any time in my life. And I didn't see many people meditating. Some people would be sitting quietly in Buddhist monasteries, that I saw, but I didn't have much interaction with them nor any relatives or any friend of mine who were doing such kind of things. So I don't remember anyone doing meditation.

IH: Growing up, what would you have thought of as meditation?

PS: Well, it's a tough question. So the idea I have of meditation might have come from different serials. We have Hindi television channels here, and they would have some kind of religious programs. There would be mythological programs where the people would meditate for years and years and get something from God himself. So for me, meditation would have been those kinds of things at that point of time. And regarding the mindfulness and Transcendental Meditation practices that we know right now, that would not have made sense to me at that time as meditation. I think the level of consciousness of the practitioner would have to be different [than an ordinary person's] for it to count as meditation for me at that time.

IH: Had you encountered mindfulness and Transcendental Meditation practices or similar practices at all growing up?

PS: No. We do not have the Nepalese equivalent of Transcendental or mindfulness-based meditation. Would I have seen a textbook or something come out in English? There was no chance of that. So I don't think I might have heard of them at that time.

IH: How does this affect the way you look at scientific research on meditation practices, which tends to focus on such practices?

PS: Well, reflecting on that, what I can say right now is that the things that are practiced in our culture are not published about most of the time. And in scientific literature, what we do is we generally tend to cite the things that are published. So, when I'm talking about a meditation-induced psychosis, I'm not talking about chanting a name of a god 108 times and having psychosis. These are biases in the scientific literature.

IH: How was the topic of meditation treated during your medical training?

PS: It was talked about more as a part of academic discussion rather than day-to-day practice. But there began to be a lot of patients asking us whether they should meditate for anxiety, whether meditation cures anxiety and depression. Those kinds of questions would come up frequently. The simple approach we had was to answer, "Well, meditation is good for general health. It's like eating a good diet. It's like having a good night's sleep. So meditation would be good for any disease—even for hypertension or diabetes it would be good—but that doesn't mean that it *cures* depression or it cures anxiety." So that would be our general advice to our patients. And that's what we had been taught by our professors. There were some residents who would be more interested in this kind of discussion, who believed that music therapy or meditation would be better than other psychotherapeutic processes. There were some individuals who believed that, but we didn't have much discussion other than an academic one regarding this.

IH: When you heard professors describe meditation as essentially part of good "mental hygiene" in this way, what kind of meditation were they referring to?

PS: I think what we understood that kind of meditation to be was simple breathing and relaxation exercises. And then whenever we would tell the patient it's good for hypertension or something, we would mean the relaxation exercise or breathing exercise. That would come up on television as well—for example, Ramdev Baba was active in India then preaching that yoga was beneficial. That was what we meant by meditation, so if the patient would ask about meditation we would have answered in that way.

But then that changed after we saw some cases of meditation-induced psychosis. After that, then we sometimes would tell the patient not to do "hard meditation" (that was the phrase we used) or meditate without taking food or without sleeping. Don't do such kinds of hard meditation. Soft forms of meditation like breathing and relaxation, you can do them.

IH: How was "the religious" or "spiritual"—people's religious practice or religious affiliation—treated in your medical training? Was there any discussion of avoiding pathologizing religious practice?

IH: We did not have much discussion regarding the culture or religion of a patient. We mostly discussed the social issues, compliance issues, we discussed the family issues. Religion-wise we didn't have much discussion. However, I forgot to mention that, during my childhood, I would see a lot of people having transient possession spells in the temples. We would get such kinds of patients during my residency—that was the culture—and we wouldn't pathologize those things because it's a culturally acceptable thing. Having one or two transient possession spells in a temple is looked at as fine. For us, it's no problem because all the people believe in that. So, actually, we would bring some awareness of religious concerns [to our clinical practice] there. And then, while talking about [the symptoms of] overvalued ideas and delusions, we would consider the religious context for that person. But generally, there was not discussion of whether to pathologize or not pathologize the religious practice. We would stick to [the diagnostic criteria in] *ICD* and then manage accordingly.

IH: How did you come to work on meditation-related difficulties?

PS: Regarding my work on meditation and psychosis, that started when I was in the second year of my residency when I came across a patient who had symptoms. What happened was, there was a patient on the ward who came with psychosis, and it was a "frank schizophrenia." And when inquiring, it was seen that he used to do intense meditation for around five to six hours a day and that increased up to twelve hours a day as well. So that was quite intense. Then, what we saw was that in some way the meditation was linked to the psychosis. We couldn't make out whether the meditation was due to psychosis or psychosis came as a result of meditation. Then what happened was we started him on some antipsychotics and after that he became well. And after a few months he was back again. He was taking medication, and he had started meditation again. It was this second time that he came that we concluded that meditation could be contributing in some way to the psychosis. And we presented this case at the grand rounds there at AIIMS. And then we thought of writing it and, luckily, the *Irish Journal of Psychological Medicine* was willing to accept it and we published it there.[3] After that, while reviewing, we found that there were other cases in the literature that saw some association of meditation with psychosis.

We hypothesized that it is meditation that brings an altered state in the mind that is in some way contributing to psychosis. And we also saw that there was some kind of time correspondence. There would be some time the patient would be involved in meditation and then there would be some event of psychosis. But in most of the literature, more than 90 percent of the people who had meditation-induced psychosis—or as I would like to call it a "meditation-associated psychosis"—had some kind of vulnerability already present. Vulnerability in terms of having previous episodes of psychosis; having a family history of psychosis, having some personality issues, taking some kind of drugs to get into an altered state like, say, cannabis, which is taken widely among people meditating in our part of the world. So there was some kind of predisposition. And for those who were not predisposed, there was some kind of sleep deprivation, there was some kind of food deprivation, some kind of sensory deprivation.

[After doing this research and presenting our findings,] I started practicing in Nepal and while practicing in Nepal I saw a few similar cases. We reported around on three or four cases in which there were similar findings to what were seen in India. However, ultimately what we thought was if meditation *is* causing psychosis, it's very difficult to prove. We can't have a case and control group and send somebody to meditate and induce psychosis. It would be very difficult to make an experiment which would *prove* that meditation causes psychosis or that psychosis would lead to meditation.

IH: Do you have any reaction to the fact that there is so much more attention to the positive benefits of meditation than its negative side effects?

PS: Yeah, I've seen people being antagonistic to me, people who are doing meditation and even when I posted my paper on Facebook there were reactions like "Buddha didn't have psychosis" and these kinds of things. But my reaction was like, okay, I looked into the evidence and the evidence suggested some relation is there. We don't know if it's causation or not, but some kind of association is there. My reaction was as a basic sciences student not more than that. The general notion about meditation is that it's good for you. And there is some research being done showing the positive aspects. And then the meditation centers where people are going to would not allow us to do some research on psychosis because if some positive correlation occurs, then their business is down. This difficulty is always there.

IH: Can you say more about these centers?

PS: There's a rampant wave of unsupervised meditation going on now, that's for sure. And there has been the establishment of multiple vipassana centers in Nepal. And what they do is they cut off the participants there from all their social life for a few days. And then, for the first session, I heard that they practice total sensory deprivation for one hour and, with time, it increases. And a lot of people have been going there. Most of the people say that it's good for them; it brings peace to them. But there have been people who believe that their anxiety has been triggered or psychosis has flared up while there. We see a lot of cases. And the kind of meditation [practiced at these centers] is not the type that is described in the scriptures or religious books, where there is supervision [so that meditators would not experience harm]. These are all motivated by business purposes. And, I'm really, really against these businesses running meditation centers.

And so I think all of this might have created a publication bias and people are not wanting to believe that meditation has some adverse effect. You know, the public has been brought up believing that the meditation is good, God says do meditation, the sages do meditation. And if we tell them that meditation is bad, then they're not going to believe that unless they face it themselves. This is what I see in the day-to-day clinical practice. People I see are trying to believe that meditation would cure their bipolar disorder, that meditation would cure their depression—such a notion is always there. And even on Facebook and social media it's like, "Don't go for medication, don't go for therapy. Go for meditation or go for some kind of relaxation exercise." Those kinds of notions are there in the public; it's kind of herd mentality right now. Especially in Nepal; I don't know about other parts of the world. So there's a general bias. Most of the people would not want to take allopathic medication or the medication that the drug companies make. They want to take something ayurvedic, something made from herbs. In the general public, this herd mentality is always there.

I see a lot of people posting [on social media] about anxiety or posting about depression . . . that "I became well" [after meditating]. Some kind of relaxation might have worked for them, aided their depression that's for sure. But then nobody's willing to talk about meditation-induced harm because that would be anti-majority. I remember one event with the Transcultural Psychosocial Organization.[4] I was project manager there and I was told to present something, so I presented on this topic [of meditation-induced harm]. And then there were some staff who were not at all interested or even arguing about those facts that I presented. I simply had to say, "These are the facts I researched; it's not I who made these facts."

But then there were also people responding [to my research] saying, "Thank you so much for writing about this." . . . I found some positive responses from people in Nepal . . . and people across the world recognizing what I had written during the time of residency and that made me really happy. And so I thought meditation-associated psychosis could be a field that my team could pursue. But we don't have that luxury here to do research in a single field, you know. This would otherwise be an area of interest to me.

And so, after that, I taught about this topic to my students in my hospital. And though there have been miniscule reports on it throughout the world, we continue to see a lot of cases here accelerated by meditation. Let's say, every three or four months, we see a case. And we have not reported, we have not been able to create that pool of data, but I think we should do that as well.

IH: You might see an additional case every three months maybe?

PS: Yeah, three to six months, let's say. We see cases regularly.

IH: Following up on what you've said about your case studies, why do you think it's important to distinguish when delusions are consistent with a patient's religious background?

PS: Oh, well, biologically speaking, that would make no sense at all because delusions are delusions; it's all neurochemicals. But if it's meditation induced or, say, psychosis related to meditation, then we might expect that there should be some kind of religious theme or a theme related to the social or religious background. One would expect that the social context or the religious context would come up once in a while.

IH: Can you say more about what you mean when you say, "It's all neurochemicals"?

PS: Well, when we look at psychosis as an interplay of chemicals only, then the content of the delusions would not matter at all. If there's a dopaminergic surge or an increase in dopaminergic neurons, then the delusion would occur, and the content wouldn't matter to us if we talked about only biology. And then, in treatment, we'd give antipsychotics and be finished. But when we look into the cultural context, the social context, then the delusion, however bizarre it may sound, should have some kind of link with the patient's understanding of [their] culture, some understanding of [their] religion. If some kind of theme regarding his religious beliefs comes along with meditation, then in that case, I think that it would make more sense for meditation to have caused or to be associated with that. So if I am meditating and I have a delusion that God is talking to me, that would make more sense in terms of my cultural background rather than saying that aliens are speaking to me. But, either way, we're giving antipsychotics for both.

IH: So do you believe that contemporary meditators are experiencing the same thing as meditators in the past, even in premodern or ancient times, who described distressing meditation experiences?

PS: I strongly believe that. I believe that if [meditation] is the cause, then the effect should be the same and it should be replicable throughout the generations. Test-retest validity, test-retest reliability should be there for any phenomenon to say that it's a cause and effect.

IH: It has been suggested that meditators in the United States, predominantly of European descent, are experiencing adverse effects because they are using practices against their intended aims. Have you heard this theory, and do you have any reactions to it?

PS: Well, not exactly that theory, but what I've heard, or what I've read commentary on, is that things that Hindus or Buddhists practice here as part of religion, is now being used as part of therapy. So what we were doing thousands of years ago, people are doing right now in the name of therapy. In my personal opinion, whatever works, whatever brings peace of mind is fine for the people. It's okay.

But I don't believe what you said in that theory, that meditation was made to be for one purpose and if done for another purpose it creates havoc in the mind. I don't believe that. Because I believe totally in the biological basis, and I believe that the vulnerability factors would have to be there. So, if somebody is not vulnerable and is doing twelve hours of meditation, I don't think that would make them psychotic. Some kind of vulnerability is always needed for a person to become psychotic, for anxiety to happen or depression to happen. That's my belief and I believe most of the theories and most of the research also back that up. And what I believe ultimately as a clinician, I would say what I find more important, is to know whether the person is vulnerable or not. And then the question is whether for them to continue or to stop the meditation. We need to be clinically active, rather than focused on the theoretical aspect. As I'm a clinician, I might be biased. I saw around fifty to sixty patients just today. It's difficult in this part of the world. We don't have that luxury you do of spending one or two hours with the patient.

IH: Is your observation that meditators with adverse experiences have a preexisting vulnerability derived from your clinical experience? Other psychological researchers have found that there are meditators-in-distress who do not report a preexisting vulnerability.

PS: Yeah, it could be my bias. I've seen the patients; I've not seen the general population. I see a patient and take a history. If somebody tells that [they have meditated] I go deeper into that because that's my interest. [Another physician] might not even notice that and might be treating psychosis without realizing this fact.

IH: How would you respond to a meditation teacher encouraging one of your team's patients to continue meditating, telling them that distressing or challenging meditation experiences can be a sign of progress on a contemplative path?

PS: I would ask the patient to completely stop meditation. Psychosis is creating distress, and if something distressful is happening, we need to treat that condition rather than thinking that distress will lead to a greater good. So I think I would be completely against [what the meditation teacher was encouraging]. I would try to psycho-educate the patient.

IH: But if the focus is on the patient's distress, what if a patient is, for example, experiencing euphoric mania and does not believe that they are experiencing distress at all (even as their family, for example, is deeply concerned, that they are not eating, not sleeping, etc.)?

PS: Well, what we have here is a little bit different than how psychiatrists practice in the West or the U.S. If we get consent from family members, we can admit the patient. That way, we're doing a lot of good to the patient. We even can physically restrain the patient by getting consent from the family members.

There might be some bad aspects to [this approach]. But, as a whole, families are more involved in the treatment. There have been many patients to whom I prescribe antipsychotic medication—and so this might seem a little bit off to you; you might not like that I would do this—but there are a lot of patients who are doing well with surreptitious medication. Like, other family members put some tablets in food and gives it to the patient unknowingly. We argue that if the patient's sense of reality has been lost, then it's up to the family members to decide on their behalf. So, [for example], in a case of a manic episode, what we do is we might admit such patients on our ward and give medication and after sanity has been restored then we can psycho-educate the patient [about the dangers of meditation] as well. I think it's a good part [of working] here.

IH: Do you ever have concerns about the risk of pathologizing religiosity when treating challenging and distressing meditation experiences?

PS: We're not pathologizing the religion; what we are pathologizing is the psychopathology that came [after meditating]. So it's nothing against religion and nothing against meditation. If somebody has no reaction to religious retreats, or no reaction to meditation, or it's creating good things for them, then I don't think any psychiatrist or psychologist would be bothered to intervene into that.

IH: So, for you, it goes back to the reported outcome of meditating, whether meditating "is creating good things" for the practitioner is the way you'd put it?

PS: Yeah, I'd bring in the definition of mental disorder: If it is causing dysfunction in any way, then we pathologize irrespective of the person's mood, let's say. We were talking about mania [which can include euphoria, but] if it's causing dysfunction, then we are against that dysfunction. We're against that psychopathology.

For mental illness there's a clear distinction. There are a cluster of symptoms, there's dysfunction, and it occurs for some duration of time. What the *DSM* or *ICD* tells us is that if there's dysfunction, it is psychopathology. Rather than pathologizing the religious experience, they're pathologizing the dysfunction in that person due to those experiences, whatever the experience might be. So I think depersonalization, derealization, or transient possession spell for a short period of time wouldn't warrant a diagnosis. But if there are clear cut psychotic symptoms—delusion, hallucinations, or disorganized behavior, disorganized speech, symptoms of formal thought disorders—such kind of symptoms objectively indicate that whatever the experience of the person that caused this psychopathology may be, that person needs help. Any person who needs help for their psychopathology, we need to pathologize them, otherwise providing help won't make any sense for them.

IH: The tricky thing is if we are using dysfunction and functional impairment—disruption to relational functioning or occupational functioning—to distinguish mental illness, well, the history of religious traditions is full of people who look functionally impaired, who leave their families and daily lives and occupations to go off in the forest and don't eat or sleep for days and report encounters with spirits. But those people claim to actually be functioning at a higher level than anyone else in their community.

PS: It's very difficult to say. Yeah there are those sorts of people. But the definitions we use here are: if there is a change in the behavior, thought, or emotions from the previous self, and if it is not keeping with the social cultural background, then we consider it psychopathology. But there would be some cases where we might need a lot of discussions about this. I think it's very difficult to give an answer in black and white. There will definitely be a sense of gray because we do not have an exact measure. If we take blood pressure, we have an exact measure—like 150/90 is hypertensive—but for psychosis, we do not have that. It completely becomes based on the discussion of the clinical team whether to pathologize or not. So, I don't have an exact answer for this.

IH: Do you think that it is important to distinguish whether certain meditation experiences are religious experience or mental illness?

PS: Whether it's a pathology or not is a very, very important thing because the management of the patient or the dealing with the patient will be completely different when we consider it to be normal religious experience versus psychopathology. But there's definitely a thin line between normality and pathology as highlighted by the transient possession spells that people have always experienced regardless of meditation. The distinction is needed, but it would not be very easy to distinguish unless we get a neurobiological substrate on that, unless we get a substrate that tells us definitively that it's a pathology. Until then, the question still will depend on the clinical judgment of the clinician or clinical judgment of a team of clinicians.

IH: Do you think that there could be resources in religious traditions for how to respond to people struggling with meditation difficulties?

PS: We've come far from that time where people with psychosis would be kept in a madhouse or kept on a separate island. Our understanding has improved regarding mental health; we all know that. And, I don't know since I've not researched it, but there might be some remedies for adverse meditation experiences in scriptures. I think there have been a lot of improvement in the development of a scientific understanding of mental illnesses. The main question still remaining is whether to pathologize it or not, and then if there are any remedies [in texts typically defined as religious] for that it would make sense.

IH: If we define a certain experience as mental illness, as psychosis, does that mean the psychiatrist would be best equipped to respond to it, whereas if we see it as a religious experience a religious teacher would be better suited?

PS: For that, I would say that I think the clinicians and the religious scholars should sit together. It's not like a clinician is doing their thing and the religious person is doing their thing, and they can't go hand in hand. They're not mutually exclusive. And I'll give you some examples. Like, on our wards, there are some people who believe that they should see a faith healer. And what we do is we give them a leave of two or three hours to go to a faith healer and we tell them not to spend much money on them and then to come back to the ward again. And this is helping in some way. We can't discount their belief. This has been helpful in our context. So if a person comes with a problem, and if there are some remedies in the religious books and some with the clinician, I think the both should be tried. It's like trying [talk] therapy and antipsychotic medication together. If it's doing no harm then, the bottom line is that it should not be mutually exclusive.

Notes

1. Of course, it is notable that Sharma uses the language of "transient possession," which itself is a common phrase in recent biomedical literature.
2. Pawan Sharma, interviews by author, conducted in English via video conference in Kathmandu on September 22, 2022, September 28, 2022, October 17, 2022, and January 1, 2023.
3. Sharma, Pawan, S. Singh, S. Gnanavel, and N. Kumar, "Meditation—a Two Edged Sword for Psychosis: A Case Report," *Irish Journal of Psychological Medicine* 33 (2016): 247–249.
4. This is a nongovernmental organization that works in community mental health (see Transcultural Psychosocial Organization, www.TPONepal.org, last accessed June 30, 2025).

Chapter 21

Navigating Enduring Challenges from Meditation Retreats

Interviews with Three Western Practitioners from the Varieties of Contemplative Experience Study

JARED R. LINDAHL, NATHAN E. FISHER, DAVID J. COOPER, AND WILLOUGHBY B. BRITTON

The Varieties of Contemplative Experience (VCE) is a mixed-methods research study of interviews with sixty-eight meditation practitioners and thirty-three meditation experts from Theravāda, Zen, and Tibetan Buddhist traditions in the West.[1] This chapter begins by concisely introducing the study's methods and findings. Then we briefly situate our data in the context of Buddhist modernism in the West. Finally, we provide background information on each of the meditation practitioners we have selected for inclusion in this volume and how they are related to the overall study findings.

Interviews with meditation practitioners and meditation experts were conducted by the authors of this chapter from 2010 to 2016. Study participants were recruited through snowball sampling, with the majority living in the United States and practicing or teaching among American Buddhist communities. To qualify, meditation practitioners had to be able to report on meditation-related effects that were challenging, difficult, distressing, or impaired functioning. Semistructured interviews were organized around four primary topics: (1) the interviewee's personal background and meditation practice history; (2) a phenomenological description of their meditation-related challenges; (3) how they and others (such as meditation teachers or doctors) appraised and responded to those challenges, including what they think caused or exacerbated them; and (4) what remedies they found helpful or unhelpful for managing or mitigating challenges.[2] Meditation practitioners who qualified for inclusion in the study also filled out a forty-three-item questionnaire. Although meditation was in some cases not the sole precipitating factor, a seven-item causality assessment was used to ensure that challenges could not be fully attributed to other causes, such as psychiatric, medical, or trauma history.

Qualitative thematic analysis of the more than one hundred interviews that constitute the VCE dataset yielded fifty-nine distinct types of meditation-related challenges; twenty-six influencing factors that could act as risk factors for the development or exacerbation of challenges, as remedies for mitigating challenges, or both; and eleven criteria for establishing differential diagnoses or determining the need for intervention.[3] Meditation-related challenges were reported across seven domains of human experience, including perceptual changes (such as hypersensitivity and distortions in space and time), cognitive changes (such as delusion-like ideation and impairments to executive functioning), emotional changes (such as fear and reexperiencing of traumatic memories), somatic changes (such as energy-like somatic experiences and involuntary movements), conative changes (such as a lack of drive or pleasure), changes to senses of self (such as changes to sense of embodiment and loss of sense of ownership over thoughts or emotions), and social changes (such as social and occupational impairment or problems with integration following retreat). Influencing factors were practitioner-level (such as psychiatric or trauma history), practice-related (such as type or amount of meditation practice), relationship-based (such as with teachers or members of the practice community), and health behaviors (such as changes to diet or medication). Finally, while some decisions concerning differential diagnosis or determining the need for intervention were based upon the specific phenomenology, most took into account secondary factors such as degree of control, associated distress, or functional impairment, as well as contextual factors such as compatibility with the cultural background of the practitioner.

Although the VCE study is the largest and most comprehensive qualitative study of meditation-related challenges to date, it was not the first. For almost as long as the psychological and scientific study of meditation in the West has been taking place, there have been small studies and case reports of meditation-related problems, many of which have documented particularly severe cases treated as acute psychotic episodes occurring in the context of meditation practice.[4] Subsequent to the VCE study, research from the psychological science of meditation has continued to investigate meditation-related challenges and adverse effects through additional case reports, through survey-based studies of self-selected meditators, through epidemiological studies, and in the context of mindfulness-based clinical trials.[5]

Drawing upon the qualitative dataset as well as the historical sources often mentioned by meditation practitioners and teachers in the study, the authors of the VCE study and their collaborators have published analyses of select meditation-related challenges (including visual lights and other simple hallucinations, changes in sense of self, energy-like somatic experiences, fear and terror, and delusion-like ideation);[6] the role of key influencing factors (including trauma history, worldviews, and relationships with meditation teachers);[7] and criteria for establishing differential diagnoses or determining the need for intervention.[8] The present chapter takes a different approach by providing extensive portions of interview transcripts from three different meditation practitioners.[9] The interviews were chosen in order to illustrate (1) a range of meditation-related challenges; (2) different types and degrees of impact on behavior and functioning; (3) how interpretations of challenges are shaped through social interactions; (4) the contribution of different practice-related and practitioner-level risk factors; and (5) various approaches to managing or mitigating challenges.

Unlike other sources translated in this volume from Buddhist Asia, these data are drawn from Buddhism in the West. Scholars have characterized contemporary Western Buddhism as being significantly influenced by "Buddhist modernism."[10] Indeed, many of the hallmarks of Buddhist modernism are present throughout the VCE dataset. These include detraditionalization; psychologization of Buddhist teachings; an emphasis on individual meditative experiences and their impacts; interactions with biomedical, psychological, and neuroscientific worldviews and institutions; an embrace of the rhetoric of the authority of science; and the association of meditation not just or primarily with religious goals but also with modern Western notions of health and well-being. This situates the problem of "meditation sickness" in a very different context, as contemporary practitioners in the West may have different notions of what constitutes the nature and purpose of "meditation" as well as what constitutes "sickness" and how to manage it. In a context in which the worldviews that underpin and motivate the practice of meditation are quite distinct, traditional remedies for meditation sickness may be limited in their applicability. Through these interviews, we present a range of perspectives on this issue as all three practitioners navigated religious frameworks within and beyond Buddhism as well as biomedical treatments and interpretations, each coming to their own conclusion about the nature and significance of their challenges.

The first meditation practitioner is a fifty-six-year-old white female who was raised in an observant Protestant household in the United States. She did not have a history of trauma or mental illness, nor was there a history of mental illness in her family. She became interested in meditation in her early twenties, in the 1970s, and started out studying with Tibetan Buddhist teachers who passed through her home region. A few decades later, she met an American

Theravāda Buddhist teacher and was encouraged to sign up for a ten-day insight (*vipassanā*) meditation retreat. Although she found it extremely difficult to maintain the discipline of that first retreat, she persevered. Subsequently, she made a commitment to undertake a ten-day retreat every year. Then, after twenty-five years and between one and five thousand hours of prior Buddhist meditation practice, she aspired to undertake her first three-month retreat with teachers she had worked with previously. Her motivation for undertaking a longer retreat was that she "wanted to get to this place where I was able to maintain a sense of peace regardless of circumstances," although she admits she was "probably both greedy and impatient" and "wanted to get there quickly." The main challenges she reports in this interview started during the first month and a half of this three-month insight meditation retreat and continued for many months after she left the retreat.

The second meditation practitioner is a fifty-three-year-old white female who was raised in a largely nonreligious American household with "one atheist and one very lazy Catholic." She reported not having a diagnosed mental illness and not having been exposed to a known traumatic event. However, she also reported that during her teenage years and into part of her adulthood, she engaged in "a low level of cutting behavior." She started a regular meditation practice in her mid-forties because of a "typical midlife thing where you woke up one day and realize your relationships are completely superficial and you're gonna die someday, and you want to do something to create some meaning in your life." A friend introduced her to a nearby Zen temple where she "began very step-by-step," slowly increasing her practice amount over a few years. During this process, she became a formal student in that community. Over the course of about four years, she participated in the occasional *sesshin* and maintained a daily sitting practice of "twice a day either for an hour or at least a half an hour." She also estimated her lifetime practice hours at the time of the interview to be between one and five thousand. Her meditation-related challenges first arose in the context of daily practice and developed further during her next *sesshin*.

The third meditator is a twenty-two-year-old American white male university student. He is close with his family, who all lived together at the time of the interview. He was raised Jewish, although his family was "not very observant." He reported having had a period of depression in middle school that was treated with herbal remedies for a year or two. He remarked that anxiety and depression were not uncommon in his immediate family. Otherwise, he thought he had a "very good childhood" with "loving parents" and did not report any history of trauma. He began meditating regularly at around age fifteen, about a year after he first started participating at a local insight meditation center. At age eighteen, he undertook his first retreat, a ten-day course in *vipassanā* meditation, at which point his meditation-related challenges arose. Since then, he described himself as "sort of like the classic American: being a religious consumer, just taking little bits and pieces from things," and he has continued to practice meditation on short-term retreats in Asia and in the United States.

These three interviews with meditation practitioners are representative of the broader VCE dataset in certain respects but not in others. While male and female practitioners from Zen and Theravāda lineages are included in the following interviews, no interviews with a Tibetan Buddhist practitioner are included here. We chose to feature practitioner interviews rather than "expert" interviews with meditation teachers and clinicians, which provided a different perspective on how they manage and interpret meditation-related challenges in others. The meditation practice background of all three practitioners presented here was much less than typical, especially the third practitioner, who was on his first intensive retreat. The majority of practitioners in the VCE study reported having a lifetime estimated meditation practice background of five to ten thousand hours or more, and 60 percent of the practitioners interviewed were themselves meditation teachers. Although the majority of practitioners in the VCE study similarly described challenges that first arose during or immediately following meditation retreats, this was not universal; there were also practitioners for whom challenges arose in the context of a daily meditation practice and from less than one hour per day of practice.

Regarding the main types of challenges reported in these interviews, the energy-like somatic experiences and associated physiological and emotional challenges described in the first two interviews were relatively common. The depersonalization-like phenomenology and hypersensitivities to emotional and perceptual stimuli reported in the third interview were also reported by many other practitioners. The additional challenges all three practitioners described in making sense of their experience, as well as the ways in which meditation communities sometimes failed to provide adequate meaning-making and other forms of support, were also recurring themes. These three practitioners reported engaging in a range of possible remedies, including changes in meditation practice approach, grounding activities, and health behaviors such as changes to diet, physical activity, and the use of pharmaceutical medications. Finally, these interviews illustrated a range of functional impairment associated with meditation-related challenges. The first meditation practitioner estimated her impairment lasted from one to three years, the second from three to six years, and the third, which was a much more mild and transient case, approximately one month. None of these cases required in-patient hospitalization, which was reported among the more severe cases of the VCE dataset.

Further Reading

Compson, Jane. 2018. "Adverse Meditation Experiences: Navigating Buddhist and Secular Frameworks for Addressing Them." *Mindfulness* 9:1358–1369.

Lambert, D., N. H. van den Berg, and A. Mendrek. 2023. "Adverse Effects of Meditation: A Review of Observational, Experimental and Case Studies." *Current Psychology* 42:1112–1125.

Lindahl, Jared R., Willoughby B. Britton, David J. Cooper, and Laurence J. Kirmayer. 2021. "Challenging and Adverse Meditation Experiences: Toward a Person-Centered Approach." In *The Oxford Handbook of Meditation,* edited by Miguel Farias, David Brazier, and Mansur Lalljee. Oxford University Press.

Lindahl, Jared R., David J. Cooper, Nathan E. Fisher, Laurence J. Kirmayer, and Willoughby B. Britton. 2020. "Progress or Pathology? Differential Diagnosis and Intervention Criteria for Meditation-Related Challenges: Perspectives from Buddhist Meditation Teachers and Practitioners." *Frontiers in Psychology* 11:1905.

Lindahl, Jared R., Nathan E. Fisher, David J. Cooper, Rochelle K. Rosen, and Willoughby B. Britton. 2017. "The Varieties of Contemplative Experience: A Mixed-Methods Study of Meditation-Related Challenges in Western Buddhists." *PLoS ONE* 12 (5): e0176239.

Female, Aged Fifty-Six, Theravāda Buddhist Tradition[11]

MP1: The first week at [name of retreat center], I had a nightmare every night, four nights in a row. And I went to my teachers every day, and I said, "I had a nightmare, and I don't have nightmares. This is completely out of the ordinary for me. I don't have nightmares." And I remember saying, "I don't think I should stay at this retreat this long. It's too long." And their response was "Long retreats are really hard. People often have cold feet when they come in, and you're just afraid." And I remember finally saying, "You know what, I'm the student here, you're the teacher. I surrender to whatever it is that you guide me to do." And they encouraged me to stay for the whole retreat.

It was a very difficult retreat, a *very* difficult retreat. I couldn't break into any places of peace. I was just struggling. But I'm a really good student. If I decide to do what I'm told, I'll do what I'm told. And so I did what I was told, and I did my practices very religiously. And I did the retreat very well. As a number of weeks went on, I became more and more sensitive, and they told me—because I was so sensitive, they pulled me out of the meditation hall. And they said I wasn't to meditate in the meditation hall anymore—I was too sensitive—and to spend more time out in nature and more time meditating by myself in the room away from other people.

INT: How did they know that you were more sensitive?

MP1: Well, you go and you report every other day. You have a meeting with your teacher every other day. And so I would go, and I would report my experiences. I remember a lot of grief was coming up, although it wasn't associated with any memory. It was just grieving coming up. I assume it was based upon my reports that they said that. And I continued to struggle. It wasn't an easy retreat; I wasn't at peace. I continued to have a lot of anxiety, a lot of dread. I had a lot of dread the whole retreat.

INT: Do you know what the dread was about? Or did it have any content?

MP1: No. It was like a nameless dread. The way I've interpreted it is I was really dealing in a huge way with doubt. About five weeks into the retreat, I was sitting in my room one night. And I'm very comfortable sitting. I'm a teacher [of young children]—"criss-cross applesauce" with my legs, you know, in a yogi position—I can sit that way forever. So I was sitting on my bed, I was sitting in that position, and all of a sudden, I felt my body—I was on the bed, maybe six inches from the wall, and I felt this energy come up into my body and *bang* my back against the wall. And I remember it because, you know, it's a silent retreat, and it made a loud noise when I banged my back against the wall. I was banged against the wall four or five times, and then my head got thrown backward. Like, pushed back as far as it could be. And my mouth dropped open, and I just shook for a while. And it was bizarre.

Every evening there was an hour talk, and in one of the talks they said, "You know, when they go to Asia and meditate for two or three years, there would be strange experiences. Sometimes there'd be strange things you'd see, strange things you'd hear. Sometimes your body would do really strange things. And you just observe it all." So I just observed it all. I remember thinking "This is pretty dramatic. God, this is pretty dramatic! But I'm just observing it." And then my body would calm down for a period.

INT: So can you tell me about how long? It sounds like you're having a convulsion.

MP1: I'm going to think it maybe lasted maybe two or three minutes. And then my body would calm down, I would say, for about fifteen minutes. And then I'd feel the energy coming again, and it would do it again, and then my body would calm down. And I think that maybe happened two or three or four times.

I cannot sleep during meditation retreats, so one of the things that I do do during meditation retreats is I get a prescription for sleeping pills, so I'll get at least a couple of hours of sleep. So at the end of that night, I took a sleeping pill, and I went to sleep for four or five hours, which I did every night, and I woke up at about five o'clock the next morning.

And then I did the same thing. I didn't go to the meditation hall. I sat in my bed, and I started meditating and within an hour the same energy started again, but this time, rather than pushing me back and throwing my neck back, it was more of like a DNA circular motion. And it literally twisted my body back and forth and back and forth and back and forth and back and forth and back and forth and back and forth [*spoken rapidly*]. All the spit in my mouth, it was just spraying back and forth and back and forth [*spoken rapidly*] out of my mouth. And I thought that was a little vulgar. But, anyway, I did the same thing: I just watched it. And it was similar to the night before. It would happen, and my body would shake back and forth and back and forth and back and forth and back and forth and back and forth and back and forth and back and forth [*spoken rapidly*] for, I don't know, I think it was probably just a couple of minutes. And then it would subside for about fifteen minutes. And the same thing, thinking "You know what? This is pretty dramatic again." And I remember kind of having this conversation with "God," thinking, "This is pretty dramatic. You must really have a good sense of humor." But I did what you are taught to do in *vipassanā:* I just observed it and didn't make any stories about it.

INT: And did you tell any teachers?

MP1: No, I didn't at that time. Okay, so in a retreat you get different jobs you are supposed to do. Well, I was on the kitchen that morning, and I was supposed to be doing kitchen duty. So I was walking towards the kitchen, and on the way I met my teacher. And I said to my teacher, "You know, I just need for you to know that my body is doing really strange things." Kind of like they said your body might do strange things. I said, "I don't know how to describe it, other than it's like my body is in convulsions on its own. It just does these things." And, when I told her that, she immediately said, "We need to pull you out of the retreat."

INT: Did she tell you why?

MP1: No. And she said, "I want to have somebody be with you all day long." The retreats are really well setup: They had somebody there who had gone through "difficult experiences" that was there twenty-four hours. I had never met her, but she spent the day with me, I think probably observing me and collecting data on me. She was very wonderful. I really, really liked her. And she shared her experience that she had. . . . So I spent the day with her. I remember in the evening they had me go with another teacher and was walking with me. I remember they told me that the reason they put me with this teacher was she had been sexually abused and had unsurfaced some memories.

I didn't have any early life traumatic incidents. I was kind of confused by that. I didn't know why they put me with her because my body was just doing strange things. . . .

At the end of the day, they asked me if I wanted to reintegrate—you know, come down. I said, "Yes." They pulled in a psychiatrist. I remember when the psychiatrist came, he asked me what my name was, you know, where I was, I was very cognizant. I mean, my brain was functioning fine. The psychiatrist thought I was perhaps bipolar—I remember [him] saying that—and I was sent home. That was the experience, up to being sent home.

INT: The psychiatrist thought you were bipolar?

MP1: I remember that's what he wrote up. That perhaps I was bipolar.

INT: But you have no history of bipolar disorder.

MP1: No, none at all. I have a history of some anxiety. But no depression, no mania. Some anxiety, and a lot of energy. I've always had a lot of energy.

When I came home, I didn't want to tell anybody. It was right before Christmas, and on Christmas Day, when I was with my family, I ended up telling everybody because I really couldn't keep it together anymore. They were very, very concerned. And they called a therapist that we all knew. She has been a therapist for many, many years, but she is also very active in the Sufi tradition. . . . She was just leaving at that time to be part of a month[long] Sufi retreat or something like that. She said, "You need to continue to take the antipsychotic medication" that they got for me when I was in [location of retreat center]. And she said, "You need to go and see a therapist."

INT: Wait, so they gave you antipsychotic medication at [name of retreat center]?

MP1: Yes. The psychiatrist there put me on Zyprexa. . . . Everybody at [name of retreat center] was very nice. They were really very, very nice. I have very positive things to say about their support of me, their interaction with me. They treated me very kindly; they were very attentive.

Then I went home. I tried to go see different therapists. It was weird, you know? It was going and seeing Western psychologists that believed there was a traumatic event that got unearthed, and there wasn't any traumatic event that got unearthed. I have nice mothers and fathers. I had a very nice childhood. I was fortunate in that way. And finally, [name of family therapist] came back from her retreat. When I went to see her, I told her my experience, and her response was twofold. Her first response was "You had a kundalini release." It was the first time I was aware of the word. And she said, "This happened to me about thirty years ago and, to this day, I've never figured out why I went through that hell." Or maybe she told me this later. She told me it about a year later, actually. She said, "Until that day, when I was meeting with you, and I did it because

I knew where you were at, and I knew what I needed to do to support you." And I met with her weekly. . . .

And the second thing—the big thing that I remember from that—was she had a lot of anger. She had a lot of anger that it happened to me. She had a lot of anger about the inappropriateness of having some individuals attend month retreats, six-week retreats, or twelve-week retreats. She said, "The mind is a powerful thing, and you don't play with people's minds." And, even though perhaps 95 percent of people can go and do a month retreat or a six-week retreat or a twelve-week retreat and not [have this] happen, there are people that they're too sensitive. And there's energies out there that you don't want to deal with unless you're masterful or are with a master that can deal with them. And she had a lot of anger. She really had a lot of anger at the *vipassanā* community because she said that this has happened to other people, and it's not appropriate. It's irresponsible on the part of teachers. . . .

I ended up working with her for a year. I wasn't able to go back to work. I mean, I couldn't work. I couldn't cook. I couldn't do anything.

INT: Why? What was going on?

MP1: I was outside of my body, and I couldn't get back inside. I was about eight to ten inches to the right. And I couldn't get in. It was like being in a hell realm. My mind functioned okay, not great. But, as I said, I could tell you things. My body was 100 percent fine; it functioned completely well. What was severed for me was my emotional body. I had two young children; I couldn't feel anything about them. I couldn't connect with them. I went through all of the routines, you know: the bedtime routine, getting them ready and kissing them and all of that stuff. But there was no emotional connection. It was like I was dead. It was really like the living dead. It was like being in the hell realm for a year. It was like the living dead. Except for about ten minutes in the evening. For some reason, I would slip back in for about ten minutes, and it was like suddenly I was myself. I could feel my kids, and I felt alive. And then I'd slip back out.

So what happened then, based upon that going on for three or four or five months, I developed a secondary intense anxiety disorder because I was afraid I was never going to be okay, which probably exacerbated what was going on anyways. After a year, I was able to go back to work. After six months, I came back, I slipped back; I was back in my body. And then, over the next two or three months, I'd go out sometimes, and come in sometimes, and then I was pretty much back in. My mind was functioning probably at 60 percent capacity, and I was able to go back to work. And so I went back to work. And so on the surface, everything looked like normal. I was back at work. I was able to connect with the kids. I was able to cook and do what I needed to do. And I would say about a year later, maybe a year and a half, I felt like I was reintegrated, to use that term.

INT: And during that year, were you still having convulsions?

MP1: No, it never happened again after that. It was only that evening and the following early hour morning.

INT: Okay, and you had a feeling like you were eight to ten inches to the right of your body and severed from your emotional connection—you couldn't connect with things. What was your sense of time like? Was there any change in that?

MP1: I don't recall.

INT: Okay, and your memory, and your ability to think?

MP1: I could think. I could answer factual questions. I *was* kind of manic when I came back. *Everything* was significant. When I came back from the retreat—my husband likes to tell this story, and I actually think there's something to this, still—where I called him up, and I said, "Have you ever looked at the dollar bill?" I said, "If you look at the dollar bill . . ." Anyway, I went through all of the symbols on the dollar bill, and I told them not only how they had a level of interpretation in terms of our government and democracy, but how it revealed all spiritual values that were being manifested in this country through the forefathers that founded this country, and all of that is there on the dollar bill. And so I did a long, lengthy interpretation of the dollar bill and the significance that it has and the spiritual significance. And when I came back, I was doing a lot of that. And that lasted maybe a month, you know—these amazing insights and connections and things.

And then that died down, and I was just left with the deadness of . . . none of that anymore. I mean—and this way it almost does sound bipolar, if I think about it—I had that mania, and then I was left with the deadness. I wasn't depressed, though. I didn't feel depressed. I felt outside of my body and living dead. No emotion. No connection with that which was important and live and real. And I couldn't focus. I remember the only time I could focus, actually, was when I was in front of the computer screen. I'm a teacher, and learning about ADHD children and how the screen helps them focus. I think when your mind is kind of shattered like that, for some reason the computer screen can help you focus.

I also remember [name of family therapist] trying to describe this to me, and she said, "You know, imagine as if your mind had just gotten struck by lightning, and all of these little neurological connections got shattered all over. What we're going to need to do is slowly, slowly, slowly, slowly bring those back together. And it's going to take a while. And you're going to need to eat meat. And I want you to garden. And I want you to do exercise every day. And take sleeping pills and sleep. And you'll take your antipsychotic medication—it's really important"—I hated the meds—"It's really important that you do this, and you're going to come and see me." So she kind of set up a therapy structure for me.

Something else I did—this is important—I went and saw a doctor. A homeopathic physician, a classical homeopathic physician . . . I told him my story also. He also said, "You had a kundalini release." He also said, "Something needs to be done about this; this happens too frequently." And he kind of reiterated everything that [name of therapist] had said. He wouldn't treat me homeopathically. He felt like it was too extreme, that I needed to stay on the antipsychotics. He put me on pretty intense antianxiety medication as well.

INT: Do you remember which drug that was?

MP1: I don't remember what drugs I was on that time [*pauses*]. Zyprexa. Effexor was the anti[anxiety medication]. I had actually been on Effexor before that, but he probably upped the dosage. And my husband was great. My husband spent a lot of time with me; I have a very supportive husband. Gave me massages continuously, you know, just to try to keep the body going.

My interpretation of what happened was that I had a kundalini release. That's what I think now because I've had a number of people tell me that. I don't know how to interpret my experience. The story that I've made up about it is that I was existing in a hell realm of doubt. And the reason why I say that is because I come from a long lineage of ministers—Mennonite background, pacifistic in orientation, but for the last couple generations became United Church of Christ. Like, my dad was a United Church of Christ minister. Very rational. I think that the whole "Is God dead?" movement, you know—they questioned that because their sense of spirituality was so rational versus mystical. I'm my dad's daughter. We both are drawn towards big questions of life. He does it rationally; I do it more from a mystical standpoint. So that's how I've interpreted it. That somehow I got caught in doubt, and I couldn't get out of it. That's the only way that I've made sense of it, for myself. . . .

I did call [name of retreat center] after I met [name of therapist], because I wanted them to know once I'd found out what happened to me. I wanted them to know, you know? So I wanted to give them that information. I called [name of retreat center], and I said to [name of meditation teacher], or whoever it was. I said to somebody, "This is what happened to me: I had a kundalini release." It was like, "I know now!" I was like an excited little kid: "I know now!" And they said they don't believe in kundalini releases.

When [name of meditation teacher who encouraged her to go on first *vipassanā* retreat] came back, maybe five or six years ago, I also made a point to find her. And I wanted to tell her my experience. I have no blame towards anybody. I think they treated me the best that they knew how. But what happened was significant, and I thought she should know. And she gave me a very cold shoulder also. So that was my two experiences with [name of retreat center].

INT: What do you mean by cold shoulder?

MP1: She didn't say what you said: "Give me more information. What did you learn?" It was like she didn't want to hear: "Who are you, and why do I want to hear what you have to say?" I mean, I don't remember exactly, but I remember just feeling like, "Oh well, I tried." And, and honestly, I think part of it is legal [*long pause*]. I think they have to be careful. They have to protect themselves, and they don't want lawsuits.

Okay, so how do I think we need to respond? I think we need to educate. I don't think we need to sue people when things like this happen. However, I understand that in the United States of America, that's the common way to respond. And people—like [name of retreat center]—that have a message that they want to share; they don't want to get sued. So perhaps there are things that they need to do legally that I'm not aware of. That said, I think it's *really important* that meditation teachers get educated on some of the dangers of meditation. . . .

Where had somebody known those skills, or had information—I mean, I'm not a kundalini expert by *any* stretch of the imagination. Everything I know about it I've told you. But, again, if teachers are trained that sometimes this happens, and here are some different strategies of how to deal with it, of how to respond. Rather than say, "We don't believe in kundalini. We think you're bipolar," and put you on antipsychotic medication and send you home.

Female, Aged Fifty-Three, Zen Buddhist Tradition[12]

MP2: I began experiencing incredible upward energy in meditation—like, too much energy—that my body couldn't hold. It was like being in a riptide, or almost in a huge wind. Somewhere between a wind and a tide. And I mentioned it to my teacher many times, and we talked about grounding.

And then, when I was at a *sesshin*, I came into the *dokusan* and said, "I can't take this; it's just too much energy. I keep wanting to make it go down, and it just wants to go up." And he said, "Well, okay, let it do what it wants to do." And I went back to my seat, and I took my . . . something . . . and I kind of put it into my belly, and I was like scrubbing it. And then I got plugged into some energy outlet, and it was literally like having a river—a river of energy, like thousands of volts of energy—go up through my right leg and across my abdomen and up through my head. It was like being a rocket ship. You know when people go into outer space, and you see the end of the rocket ship and all the stuff coming out? It's like that, except all the stuff was going up. And that lasted quite a few hours. And it felt *great,* because my body was completely relaxed, and this thing just went through. But after that I became very, very destabilized, very volatile, and my teacher dismissed me. He said, "I don't think meditation is very good for you right now, and I think you should not do it." So that was energetically one thing that happened, and at the same time—

INT: Can I just back you up real quick? So at this point you had been slowly, incrementally increasing the meditation. Was this the first weeklong retreat you had been on?

MP2: No, I had definitely done other ones. I would have to remember how many I had done. At the place I was meditating, they wanted you to do at least one a year, but I did at least two a year. So I would say this was the fourth or fifth weeklong. Yeah, something like that.

INT: So you had never had an experience of this kind of sensation before on any of the other retreats?

MP2: No, but I had for a long, long time had this incredible updraft, which I not only had during meditation, but not in meditation. So I would feel this updraft—that's the only way I can describe it.

And analogous to this whole energetic thing was, later on, I began to experience—what many people experience in meditation—was excruciating body sensations. My entire body would fill up in the meditation session with tension, like a bathtub. So by the end of the half-hour period, I would be completely immobilized. . . . Contiguous with all of this energy would be a constriction of the body. And it's normal for people to have that. That's something a lot of people go through. Mark Epstein talks about that in his book—you know, these early body memory kinds of things.

But in my case, after this big updraft, I took a little break, and then I came back to meditation. I took a couple months off and then I came back. And that was a mistake. I made a mistake. Because when I came back, I was still destabilized and, instead of this incredible tension clearing—often it will clear if you work with a therapist—instead I developed an intense body thing where my system—my own body—yanked on me. It yanked and pulled me over to the side. And this was extremely, extremely upsetting.

INT: Can you describe that a little bit more?

MP2: Yes, so it would happen sometimes in the *zendo,* and sometimes it would happen out of the *zendo.* On my left side, it was like there was a hand in there that was *grabbing.* It grabbed my muscles and *yanked* them. Or *squeezed* them.

They would get incredibly squeezed. Again, like a vise or hand. As if you were a very small thing, and then you were being squeezed in a fist. Or yanked, like yanking on a rope or something like that. So I would end up kind of pitched over to the left and frozen there. And that was extremely distressing.

INT: And was that painful?

MP2: Very painful. Very, very painful.

INT: But that would just happen while meditating?

MP2: It would happen while meditating, and also it would happen not while meditating. And I understand the mechanics of why it happens. When the body memories came up, my meditation teacher told me, "You need a therapist. I really recommend that you find a therapist now." Unfortunately, the first therapist I found was not the right therapist for me. So instead of clearing, the things got worse. And I don't think my meditation center was really set up to cope with somebody that was having this kind of thing, so I had to find a better therapist but, unfortunately, I was in a pretty bad state.

But my sense of it was that, because I was so energetically destabilized, that when the trauma material came up, as it does for most people who have trauma in their backgrounds and who have tried these meditation practices, hopefully the stuff is gonna clear. But because of the energetic destabilization, I just got more destabilized. So that was 2011, then 2012, and now it's 2014, and I have to say that I'm really still trying to recover. I haven't recovered. And I don't have a meditation practice right now because I'm trying to recover.

INT: So you haven't meditated since two years ago?

MP2: I would say the last time I really, really tried was somewhere in 2012. Because I can't sit up. It's really hard for me to sit down now because of the contractions, and how long the muscles have been in contraction. And believe you me, I've done lots and lots of Somatic Experiencing and therapy and bodywork and cortisone shots [*laughs*]. I mean, it's not like I've just sat and am eating ice cream on the couch. So I am just interested because I am very, very flummoxed. I'm sure you guys have read that book *Spiritual Emergency?*

INT: Mm hm.

MP2: Yeah, so lots of people have energetic experiences where they feel voltage. Lots of people have trauma memories come up. That's not unusual. That's a part of the practice. So why are some of us so destabilized and really have difficulty coping with that and recovering from it, and why do other people kind of move through it? I'm flummoxed. I don't understand. That's really my question. The place where I was practicing was very robust, a place with people with a lot of experience. So I saw a lot of my peer group move through these experiences, and I have not moved through them. And I don't understand. I don't understand [*sounds distressed*].

INT: And so, in that first period, though, if you couldn't use the word energy, how would you describe?

MP2: Oh, before the voltage? Before being plugged into the voltage?

INT: Mm hm.

MP2: Hm, I would say, current. But in the sense of water, not electricity. If you combined water and wind. And you know how it is when you walk against a very, very strong wind? Well, I was sitting down, and there was this very, very strong wind *in* me. So I was sitting down, and this very strong wind was moving up. So I was trying to stay seated, and the wind was moving up. It was like a very strong wind. Or, if you took a branch, and you put it in a current, and the current gets stronger, you know how the branch will vibrate? That's kind of the way I felt.

INT: So was your body actually vibrating? Or did it feel like that?

MP2: No, it didn't feel like it was vibrating. It felt more like it was overstuffed.

INT: Overstuffed?

MP2: Yes, like a balloon that was blown up too big. Yes, like a balloon or a membrane that had too much water or wind in it, and it was like it was going to explode.

INT: And was that feeling all throughout your body, or was it in just particular parts?

MP2: It was mostly from the pubic bone upward. And also there was a feeling, especially on the left, which was weak in the left flank, that was like a tearing. Like if you have a riverbank and there's rapids going by, you know how the riverbank will fall into the water? It kind of felt like that. Like this riverbank is running, and my muscles were being kind of torn at.

INT: And this was just on your left side?

MP2: Mostly on the left, though I would feel it all through.

INT: And so you said that this was happening while you were on the cushion and off the cushion, while you weren't—

MP2: Yes, the updraft. That's what I would call it. That would often—and that still happens. Like, if I get on the subway, or if I get impatient, I will get a strong updraft. And I've asked people about it. The acupuncturists said it has to do with the vascular system, and the way my nervous system is operating, which creates this sort of strange . . . I mean, I've been also to medical doctors, and when I describe that, they just look at me as if I'm nuts. But the acupuncturists seem to understand more.

INT: And would it get worse or better when you would actually be meditating?

MP2: Worse, much worse. Amplified, definitely amplified.

INT: And can you remember the first time that you noticed this happening?

MP2: I would say somewhere in 2010, because I had done, in 2009, a month-long residency at the monastery, and didn't really have it then. But the very beginnings of it came in terms of an incredible tightening of the throat in meditation. I talked to a kind of healer, somebody who went to the Barbara Brennan school for people who do bioenergetics, and they say often that the throat will close or have this incredible constriction because the body is trying to keep the organism from remembering trauma material. The way of trying to cut off the experience from arising in consciousness. So at the time I didn't know that; it was only an unbelievably horrible sensation.

I could always breathe, so it's not like you're being strangled, but the throat absolutely closing up like a vise. And then incrementally, over time, both the energetic updraft and the tightening of the body became more and more global.

INT: And how long would it last when your throat would close up or would tighten?

MP2: That would last a whole period, a whole meditation period, and because I was at the monastery then, at least throughout the day. And then it also began to happen just in life. Again, I have to say that when I talk to fellow students, this is kind of a *normal* thing, this kind of body constriction. To me, the out-of-the-normal thing is that I am kind of impaired now, and I never could work through it. . . .

Why I am so curious is that so many things that I've read, and talking to my fellow students, it's also a thing that many, many people go through, but they *pass through.* Some people pass through in one meditation period. Some people it's a longer thing. But, for me, I've been semi-impaired for like a couple years now. That's what I don't understand.

INT: And the technique that you described about scrubbing, is that something you just invented, or . . . ?

MP2: [*Laughs.*] Literally, that was just like a four-year-old playing around with an electrical socket. I had no idea what I was doing.

INT: So had you tried other things first, or was that the first thing you went for?

MP2: No, that was the first thing I tried in terms of like, "Let's see, let's let it do what it wants to do." And that was just the first thing I tried.

INT: And you went to your left side because that's where you had been feeling a lot of the constriction?

MP2: Lots of constriction and also lots of imagery would come out of that part of the body.

INT: Can you describe that a little bit?

MP2: Well, different things would come out of there, different images. Sometimes it would be very reptilian images. A lot of like prehistoric fish would kind of come out of there. Once I had, again to the left, kind of like an auditory hallucination. A very, very deep voice. And it wasn't a voice in my head; it was actually a voice outside of my head. It was very startling.

INT: And the images, were they internally generated, or were those things you were seeing with your eyes?

MP2: No, I would just be seeing them. They would just appear.

INT: With your eyes closed?

MP2: Yes, eyes closed or eyes down.

INT: And how were you knowing that they were coming out of your left side? Was it something you could feel?

MP2: Yeah, I don't know, that's just definitely where they were coming from. I think just because we hold a lot of things in our bodies, and they're held in certain places in our bodies, so it's just things coming up out of the body.

INT: So how long did that experience last?

MP2: It lasted a couple hours. Only a couple hours. Again, after we're done, I'd like to ask you, because it's strange to me. But I know after that I became very, very emotionally volatile and more and more unstable until, I think, it was like the early summer.

INT: So that continued off the retreat for another few weeks or few months?

MP2: Off the retreat, yeah, a few months. Until my meditation teachers told me to take a break.

INT: And you continued the same amount of meditation through that time, about a half an hour to an hour a day?

MP2: Yeah.

INT: And so, in terms of feeling destabilized, you said you were feeling more reactive?

MP2: Yes, more destabilized and more reactive [*long pause*]. You know, like a banshee? I don't know if I'm using the right word, but like a banshee. Like a lady with her hair all wild? There was a sort of thing like being very smoky, very dispersed . . .

INT: That's how you were feeling, you mean?

MP2: Yes, that's how I was feeling. Or else very depressed. So kind of wildly swinging between things.

INT: So swinging between depression and—

MP2:—and this sort of wild crying or hysteria.

INT: So there wasn't really any kind of euphoria or anything?

MP2: No, unfortunately the only euphoria I felt was during the actual event. That was like, "Wow! This is great!" [*laughs*]. And I actually projected that. I was like: "Oh, this is so great. I must be getting rid of so much crap because this voltage is just clear." But it didn't work out that way.

INT: So that was in the spring. You were swinging and having emotional reactivity, or kind of swings, through into the summer when your teacher told you to stop meditating.

MP2: Right.

INT: And then you started meditating again that following winter. And then you said afterwards you felt that was a bad idea at that point?

MP2: [*Sighs.*] That was a bad idea.

INT: And what was your experience at that time?

MP2: Because, after I came back, the sort of crushing body sensations, and the yanking and pulling . . . it just was completely counterproductive. I would come, and I would try, and then I'd get yanked, and then I would stop, and then I would come again and try again. And I just kept trying, and it really was very counterproductive. And one day I just stopped altogether.

INT: Were you working with a teacher at that point in time?

MP2: I was, and I would say . . . [*long pause*] I remember talking to my teacher about this, you know, sort of processing it together, that when I came back—because many people have gone through a lot of stuff, and sometimes they would have to leave the monastery, or leave the site and go take care of those things. And many students have had this, and then they would come back. And I think, because I couldn't come a lot, he just sort of trusted that "okay, she went and dealt with her stuff and now she's back, doing what she can." So I don't think he realized the severity of what had happened. Plus, these people have to deal with dozens and dozens and dozens of people. You're in a big, big family, and you're not the only kid there [*laughs*]. You're not in a small family; you're in a big family.

INT: The last thing, in terms of phenomenology, that I wanted to follow up with you on was, again, you had talked about traumatic memories coming up, and, if you remember, kind of at what point did they come up, and how they came up, and in what context?

MP2: The very beginning of when they came up was with the throat closing in 2009. And *very* slowly, *very* incrementally, the body tension . . . I never, ever had what we call a memory. What we think of as a memory is when you see a picture, or you smell something. You know what I mean? My memory was completely somatic in that it was crushing tension in the body—crushing, like in a vise—which then, by 2012, had become yanking.

INT: Oh, okay, gotcha. So you never had a specific event or something come back to you?

MP2: No.

INT: But you feel that this is the physical manifestation of a memory?

MP2: I think it is the physical manifestation of early conditioning. Early global conditioning. Preverbal. Because there is no language for it. And, as far as I can tell, from what I've read. . . . Okay, a person, if you look at a spectrum of light, there's the spectrum of light that we can see, and then there's the infrared light. That's the part of our personality that can't be seen until you start to meditate. The body part is like infrared and then there is ultraviolet light. Many people have ultraviolet experiences, which are maybe the more blissful ones. But mine were in this infrared thing where there's only body sensations. No pictures. They take place in a kind of blackness, and it's terrifying. It's extremely terrifying.

INT: So I hadn't heard you mention that aspect of these experiences so far. So was it the constriction and yanking, specifically, that was frightening or . . . ?

MP2: Yes, and that it also happened without my will. It happened by itself, inexorably. And I've read a lot about it: Peter Levine and Somatic Experiencing, and Mark Epstein talks about it. But I would say that, when it was happening to me then, I didn't know what was happening. I had no context for it. I thought I was doing something wrong. Something was wrong. Terribly wrong. All because: Isn't meditation supposed to be relaxing?

INT: And you were talking with your teacher at this time, too, so what were they saying about this?

MP2: Well, he did say, "This is something that people go through, and you kind of have to go through it. And you need a therapist." And I would say, for me, there is something in the experience, maybe because of the time in my life. I came to meditation very late. Maybe because of the cutting behavior, and because of the level of amnesia that I had. I had not been in therapy or touched this material or known it was there, so I think there was something in that. That it was so new to me that I couldn't hold it. And, in the energetic destabilization that was happening at the same time, there was no way for me to hold what was coming up. There was no space to hold it.

INT: At the time, or even now, do you have an interpretive framework or container for the energetic kind of stuff?

MP2: You know, I really don't [*sounds distressed*], and I just am totally puzzled. I really am. I mean, I did qigong. I did some other things, like, "Okay, I'm going to go do tai chi," and I have to say, I didn't find it very helpful. Because, at the end of a qigong session, I would have this terrible overstuffed feeling, or too full. And I thought, "Hm, do I have something organically awry in my spinal column? Is there some compression? Do I have a hormonal imbalance because I am a fifty-three-year-old menopausal lady?" And so I'm just totally curious about what the heck this is, because I still have it, and I have it all the time.

INT: You mentioned Somatic Experiencing, you mentioned going to a Western medical doctor, an acupuncturist, doing qigong, doing tai chi—were there things that were particularly helpful or anything that made it worse, or was particularly unhelpful?

MP2: I think acupuncture has been very helpful. I came to acupuncture because I read in the *Spiritual Emergency* book that when people have these surges, that acupuncture can help. I also read that gardening and things like that can help. I've done things like cooking, walking, trying to feel connected to the earth. I would go to the park. I would lie down on the grass, put my belly button to the earth. I've done quite a lot with trees.

INT: And has any of that been helpful?

MP2: Yes, that's been helpful. I would say the Somatic Experiencing has been helpful. Lying on the earth. I've become a big tree-hugger. I would say those are very helpful.

INT: Well, good, I'm happy to hear that those things are. Was there anything else particularly unhelpful or that has made it worse or did nothing?

MP2: Sitting at a computer is really yucky. All electronic things. Well, one: We weren't meant sit down, and looking at the screen and the fuzziness of that. That's difficult. I am very, very flummoxed why qigong and tai chi and all those things I didn't find helpful. I'm wondering if I didn't stick with it long enough, but I went for a couple months and did various qigong forms. I would say I am still looking. Kind of still looking . . .

INT: Okay, so again thank you so much for sharing. The last question in terms of the formal interview would be: You mentioned feeling a lot of impairment from these symptoms. So has there been or is there now a period of time where you felt you have been unable to work, or that your ability to work or function otherwise has been decreased in some way?

MP2: Absolutely, absolutely. Okay, I used to be a performer. In November of 2011, I was performing at [name of performance venue]. That is a very prestigious venue. I'm standing on stage in front of like a thousand people, and this energetic updraft is happening to me onstage. Not the voltage, but the sort of watery, windy current. So that's really weird to me because my experience with performing is: Once you walk on stage, whatever is happening . . . I've seen people who had their backs thrown out and they get on stage and they're fine. So there's an ability to be on stage and it doesn't matter. If you have a broken ankle, who cares, wrap it up and get out there and do your job. So that this would happen on stage was extremely troubling to me. And since, I would say, 2012, when the yanking started to happen, I really haven't been able to work full-time. And I can't sit down. I haven't sat down comfortably for a year. So I'm not dying. All my organs work. I have no organ failure. But I have neuromuscular difficulties.

Male, Aged Twenty-Two, Theravāda Buddhist Tradition[13]

MP3: So I began the retreat, not having had done a retreat before, but thinking that it would be fine because I had done some meditation. I wasn't really apprehensive about it; I just sort of did it without thinking too much. I assumed that only good things could come of it—that even if it was difficult somehow, it would still be helpful for me in some way. And I guess I can overwork myself sometimes. Like it happens with schoolwork, for example. I get sort of very obsessed and driven to do something, and I think something kind of similar to that maybe happened on this retreat.

So the instructions, as you probably know, the first four days are the breath, *ānāpāna,* watching the breath at the tip of the nostrils. So I got very determined in doing that. I was really not going to let my mind wander for one breath. And, of course, it did, but I think I got like very into that. And I think I somehow attained some pretty nice states of calm. Not like the *jhāna*s or anything, but definitely not a normal experience of calm that I had had before. Oh, and the other thing I should mention is this: The time I did this retreat was right before college acceptances were coming out. So I think I was kind of high-strung and anxious, even if I may not have realized it completely.

INT: So what I'm hearing is that you kind of went into this with a certain degree of intensity or determination, and you feel like that was at least some variable amidst all the types of changes that happened. Is that right?

MP3: I think so. I would say so. So everything was going pretty much fine. I think it was on the fourth day that this happened. What I remember was the day before the actual *vipassanā,* which for him [primary teacher in the tradition] means the body scanning. So I had this experience where I was sort of noticing one of the sensations. I guess maybe it was the day that we were transitioning to *vipassanā.* We were observing sensations below the bottom of the nostril, like above the upper lip. I was just observing little sensations, like muscle twitches there. I don't really know what they are. And then, all of a sudden, this image of my mother's face popped into my mind. And she just looked normal, but for some reason I had the feeling that she was dead. And I knew that she wasn't actually dead, but it felt as if she had died, for some reason. And this was not preceded by anything strange happening; it just sort of came all of a sudden. And then I felt very intense sadness—sensations in my heart. And I started crying, just right in the meditation hall. And I couldn't really stop crying. And then, the rest of the day, I sort of recovered from it. It sort of went away, and I realized that she didn't actually die. So I wasn't concerned that she died, but I was just sort of a little bit shaken up by this intense emotional experience. It was also just strange, because nothing actually happened, but I felt really, really sad.

INT: Can you just, to the best of your recollection, walk me through what it felt like to have the onset of this image? How did it relate to the kind of technique you were doing?

MP3: Sure. I guess my understanding is that it didn't really relate to the technique. I mean, the technique is observing sensations, which is like a feeling tone, like a touch. It's not a touch. I don't even know what sense it is. It's like an internal body sense. And the image of my mother was like a visual image, and it didn't correspond in any way to any of the sensations that I was observing. It wasn't like I was observing one sensation that was my mother's face or something like that; it just kind of jumped to a different . . .

INT: And did the emotional component come right away, too, or was that sort of derivative?

MP3: No, it came right away. It was concurrent with the appearance of my mother's face, the sort of sadness.

INT: And the sense that she was dead? That was all there at the same time, too?

MP3: Yeah, that was all there at the same time.

INT: Okay. All right, so what happened next?

MP3: So I kept doing the course. I think I actually went to the teacher—actually, the assistant teacher—because they have that time you can talk to the assistant teacher during lunch. And I asked him, "I had this weird thing where I thought my mother died, and I started crying. Is that normal? Should I be concerned? Am I doing the technique right?" And he just said, "Yeah, you're doing it right. It's fine." So I figured it was almost maybe a good thing, like it was some sort of breakthrough.

Although I was really sad, it also was intense in the kind of way that maybe, as a teenager, I was thinking, "Oh, meditation retreats should be really intense. So maybe it was some sort of like crazy, spiritual breakthrough or something." So I think at some point I thought it maybe was like a good thing. And then I think I kind of even tried to have *more* experiences like that—not that I could make them come about but just sort of this like drivenness to follow the sensations and not get caught up in thoughts, or just keep going back to the sensations over and over again.

And so what started happening was that I would have these similar episodes as this first one that I just described, where I would experience different emotions—it could be anger or sadness or joy or lust. Just the whole gamut of emotions would come—not all at once, but separately, in very intense episodes. So if I was experiencing anxiety, for example, it felt almost like I was having a panic attack. I've never had a panic attack outside of retreat like this, but my body would shake, and I would be sweating. But I thought it was somehow part of the purification process or something, and that it was like something that I needed to go through. But this kept happening. And I guess it maybe happened once or twice a day for the next six days of the retreat.

[At] the end of the retreat, when we started—when we broke the silence, I was rather zoned. Like, I couldn't communicate with people, really. I didn't quite realize how out of it I had become. Like, people would walk up to me and say, "Hey, how was the retreat? It's nice that it's over," or something like that. And I just couldn't respond. I couldn't say, "Oh, it was good, and I had some weird experiences." I was almost speechless. And then I felt very disconnected from everyone, because I couldn't interact with people normally. And I became concerned about myself.

And, I also became concerned about losing the sort of intensity of the practice that I thought I had achieved, I guess. I remember sitting in a room. I think there was some talk they were giving on the last day on the history of the tradition or something. I remember sitting in a room with twenty other people and one person talking. It's hard, I can't remember exactly what it felt like, but I think my eyes kept moving to all the different light sources in the room, kind of uncontrollably, but like sequentially. It would be like one light source and another light source. And it felt like I didn't have control of what my eyes were doing. And I felt that everyone—every person—and the whole external, material world was somehow like flat. It had no depth to it. It was just sort of this lifeless picture. It didn't feel like the people there were real, whatever real means. But I felt like I couldn't connect. I felt totally isolated inside all these body sensations I had been observing, and they were the only things I felt like I could experience directly. And I became very anxious and distraught, because it was really frightening.

And then I think I went to the information desk, and I said something like, "I need help." And then someone there took me on a walk, which *sort of* helped. It was helpful to go on a walk, and sort of just grounding. But it didn't solve the problem. So when I came back I felt isolated. And the more strange that I felt, the more worried I became about how I was feeling. But I guess I was still thinking, "Oh, maybe this is just something that will go away, or it's just a natural part of this." I didn't realize. If something like this had happened to me at this point in my life, I would probably be concerned and try to get help for it, but I wasn't completely clear that I needed that at the time.

INT: Yeah, well, it sounds like you had had a wide range of experiences over the last couple of days. Were you seeing it like just another one of those, and that it was probably going to pass like the other ones passed? Is that what you were anticipating?

MP3: I think so, yeah. I was thinking of it like that. Or I was thinking of it like that I did all the instructions right, and if this was the result then it was definitely supposed to happen. And if people thought it was strange, then they didn't understand or something. Like, I thought I was really good at doing the technique. Kind of like a hubristic kind of thing.

INT: Uh huh. What kind of feedback did you get from the people you talked to about it? You said you went on a walk with your course manager or someone. Were you telling them what you were feeling like at that time?

MP3: Yeah, yeah, I think I tried to tell them all these things, although I actually can't remember a lot of what we talked about on the walk. Not just because it was so long ago, but I think even closer to when this happened, my memory wasn't recording things very well for some reason. But I remember him saying, "You're not the only one that this"—whatever *this* is—"has happened to." "This," I guess, meaning a strange, intense experience. "You're not the only one who this has happened to. And most of the other people who have an issue like this are young men, because they're very macho and strive a lot." I think I remember him saying something like that.

INT: Okay, interesting. And that was specifically about how you were feeling, that people didn't seem real? Or was that about the sort of broader range of emotional experiences that you had had over the last couple of days?

MP3: I think it's the latter: the broader range of experiences. I'm not sure I was able to describe to him exactly how I felt, about people not seeming real. I can't really remember what I spoke with him about.

INT: These sound like, to me, two pretty different experiences in the sense that one pattern you were having was these really intense emotional experiences. You said when it would be anxiety-related it would feel almost like a panic attack, but you would go through these different emotions. I guess I'm wondering if this experience you had at the end of the course in relationship to not feeling like you could communicate with people, not feeling like people were real—did that also have a strong emotional component, or was there less emotion than usual to that experience?

MP3: I guess there was less emotion than in the other experiences that I had. I guess I would say I was anxious, although I wasn't in touch with it at the time. Like, in some ways I felt like I was—what's that—is it called depersonalization? Yeah, the state in which one's thoughts and feelings seem unreal, or not to belong to oneself. So I felt like I wasn't connected to what I was feeling. So even if I felt anxious, I couldn't acknowledge it. I mean, I guess maybe I was suppressing it, but that's an interpretation. I don't really know.

INT: Okay, feel free to recount the other changes that you wanted to make sure to say. It sounds like the story is not quite over yet.

MP3: So I think it's like day ten when you break silence. And you stay that night. So this whole day happened of feeling very strange and not being able to connect with people. And then that night, when I'm technically still on the retreat even though we had broken silence, when I laid down in my bed I looked at my body and had this same sort of feeling that I was dead, even though, well, first of all I knew I wasn't dead, and second of all it's not like my body looked like it was decayed or anything. It looked exactly as it normally does. But I just had this feeling that I was dead, and it was sort of unshakable. I couldn't convince myself. I guess I thought I was dying somehow.

And I felt this very intense pressure on my chest. I was really, really scared, and I couldn't just snap out of it. I tried to think of my favorite song, or I tried do some stretching to get my body active or something, but I couldn't shake this feeling. And then I eventually let go or whatever. I'm not really sure what I did, but I guess I gave up resisting the feeling, and it sort of went away. And there was a turn-around point, but it didn't all of a sudden go away.

But I couldn't go to sleep that night at all. I was trying to lie down and go to sleep but I ended up walking around. And I ran into another student on the course who was also up for whatever reason. I think I ran into him in the bathroom, and I was like, "Hey, I don't know what is going on. I feel really, really weird." He was sort of the first person I found who I could speak to, and it turned out he had done a lot of [name of tradition] retreats. And he was like, "Oh, this happens sometimes. You should go see the teacher."

So he took me to the assistant teacher's bedroom and opened the door, and the assistant teacher sat up on his bed in half-lotus or whatever. And was sort of like, "Oh, what can I do to help?" and had me sit down on the floor in front of him. But at this point I was very out of sorts and scared and confused. And somehow this image of this assistant—oh, he also never turned the light on—so this image of the silhouetted assistant teacher sitting up on the bed somehow was very, very scary to me. And so all of my fear about all of these weird experiences I'd been having got pegged onto the teacher. But at the same time, I knew that that had happened. I didn't run away from the teacher. I remember telling the teacher something like that. I said, "I am really, really afraid of you, but I don't think I actually am. But it feels like I'm really afraid of you." I don't know, something really strange like that. So the teacher and I went on a walk for like half an hour. And then we ended up going back inside, and he talked to me for a while, until I calmed down a little bit. And then I tried to go back to sleep. I don't think I slept at all that night.

And then, woke up the next morning, tried to drive home, but I couldn't concentrate on the road. I sort of was too involved in all these bodily sensations, and I just couldn't concentrate, so I had to pull over. My parents came and picked me up. It was like a two-hour drive. But that's the end of the retreat stage, I guess, although there were definitely still weird things that happened after the retreat.

INT: So, all right, you were saying that as you were driving, you felt like you had this hyper-awareness of sensations, and that was distracting you from being able to drive. Were you too much in your body at that point? What was that like?

MP3: That's what it felt like, yeah. That's what it felt like. It felt like I couldn't put my attention on anything other than my body sensations. Although there may have been other things going on as well, but that was what I thought was going on.

INT: And was that something that had been happening the last day of the course as well, while you were feeling disconnected from people, this heightened awareness of your body, or did that have varying degrees of clarity or intensity?

MP3: No, I think it was ongoing, this sense that my body sensations were the only thing that was real or something like that. It wasn't an issue when I was on the silent part of the retreat, because I didn't have to do anything, I guess. But as soon as I started having to interact with people I found it really hard and kind of destabilizing and disorienting, because I felt like the only thing I could connect to was my body sensations. So that was like an ongoing thing. . . .

If I can remember correctly, I was still trying to keep paying attention to the body sensations, which was hard to do if I also wanted to talk to people. It was sort of overwhelming, I guess. Because also, as you maybe know, there is some relation between your emotional affect and your body sensation. So if you're aware of all these different body sensations, it can give you some sort of clue into how you're feeling emotionally, and so I guess I felt like I was an open canvas. I had no defense mechanism or boundaries between me and other people, so interacting with someone—just looking into somebody's eyes and connecting with them felt like this huge onslaught. I didn't know where the emotions were coming from—I guess they were my emotions—but it felt just extremely emotionally intense. I had such heightened awareness of all my emotions that it just felt so intense to interact with people. I physically could move my mouth, but I had trouble finding words that I could use to communicate with people.

INT: So I think we left off in the sequence of things that your parents came and picked up after you pulled off on the side of the road. What happened over the next couple hours, days, weeks—however long you feel like there was still a connection to these changes that you felt like you experienced on the retreat?

MP3: Yeah, so my parents came, and they came with my sister, too, because they probably figured, "Well, she doesn't need to come, but if we just leave her at home then she'll probably be even more freaked out." And they came, and they gave me a hug, and I guess they thought that would help, but it didn't really help because I felt overly hypersensitive to my own emotions. I felt like I was somehow picking up other people's emotions, but I don't really know if that was true.

But my parents were very, very anxious because it turns out the center had called them saying, "Your son is having an issue. You should call him because he might not be able to drive home," which is a horrible thing to hear if you're somebody's parent. And then I had also called them saying, "I need help. Can you pick me up?" So they were like, "What the hell has happened to our kid?" As I said before, my mom is just a very anxious person in general. So when they came things kind of got even worse, because they were anxious, and I was anxious myself, and I felt somehow that I was becoming more anxious by being around them.

And this is sort of when I began to start trying to interpret what had happened, in terms of: Was this part of the retreat experience, or was this some sort of weird side effect thing that happened that wasn't supposed to happen? And then my parents were definitely of the opinion that this was not supposed to happen, and I should be concerned about my health. And up to that point I hadn't really thought that. I had thought that it was sort of concerning and strange, but it was somehow normal, and fine, and it wasn't really a big issue. But the more they kept saying it was a big issue, the more I became convinced that it was a big issue, and the more concerned I became. And this was all in the course of driving back and that day.

And then I think I finally went to sleep, and I think I just slept a lot for the next couple of days. And I don't even remember what I did over those next couple of days. But I still felt very strange, and still this issue of being hypersensitive, and things being kind of just intense. Sometimes things being very clear, having very clear sensory perceptions—the kind of things that can happen on retreat, but it's sort of like you can't turn it off, almost. So it's not helpful to be incredibly sensory aware when you're walking in a city, for example. Just too intense, I guess—or at least it was for me. So that took a while to resolve. . . .

INT: Okay. I guess the one piece of the puzzle that I need to fit in somewhere is: You said earlier on, at the beginning of the interview, that you ended up being given a low dose of Abilify. When did that happen?

MP3: I think that happened between a week and a month after the retreat. I started seeing a psychiatrist within a week from the retreat ending. And he kept asking me what had happened, and basically his hypothesis was that it was an episode of mania. What happened does have some similarities to mania, or maybe it *was* mania—I really don't know. So he prescribed Abilify within a month of the retreat ending. I guess he was just thinking I'd take it to get myself more stable and then be weaned off of it, which is what happened.

INT: Two questions about that. What symptoms were you still having? You talked about this ongoing perceptual and emotional sensitivity—is that mostly what was happening at this period of one month after? And how did you come to the decision to see this psychiatrist? Did your mom encourage you to do that since she's a psychiatrist as well? Walk me through a little bit more how that all unfolded.

MP3: So she basically forced me to see a psychiatrist. I mean, I wasn't going to resist it, but it was totally her idea and her decision. She was like, "You need help. You need to see the psychiatrist." Which really concerned me, of course, because I thought I was doing a meditation retreat and was becoming more enlightened or something, and that the last thing that was going to happen was that I was going to become mentally ill from doing a meditation retreat. So it was her thing with that.

And it also just felt like my world had been turned upside down in terms of everything I thought that I had trusted. It was like I couldn't trust. Because I had trusted the Buddhist tradition, and I had trusted [name of primary teacher in tradition], or whatever, and now this thing that I had put so much effort into was somehow harmful to me. And I didn't know if I could trust my parents, because they were saying something bad had happened, but I wasn't really sure if it was bad. And I had this crisis of how to make meaning out of this experience. I guess that was the biggest symptom that I had. It wasn't like I was having these emotional, intense episodes, but it was just like how to make sense of all of it was what was distressing to me.

INT: Yeah, no, I feel like we've been sort of continually bracketing that issue, but maybe it's time to talk about it directly, since the second part of the interview is to talk more explicitly about the interpretations. . . .

MP3: Yeah, I would say my interpretation has evolved a lot. At the time these experiences happened, my interpretation was something like, "Oh, they're just natural stages on the path of Buddhist practice." And then, when I started interacting with my parents, I sort of thought they might be natural stages on the Buddhist path, but then also had this other idea introduced of maybe they're somehow like dangerous, pathological experiences, but I wasn't really sure. And then the psychiatrist was leaning more towards like: This is pathological. But I didn't really know if I believed that, I guess.

Within a month or two after the retreat, I began going to see [name of meditation teacher] at [name of American insight meditation center] to ask him for guidance about what had happened. And I sort of took his point of view, which was: This wasn't a great thing to have happened. Like, it doesn't have to be a stage on the Buddhist path. It wasn't like a good thing that you need to go through, or something like that. That there are different ways to manage this on the retreat, and the retreat teacher could have done a better job explaining the instructions and how to calm myself down or whatever. But, that said, it still does happen to people on retreats and it's not indicative of mental illness. It's just something that can happen on retreats, that happens to Westerners, and also I think can happen to Asian Buddhists as well—maybe less frequently. But that's sort of the lens that I sort of took up. I guess it was pretty close to the way I interpret it now.

INT: Why did you decide to take the Abilify if you were in between these different frameworks? And did this encounter with your teacher afterwards, was that part of the process of stopping taking the medication, ultimately?

MP3: Yeah, yeah. So I didn't want to take the Abilify. I did not think it was necessary. But also that's the classic sign of being insane, when you think that you are sane. So my parents were like, "Yeah, forget about it. You need this medication and you will take this medication, regardless of what you say." And I guess technically I was over 18, so I could have decided not to, but I think the psychiatrist convinced me. I don't think I was totally convinced by the pathological framework, but I was at least convinced of the possibility that that might be correct, and therefore that it might be a good idea to take the medication. I think I resisted it a lot, but I also saw the wisdom of: If you have something strange happen and then you go see the psychiatrist and they give you medication, then it's not going hurt that much to—Maybe I needed the medication. In retrospect, I don't think I did. And my parents even have agreed—I think even the psychiatrist has agreed—that I did not need the medication. But at the time they were concerned that I had bipolar disorder, and that they wanted to bring me down from what they thought was a manic episode.

INT: And did you describe to them the sense that you had of other people not being real, or your body not being real? Did they get that information? The things that you previously described as relating to depersonalization? Or were they just hearing about the hypersensitivity to the sensations and emotions that you were experiencing later on?

MP3: That's a good question. So I think the psychiatrist, he definitely heard about all of it. I mean, I told him everything. My parents, I think the day I came home they were concerned about how I was acting. I guess I was sort of not normal; I couldn't speak and be relaxed and friendly like normal. So I tried to explain to them, "Oh yeah, these strange things happened on the retreat and that's why I can't be normal right now." But the more I would explain to them, the more deeply freaked out they would become. So even to this day, I don't think I've explained most of these things in that much detail, because they just think it's crazy talk, basically. It's scary for them to hear. But I think they've heard some of it. But, yeah, that's a good question.

INT: Okay. Anything else you want to say about the types of interpretations you were given by the teachers? It seems that at some point, since they called your parents, they also came to some conclusion that you were having some sort of problem. So I'm wondering if that was ever communicated to you directly, or if you were surprised to hear that your parents got a call warning them about you?

MP3: Yeah. You know, I was surprised, because they never communicated it to me directly, either on the retreat or after the retreat, at all. So I feel like that's not the best thing. They didn't really offer me any framework at all, either a positive one or a negative one, about how to interpret this experience. . . .

INT: Okay. Our last set of questions is on things you found helpful or unhelpful in navigating these experiences. That could be a whole range of things. I mean, you've talked to teachers, you talked to your parents, you talked to psychiatrists, you were on medication for a while. If you could just walk us through what types of things you found helpful at the time, or in retrospect, and what kinds of things you would have liked to have had happen that you didn't have access to or have happen. So any comments you have about remedies for negotiating what you went through on this course.

MP3: Yeah, no, that's a good question. Well, I guess, for me, because I was in this limbo between wondering if people were right in thinking that I had some mental illness, versus just having had a strange experience. Like, it wasn't even the experience so much that was the issue for me. It was the interpretation of it that was the issue. So I guess what I found the most helpful was when I realized that I'm not the only one who has had an experience like this, and that people have these experiences sometimes on meditation retreats, and they're not ideal and they can be mitigated—and I think that they should be mitigated—but they also can happen sometimes, and it's probably not good for you, but I don't think it's really long-term bad for you. I think my parents were concerned either that it was the first episode of bipolar mania, or that it was making me more prone to something like that. I don't have evidence for this, but I don't see why it would. I don't really see that there's evidence for their position either, really.

First of all, talking to meditation teachers who have dealt with students who have had similar experiences, talking to other meditators who have had similar experiences, we shared our stories. And when you have someone who can listen . . . And even like this interview is sort of therapeutic because I got to say all of these things, and you just sort of listened to it, and you're not freaked out by it. And that even happened the night I came home. My best friend at the time came over, and he doesn't really meditate at all but he's done a lot of psychedelic drugs. So I was describing to him all these strange things that had happened, and he just sort of listened very openly, without judging them. And that was really helpful for me. But it was really not helpful when people tried to put everything I said into some sort of box, like: "Oh, you said this, so you were depersonalized, and then you had a panic attack, and now you're manic." That was not helpful for me.

INT: Did anyone ever give you an explicitly Buddhist framework about these signifying some type of progress or some type of attainment or anything like that, whether that's within the [name of tradition] framework or beyond it?

MP3: No. No one did, actually.

INT: Okay. So more what you heard was that this kind of thing can happen, basically, but they didn't tell you what it meant?

MP3: Basically, yeah. So in terms of where I got this idea that this kind of thing can happen, it was from [name of meditation teacher at American insight meditation center], who basically said it's something that can happen when you have an imbalance of mental faculties. Like: You have too much mindfulness and not enough—I actually forget what he said. But there's the seven factors of awakening, and basically, they don't develop at the same rate. So if you have some developing at a faster rate than others, you're kind of growing in this mismatched, this disproportionate way, and then they can result in . . . basically, it was explained to me as a result of an imbalance of mental faculties, so not like an attainment at all—like the opposite of that. Not like something that I needed to feel bad about, but just like a natural thing that happens when things get out of whack.

INT: Okay. And I thought I remembered that you said that the teachers on the course that you talked to, they also acknowledged that this type of thing could happen, or did happen, as an outcome of doing the practice. Did they say much more than that? And what did they tell you to do about it, if anything?

MP3: First of all, they didn't say much more about it, but I guess the implication was that this sort of thing can happen. Like: It's not a good thing that it happens, but it can happen, but you shouldn't worry about it too much, was sort of what was implied there. In terms of what to do about it, they just were like, "Relax, don't worry." I guess they said going on a walk; that was good. They didn't have a lot of other recommendations. Although I think I've read some since then. Like eating a lot can help if you feel very light and not very grounded. Doing vigorous exercise, I think, can help. But they didn't tell me these things; I read about them.

INT: Okay. And did the walk have the anticipated effect of grounding you or calming you down at all?

MP3: I think it did, but it was just like a drop in the bucket at that point. Although later, going on walks, when I was more stable, it did help.

INT: Okay. Let's see. Anything else that you think now would have been helpful that you wish you had been told or had been offered? Or any other things that you think could or should be in place for other people going through these types of experiences?

MP3: I think so. Maybe if it was explained to me beforehand that something like what happened to me was possible. And second of all, that it's not something that's desirable or required. And third: what to do to mitigate it. So the kind of questions that you just asked. I think that would be really helpful.

Notes

1. The summary of study subjects, methods, and results discussed herein is presented in full in Lindahl et al. (2017). The main study recruited twenty meditation practitioners each from among Theravāda, Zen, and Tibetan Buddhist traditions, along with thirty-one experts (Buddhist meditation teachers or clinicians); a subsequent replication study sampled an additional eight practitioners and one expert from the tradition of *vipassanā* meditation as taught by S. N. Goenka.
2. Interviews with meditation experts (teachers and clinicians) followed a similar structure but focused on meditation-related challenges that experts had observed and managed in their students or patients.
3. The complete taxonomy of phenomenology and influencing factors can be found in Lindahl et al. (2017), and the differential diagnosis criteria are presented in Lindahl et al. (2020).
4. Many of these studies are cited or reviewed in Lindahl et al. (2017, 2021); Compson (2018); Farias et al. (2020); and Lambert et al. (2021).

5. For survey-based studies, see Cebolla et al. (2017); Schlosser et al. (2019); and Goldberg et al. (2021). For research in clinical contexts, see Baer et al. (2019) and Britton et al. (2021); see Farias et al. (2020) for a review.
6. Lindahl et al. (2014); Lindahl and Britton (2019); Cooper et al. (2021); Lindahl, Britton, and Cooper (2023); and Solomonova et al. (2025).
7. Lindahl (2017); Lindahl et al. (2023); Palitsky et al. (2023); and Canby et al. (2025).
8. Lindahl et al. (2020).
9. Although interview transcripts are to a great extent presented verbatim and as they unfolded, some sections of each interview were summarized in the introduction, and other sections have been omitted for brevity. Minor edits have been made for clarity and readability. Where necessary, they have also been edited in order to preserve anonymity.
10. See, in particular, Sharf (1995), McMahan (2008, 2011), and Thompson (2020).
11. Interview conducted via telephone by Willoughby Britton, February 10, 2011.
12. Interview conducted via video conferencing by Nathan Fisher, March 4, 2014.
13. Interview conducted via video conferencing by Jared Lindahl, August 2, 2016.

References

Abe, Ryuichi. 1999. *The Weaving of Mantra: Kukai and the Construction of Esoteric Buddhist Discourse.* Columbia University Press.

Agsar, Wendy Biddlecombe. 2021. "Buddhism's Biggest Open Secret." *Tricycle: The Buddhist Review.* Accessed January 28, 2024. https://tricycle.org/magazine/meditation-sickness.

Ahn, Jun. 2007. "Malady of Meditation: A Prolegomenon to the Study of Illness and Zen." PhD diss., University of California, Berkeley.

Ahn, Juhn Y. 2008. "Zen and the Art of Nourishing Life: Labor, Exhaustion, and the Malady of Meditation." *Japanese Journal of Religious Studies* 35 (2): 177–229.

Ahn, Jun. 2014. "Meditation Sickness." In *The Oxford Handbook of Meditation,* edited by Miguel Farias, Mansur Lalljee, and David Brazier. Oxford University Press.

Ahn, Jun. 2017. "Getting Sick Over Nothing: Hyesim and Hakuin on the Maladies of Meditation." In *Buddhism and Medicine: An Anthology of Premodern Sources,* edited by C. Pierce Salguero. Columbia University Press.

Aitken, Robert. 1994. *The Practice of Perfection: The Pāramitās from a Zen Buddhist Perspective.* Pantheon.

Akanuma, Chizen. (1930) 1994. *A Dictionary of Buddhist Proper Names.* Sri Satguru.

Anālayo, Bhikkhu. 2011. *A Comparative Study of the Majjhima-nikāya.* Vols. 1–2. Dharma Drum.

Anālayo, Bhikkhu. 2012. "The Historical Value of the Pāli Discourses." *Indo-Iranian Journal* 55:223–253.

Anālayo, Bhikkhu. 2014. "The Mass Suicide of Monks in Discourse and Vinaya Literature." *Journal of Chinese Buddhist Studies* 7:11–55.

Anālayo, Bhikkhu. 2017. *A Meditator's Life of the Buddha, Based on the Early Discourses.* Windhorse.

Anālayo, Bhikkhu. 2019a. *Mindfulness of Breathing: A Practice Guide and Translations.* Windhorse.

Anālayo, Bhikkhu. 2019b. "Brahmā, Śakra, and Māra." In *Brill's Encyclopedia of Buddhism,* Vol. 2, *Lives,* edited by Jonathan A. Silk, Richard Bowring, Vincent Eltschinger, and Michael Radich. Brill.

Anālayo, Bhikkhu. 2020. "Peyāla in the Skandha-saṃyukta, Contraction and Expansion in Textual Transmission." In *Research on the Saṃyukta-āgama,* edited by Bhikkhunī Dhammadinnā. Dharma Drum.

Anālayo, Bhikkhu. 2021a. "The Buddha's Pre-Awakening Practices and Their Mindful Transformation." *Mindfulness* 12:1892–1898.

Anālayo, Bhikkhu. 2021b. "The Dangers of Mindfulness: Another Myth?" *Mindfulness* 12:2890–2895. https://doi.org/10.1007/s12671-021-01682-w.

Anālayo, Bhikkhu. 2022. *Early Buddhist Oral Tradition: Textual Formation and Transmission.* Wisdom.

Baer, Ruth, Catherine Crane, Edward Miller, and Willem Kuyken. 2019. "Doing No Harm in Mindfulness-Based Programs: Conceptual Issues and Empirical Findings." *Clinical Psychology Review* 71:101–114. https://doi.org/10.1016/j.cpr.2019.01.001.

Baer, Ruth, Catherine Crane, Jesus Montero-Marin, Alice Phillips, Laura Taylor, Alice Tickell, Willem Kuyken, and the MYRIAD Team. 2020. "Frequency of Self-Reported Unpleasant Events and Harm in a Mindfulness-Based Program in Two General Population Samples." *Mindfulness* 12:763–774. https://doi.org/10.1007/s12671-020-01547-8.

Ba Khin, U. n.d. [1960?]. *Discourses from a Ten-Day Vipassanā Course at the International Meditation Centre, Rangoon.* Seven CDs with two tracks each. International Meditation Centre.

Benn, James A. 2008. "Another Look at the Pseudo-Śūraṃgama Sūtra." *Harvard Journal of Asiatic Studies* 68 (1): 57–89.

Benn, James A. 2024. "'Lengyan jing': Chinese Buddhist Apocryphon or Late Mahāyāna Sutra." *International Journal of Buddhist Thought & Culture* 34 (2): 81–117.

Bernot, Lucien. 1967. *Les paysans arakanais du Pakistan oriental: L'histoire, le monde végétal et l'organisation sociale des réfugiés Marma (Mog).* Mouton.

Bhikshu Dharmamitra, trans. 2008. *The Essentials of Buddhist Meditation: A Classic Śamatha-Vipaśyanā Meditation Manual: The Essentials for Practicing Calming-and-Insight and Dhyāna Meditation, by the Great Tiantai Meditation Master and Exegete: Śramaṇṇa Zhiyi (Chih-I) (538–597 CE).* Kalavinka Press.

Bingenheimer, Marcus. 2011. *Studies in Āgama Literature with Special Reference to the Shorter Chinese Saṃyuktāgama.* Xinwenfeng.

Birnbaum, Raoul. 1989. "Chinese Buddhist Traditions of Healing and the Life Cycle." In *Healing and Restoring: Health and Medicine in the World's Religious Traditions,* edited by L. E. Sullivan. Macmillan.

Bodhi, Bhikku. 2000. *The Connected Discourses of the Buddha.* Wisdom.

Brac de la Perrière, Bénédicte. 1989. *Les Rituels de Possession en Birmanie: Du Culte d'État aux Cérémonies Privées.* Éditions Recherche sur les Civilisations.

Britton, Willoughby B. 2019. "Can Mindfulness Be Too Much of a Good Thing? The Value of a Middle Way." *Current Opinions in Psychology: Special Issue on Mindfulness* 28:159–165. https://doi.org/10.1016/j.copsyc.2018.12.011.

Britton, Willoughby B., Jared R. Lindahl, David J. Cooper, Nicholas K. Canby, and Roman Palitsky. 2021. "Defining and Measuring Meditation-Related Adverse Effects in

Mindfulness-Based Programs." *Clinical Psychological Science* 9 (6): 1185–1204. https://doi.org/10.1177/2167702621996340.

Broughton, Jeffrey L. 2023. *The Recorded Sayings of Chan Master Zhongfeng Mingben.* Oxford University Press.

Broughton, Jeffrey L., and Elise Yoko Watanabe. 2017. *The Letters of Chan Master Dahui Pujue.* Oxford University Press.

Buddhaghosa, Bhikkhu. (1956) 2010. *The Path of Purification: Visuddhimagga.* Buddhist Publication Society.

Burnouf, Eugène. 2022. *Aṣṭasāhasrikā Prajñāpāramitā: La perfection de sagesse en huit mille stances.* Edited by Guillaume Ducoeur. Université de Strasbourg.

Buswell, Robert E., and Donald S. Lopez. 2013. *The Princeton Dictionary of Buddhism.* Princeton University Press.

Byrne, Christopher. 2019. "Verses of Silent Illumination: Hongzhi Zhengjue's Poetic Vision of Caodong Zen." *International Journal of Buddhist Thought and Culture* 29 (2): 171–205.

Canby, Nicholas K., Jared R. Lindahl, David J. Cooper, Nitai Joseph, Roman Palitsky, and Willoughby B. Britton. 2025. "The Teacher Matters: The Role and Impact of Meditation Teachers in the Trajectories of Western Buddhist Meditators Experiencing Meditation-Related Challenges." *Contemporary Buddhism* 25 (1–2): 9–53. https://doi.org/10.1080/14639947.2025.2485677.

Cassaniti, Julia. 2018. *Remembering the Present: Mindfulness in Buddhist Asia.* Cornell University Press.

Cebolla, Ausiàs, Marcelo Demarzo, Patricia Martins, Joaquim Soler, and Javier Garcia-Campayo. 2017. "Unwanted Effects: Is There a Negative Side of Meditation? A Multicentre Survey." *PLOS ONE* 12 (9): e0183137. https://doi.org/10.1371/journal.pone.0183137.

Chakma, Jointu. 2016. "The Concept of Mind (Citta) in Early Buddhism." *Journal of International Buddhist Studies College* 2 (1): 92–103.

Chen Ming. 2013. *Zhonggu yiliao yu wailai wenhua.* Peking University Press.

Chen, Nancy N. 2003. *Breathing Spaces: Qigong, Psychiatry, and Healing in China.* Columbia University Press.

Chenagtsang, Nida. 2018. *Karmamudra: The Yoga of Bliss (Sexuality in Tibetan Medicine and Buddhism).* Sky Press.

Chenagtsang, Nida. 2023. *G.yu thog snying thig gi phyag rdzogs kyi 'grel ba nyi zla'i 'od snang* (Light of the sun and moon: A commentary on the Mahamudra and Ati Yoga teachings of the Yuthok Nyingthig). Sky Press.

Chenagtsang, Nida. 2024. *Foundations of Sowa Rigpa: A Guide to the Root Tantra of Tibetan Medicine.* Sky Press.

Cheung, Kin. 2022. "Miracle as Natural: A Contemporary Chinese American Religious Healer." In *Miracles: An Exercise in Comparative Philosophy of Religion,* edited by Karen R. Zwier, David L. Weddle, and Timothy D. Knepper. Springer International.

Cheung, Kin. 2023. "A Chinese American Religious Healer: Toward Filial Ethnography." In *The Familial Occult: Explorations at the Margins of Critical Autoethnography,* edited by Alexandra Coţofană. Berghahn Books.

Cheung, Kin. 2024. "Buddhist Healing in the Community: A Chinese American Healer in New York City." In *Buddhism and Healing in the Modern World,* edited by C. Pierce Salguero, Kin Cheung, and Susannah Deane. University of Hawai'i Press.

Cheung, Kin. Forthcoming. "Healing (with) *Qi* via *Qigong,* Acupuncture, and *Fengshui:* Code-Switching and the Case of a Chinese American Healer." In *Subtle Energies in Therapy, Spirituality, Arts, and Politics, 1800–Present,* edited by Julian Strube, Marleen Thaler, and Dominic Zoehrer. Numen Book Series: Studies in the History of Religions. Brill.

Cheung, Kin, and C. Pierce Salguero. 2019. "Interview with a Contemporary Chinese American Healer." In *Buddhism and Medicine: An Anthology of Modern and Contemporary Sources,* edited by C. Pierce Salguero. Columbia University Press.

Chit Tin, U., ed. 1999. *Truth Must Triumph: A History of the Worldwide Dhamma Mission of Sayagyi U Ba Khin.* International Meditation Centres in the Tradition of Sayagyi U Ba Khin.

Chui, Antonio Ka-meng. 2018. "The Tantric Management of 'Life-Wind Illness' (*srog rlung nad*) in the Tibetan Tradition: An Interplay of Vajrayāna Ideation and Healing." PhD diss., University of Hong Kong.

Coderey, Céline. 2012. "The *Weikza's* Role in Arakanese Healing Practices." *Journal of Burma Studies* 16 (20): 181–211.

Coderey, Céline. 2015. "Coping with Health-Related Uncertainties and Risks in Rakhine (Myanmar)." *Health Risk & Society* 17 (3–4): 263–284.

Coderey, Céline. 2017. "The (Buddhist) Grammar of Healing: Building Therapeutic Efficacy in the Pluralistic Context of Rakhine, Myanmar." *Asian Medicine* 12 (1/2): 1–32.

Coderey, Céline. 2020. "Healing the Whole: Questioning the Boundaries Between Medicine and Religion in Rakhine, Western Myanmar." *Journal of Southeast Asian Studies* 51 (1/2): 49–71.

Coderey, Céline. 2023. "Questioning Boundaries Between Medicine and Religion in Myanmar." In *Situating Medicine and Religion in Asia,* edited by M. S. Baker. Manchester University Press.

Coderey, Céline. Forthcoming 2026. *The Power of Remainder: Politics and Poetics of Healing in Buddhist Myanmar.* University of Hawai'i Press.

Collins, Steven. 1982. *Selfless Persons: Imagery and Thought in Theravāda Buddhism.* Cambridge University Press.

Compson, Jane. 2018. "Adverse Meditation Experiences: Navigating Buddhist and Secular Frameworks for Addressing Them." *Mindfulness* 9:1358–1369. https://doi.org/10.1007/s12671-017-0878-8.

Conze, Edward. 1958. *Aṣṭasāhasrikā Prajñāpāramitā: The Perfection of Wisdom in Eight Thousand Slokas.* Asiatic Society.

Cooper, David J., Jared R. Lindahl, Roman Palitsky, and Willoughby B. Britton. 2021. "'Like a Vibration Cascading Through the Body': Energy-Like Somatic Experiences Reported by Western Buddhist Meditators." *Religions* 12 (1042): 1–27. https://doi.org/10.3390/rel12121042.

Curley, Melissa Anne-Marie. 2024. "A Cure for Mindfulness: Buddhism, Anxiety, and the Problem of Work in Modern Japan." *Buddhism & Medicine in the Modern World,* edited by C. Pierce Salguero, Kin Cheung, and Susannah Deane. University of Hawai'i Press.

Deane, Susannah. 2018. *Tibetan Medicine, Buddhism and Psychiatry: Mental Health and Healing in a Tibetan Exile Community.* Carolina Academic Press.

Deane, Susannah. 2019. "Rlung, Mind, and Mental Health: The Notion of 'Wind' in Tibetan Conceptions of Mind and Mental Illness." *Journal of Religion and Health* 58 (3): 708–724. http://www.doi.org/10.1007/s10943-019-00775-0.

Deane, Susannah. 2025. *Illness and Enlightenment: Exploring Tibetan Perspectives on Madness in Text and Everyday Life.* Berghahn Books.

Demiéville, Paul. 1985. *Buddhism and Healing: Demiéville's Article 'Byō' from Hōbōgirin,* Translated by Mark Tatz. University Press of America.

Despeux, Catherine. 2006. "The Six Healing Breaths." In *Daoist Body Cultivation: Traditional Models and Contemporary Practices,* edited by L. Kohn. Three Pines Press.

Despeux, Catherine. 2015. "Symbolic Pregnancy and the Sexual Identity of Taoist Adepts." In *Transforming the Void: Embryological Discourse and Reproductive Imagery in East Asian Religions,* edited by Anna Andreeva and Dominic Steavu. Brill.

Despeux, Catherine. 2019. *Taoism and Self Knowledge: The Chart for the Cultivation of Perfection (Xiuzhen tu).* Translated by Jonathan Pettit. Brill.

Despeux, Catherine. 2020. "Buddhist Healing Practices at Dunhuang." In *Buddhist Healing in Medieval China and Japan,* edited by C. Pierce Salguero and Andrew Macomber. University of Hawai'i Press.

Dhammajoti, Bhikkhu K. L. 2021. "Meditative Experiences of Impurity and Purity: Further Reflection on the *Aśubhā* Meditation and the *Śubha-vimokṣa.*" *Religions* 12 (86): 1–32.

DiSimone, Charles. 2023. "Manuscript Discoveries at Mes Aynak." *Journal of the International Association of Buddhist Studies* 46:121–176.

Dreissens, Georges. 2007. *La Noble Perfection de Sagesse en Huit Mille Versets.* Éditions Vajra Yogini.

Dreitlein, Thomas Eijo. 2011. *Beginner's Handbook for the Shido Kegyō of Chūin-ryū.* Kōyasan Shingon-shū Sōhonzan Kongōbu-ji Kyōgaku-bu.

Dutoit, Julius. 1905. *Die duṣkaracaryā des Bodhisattva in der buddhistischen Tradition*. Verlag von Karl J. Trübner.

Endo, Toshiichi. 2013. *Studies in Pali Commentarial Literature, Sources, Controversies and Insights*. Centre of Buddhist Studies.

Eskildsen, Stephen. 2008. "Some Troubles and Perils of Taoist Meditation." *Monumenta Serica* 56 (1): 259–291.

Falk, Harry, and Seishi Karashima. 2012. "A First-Century *Prajñāpāramitā* Manuscript from Gandhāra—*Parivarta* 1 (Texts from the Split Collection 1)." *Annual Report of the International Research Institute for Advanced Buddhology at Soka University* 15:19–61.

Falk, Harry, and Seishi Karashima. 2013. "A First-Century *Prajñāpāramitā* Manuscript from Gandhāra—*Parivarta* 5 (Texts from the Split Collection 2)." *Annual Report of the International Research Institute for Advanced Buddhology at Soka University* 16:97–169.

Farias, M., E. Maraldi, K. C. Wallenkampf, and G. Lucchetti. 2020. "Adverse Events in Meditation Practices and Meditation-Based Therapies: A Systematic Review." *Acta Psychiatrica Scandinavica* 142 (5): 374–393. https://doi.org/10.1111/acps.13225.

Fisher, Nathan. 2011. "The Dark Night of the Soul in Abrahamic Meditative Traditions." *The Oxford Handbook of Meditation*, edited by Miguel Farias, Mansur Lalljee, and David Brazier. Oxford University Press.

Foxeus, Niklas. 2013. "Esoteric Theravada Buddhism in Burma/Myanmar." *Scripta Instituti Donneriani Aboensis* 25:55–79.

Furth, Charlotte. 1999. *A Flourishing Yin: Gender in China's Medical History, 960–1665*. University of California Press.

Garrett, Frances, and Vincanne Adams. 2008. "The Three Channels in Tibetan Medicine, with a Translation of Tsultrim Gyaltsen's a 'Clear Explanation of the Principal Structure and Location of the Circulatory Channels as Illustrated in the Medical Paintings.'" *Traditional South Asian Medicine* 8:86–115.

Gerke, Barbara. 2013. "On the 'Subtle Body' and 'Circulation' in Tibetan Medicine." In *Religion and the Subtle Body in Asia and the West*. Routledge.

Germano, David, and Nicolas Tournadre. 2010. "THL Simplified Phonetic Transcription of Standard Tibetan." The Tibetan & Himalayan Library. Last modified February 1, 2010. https://www.thlib.org/reference/transliteration/#!essay=/thl/phonetics/all/.

Gethin, Rupert M. L. 1997. "Cosmology and Meditation: From the Aggañña-Sutta to the Mahāyāna." *History of Religions* 36 (3): 183–217.

Gethin, Rupert M. L. 2001. *The Buddhist Path to Awakening*. Oneworld.

Goldberg, Simon B., et al. 2021. "Prevalence of Meditation-Related Adverse Effects in a Population-Based Sample in the United States." *Psychotherapy Research* 32 (3): 291–305. https://doi.org/10.1080/10503307.2021.1933646.

Goldberg, Simon B., Sin U. Lam, Willoughby B. Britton, and Richard J. Davidson. 2022. "Prevalence of Meditation-Related Adverse Effects in a Population-Based Sample in the United States." *Psychotherapy Research: Journal of the Society for Psychotherapy Research* 32 (3): 291–305. https://doi.org/10.1080/10503307.2021.1933646.

Gombrich, Richard. 2009. *What the Buddha Thought.* Equinox.

Greene, Eric M. 2016. "Visions and Visualizations: In Fifth-Century Chinese Buddhism and Nineteenth-Century Experimental Psychology." *History of Religions* 55 (3): 289–328.

Greene, Eric M. 2017. "Healing Sicknesses Caused by Meditation: 'The Enveloping Butter Contemplation' from the 'Secret Essential Methods for Curing Meditation Sickness.'" *Buddhism and Medicine: An Anthology of Premodern Sources,* edited by C. Pierce Salguero. Columbia University Press.

Greene, Eric M. 2021a. *Chan Before Chan: Meditation, Repentance, and Visionary Experience in Chinese Buddhism.* University of Hawai'i Press.

Greene, Eric M. 2021b. *The Secrets of Buddhist Meditation: Visionary Meditation Texts from Early Medieval China.* Classics in East Asian Buddhism. University of Hawai'i Press.

Grof, Christina, and Stanislav Grof. 1989. *Spiritual Emergency: When Personal Transformation Becomes a Crisis.* Putnam.

Gutman, Pamela. 2001. *Burma's Lost Kingdoms: Splendours of Arakan.* Allen & Unwin.

Guy, John. 2023. *Tree and Serpent: Early Buddhist Art in India.* Metropolitan Museum of Art.

Gyatso, Geshe Kelsang. 1994. *Tantric Grounds and Paths: How to Enter, Progress on, and Complete the Vajrayana Path.* Tharpa.

Harrison, Paul. 1978. "Buddhānusmṛti in the Pratyutpanna-buddha-saṃmukhāvasthita-samādhi-sūtra." *Journal of Indian Philosophy* 6:35–57.

Haskel, Peter. 2013. *Sword of Zen: Master Takuan and His Writings on Immovable Wisdom and the Sword Taie.* University of Hawai'i Press.

Helderman, Ira. 2024. "The Average Meditator and What No One Is Talking About: Framing the Adverse Effects of Meditation in American Popular Media." *Buddhism & Medicine in the Modern World,* edited by C. Pierce Salguero, Kin Cheung, and Susannah Deane. University of Hawai'i Press.

Hirota, Dennis, ed. 1997. *Collected Works of Shinran.* Vol. 1. Jōdo Shinshū Hongwangji-ha.

Hori, Victor Sōgen. 2003. *Zen Sand: The Book of Capping Phrases for Kōan Practice.* University of Hawai'i Press.

Horner, I. B., trans. (1938) 1949. *The Book of the Discipline (Vinaya-Piṭaka).* Vol. 1, *Suttavibhaṅga.* Published for the Pali Text Society by Luzac & Company. https://doi.org/10.1371/journal.pone.0216643.

Huang Boyuan. 2000. "Zhiyi yixue sixiang zhi yanjiu—yi 《Mohe zhiguan》 'Guanbing huanjing' wei zhongxin" (A study on Zhiyi's thought of medical science—focus on "Contemplation in a State of Illness" of *Mo-ho-chih-kuan*). Master's thesis, Huafan Daxue.

Huang, Shi-shan Susan. 2012. *Picturing the True Form: Daoist Visual Culture in Traditional China.* Harvard University Asia Center.

Hüsken, Ute. 2007. *When Rituals Go Wrong: Mistakes, Failure, and the Dynamics of Ritual,* edited by Ute Hüsken. Brill.

Ingram, Daniel M. 2018. *Mastering the Core Teachings of the Buddha: An Unusually Hardcore Dharma Book.* Rev. and expanded ed. Aeon.

James, Steve. 2023. "Ep. 228: Dzogchen & Dark Retreat." Interview with Nida Chenagtsang and Justin Von Bujdoss. *Guru Viking.* Podcast, 2:26:50. November 17. https://www.guruviking.com/podcast/ep228-dzogchen-dark-retreat-dr-nida-chenagtsang-and-justin-von-bujdoss.

Jamgön Kongtrul Lodrö Tayé. 1976–1980. "Rdzogs chen yang ti nag po'i mun khrid kyi zhal shes snyan khungs brgyud pa'i man ngag sangs rgyas zhag bdun gyis sgrub thabs" (The Sādhanā through which Buddhahood is realized in seven days: A pith teaching of Dzogchen dark retreat instructions, based on the heard lineage of oral explanation). In *Rin chen gter mdzod chen mo* (*The great treasury of precious Termas*). Stod lung mtshur phu'i par khang/dpal spungs dgon pa'i par khang.

Jamgon Mipham. 2015. *White Lotus: An Explanation of the Seven-Line Prayer to Guru Padmasambhava.* Translated by Padmakara Translation Group. Shambhala.

'Jig rten mgon po Rin chen dpal. 2008. *Dmigs pa gegs sel chen mo.* Compiled by Grub dbang Nub sprul dkon mchog bstan 'dzin. Srong btsan dpe mdzod khang.

Joffe, Ben. 2019a. "Dr Nida Chenagtsang's Research into Reviving Yookchö or Tibetan Stick Therapy." *A Perfumed Skull* (blog), October 13. https://perfumedskull.com/2019/10/31/dr-nida-chenagtsangs-research-into-reviving-yookcho-or-tibetan-stick-therapy/.

Joffe, Ben. 2019b. "White Robes, Matted Hair: Tibetan Tantric Householders, Moral Sexuality, and the Ambiguities of Esoteric Buddhist Expertise in Exile." PhD diss., University of Colorado at Boulder.

Kilty, Gavin, trans. 2004. *Ornament of Stainless Light: An Exposition of the Kālacakra Tantra.* By Khedrup Norsang Gyatso. Wisdom.

Kornfield, Jack. 1993. *A Path with Heart: A Guide Through the Perils and Promises of the Spiritual Life.* Bantam.

Kortava, David. 2021. "Lost in Thought: The Psychological Risks of Meditation." *Harper's Magazine.* Accessed January 28, 2024. https://harpers.org/archive/2021/04/lost-in-thought-psychological-risks-of-meditation/.

Kritzer, Robert. 2023. "Worms in *Saddharmasmṛtyupasthānasūtra.*" In *Burlesque of the Philosophers: Indian and Buddhist Studies in Memory of Helmut Krasser,* edited by Jowita Kramer, Vincent Eltschinger, Parimal Patil, and Chizuko Yoshimizu. Projekt Verlag.

Kūkai. 2010. "The Meanings of Sound, Letter, and Reality (Shōjijisōgi)." In *Kukai on the Philosophy of Language,* edited and translated by Shingen Takagi and Thomas Eijo Dreitlein. Keio University Press.

Kurata Hyakuzō. 1932. *A Heaven for the Anxious: My Experience of Being Cured Without Being Cured.* Senshinsha.

Kurata Hyakuzō. 2013. *Religion and Life as One.* In Vol. 10, *Sekai kyōyō zenshū.* Aozora Bunko. www.aozora.gr.jp/cards/000256/card43463.html.

Kvaerne, Per. 1995. *The Bon Religion of Tibet: The Iconography of a Living Tradition.* Serindia.

Lai, Karyn. 2007. "Ziran and Wuwei in the Daodejing: An Ethical Assessment." *Dao* 6 (4): 325–337.

Lambert, D., Nicholas H. van den Berg, and Adrianna Mendreka. 2021. "Adverse Effects of Meditation: A Review of Observational, Experimental and Case Studies." *Current Psychology* 42:1112–1125.

Lambert, D., Nicholas H. van den Berg, and Adianna Mendrek. 2023. "Adverse Effects of Meditation: A Review of Observational, Experimental and Case Studies." *Current Psychology* 42:1112–1125. https://doi.org/10.1007/s12144-021-01503-2.

Legge, James. 1879. *Sacred Books of the East.* Vol. 3. Accessed November 22, 2023. https://ctext.org/shang-shu.

Legge, James, trans. 2013. *Confucian Analects, the Great Leaning and the Doctrine of the Mean.* Dover.

Li Chan. 2006. *Yixue rumen.* Modern edition of the Ming dynasty text, arranged by Tian Daihua et al. Renmin weisheng chubanshe.

Lindahl, Jared R. 2017. "Somatic Energies and Emotional Traumas: A Qualitative Study of Practice-Related Challenges Reported by Vajrayāna Buddhists." *Religions* 8 (8): 153. https://doi.org/10.3390/rel8080153.

Lindahl, Jared R., and Willoughby B. Britton. 2019. "'I Have This Feeling of Not Really Being Here': Buddhist Meditation and Changes in Sense of Self." *Journal of Consciousness Studies* 26 (7–8): 157–183.

Lindahl, Jared R., Willoughby B. Britton, and David J. Cooper. 2022. "Fear and Terror in Buddhist Meditation: A Cognitive Model for Meditation-Related Changes in Arousal and Affect." *Journal of Cognitive Historiography* 7 (1–2): 148–171. https://doi.org/10.1558/jch.22807.

Lindahl, Jared R., Willoughby B. Britton, David J. Cooper, and Laurence J. Kirmayer. 2021. "Challenging and Adverse Meditation Experiences: Toward a Person-Centered Approach." In *The Oxford Handbook of Meditation,* edited by Miguel Farias, David Brazier, and Mansur Lalljee. Oxford University Press.

Lindahl, Jared R., David J. Cooper, Nathan E. Fisher, Laurence J. Kirmayer, and Willougby B. Britton. 2020. "Progress or Pathology? Differential Diagnosis and Intervention Criteria for Meditation-Related Challenges: Perspectives from Buddhist Meditation Teachers and Practitioners." *Frontiers in Psychology* 11:1905. https://doi.org/10.3389/fpsyg.2020.01905.

Lindahl, Jared R., Nathan E. Fisher, David J. Cooper, Rochelle K. Rosen, and Willoughby B. Britton. 2017. "The Varieties of Contemplative Experience: A Mixed-Methods Study of Meditation-Related Challenges in Western Buddhists." *PLoS ONE* 12 (5): e0176239. https://doi.org/10.1371/journal.pone.0176239.

Lindahl, Jared R., Christopher T. Kaplan, Evan M. Winget, and Willoughby B. Britton. 2014. "A Phenomenology of Meditation-Induced Light Experiences: Traditional Buddhist and Neurobiological Perspectives." *Frontiers in Psychology* 4 (973): 1–16. https://doi .org/10.3389/fpsyg.2013.00973.

Lindahl, Jared R., Roman Palitsky, David J. Cooper, and Willoughby B. Britton. 2023. "The Roles and Impacts of Worldviews in the Context of Meditation-Related Challenges." *Transcultural Psychiatry* 60 (4): 637–650. https://doi.org/10.1177/13634615221128679.

Lo, Yuet Keung. "From a Dual Soul to a Unitary Soul: The Babel of Soul Terminologies in Early China." *Monumenta Serica* 56 (2008): 23–53.

Loizzo, Joseph J. 2016. "The Subtle Body: An Interoceptive Map of Central Nervous System Function and Meditative Mind-Body-Brain Integration." *Annals of the New York Academy of Sciences,* 1–18.

Love, Shayla. 2018. "Meditation Is a Powerful Mental Tool—and for Some People It Goes Terribly Wrong." *Vice.* Accessed January 28, 2024. https://www.vice.com/en/article /vbaedd/meditation-is-a-powerful-mental-tool-and-for-some-it-goes-terribly-wrong.

Lu, K'uan Yü. 1964. *The Secrets of Chinese Meditation: Self-Cultivation by Mind Control as Taught in the Ch'an, Mahāyāna and Taoist Schools in China.* Rider.

Luhrmann, T. M., and Rachel Morgain. 2012. "Prayer as Inner Sense Cultivation: An Attentional Learning Theory of Spiritual Experience." *Ethos* 40 (4): 359–389.

Lutkajtis, Anna. 2020. *The Dark Side of Dharma: Meditation, Madness and Other Maladies on the Contemplative Path.* Aeon.

Madsen, Richard. 2007. *Democracy's Dharma: Religious Renaissance and Political Development in Taiwan.* University of California Press.

Marek, Todd, and Charles Jamyang Oliphant of Rossie. 2017. "Treating Disorders of the Subtle Winds in Tibetan Buddhism." In *Buddhism and Medicine: An Anthology of Premodern Sources,* edited by C. Pierce Salguero. Columbia University Press.

McMahan, David. 2008. *The Making of Buddhist Modernism.* Oxford University Press.

McMahan, David. 2011. "Buddhism as the 'Religion of Science': From Colonial Ceylon to the Laboratories of Harvard." In *Handbook of Religion and the Authority of Science,* edited by Jim R. Lewis and Olav Hammer. Brill. https://doi.org/10.1163/ej .9789004187917.i-924.38.

McRae, John R., trans. 2000. *The Platform Sutra of the Sixth Patriarch.* Numata Center for Buddhist Translation and Research.

McRae, John R. 2003. *Seeing Through Zen: Encounter, Transformation, and Genealogy in Chinese Chan Buddhism.* University of California Press.

Mettanando Bhikkhu. 1999. *Meditation and Healing in the Theravada Buddhist Order of Thailand and Laos.* n.p.

Millard, Colin. 2013. "Bon Religion in Reb Kong." In *Monastic and Lay Traditions in North-Eastern Tibet,* edited by Yangdon Dhondup, Ulrich Pagel, and Geoffrey Samuel. Brill.

Mi nyag Grags pa rdo rje. 2008. *Gegs sel gyi man ngag nor bu'i phreng ba,* Sakya Lamdre Collections, v. 43, p. 329-397. Sachen International.

Mitra, Rajendra Lal. 1888. *Aṣṭasāhasrikā: A Collection of Discourses on the Metaphysics of the Mahāyāna School of the Buddhists Now First Edited from Nepalese Sanskrit mss.* Bibliotheca Indica; Asiatic Society.

Mitsui Eikō. 2016. *Kajikitō no genri to jisshū* (Principles and practice of blessing prayer). Kōyasanshuppansha.

Mori, Sodo. 2007. "Recent Japanese Studies in the Pali Commentarial Literature: Since 1984." *Journal of the Pali Text Society* 29:175–190.

Morita Shōma. 1998. *Morita Therapy and the True Nature of Anxiety-Based Disorders (Shinkeishitsu).* Translated by Akihisa Kondo and edited by Peg Le Vine. State University of New York Press.

Muller, A. Charles, trans. 2013. *The Diamond Sutra.* http://www.acmuller.net/bud-canon/diamond_sutra.html.

Ñāṇamoli, Bhikkhu, and Bhikku Bodhi, trans. (1995) 2009. *The Middle Length Discourses of the Buddha.* Wisdom.

Nattier, Jan. 2003. "The Ten Epithets of the Buddha in the Translations of Zhi Qian." *Annual Report of the International Research Institute for Advanced Buddhology at Soka University* 6:207–250.

Norman, Kenneth R. [1984] 1992. "The Value of the Pāli Tradition." In Vol. 3, *Collected Papers,* edited by Kenneth R. Norman. Pali Text Society. Originally published in *Jagajjyoti, Buddha Jayanti Annual,* 1984.

Orzech, Charles D., Richard K. Payne, and Henrik Sørensen. 2011. "Introduction: Esoteric Buddhism and the Tantras in East Asia: Some Methodological Considerations." In *Esoteric Buddhism and the Tantras in East Asia,* edited by Charles D. Orzech, Henrik Sørensen, and Richard K. Payne. Brill.

Pagis, Michal. 2014. "Evoking Equanimity: Silent Interaction Rituals in Vipassana Meditation Retreats." *Qualitative Sociology* 38 (1): 39–56.

Palitsky, Roman, David J. Cooper, Jared R. Lindahl, and Willoughby B. Britton. 2023. "Relationships Between Religious and Scientific Worldviews in the Narratives of Western Buddhists Reporting Meditation-Related Challenges." *Journal of Contemplative Studies.* https://doi.org/10.57010/GDCW6138.

Partikova, Veronika, and George Jennings. 2018. "The Kung Fu Family: A Metaphor of Belonging Across Time and Place." *Revista de Artes Marciales Asiáticas* 13 (1): 35–52.

Patton, Thomas Nathan. 2014. *The Buddha's Wizards: Magic, Protection, and Healing in Burmese Buddhism.* Columbia University Press.

Payne, Richard K. 2015. "Introduction." In *Homa Variations: The Study of Ritual Change Across the Longue Durée,* edited by Richard K. Payne and Michael Witzel. Oxford University Press.

'Phags pa shes rab kyi pha rol tu phyin pa brgyad stong pa (Āryāṣṭasāhasrikāprajñāpāramitā). BDRC Work Number: WA0RK0012. As transmitted in the *Bka' 'gyur (sde dge par phud)* (Dergé Kangyur), BDRC Version Number: MW22084_0012.

Pregadio, Fabrizio. 1995. "The Representation of Time in the *Zhouyi Cantong Qi*." *Cahiers d'Extrême-Asie*, no. 8: 155–173.

Pregadio, Fabrizio, and Lowell Skar. 2000. "Inner Alchemy (*neidan*)." In *Daoism Handbook*, edited by Livia Kohn. Brill.

Prost, Audrey. 2006. "Causation as Strategy: Interpreting Humours Among Tibetan Refugees." *Anthropology & Medicine* 13 (2): 119–130.

Pu, Chengzhong. 2013. "Chinese Versions of Virūḍhaka's Massacre of the Śākyans: A Preliminary Study." *Indian International Journal of Buddhist Studies* 14:29–47.

Qin Bowei. (1929) 2007. *Qing-dai mingyi yihua jinghua*. Beijing renmin weisheng chubanshe.

Rahula, W. 1974. *What the Buddha Taught*. Grove Press.

Reynolds, David K. 1982. *The Quiet Therapies: Japanese Pathways to Personal Growth*. University of Hawai'i Press.

Rhys Davids, Thomas W. 1880. *Buddhist Birth-Stories (Jataka Tales): The Commentarial Introduction Entitled Nidāna-Kathā the Story of the Lineage*. George Routledge & Sons.

Rosenthal, Randy. 2021. "Can Meditation Actually Be Dangerous?" *Lion's Roar: Buddhist Wisdom for Our Time*. Accessed January 28, 2024. https://www.lionsroar.com/can-meditation-actually-be-dangerous.

Rozenberg, Guillaume. 2010. *Renunciation and Power: The Quest for Sainthood in Contemporary Burma*. Yale University Press.

Rozenberg, Guillaume. 2015. *The Immortals: Faces of the Incredible in Buddhist Burma*. University of Hawai'i Press.

Salguero, C. Pierce. 2009. "The Buddhist Medicine King in Literary Context: Reconsidering an Early Medieval Example of Indian Influence on Chinese Medicine and Surgery." *History of Religions* 48 (3): 183–210.

Salguero, C. Pierce. 2010. "Buddhist Medicine in Medieval China: Disease, Healing, and the Body in Crosscultural Translation (Second to Eighth Centuries C.E.)." PhD thesis, Johns Hopkins University.

Salguero, C. Pierce. 2014. *Translating Buddhist Medicine in Medieval China*. University of Pennsylvania Press.

Salguero, C. Pierce, ed. 2017. *Buddhism and Medicine: An Anthology of Premodern Sources*. Columbia University Press.

Salguero, C. Pierce. 2023. "'Meditation Sickness' in Medieval Chinese Buddhism and the Contemporary West." *Journal of Buddhist Ethics* 30:169–211. Accessed January 28, 2024. https://blogs.dickinson.edu/buddhistethics/files/2023/08/Salguero-Finalized-ms-for-publication47.pdf.

Samuel, Geoffrey. 2019. "Unbalanced Flows in the Subtle Body: Tibetan Understandings of Psychiatric Illness and How to Deal with It." *Journal of Religion and Health* 58 (3): 770–794. http://www.doi.org/10.1007/s10943-019-00774-1.

Sander, Lore. 2000. "Fragments of an *Aṣṭasāhasrikā* Manuscript from the Kuṣāṇa Period." In Vol. 1, *Manuscripts in the Schøyen Collection I—Buddhist Manuscripts,* edited by Jens Braarvig. Hermes.

Sander, Lore. 2002. "New Fragments of the *Aṣṭasāhasrikā* of the Kuṣāṇa Period." In Vol. 2, *Manuscripts in the Schøyen Collection III—Buddhist Manuscripts,* edited by Jens Braarvig. Hermes.

Sandilands, Olivier, and Daniel M. Ingram. 2024. "Documenting and Defining Emergent Phenomenology: Theoretical Foundations for an Extensive Research Strategy." *Frontiers in Psychology* 15:1340335. https://doi.org/10.3389/fpsyg.2024.1340335.

Satha-Anand, Suwanna. 1999. "Truth over Convention: Feminist Interpretations of Buddhism." In *Religious Fundamentalisms and the Human Rights of Women,* edited by C. W. Howland. Palgrave.

Scheid, Volker. 2020. "The Neglected Role of Buddhism in the Development of Medicine in Late Imperial China Viewed Through the Life and Work of Yu Chang (1585–1664)." *Bulletin of the History of Medicine* 94 (1): 1–28.

Schlosser, Marco, Terje Sparby, Sebastjan Vörös, Rebecca Jones, and Natalie L. Marchant. 2019. "Unpleasant Meditation-Related Experiences in Regular Meditators: Prevalence, Predictors, and Conceptual Considerations." *PLOS ONE* 14 (5): 0216643.

Scott, Anthony. 2023. "The Politics of Pali Commentary: Canon-Making, Monastic Reform, and Religious Revival in the Mingun Jetavana Sayadaw's *Milindapañha-aṭṭhakathā.*" PhD diss., University of Toronto.

Sekiguchi Shindai. 1954. *Tendai shōshikan no kenkyō.* Sankibō busshorin.

Sharf, Robert. 1995. "Buddhist Modernism and the Rhetoric of Meditative Experience." *Numen* 42 (3): 228–283. https://doi.org/10.1163/1568527952598549.

Sheng, Yen. 2003. *Chan Wisdom: Conversations with Master Sheng Yen.* Dharma Drum.

Shimoizumi Zengyo. 2021. *Fudō Myō-ō: Chie to Chikara no Hotoke no Subete.* 4th ed. Shunjusha.

Simonis, Fabien. 2015. "Ghosts or Mucus? Medicine for Madness: New Doctrines, Therapies, and Rivalries." In *Modern Chinese Religion I: Song–Liao–Jin–Yuan (960–1368 AD),* edited by P. Marsone and J. Lagerwey. Brill.

Skidmore, Monique. 2002. "Menstrual Madness: Women's Health and Well-Being in Urban Burma." In *Women's Health in Mainland Southeast Asia,* edited by A. Whittaker. Haworth Medical Press.

Solomonova, Elizaveta, Jared R. Lindahl, Ian Gold, David J. Cooper, Charlotte Little, Damian Arteca, Chenxi Cao, and Willoughby B. Britton. 2025. "'I Was Trying to Save the World': Delusion-like Ideation and Associated Impacts Reported by Western Practitioners of Buddhist Meditation." *Frontiers in Psychology* 16:1644684. https://doi.org/10.3389/fpsyg.2025.1644684.

Spiro, Melford E. 1967. *Burmese Supernaturalism: A Study in the Explanation of Reduction of Suffering.* Prentice-Hall.

Spiro, Melford E. 1971. *Buddhism and Society: A Great Tradition and Its Burmese Vicissitudes.* Allen and Unwin.

Stanley-Baker, Michael. 2022. "Qi: A Means for Cohering Natural Knowledge." In *Routledge Handbook of Chinese,* edited by Vivienne Lo, Michael Stanley-Baker, and Dolly Yang. *Medicine.* Routledge.

Stevenson, Daniel B., and Neal Donner. 1993. *The Great Calming and Contemplation: A Study and Annotated Translation of Chih-i's Mo-ho chih-kuan.* Vol. 3. Kuroda Institute Classics in East Asian Buddhism. University of Hawai'i Press.

Stuart, Daniel M. 2020. *S. N. Goenka: Emissary of Insight.* Shambhala.

Stuart, Daniel M. 2024. "Local Cure, Global Chant: Performing Theravadic Awakening in the Footsteps of the Ledi Sayadaw." *Numen* 71 (2–3): 256–302.

Swanson, Paul L. 1997. "What's Going on Here? Chih-i's Use (and Abuse) of Scripture." *Journal of the International Association of Buddhist Studies* 20 (1): 1–30.

Swanson, Paul L. 1999. "Dry Dust, Hazy Images, and Missing Pieces: Reflections on Translating Religious Texts." *Nanzan Bulletin* 23:29–43.

Swanson, Paul L. 2007. "Ch'an and Chih-kuan: T'ien-t'ai Chih-i's View of 'Zen' and the Practice of the *Lotus Sutra.*" Special issue, *Tendai Bulletin,* 143–164.

Swanson, Paul L. 2018. *Clear Serenity, Quiet Insight: T'ien-t'ai Chih-i's "Mo-ho chih-kuan."* Vol. 3. 3 vols. University of Hawai'i Press.

Tambiah, Stanley. 1970. *Buddhism and Spirit Cults in Northeast Thailand.* Cambridge University Press.

Tanahashi, Kazuaki, ed. 2013. *Treasury of the True Dharma Eye: Zen Master Dōgen's Shōbō Genzō.* Shambhala.

Tessenow, Hermann, and Paul U. Unschuld. 2008. *A Dictionary of the Huang Di Nei Jing Su Wen.* University of California Press.

Thompson, Evan. 2020. *Why I Am Not a Buddhist.* Yale University Press.

Unschuld, Paul U. 1986a. *Medicine in China: A History of Pharmaceutics.* University of Chicago Press.

Unschuld, Paul U. 1986b. *Nan-Ching: The Classic of Difficult Issues (with Commentaries by Chinese and Japanese Authors from the Third Through the Twentieth Century).* University of California Press.

Unschuld, Paul U. 2003. *Huang Di Nei Jing Su Wen: Nature, Knowledge, Imagery in an Ancient Chinese Medical Text.* University of California Press.

Unschuld, Paul U. (1985) 2010. *Medicine in China: A History of Ideas.* 2nd ed., with a new preface. Comparative Studies of Health Systems and Medical Care. University of California Press.

Unschuld, Paul U., and Hermann Tessenow, in collaboration with Zheng Jinsheng. 2011. *Huang Di nei jing su wen: An Annotated Translation of Huang Di's Inner Classic—Basic Questions*. University of California Press.

Vaidya, P. L. 1960. *Aṣṭasāhasrikā Prajñāpāramitā with Haribhadra's Commentary Called Āloka*. Buddhist Sanskrit Texts 4. Mithila Institute of Post-Graduate Studies and Research in Sanskrit Learning.

Vipassana Research Institute. (1991) 1994. *Sayagyi U Ba Khin Journal, a Collection Commemorating the Teaching of Sayagyi U Ba Khin, Published to Mark the Twentieth Anniversary of His Demise*. Vipassana Research Institute.

Waddell, Norman. 2002. "Hakuin's Yasenkanna." *Eastern Buddhist*, new series, 34 (1): 79–119.

Wang, Guangxi. 2012. *Chinese Kung Fu*. 3rd ed. Cambridge University Press.

Weber, Daphne. 2024. "ExBodiment: Transformed Subjectivities in a Thai Bhikkhuni Temple." PhD diss., Washington State University.

Wilson, Jeff. 2014. *Mindful America: The Mutual Transformation of Buddhist Meditation and American Culture*. Oxford University Press.

Winiger, Fabian. 2017. "'When the Spirit Cannot Feel The Body': Overcoming Cartesian Mind-Body Dualism with Qigong Practice." *Staps* 117–118 (3): 127–140.

Wogihara, Unrai. 1932–1935. *Abhisamayālaṃkār'āloka Prajñāpāramitāvyākhyā (Commentary on Aṣṭasāhasrikā-Prajñāpāramitā) by Haribhadra Together with the Text Commented on*. Toyo bunko.

Wright, Dale S. 2009. *The Six Perfections: Buddhism and the Cultivation of Character*. Oxford University Press.

Yamada, Mumon. 1977. *How to Practice Zazen: Taken from the Lectures on the Zazengi*. Translated by Nishimura Eishin. Institute for Zen Studies.

Yamada, Mumon. 2012. "My Spiritual Home: The Autobiography of Yamada Mumon Rōshi." Translated by Thomas Kirchner. *Annual Report of the International Research Institute for Zen Buddhism* 7.

Yamada, Mumon, Sōgen Ōmori, and Hirata Seikō. (1982) 2008. *Recommendations for Zazen (Zazen no susume)*. 8th ed. Institute for Zen Studies.

Yamano Toshirou. 1985. "Tendai Chigi no igaku shisō josetsu." *Shinshū Sōgō Kenkyūjo kenkyū kiyō* 3:115–142.

Yangönpa Gyalwa. 2015. *Secret Map of the Body: Visions of the Human Energy Structure*. Translated from the Tibetan and annotated by Elio Guarisco. Shang Shung.

Ye, Shaoyong. 2013. "Aṣṭasāhasrikā Prajñāpāramitā." In *Xinjiang Manuscripts Preserved in the National Library of China: Sanskrit Fragments and Kharoṣṭhī Documents*, edited by Duan Qing and Zhang Zhiqing. Series of Sanskrit Manuscripts & Buddhist Literature 3. Research Institute of Sanskrit Manuscripts and Buddhist Literature.

Yongey Mingyur Rinpoche. 2019. *In Love with the World: A Monk's Journey Through the Bardos of Living and Dying*. With Helen Tworkov. Random House.

Yoshizawa Katsuhiro. 2000. *Yasenkanna.* Zenbunka kenkyūsho.

Yü, Ying-Shih. 1987. "'O Soul, Come Back!' A Study in the Changing Conceptions of the Soul and Afterlife in Pre-Buddhist China." *Harvard Journal of Asiatic Studies* 47 (2): 363–395.

Yuasa, Yasuo. 1993. *The Body, Self-Cultivation, and Ki-Energy.* Translated by Shigenori Nagatomo and Monte S. Hull. State University of New York Press.

Yuthok Yönten Gönpo. 2011. *The Root and Explanatory Tantra from the Four Tantras of Tibetan Medicine.* 2nd ed. Translated by Men-Tsee-Khang Translation Department. Men-Tsee-Khang Publication Section.

Yuthok Yönten Gönpo. 2017. *The Oral Instruction Tantra from the Four Tantras of Tibetan Medicine.* Translated by Men-Tsee-Khang Translation Department. Men-Tsee-Khang Documentation and Publication Department.

Yuthok Yönten Gönpo. 2023. *Gyu thog snying thig* (The heart-essence teachings of Yuthok, a.k.a. the Yuthok Nyingthig). With Sumtön Yeshé Zung. Sky Press.

Zacchetti, Stefano. 2003. "The Rediscovery of Three Early Buddhist Scriptures on Meditation: A Preliminary Analysis of the *Fo Shuo Shi'er Men Jing* Translated by An Shigao and Their Commentary Preserved in the Newly Found Kongō-Ji Manuscript." *Journal of the International Research Institute for Advanced Buddhology at Soka University* 6:251–300.

Zacchetti, Stefano. 2015. "Prajñāpāramitā Sūtras." In *Brill's Encyclopedia of Buddhism.* Vol. 1, *Literature and Languages,* edited by Jonathan A. Silk, Oskar von Hinüber, and Vincent Eltschinger. Brill.

Zhang Jiebin. 1999. *Jingyue quanshu.* In *Jingyue yixue quanshu,* compiled by Li Zhiyong et al., 813–1831. Modern edition of the Ming dynasty text. Zhongguo zhongyiyao chubanshe.

Zhao Jinwei and Zhong Suya. 2021. "Wan-Qing yilai Putuoshan de foyi huodong." *Zhonghua yishi zazhi* 51 (1): 276–281.

Zhong yi da ci dian. 1995. Ren min wei sheng chu ban she.

Zhou, Yiqun. 2011. "Temples and Clerics in 'Honglou meng.'" *Harvard Journal of Asiatic Studies* 71 (2): 263–309.

Zurkhar Nyamnyi Dorjé. 2005. *Man ngag bye ba ring bsrel pod chung rab 'byams gsal ba'i sgron me* ("Tens of millions of pearl relics pith instructions," the lesser, infinitely illuminating lamp volume, a.k.a. the *Mengngak chewa ringsel*). Mi rigs dpe skrun khang (Ethnic Minorities Publishing House).

Zysk, Kenneth G. 1993. *Religious Medicine: The History and Evolution of Indian Medicine.* Transaction.

Contributors

JUHN Y. AHN is an associate professor of Buddhist and Korean studies at the University of Michigan and the author of *Buddhas and Ancestors: Religion and Wealth in Fourteenth-Century Korea; Transgression in Korea: Beyond Resistance and Control;* and *Gongan Collections I: Collected Works of Korean Buddhism,* Vol. 7–1. His current research focuses on the economic history of Korea during the Goryeo period (918–1392), reading practices in Song-dynasty (960–1279) Chan Buddhism, and the cultural history of weather and wealth during the Joseon period (1392–1910) in Korea.

BHIKKHU ANĀLAYO has recently retired from the position of professor of Buddhist studies at the University of Hamburg. His over five hundred publications are mainly on early Buddhism, with a special interest in meditation and the role of women.

JAMES A. BENN is a professor of Buddhism and East Asian religions at McMaster University. He studies Buddhism and Daoism, focusing on bodily practice, apocryphal scriptures, and the religious dimensions of commodity culture. He is the author of *Burning for the Buddha: Self-Immolation in Chinese Buddhism* and *Tea in China: A Religious and Cultural History.*

WILLOUGHBY B. BRITTON is an associate professor of psychiatry and human behavior in the Warren Alpert Medical School at Brown University. She designed the Varieties of Contemplative Experience Study and conducted most of the early interviews. Britton is also the founder of Cheetah House (www.cheetahhouse.org), a nonprofit that supports meditators-in-distress.

DAVID CARPENTER (PhD, University of Chicago, 1987) taught at Saint Joseph's University in Philadelphia from 1986 until his retirement in 2024, teaching courses on Hinduism, Buddhism, and the comparative study of contemplative practices. His current research focuses on the meditative manuals of Zhiyi, founder of the Tiantai school of Chinese Buddhism.

DIXUAN CHEN is an assistant professor of East Asian religions at Grinnell College, Iowa. Her research focuses on Chinese Buddhist beliefs and practices related to medicine, meditation, and gender. Recently awarded the Harris

Fellowship, she is currently studying the intersection between Buddhist meditation and Chinese medical knowledge.

KIN CHEUNG is an associate professor of East and South Asian religions at Moravian University. He researches how contemporary people use Buddhist doctrine and ritual practices in Chinese and American contexts as well as transnational networks. He has published on Buddhists engaging with healing, meditation, ethical dilemmas, economics, capitalism, and secularism.

CÉLINE CODEREY is a research fellow and a lecturer at the National University of Singapore. She received her PhD in anthropology from the University of Provence and her MA in psychology from the University of Lausanne. Her field of expertise spans from medical anthropology and anthropology of the body to the anthropology of dance.

DAVID J. COOPER is a research associate in the Clinical and Affective Neuroscience Laboratory at Brown University. He has been involved with the Varieties of Contemplative Experience research project since 2014 and has contributed to all aspects of the project, from conducting practitioner and expert interviews to qualitative data analysis to manuscript writing.

MELISSA ANNE-MARIE CURLEY is an associate professor in the Department of Comparative Studies at Ohio State University. Her work focuses on the uses of Buddhist repertoires in modern and contemporary Japan. She is currently developing a project on bodily relics and the role of Buddhist temples as modern memory institutions.

BRYAN DE NOTARIIS received a PhD from the University of Turin (Italy), with a dissertation on the extraordinary capacities developed in the Buddhist path of liberation, analyzing both canonical and commentarial sources of the Theravāda Buddhist tradition. Later, he was awarded a postdoctoral fellowship at the Ca' Foscari University of Venice (Italy) to study grape wine in the Gandhāra area through the analysis of literary sources and a second one to study nonhuman animals in Indian literature.

LESLIE E. DE VRIES is visiting lecturer at KU Leuven (Belgium), where he teaches Asian religions. His research focuses on interactions between the Three Teachings and medicine in Ming and Qing China. He also publishes on the history of medicine in Vietnam.

SUSANNAH DEANE received her PhD from Cardiff University in 2015. She is the author of multiple articles and book chapters based on her doctoral and postdoctoral research on notions of mental health, illness, and healing in contemporary Tibetan communities. Her second monograph, *Illness and Enlightenment: Exploring Tibetan Perspectives on Madness in Text and Everyday Life,* was published in early 2025.

CHARLES DISIMONE is an associate professor of Buddhist studies and Indology at Ghent University and is the principal investigator of the European Research Council funded project "Corpora in Greater Gandhāra: Tracing the Development of Buddhist Textuality and Gilgit/Bamiyan Manuscript Networks in the First Millennium of the Common Era." His research interests include the applications of philological, codicological, and critical analysis of Buddhist sutra manuscripts and literature, both Mahāyāna and Mainstream.

NATHAN E. FISHER recently completed his PhD in religious studies from the University of California, Santa Barbara. After conducting numerous interviews for the Varieties of Contemplative Experience research project and coauthoring the overall results paper, he conducted a replication study of practice-related challenges among the contemplative traditions of Judaism, Christianity, and Islam.

ERIC GREENE is an associate professor of religious studies at Yale University. His research focuses on all aspects of medieval Chinese Buddhism, with a particular emphasis on meditation, Chan (Zen), early commentarial literature, and the history of Chinese Buddhist translations practices.

IRA HELDERMAN is an adjunct professor of religious studies at Vanderbilt University and is a practicing psychotherapist. His research examines how psychotherapists' definitions of what is and is not religious shape their approaches to healing and illness. He is the author of *Prescribing the Dharma: Psychotherapists, Buddhist Traditions, and Defining Religion* (2019).

BEN P. JOFFE holds a PhD in cultural anthropology from the University of Colorado, Boulder. He works as a translator and editor for Sky Press and as a curriculum developer for Sowa Rigpa Institute, organizations devoted to the study and practice of Tibetan meditative and healing traditions.

JARED R. LINDAHL is a visiting assistant professor in the Department of Religious Studies at Brown University. Since 2014 he has been directing the qualitative data analysis and academic writing for the Varieties of Contemplative Experience research project. He also conducted some of the interviews with both meditation practitioners and meditation experts.

LEO W. LOK (MACOM) is a practitioner and independent scholar of Chinese medicine. A native speaker and reader of Chinese languages, Leo has studied with renowned translators such as Dan Bensky. His main area of interest is the textual analysis and translation of premodern Chinese medical literature.

FRANCISCO FIGUEROA MEDINA is a PhD candidate at Kyoto University. His research focuses on the history of meditation manuals and lay meditation groups of the Rinzai Zen school in postwar Japan.

NATHAN JISHIN MICHON is a lecturer with the KYOEN Institute in Kyoto, Japan, where they also run the Japan Inward Journeys initiative. They previously served as a JSPS postdoctoral fellow at Ryukoku University and edited volumes such as *Refuge in the Storm: Buddhist Voices in Crisis Care* and *A Thousand Hands: A Guidebook to Caring for Your Buddhist Community.*

SWE SWE MON is an associate professor of Buddhist studies at the Institute of Buddhist Psychology, Shan State, Myanmar, as well as translator and editor of the Pariyatti Organization, Mahasi Meditation Center, Yangon, Myanmar.

TRANG T. D. NGUYEN is a PhD candidate at the University of Vienna. Her research focuses on the ideas and practices of Trúc Lâm, a contemporary meditation-based Vietnamese Buddhist tradition strongly influenced by Chinese Chan Buddhism.

C. PIERCE SALGUERO (PhD, Johns Hopkins School of Medicine, 2010) is a professor of Asian history and health humanities at Pennsylvania State University's Abington College near Philadelphia. He is the author of numerous books and articles on Buddhist medicine in medieval China and globally and is also the editor in chief of the journal *Asian Medicine.*

MICHAEL R. SHEEHY is a research assistant professor and the director of research at the Contemplative Sciences Center, University of Virginia. He studies Tibetan contemplative practices and the relevance of meditation research to the humanities, health sciences, and cultural psychology. He is editor in chief of the *Journal of Contemplative Studies.*

DANIEL M. STUART is an associate professor of religious studies at the University of South Carolina. He studies the history of traditional Buddhist contemplative practices from their origins in premodern South Asia into the global present. He is the author of *Insight in Perspective, S. N. Goenka: Emissary of Insight, The Stream of Deathless Nectar, A Less Traveled Path,* and *Thinking About Cessation.*

PAUL L. SWANSON was a research Fellow at the Nanzan Institute for Religion and Culture for over thirty-five years, where he edited the *Japanese Journal of Religious Studies.* His publications include *Pruning the Bodhi Tree,* the

Nanzan Guide to Japanese Religions, translations for the *BDK English Tripitaka,* and *Clear Serenity, Quiet Insight,* a fully annotated translation of Zhiyi's *Mohe zhiguan.*

DAPHNE WEBER is a PhD candidate at Washington State University. Her research focuses on Thai bhikkhuni and the transformative process women go through when they receive ordination. She has developed the theory of ExBodiment, confronting the juxtaposition of culture and agency as it relates to personal experience.

Index